INVITATION TO THE SOCIOLOGY OF INTERNATIONAL LAW

Invitation to the Sociology of International Law

MOSHE HIRSCH

OXFORD
UNIVERSITY PRESS

OXFORD
UNIVERSITY PRESS

Great Clarendon Street, Oxford, OX2 6DP,
United Kingdom

Oxford University Press is a department of the University of Oxford.
It furthers the University's objective of excellence in research, scholarship,
and education by publishing worldwide. Oxford is a registered trade mark of
Oxford University Press in the UK and in certain other countries

First published 2015
First published in paperback 2017

Published in the United States of America by Oxford University Press
198 Madison Avenue, New York, NY 10016, United States of America

British Library Cataloguing in Publication Data
Data available

Library of Congress Cataloging in Publication Data
Data available

ISBN 978–0–19–968811–1 (Hbk.)
ISBN 978–0–19–881363–7 (Pbk.)

To my family

Preface

My interest in the sociology of international law grew out of reading some studies in the early 2000s, comparing rational choice and sociological analyses of social phenomena. Following some research work on the rational choice model and international law, the thick and richly textured account of the 'homo sociologicus' inspired my first expeditions into the sociological dimension of international law. My early research work in that field convincingly revealed that international legal actors do not operate in a social vacuum, and that socio-cultural factors significantly influence the formation, interpretation, and implementation of international law. Those early studies, along with feedback from colleagues, and the relatively scant attention paid in the literature, persuaded me that sociological literature provides valuable tools for a meaningful analysis of international law. And of no less importance, that literature also exposes the social limits of international legal rules. After some further publications and conference papers exploring the interactions between international law and socio-cultural factors and processes, I decided in 2012 to embark on preparing a book devoted to the sociological study of international law.

Many people have contributed in one way or another to the long process of writing this book. I am particularly indebted to my colleagues who provided valuable comments on earlier draft chapters and research assistants who helped me at various stages of this study. Chapter 2 draws substantially on an article published in the *European Journal of International Law* in 2008 and it benefited from the attention of anonymous referees and staff editors. I am particularly grateful to Joseph Weiler, Benedict Kingsbury, and Robert Howse (of the New York University Law School) with whom I discussed various issues arising from earlier drafts of this article. Chapter 3 greatly benefited from helpful comments provided by Vered Vinitzky-Seroussi, Orit Gazit, and Nir Rotem (of the Hebrew University Department of Sociology), Ron Levi (of the University of Toronto School of Global Affairs), and Sungjoon Cho (of the IIT Chicago-Kent College of Law). Section V of this chapter addresses Argentina's attitude towards investment awards, and I am indebted to Oscar Garibaldi (arbitrator, retired partner of Covington & Burling LLP) and Jorge Viñuales (of the University of Cambridge Faculty of Law) for their helpful comments on this section. Orit Gazit (of the Hebrew University Department of Sociology) and Guy Harpaz (of the Hebrew University Law Faculty) offered useful comments on earlier drafts of Chapter 4, and I am also grateful to Yuval Shany (of the Hebrew University Law Faculty) for his comments on Section IV(b) of this chapter. Chapter 5 expands on a chapter published in the book *Multi-Sourced Equivalent Norms* edited by Yuval Shany and Tomer Broude (of the Hebrew University Law Faculty) and it benefited from comments provided by both of them. Comments were also provided by the anonymous referees of the Oxford University Press and they are highly appreciated.

Many thanks are due to the excellent research assistants of the Hebrew University Law Faculty for their tremendous help during the various stages of the preparation of this book. Ohad Abrahami's painstakingly detailed work on this book's bibliographical sources during several stages of this study (and in particular during this work's final stages), along with his sound editing advice, were invaluable in bringing this manuscript into print. Hila Levi, Anna Lechermann, Pablo Robles, and Oscar Weller provided outstanding research assistance during the preparation of Chapter 4. Shani Friedman, Jacob Jordan, and Doron Pe'er also assisted me during diverse stages of the research work. Funding support for the research of this book has been provided by the Maria Von Hofmannsthal Fund in memory of Emilio Von Hofmannsthal, and this kind support is gratefully acknowledged. I am also grateful to the editors at Oxford University Press, John Louth, Merel Alstein, and Emma Endean, who supported the project. Thanks also go to Keerthana Christopher and Saipriya Kannan and the production team for preparing the manuscript for publication. And above all, love and gratitude to my wife, Idit, who accompanied and assisted me in so many ways, along each step of the way.

Moshe Hirsch

Jerusalem
Winter 2015

Table of Contents

Table of Cases

INTERNATIONAL

International Court of Justice (ICJ)

Human Rights Committee

International Centre for Settlement of Investment Disputes (ICSID)

Table of Treaties and other Instruments

UNITED NATIONS SECURITY COUNCIL

UNITED NATIONS GENERAL ASSEMBLY RESOLUTIONS

INTERNATIONAL LAW COMMISSION

UNITED NATIONS COMMISSION ON INTERNATIONAL TRADE LAW (UNCITRAL)

WORLD TRADE ORGANIZATION (WTO)

EUROPEAN UNION LEGISLATION

OTHER DOCUMENTS

List of Abbreviations

ACP countries	79 African, Caribbean, and Pacific states
AFTA	ASEAN Free Trade Area
AJIL	*American Journal of International Law*
ASEAN	Association of Southeast Asian Nations
BITs	Bilateral Investment Treaties
CERD	Committee on the Elimination of Racial Discrimination
COMESA	Common Market of Eastern and Southern Africa
CRTA	Committee on Regional Trade Agreements
CUP	Cambridge University Press
CW	Chemical Weapons
ECB	European Central Bank
ECCHR	European Center for Constitutional and Human Rights
ECHR	European Convention on Human Rights
ECtHR	European Court of Human Rights
EDP	Excessive Debt Procedure
EFSF	European Financial Stability Facility
EJIL	*European Journal of International Law*
EJIR	*European Journal of International Relations*
EMU	Economic and Monetary Union
ESCB	European System of Central Banks
ESM	European Stability Mechanism
EU	European Union
FET	Fair and Equitable Treatment
FTAs	Free Trade Agreements
GATS	General Agreement on Trade in Services
GATT	General Agreement on Tariffs and Trade
GNI	Gross National Income
GSP	Generalized System of Preferences
HRC	Human Rights Committee
ICC	International Criminal Court
ICCPR	International Covenant on Civil and Political Rights
ICJ	International Court of Justice
ICSID	International Centre for Settlement of Investment Disputes
ICTY	International Criminal Tribunal for the Former Yugoslavia
IEL	International Economic Law
IIAs	International Investment Agreements
ILC	International Law Commission
ILM	*International Legal Materials*
ILO	International Labour Organization
IMF	International Monetary Fund
LTRO	Long-Term Refinancing Operation
MAI	Multilateral Agreement on Investment
MEFP	Memorandum of Economic and Financial Policies

MERCOSUR	Southern Common Market
MFN	Most Favoured Nation
MoU	Memorandum of Understanding
NAFTA	North American Free Trade Agreement
NGOs	Non-Governmental Organizations
OECD	Organisation for Economic Co-operation and Development
OGEMID	Oil, Gas, Energy, Mining, and Investment Disputes
OHCHR	*Office of the High Commissioner for Human Rights*
OJ C	Official Journal of the European Communities
OJ L	*Official Journal of the European Union*
OMT	Outright Monetary Transactions
OUP	Oxford University Press
PPI	Producer Price Index
RTAs	Regional Trade Agreements
SC	Security Council
SGP	Stability and Growth Pact
TPRM	Trade Policy Review Mechanism
TRIPS	Trade-Related Aspects of Intellectual Property Rights
UNCITRAL	United Nations Commission on International Trade Law
UNCTAD	United Nations Conference on Trade and Development
UNDP	United Nations Development Programme
UNHCR	United Nations High Commissioner for Refugees
UNTS	United Nations Treaty Series
WMD	Weapons of Mass Destruction
WTO	World Trade Organization
YB Eur L	*Yearbook of European Law*
YJIL	*Yale Journal of International Law*
YPF	Argentine Energy Corporation

1

Introduction

The Sociological Dimension of International Law

> An intellectual activity derives excitement from the moment it becomes a trail of discovery.… The fascination of sociology lies in the fact that its perspective makes us see in a new light the very world in which we have lived all our lives.
>
> Peter Berger, *Invitation to Sociology*[1]

I. An Invitation

International law is deeply embedded in various sociological factors and processes. Numerous international legal rules *reflect* and *affect* societal factors and processes such as norms, socialization, identity, and collective memory. Political and economic dimensions of international law are overlain with a sociological dimension, but this study focuses on the sociological dimension of international law. While the idea that international law and other societal processes are profoundly interlinked is not new, international legal literature habitually pays only scant attention to socio-cultural aspects of international law. In light of the underlying interrelationships between international law and other social factors, the book invites international law specialists to analyse international legal rules in their wider social context, and incorporate sociological tools into mainstream international law scholarship.

The book aims to introduce readers to some key sociological elements and major theoretical approaches, and illustrates their valuable contribution to international

[1] Peter Berger, *Invitation to Sociology: A Humanistic Perspective* (Anchor Books, 1963) 20–1.

legal scholarship. To exemplify the properties of the sociological analysis, the book employs sociological tools to explore diverse topics in contemporary international law, including the World Trade Organization's (WTO) rules regulating regional trade agreements; legal fragmentation and the interaction between international investment law and human rights law; impartiality of adjudicators; compliance with and breach of international law; and the European Union's rules concerning economic and monetary cooperation.

The book is not an introductory textbook and does not address all central topics in either sociology or sociology of international law. Rather, it aims to expose the readers to the sociological discipline and illustrate the potential contribution of sociological tools to international law scholarship. Readers interested in this fascinating field will have to further broaden their knowledge in both sociology and the sociological dimension of international law. As Berger explains in his *Invitation to Sociology*: 'In issuing such an invitation it is necessary to delineate the world to which the reader is being invited, but it will be clear that the latter will have to go beyond this book if he [or she] decides to take the invitation seriously'.[2]

Sociological analysis of international legal issues broadens our understanding of social factors involved in the formation and implementation of international law. Employing sociological tools may also constitute an interpretative tool to clarify the content of international legal provisions, such as rules regarding succession of states and the definition of various social groups (e.g., 'indigenous peoples' and 'minority groups') in diverse international legal instruments. A sociological examination may also suggest some better legal mechanisms for coping with new challenges faced by international law, such as improved regulation of regional trade agreements or enhancing compliance with international law.

While sociological analysis provides a set of valuable tools for inquiry into various international legal spheres, this study does not aim to substitute economic, political, or other modes of analysis drawn from other disciplines, but rather to cast light on the under-explored sociological dimension of international law.

A sociological exploration of international law cannot limit itself to the analysis of official legal texts (such as treaties or decisions by judicial tribunals) and their interrelationships. Although these sources of 'lawyers' law' remain important, unofficial sources of 'living international law' should also be carefully studied. Sociological studies examine a broad range of sources as well as informal normative processes (such as social control or socialization) which motivate and constrain actors in the international legal system. Of no less importance, sociological analysis can further our understanding of the social limits of international law. Thus, for example, it would be naïve to assume that the mere establishment of legally binding rules is sufficient to engender a dramatic and meaningful normative change in a certain community (such as a state society, a regional group of states, or a particular epistemic community). In certain cases, socio-cultural factors inspire a 'cultural resistance' to the formation or internalization of international legal rules.

[2] Ibid., vii.

Unlike the early studies of the sociology of international law (mainly in early and middle of the 20th. century),[3] the following chapters draw primarily on sociological literature, and Section II of this chapter briefly exposes some central assumptions of the sociological perspective and its key concepts. The book is also informed by sociology of law literature and the social constructivist approach in international relations theoretical literature: Sections III and IV (respectively) concisely introduce these approaches. Sections II to IV are accompanied by brief references to the following chapters which employ key concepts set out in this chapter. Section V addresses some methodological issues, and presents the outline of the book.

II. The Sociological Perspective

The term 'sociology' derives from the Latin word *socius* (companion) and the Greek word *ology* (study of) and it commonly refers to the discipline that systematically studies societies, social relations, and social institutions.[4] Sociological studies address numerous issues relating to social groups and the interaction between individuals and groups, but the underlying conception was famously stated by Emile Durkheim: society is more than the individuals who compose it; society has a life of its own that stretches beyond our personal experience.[5] Thus, the fundamental idea that reverberates in countless sociological studies is that the social whole of a group is greater than the sum of its parts, and knowledge about social relations cannot be derived solely from knowledge about the individuals who compose the group.

The sociological perspective assumes that individuals' behaviour and their normative choices are significantly affected by socio-cultural factors and processes. Individuals, however, also influence their social structure.[6] Socio-cultural factors not only constrain individuals but also equip them with resources, thus enabling them to construct strategies of action. As Swidler explains in her influential book:

> [S]ettled cultures provide a 'tool kit' of resources with which people can construct diverse strategies of action; the limitations of that tool kit necessarily constrain action.... Thus

[3] The classical studies of the sociology of international law (prominently by Max Huber, Julius Stone and Bart Landheer) largely addressed the context in which international law developed, emphasizing the role of external factors (such as political, historical and philosophical considerations). For a concise examination of these studies, see Anthony Carty, 'Sociological Theories of International Law' and the references therein, *Max Planck Encyclopedia of Public International Law* (last updated March 2008), http://opil.ouplaw.com/view/10.1093/law:epil/9780199231690/law-9780199231690-e735?rskey=uV9ZYR&result=1&prd=EPIL; Jost Delbrück, 'Max Huber's Sociological Approach to International Law Revisited' (2007) 18 *EJIL* 97; Edward McWhinney, 'Julius Stone and the Sociological Approach to International Law' (1986) 9 *University of New South Wales Law Journal* 14; Bart Landheer, *On the Sociology of International Law and International Society* (Nijhoff, 1966).

[4] 'Sociology', *Oxford Dictionary of Sociology* (4th edn, OUP, 2014) 715–17; 'Sociology', *The Penguin Dictionary of Sociology* (4th edn, Penguin Books, 2000) 333; R Boudon, 'Sociology: Overview', *International Encyclopedia of the Social & Behavioral Sciences* vol 21 (OUP, 2001) 14581.

[5] Emile Durkheim, *Sociology and Psychology* (Free Press, 1953) 55.

[6] See, e.g., George Ritzer, *Introduction to Sociology* (2nd edn, Sage, 2015) 6, 25; Anthony Giddens and Philip Sutton, *Sociology* (7th edn, Polity, 2013), 8.

culture is causally significant both because the cultured capacities individuals possess constrain the strategic of action they can construct, and because available cultural resources allow individuals to initiate and cement such strategies.[7]

The weight accorded to the role of individuals in society forms a major axis of differences in sociological literature.

Core theoretical divides: Sociological theory includes diverse streams. Since the ascendancy of the structural-functional perspective[8] in the 1950s and early 1960s, no single theory has dominated the discipline, and contemporary sociology is thus marked by theoretical pluralism.[9] Several fundamental dichotomies characterize sociological theoretical literature and the two most prominent debates which cut across the whole discipline relate to the relationship between individual and society ('the structure–agency divide') and the underlying consensual or conflictual character of society ('the consensus–conflict divide').

The structure–agency debate revolves around the relationship between individuals and social structures. The principal question is—to what extent are individuals creative actors who control their life? or, alternatively—does most behaviour result from social forces beyond individuals' control? Agency-oriented approaches emphasize the active and creative aspects of human behaviour, while structure-oriented approaches underline the constraining nature of social structures on individuals.[10] Generally,[11] theories belonging to the macro-sociology tradition[12] incline to focus on large-scale social patterns, such as the social system as a whole and its functional elements. These approaches tend to emphasize the constraining power of social structures on individual choices. Individuals are largely perceived here as 'bearers' of social patterns. Micro-sociology theories[13] tend to highlight the role of individuals in society and are primarily concerned with the behaviour of individuals and small groups. Under the latter approach (which is also related to social psychology), social structures, like a society itself, are constituted and changed by interactions between individuals. Furthermore, individuals' choices are not determined by social patterns.[14]

[7] Ann Swidler, *Talk of Love: How Culture Matters* (University of Chicago Press, 2001) 104–5. See also 82–3, 104–17. See also Mario Luis Small, David J Harding and Michèle Lamont, 'Reconsidering Culture and Poverty' (2010) 629 *Annals of the American Academy of Political and Social Science* 6.

[8] On the structural-functional perspective, see Chapter 2, Section IV(b).

[9] See, e.g., Giddens and Sutton (n 6) 9; Ira Cohen, 'Sociological Theory', *The Cambridge Dictionary of Sociology* (CUP, 2006) 600; 'Sociology', *The Penguin Dictionary of Sociology* (4th edn, Penguin Books, 2000) 333, 334.

[10] Giddens and Sutton (n 6) 86; James Fulcher and John Scott, *Sociology* (4th edn, OUP, 2011) 53. See also George Ritzer and Jeffrey Stepnisky, *Sociological Theory* (9th edn, McGraw Hill, 2013) 510; Ritzer (n 6) 86.

[11] On the general resemblance between micro-level theories and agency (and between macro-level and social structure), see Ritzer (n 6) 24. On some differences between agency-structure and micro-macro linkages, see Ritzer and Stepnisky (n 10) 536–7.

[12] Both the structural-functional and the social conflict perspectives are generally considered as macro-sociological theories; see Chapter 2, Sections IV(b) and IV(d) respectively.

[13] On the symbolic-interactionist approach, see Chapter 2, Section IV(c).

[14] On the structure–agency debate, see Ritzer and Stepnisky (n 10) 488–9; Ritzer (n 6) 24–5; Giddens and Sutton (n 6) 86–7; Fulcher and Scott (n 10) 53; Reza Banakar and Max Travers, 'Introduction' in Reza Banakar and Max Travers (eds), *An Introduction to Social Theory* (Hart, 2002), 4–5; Scott Appelrouth and Laura Desfor Edles, *Classical and Contemporary Sociological*

As pointed out in Chapter 2, the structure–agency debate is closely related to the global-regional debate in international trade law. The realization that regional trade agreements often reflect and affect societal processes (such as international socialization or regional identity) brings to the fore several questions regarding the role of individual states and regions in the construction of global social structures. Thus, the WTO rules regulating regional trade agreements and their alternative interpretations reflect certain approaches to the international structure–agency debate.[15]

The second major dichotomy in sociological theory relates to the emphasis placed by social theorists on the consensual or conflictual features of society and its stratification. *Social conflict theories*[16] contend that societies are marked by inequalities and social groups struggle to gain control over various resources. Thus, culturally and economically, dominant groups impose their will on subordinate groups in society. Such approaches tend to view social order as based on manipulation and control by dominant groups, and consider social change as occurring rapidly and in a disorderly fashion (prominently, as subordinate groups overthrow dominant groups). *Consensual theories*[17] downplay social struggles and stress the integrated conception of society as well as the harmonious effect of shared values. The latter approaches underline the importance of consensus over basic values as essential for a stable and harmonious society. Social order is vital for any society and social change regularly occurs in a slow and orderly fashion.[18]

Certain social conflict features resurface in the analysis undertaken in several chapters of this work.[19] The discussion on collective memory refers, inter alia, to the fact that political leaders occasionally plan commemorative events to recruit people for their political aims (but warns against the reduction of such social memories to the political realm). And Foucault emphasizes the role of 'counter-memory', a social memory developed by a disadvantaged group which challenges the dominant group's historical narrative.[20] Similarly, Argentina's collective memory of past foreign interventions and the ensuing Calvo doctrine have contributed to the resistant approach adopted by the government of Argentina towards international investment tribunals after the financial crisis.[21]

Theory (Pine Forge Press, 2008) 12–13; Sharon Hays, 'Structure and Agency and the Sticky Problem of Culture' (1994) 12 *Sociological Theory* 57; David F Walsh, 'Structure/Agency' in Chris Jenks (ed), *Core Sociological Dichotomies* (Sage, 1998) 8.

Several leading sociologists attempted to mediate between these theoretical approaches. One of the most prominent attempts is presented in Giddens's structuration theory. See Anthony Giddens, *The Constitution of Society: Outline of the Theory of Structuration* (University of California Press, 1984) 281–354; Anthony Giddens, *New Rules of Sociological Method: A Positive Critique of Interpretative Sociologies* (Basic Books, 1976) 118–29.

15 See Chapter 2, Sections IV and V.

16 On the social conflict perspective, see Chapter 2, Section IV(d).

17 On the structural-functional perspective, see Chapter 2, Section IV(b).

18 On the consensus-conflict debate, see Ritzer and Stepnisky (n 10) 237–8; Giddens and Sutton (n 6) 91; Banakar and Traverse (n 6) 3–4; Malcolm Waters, *Modern Sociological Theory* (Sage, 1994) 219–20.

19 See, e.g., the social conflict approach to regional trade agreements, Chapter 2, Section IV(d).

20 See Chapter 3, Section II.

21 See Chapter 3, Section V.

Key concepts: *Culture* is an elusive concept and defining it is a complicated task. According to Ritzer, culture is a collection of ideas, values, practices, and material objects that are meaningful to a group of people or the entire society, and which allows them to carry out their collective lives in relative order and harmony.[22] The principal elements of culture are values, norms, material objects, symbols, and language.[23] *Values* refer to broad guidelines defining what a group considers good, desirable, right, or important. Values express the ideals of society, as well as of groups of every size.[24] The term *norm* refers to shared expectations about appropriate behaviour in a given situation, and norms guide people's social action.[25] Culture is also manifested in tangible forms, and material culture includes a wide range of items ('artefacts'), including clothes, food products, toys, and weapons.[26] A *symbol* is anything which carries a particular meaning and is recognized by people who share the same culture. Symbols are often manifested in material objects, and there is no clear dividing line between material and non-material culture.[27] A key element of symbolic culture is *language*, a set of meaningful symbols that enable communication among people. Language, especially in its written form, allows the storage and development of culture.[28]

A variety of elements of culture pervade all chapters of this book. Thus, for example, norms are extensively discussed in Chapter 6 regarding compliance, and it is clear that the interaction between international norms and international law (including 'soft' law) affects the prospects of compliance with or breach of these rules.[29] As for tangible forms of culture, collective memories are substantiated and transmitted through a wide array of practices of commemoration, including monuments and museums.[30] Language's significance is illustrated in the discussion on the investment arbitration community and its attitude to the application of human rights treaties in investment disputes.[31]

The concept of culture is closely related to the notion of *society*, a group of people who interact and share a common culture, frequently occupy a particular territorial area, and believe themselves to constitute a unified, distinct entity.[32] A prominent distinction in sociological literature relates to the differences between two types

[22] Ritzer (n 6) 109. On further definitions of 'culture', see, e.g., John J Macionis, *Sociology* (14th edn, Pearson, 2012) 54; Chris Jenks, 'Culture: Conceptual Clarifications', *The Concise Encyclopedia of Sociology* (Wiley-Blackwell, 2010) 114–15; 'Culture', in *Oxford Dictionary of Sociology* (4th edn, OUP, 2014) 146–7.

[23] Ritzer (n 6) 111. See also Macionis (n 22) 58–63. On the similar contemporary concept of 'culture' in the context of cultural rights, see Pok Yin S Chow, 'Culture as Collective Memories: An Emerging Concept in International Law and Discourse on Cultural Rights' (2014) 14 *Human Rights Law Review* 611, 621 et seq.

[24] Ritzer (n 6) 111. See also Macionis (n 22) 60.

[25] 'Norm', *Oxford Dictionary of Sociology* (4th edn, OUP, 2014) 519; 'Norm', *The Penguin Dictionary of Sociology* (4th edn, Penguin Books, 2000) 243. See also Steven P Dandaneau, 'Norms', *The Concise Encyclopedia of Sociology* (2010) 426; Macionis (n 22) 62; Ritzer (n 6) 112.

[26] Ritzer (n 6) 113–14; Macionis (n 22) 63–4.

[27] Ritzer (n 6) 114; Macionis (n 22) 58.

[28] Ritzer (n 6) 114–16; Macionis (n 22) 59.

[29] See Chapter 6, Section III(b).

[30] See Chapter 3, Section II.

[31] See Chapter 5, Section IV.

[32] 'Society', *Oxford Dictionary of Sociology* (4th edn, OUP, 2014) 711. See also Ritzer (n 6) 195.

of social groups,[33] often labelled as 'communities' and 'societies'. Though there is no clear line between these two social groups and both refer to groups of people who interact and share certain features, the term 'society' commonly denotes a larger entity than 'community' (society may thus comprise several communities).[34] The first type of social groups (*gemeinschaft* in Tönnies's famous classification—often translated as 'community')[35] commonly refers to traditional groups who live together in the same geographical area and are characterized by personal intimacy and sympathy, higher social cohesion, moral commitment, and common understanding. The second type of social group (*gesellschaft* in Tönnies' classification—often translated as 'society')[36] refers to people who may be geographically dispersed but share common interests, identities, and agreed rules; this group is also characterized by impersonal and exchange relations.[37]

Sociological analysis of international law addresses both types of social groups, and the following chapters discuss social groups which present features resembling *gemeinschaft* (such as indigenous groups)[38] as well as groups presenting features closer to *gesellschaft* (such as the investment arbitration community[39] or certain regional groups of states).[40]

Sharing a culture tends to lead people to adopt a similar worldview and behave in similar ways.[41] Such similar worldviews and behaviours may be attributed, inter alia, to social control mechanisms, socialization, or common identity. Every society deploys diverse *social control* mechanisms, that is, informal and formal means to encourage and enforce conformity to norms (including addressing norm violation).[42] *International* social control mechanisms include a broad range of practices (such as statements by international bodies expressing condemnation, 'peer review' procedures, or threats to expel members from international institutions): their significant influence on compliance with international law is addressed in Chapter 6.[43]

Newcomers to a society learn and generally come to accept the basic elements of culture through the process of *socialization*.[44] Individuals who successfully undergo

[33] On some other common divisions of societies, see, e.g., Macionis (n 22) 80 et seq.; Ritzer (n 6) 196–8.

[34] On Tönnies's definition of these social groups, see further below.

[35] Ferdinand Tönnies, *Community and Society* (Transaction Publishers, 2004) 31–64.

[36] Ibid., 34, 64–102.

[37] On this division between social groups, see Tönnies (n 35) 31–102: Ritzer (n 6) 197; Graham Crow, 'Community', *The Concise Encyclopedia of Sociology* (Wiley-Blackwell, 2010) 74, 74–5; 'Community', *The Oxford Dictionary of Sociology* (4th edn, 2014) 103–4. See also John D Kasarda and Morris Janowitz, 'Community Attachment in Mass Society' (1974) 39 *American Sociological Review* 328.

[38] See Chapter 4, Section IV(c)(iii).

[39] See Chapter 5, Section IV(a).

[40] See Chapter 2, Section IV(a).

[41] Ritzer (n 6) 109.

[42] See, e.g., Erich Goode, *Deviant Behaviour* (9th edn, Prentice Hall, 2011) 49–50; Mathieu Deflem, *Sociology of Law: Visions of a Scholarly Tradition* (CUP, 2008) 227 et seq. On social control mechanisms, see Chapter 6, Section III(c).

[43] See Chapter 6, Section III(c).

[44] Ritzer (n 6)154; Eleanor E Maccoby, 'Historical Overview of Socialization Research and Theory' in Joan E Grusec and Paul D Hasting (eds), *Handbook of Socialization* (Guilford Press, 2007) 13; Macionis (n 22) 102.

this process learn to become members of society both by internalizing the values and norms of their social group,[45] as well as by learning to perform their social roles.[46] The most influential *agents of socialization* are generally the family, education system, peer group, and the mass media.[47] As elaborated in Chapter 6, socialization is one of the influential sociological processes in the international system and it substantially affects compliance with international law.[48] Regional economic organizations occasionally function as agents of socialization, and it is particularly notable regarding the long accession process to certain international organizations (such as the EU).[49]

Social identity mediates the relationships between individuals and the social group. Personal identity differentiates one's self from other individuals and includes personal traits and the self's social categorization into social groups.[50] People also identify themselves collectively, and collective identification evokes imagery of people who resemble one another and share inter-subjective characteristics.[51] It is often impossible in reality to disentangle group identity from personal identity.[52] Two dynamic elements stand at the heart of social identity (both personal and collective)—similarity and difference. Individuals and groups need a certain level of both similarity to and differentiation from others, and social identity derives from the fundamental tension between the sense of belonging and the sense of distinctiveness.[53]

As elaborated in Chapter 4, international law often institutionalizes identities which are encoded into diverse international instruments and institutions' constituent documents.[54] The formation of certain international institutions often reflects collective identity, and membership in these groups represents various identity ties (such as regional, ideological, or historical ones). International norms often constitute a significant element of collective identity, and this is remarkable with regard to the 'constitutive norms' which define group membership. The latter feature is prominent regarding the central role of human rights protection in the EU identity, which is also employed to highlight social boundaries vis-à-vis other international actors. This identity of the EU is projected through a variety of

[45] See, e.g., 'Socialization', *Oxford Dictionary of Sociology* (4th edn, 2014) 714; Macionis (n 22) 102–3. See also Joan E Grusec and Paul D Hasting, 'Introduction' in Joan E Grusec and Paul D Hasting (eds), *Handbook of Socialization* (Guilford Press 2007) 1; 'Socialization', *Penguin Dictionary of Sociology* (4th edn, Penguin Books, 2000) 329.

[46] The term 'role' refers to socially defined expectations that a person generally follows in a particular social position (e.g., 'parent' or 'employee'). 'Role (social role, role theory)', *Oxford Dictionary of Sociology* (4th edn, 2014) 652. See also 'Role', *Penguin Dictionary of Sociology* (4th edn, 2000) 301. On 'role strain', see Chapter 6, Section IV(c).

[47] See, e.g., Ritzer (n 6) 156–61; Maccoby (n 44) 14; Macionis (n 22) 109–14.

[48] See Chapter 6, Section III(b).

[49] See Chapter 2, Section IV(a).

[50] Stephan Worchel, 'A Developmental View of the Search for Group Identity' in Stephan Worschel and others (eds), *Social Identity: International Perspectives* (Sage, 1998) 53, 55; Richard Jenkins, *Social Identity* (4th edn, Routledge, 2014) 114–15. On social identity theory, see Chapter 4, Section II.

[51] Jenkins (n 50) 104.

[52] Jan E Stets and Peter J Burke, 'A Sociological Approach to Self and Identity' in Mark Leary and June Tangney (eds), *Handbook of Self and Identity* (Guilford Press, 2002) 228.

[53] Marilynn B Brewer, 'The Social Self: On Being the Same and Different at the Same Time' (1991) 17 *Personality and Social Psychology Bulletin* 475, 475–7.

[54] On the interaction between social identities and international law, see Chapter 4, Section IV(a).

frameworks, such as the inclusion of human rights clauses in international trade treaties concluded with non-members. The motivation for and the impact of those identity-driven treaty provisions are explored in Chapter 4.[55]

Social groups often influence individual memories. Society frequently reminds us that certain historical events have taken place, provides some details of the particular occurrence, and occasionally suggests certain normative lessons drawn from this event. The construction of *collective memory* is a selective process, storing and interpreting historical events according to the distinctive features of the specific *contemporary* society. A group's memory preserves the store of knowledge from which the group derives awareness of its unity and identity. Collective memories may be transmitted through numerous practices, including various ceremonies, national holidays, the mass media, or court proceedings.[56] Chapter 3 discusses the reciprocal interactions between international law and collective memories. International legal mechanisms occasionally function as carriers of collective memory, and the memories of various social groups (including nations or regional groups) often motivate and constrain their activities in the international legal system.[57] The impact of collective memories on international law is illustrated by an examination of Germany's collective memory of the hyperinflation and its influence on the EU economic and monetary law during the Eurozone debt crisis (2009–12),[58] as well as Argentina's collective memory of past foreign interventions and its effect on the non-implementation until 2013 of a series of investment tribunals' awards.[59]

III. Law, International Law, and Culture

Sociologists of law have long emphasized that law is rooted in communities, and laws are expressive types of those communities.[60] Rosen explains:

> Indeed, it is to suggest that law is so deeply embedded in the particularities of each culture that carving it out as a separate domain and only later making note of its cultural connections distorts the nature of both law and culture.[61]

[55] See Chapter 4, Section IV.

[56] See, e.g., Jeffrey K Olick and Joyce Robbins, 'Social Memory Studies: From "Collective Memory" to the Historical Sociology of Mnemonic Practices' (1998) 24 *Annual Review of Sociology* 105, 106; Eviatar Zerubavel, 'Social Memories: Steps to a Sociology of the Past' (1996) 19 *Qualitative Sociology* 283, 286; Yael Zerubavel, *Recovered Roots* (University of Chicago Press, 1995) 6–8; Vered Vinitzky-Seroussi, 'Commemorating a Difficult Past: Yitzhak Rabin's Memorial' (2002) 67 *American Sociological Review* 30, 34–5, 51; Barry Schwartz, *Abraham Lincoln and the Forge of National Memory* (University of Chicago Press, 2000) 18. For a detailed discussion on collective memory, see Chapter 3, Section II.

[57] See Chapter 3, Sections III–V.

[58] See Chapter 3, Section IV.

[59] See Chapter 3, Section V.

[60] Roger Cotterrell, *Law, Culture and Society: Legal Ideas in the Mirror of Social Theory* (Ashgate, 2006) 117, 161. See also Mathieu Deflem, *Sociology of Law: Visions of a Scholarly Tradition* (CUP, 2008) 7–8.

[61] Lawrence Rosen, *Law as Culture: An Invitation* (Princeton University Press, 2006) xii. See also Paul Schiff Berman, 'The Enduring Connections between Law and Culture' (2009) 57 *American Journal of Comparative Law* 101.

This rich literature is mindful that the relationship between law and culture is not unidirectional: law is both affected by, and influences, cultural patterns.[62]

A central approach in law and culture scholarship is identified with the German historical school of law (dating back to the first half of the nineteenth century) which considers law as a product of a nation's culture.[63] Another central stream in this scholarship (prominently developed in the American literature in the 1980s) views law as playing a significant role in constituting culture, and influencing people's minds, practices, and social relations.[64] The above conception that law is inextricably entwined with culture should not lead to a reductionist view assuming that law is only a mirror of society. Leading sociologists of law (such as Nelken) do not accept the 'mirror theory of law' and emphasize that law does not fully reflect society.[65]

The concept of *legal culture* refers in sociology of law literature to relatively stable patterns of legally oriented social behaviour and attitudes. The identifying elements of legal culture range from facts about institutions (such as the role of courts and their involvement in the development of law) to various forms of behaviour (such as litigation) as well as aspects of legal ideas, values, aspirations, and mentalities.[66] Though numerous studies identify legal culture with national legal systems, patterns of legal culture are also sought at the international level.[67] In parallel to the sociological literature regarding the diffusion of cultural traits, sociology of law scholarship on 'legal transplants' explores various factors affecting the diffusion of laws (ordinarily among national legal systems). These factors include complementarity between the 'exporting' and 'importing' societies and their legal cultures,[68] and this literature also emphasizes the role of legal professional communities.[69] Informed by this scholarship, Chapter 5 explores some factors affecting the diffusion of legal rules across different branches of international law, particularly the disinclination of investment tribunals to apply human rights treaties in investment disputes.[70]

[62] See, e.g., Paul Schiff Berman, 'From International Law to Law and Globalization' (2005) 43 *Columbia Journal of Transnational Law* 485, 496; David Nelken, 'Towards a Sociology of Legal Adaptation' in David Nelken and Johannes Feest (eds), *Adapting Legal Cultures* (Hart, 2001) 3, 8; Berman, 'Enduring Connections' (n 61) 109.

[63] See, e.g., Menachem Mautner, 'Three Approaches to Law and Culture' (2011) 96 *Cornell Law Review* 839, 841, 844–8 and see the references therein.

[64] Ibid., 848–56.

[65] See, e.g., Nelken (n 62) 12, 15.

[66] David Nelken, 'Using the Concept of Legal Culture' (2004) 29 *Australian Journal of Legal Philosophy* 1, 3; See also Cotterrell (n 60) 81–96; Nelken (n 62) 25–6.

[67] See, e.g., Yves Dezalay and Bryant G Garth, *Dealing in Virtue: International Commercial Arbitration and the Construction of a Transnational Legal Order* (University of Chicago Press, 1996) 3 et seq.

[68] See, e.g., Pitman B Potter, 'Legal Reform in China: Institutions, Culture, and Selective Adaptation' (2004) 29 *Law and Social Inquiry* 465, 478–9.

[69] See, e.g., Nelken (n 62) 24, 42-43; Lawrence Friedman, 'Some Comments on Cottorrell and Legal Transplants' in David Nelken and Johannes Feest (eds), *Adapting Legal Cultures* (Hart, 2001) 93, 96.

[70] See Chapter 5, Section IV(b).

Early law and society scholarship emphasized non-formal rules, alternatives to legal dispute resolution, and alternatives to law. This approach constituted an obstacle to studying formal international law and institutions and, as Madsen notes, it required a 'detour' via less formalized international law to find a convergence of interests and a start to an analysis of the work of international courts.[71]

In light of the above sociological and sociology of law literature, this study's point of departure is that international law is deeply rooted in the particular socio-cultural features of various communities. Sociological factors and processes thus form an inseparable dimension of international law, and international law is both affected by and influences such factors and processes. While international law often cannot be disentangled from socio-cultural factors and processes undertaken in various international communities, it is clear that it does not fully mirror the culture of those communities. Thus, for example, certain international norms,[72] identities,[73] and collective memories[74] are *partially* institutionalized in international legal rules. Still, as elaborated throughout this study, such factors are meaningful to communities and they affect international law and its implementation.

IV. The Social Constructivist Approach in International Relations Theory

In addition to sociological and sociology of law literature, this study also draws on the constructivist approach in international relations scholarship. The social constructivist approach in international relations literature[75] has been significantly influenced by sociological scholarship.[76] Social constructivism emerged in the late 1980s, and largely developed as a critique of the realist tradition in international relations literature. Constructivism was introduced to international relations

[71] Mikael Rask Madsen, 'Sociological Approaches to International Courts' in Cesare Romano, Karen Alter, and Yuval Shany (eds), *Oxford Handbook of International Adjudication* (OUP, 2014) 338–9, 388.

[72] On the interaction between international norms and international law, see, e.g., Chapter 6, Section III(b).

[73] On the interaction between social identities and international law, see Chapter 4, Section IV.

[74] On the interactions between collective memories and international law, see Chapter 3, Section III.

[75] On some *social* elements in the neo-liberal institutional approach (and particularly regarding the factor of identity), see Jennifer Sterling-Folker, 'Competing Paradigms or Birds of a Feather? Constructivism and Neoliberal Institutionalism Compared' (2000) 44 *International Studies Quarterly* 97, 110–13. On additional international relations theoretical approaches to international law, see John Baylis, Steve Smith, and Patricia Owens, *The Globalization of World Politics* (6th edn, OUP, 2014) 91 et seq. See also Moshe Hirsch, 'The Impact of the Advisory Opinion on Israel's Future Policy: International Relations Perspective' (2005) 1 *Journal of International Law and International Relations* 319.

[76] On the links between the constructivist approach and sociology, see, e.g., Alexander Wendt, 'Collective Identity Formation and the International State' (1994) 88 *American Political Science Review* 385–6, 394. See also Robert Jackson and Georg Sørensen, *Introduction to International Relations: Theories and Approaches* (4th edn, OUP, 2010) 163. See also Chapter 4, Section III.

scholarship by Onuf (1989),[77] who coined the term, and it became influential following a series of publications by Wendt, Finnemore, Hopf, Adler, Barnett, Katzenstein, and other leading international relations scholars.

According to social constructivism, states are social actors embedded in social relations which constitute their interests and motivate them.[78] Wendt emphasizes that the international system is composed not only of physical entities and the distribution of material capabilities (such as military and economic resources), but also comprises social relationships. The critical components of the international social structure include shared inter-subjective understandings, expectations, and knowledge.[79] The physical element is part of the international system but is secondary to social and ideational elements that infuse it with meaning, organize, plan, and guide it.[80] The international system and states are not exogenously given and do not exist independently of the thoughts and ideas of the people involved; rather they are constructed by diverse historical interactions.[81] International politics and related concepts are human creations and exist as inter-subjective beliefs that are widely shared among people.[82] Thus the social world is a world of human consciousness that includes language, signals, and understanding among human beings, and especially groups such as states.[83]

Norms are of major importance in constructivist literature. Finnemore emphasizes that international politics creates normative understanding among actors that coordinate values, expectations, and behaviour.[84] Norms influence the formation of interests, and changing norms are likely to change state interests.[85] Norms do not always determine behaviour but do create permissive conditions for action.[86] Identity (and particularly collective identity) is one of the key concepts

[77] Nicolas Onuf, *World of Our Making* (University of South Carolina Press, 1989) 29–30, 35–40.

[78] See, e.g., Peter J Katzenstein, 'Introduction: Alternative Perspectives on National Security' in Peter J Katzenstein (ed), *The Culture of National Security: Norms and Identity in World Politics* (Columbia University Press, 1996) 1, 23.

[79] Wendt, 'Collective Identity' (n 76) 389; Jackson and Sørensen (n 76) 165. See also Alexander Wendt, *Social Theory of International Politics* (CUP, 1999) 94–5; Emanuel Adler, 'Cognitive Evolution: A Dynamic Approach for the Study of International Relations and Their Progress' in Emanuel Adler and Beverly Crawford (eds), *Progress in Postwar International Relations* (Columbia University Press, 1991) 44–6.

[80] Jackson and Sørensen (n 76) 165; Wendt, *Social Theory* (n 79) 165–6.

[81] Wendt, 'Collective Identity' (n 76) 386; Katzenstein (n 78) 22; Bahar Rumelili, 'Constructing Identity and Relating to Difference: Understanding the EU's' (2004) 30 *Review of International Studies* 27, 30–1; Jackson and Sørensen (n 76) 164, 172; Michael Barnett, 'Social Constructivism' in John Baylis, Steve Smith, and Patricia Owens, *The Globalization of World Politics* (6th edn, OUP, 2014) 130, 132–4.

[82] Jackson and Sørensen (n 76) 162, 166.

[83] Ibid., 165.

[84] Martha Finnemore, 'Constructing Norms of Humanitarian Intervention' in Peter J Katzenstein (ed), *The Culture of National Security: Norms and Identity in World Politics* (Columbia University Press, 1996) 153, 157–8.

[85] Ibid., 158.

[86] Ibid., 158. On the sources of norms, see also Paul Kowert and Jeffrey Legro, 'Norms, Identity and Their Limits: A Theoretical Reprise' in Peter J Katzenstein (ed), *The Culture of National Security: Norms and Identity in World Politics* (Columbia University Press, 1996) 451, 469.

in constructivist scholarship,[87] and Hopf states that 'identities are the most proximate causes of choices, preferences, and action'.[88]

From the social constructivist perspective, decision-makers in the international legal system are motivated by impersonal social factors and processes such as values, norms, and identity. Legal obligations often represent social standards of appropriate behaviour which operate in an inter-subjective framework.[89] The following chapters also draw on the rich social constructivist literature and this is particularly notable concerning compliance and deviance from international law,[90] identity of various international groups,[91] and regional trade agreements.[92]

V. Methodology, Structure, and Outline

Methodology: Sociological studies of international law broaden the options for research methods which international law scholars can apply. Research methods used in sociology may well lead to new insights regarding the evolution of international law and normative behaviour of international actors. Such methods include the examination of public records and statistics, surveys, interviews, content analysis (e.g., of visual or digital media), and secondary data analysis.[93] This book extensively employs theoretical tools and evidence drawn from sociological literature but the analysis undertaken in the following chapters does not amount to a rigorous methodological investigation. As an *invitation*, this study rather aims to expose readers to the sociological dimension of international law and illustrate the valuable potential of sociological analysis to broaden our understanding of the development and implementation of international law.

Structure: The book is divided into three major parts. The first part includes two chapters and is intended to introduce the reader to the sociological perspective. Chapter 1 briefly exposes the central assumptions and certain key concepts of the sociological perspective, and Chapter 2 presents the major theoretical approaches in sociological literature. Readers who are not familiar with the

[87] See, e.g., Wendt, 'Collective Identity' (n 76) 385; James D Fearon, 'What is Identity (As We Now Use the Word)?' (1999) Stanford University, 3 <https://web.stanford.edu/group/fearon-research/cgi-bin/wordpress/wp-content/uploads/2013/10/What-is-Identity-as-we-now-use-the-word-.pdf> accessed 8 March 2015; Thomas Risse, *A Community of Europeans? Transnational Identities and Public Spheres* (Cornell University Press, 2010) 20.

[88] Ted Hopf, 'The Promise of Constructivism in International Relations Theory' (1998) 23 *International Security* 171, 174.

[89] See, e.g., Kal Raustiala and Anne-Marie Slaughter, 'International Law, International Relations and Compliance' in Walter Carlnaes and others (eds), *Handbook of International Relations* (2002) 538, 540: Robert O Keohane, 'International Institutions: Two Approaches' (1988) 32 *International Studies Quarterly* 379, 381; Emanuel Adler, 'Cognitive Evolution: A Dynamic Approach for the Study of International Relations and Their Progress' in Emanuel Adler and Beverly Crawford (eds), *Progress in Postwar International Relations* (Columbia University Press, 1991) 44, 49–51.

[90] See Chapter 6, Sections II(b), IV(b), and V(b).

[91] See Chapter 4, Section II et seq.

[92] See Chapter 2, Section IV(a).

[93] On these and additional research methods in sociology, see Ritzer (n 6) 76–96; Giddens and Sutton (n 6) 48–61; Fulcher and Scott (n 10) 74–103.

sociological perspective and its terminology are advised to read those chapters first. The remaining chapters illustrate the contribution of sociological analysis to international legal scholarship; they are self-standing chapters and need not necessarily be read in consecutive order. The second part of the book presents two important concepts in contemporary sociology and explores their interactions with international law: Chapter 3 addresses the concept of collective memory and Chapter 4 discusses the conception of social identity. The third part examines two socio-legal themes which cross-cut through virtually all spheres of international law: Chapter 5 discusses the sociological dimension of international legal fragmentation and Chapter 6 addresses sociological factors influencing deviance and compliance with international law.

Outline: This chapter discusses the mutual links between sociology and international law and introduces some key concepts of the sociological discipline; it also briefly sets out certain basic concepts in the sociology of law scholarship and the social constructivist approach in international relations literature. Chapter 2 analyses the long-standing debate in international trade law regarding regional trade agreements (RTAs) from three major theoretical perspectives in sociological literature. The unprecedented proliferation of free trade areas and customs unions has intensified the debate among scholars and policy-makers regarding the repercussions of RTAs, and whether the WTO legal system should promote, tolerate, or restrict the formation of RTAs. The answers provided to these important questions affect the interpretation of existing WTO legal provisions regarding RTAs, and negotiations regarding future legal rules in this sphere. The chapter analyses these questions using the most influential sociological theories: the structural-functional perspective, the symbolic-interactionist approach, and the social conflict perspective. While each of these core sociological approaches underscores certain significant aspects of the global/regional debate, the chapter concludes that the symbolic-interactionist perspective should serve as a point of departure for legal and policy-making in this sphere. This chapter draws substantially on the article 'The Sociology of International Economic Law: Sociological Analysis of the Regulation of Regional Agreements in the World Trading System'.[94]

Chapter 3 explores the mutual interactions between collective memory and international law. Social groups often influence individual memories, and society often reminds us that certain historical events have taken place, provides some details of the particular occurrence, and suggests certain normative lessons arising from the event. Collective memories of various social groups often motivate and constrain their activities in the international legal system. The chapter introduces the central tenets of collective memory in sociological literature and outlines the diverse interrelationships between such memories and international law. To illustrate the significance of collective memory for international law, the chapter discusses Germany's

[94] Moshe Hirsch, 'The Sociology of International Economic Law: Sociological Analysis of the Regulation of Regional Agreements in the World Trading System' (2008) 19 *EJIL* 277.

collective memory of the hyperinflation (in 1922–3) and its considerable impact on the EU economic and monetary law, particularly during the Eurozone debt crisis (2009–12). An examination of Argentina's collective memory of foreign interventions sheds light on that memory's contribution to the hostile approach of the government of Argentina towards international investment tribunals, as well as the non-implementation of a series of International Centre for Settlement of Investment Disputes (ICSID) awards during the period of 2007–13.

Chapter 4 addresses the concept of social identity and interrelationships between identity and international law. Social identity constitutes a conceptual bridge between individuals and collective groups (like 'peoples' or 'minority groups') or between such groups. Numerous international legal rules are infused with social identities and international law often institutionalizes (to various degrees) collective identities. Diverse identities (e.g., regional, ethnic, and historical) often affect the perception, judgment, and behaviour of international legal actors. The chapter exposes the key elements of social identity in sociological and social psychology literature, and briefly discusses certain links between international law and social identity. It elaborates on the links between the EU's identity and its external trade law aimed at promoting compliance with international human rights law. The potential of social identity literature as an instrument for interpreting certain international legal provisions is illustrated here with regard to the definition of 'minority groups' as well as to rules concerning disqualification of adjudicators.

Chapter 5 examines some sociological aspects of international legal fragmentation, and particularly regarding the interaction between international investment tribunals and human rights law. Informed by sociological and sociology of law literature concerning diffusion of cultural traits, the chapter seeks to shed light on the limited diffusion of human rights norms in the investment arbitration community. It explores the investment arbitration community as a social group and discusses the impact of certain features of this group on investment tribunals' jurisprudence regarding human rights treaties. The chapter argues that the specific socio-cultural characteristics of the investment arbitration community, the socio-cultural distance between the group and the human rights community, and the strained relations between them, significantly contributed to the reserved approach of investment tribunals vis-à-vis international human rights instruments. The dynamic aspect of the relationships between these two branches of international law and the possibility of narrowing the social distance between the two communities are also addressed. This chapter draws and enlarges on the chapter titled 'The Interaction between International Investment Law and Human Rights Treaties: A Sociological Perspective'.[95]

Chapter 6 explores the complex and multi-dimensional topic of compliance with international law. Factors motivating deviance from and compliance with

[95] Moshe Hirsch, 'The Interaction between International Investment Law and Human Rights Treaties: A Sociological Perspective' in Yuval Shany and Tomer Broude (eds), *Multi-Sourced Equivalent Norms* (Hart, 2011) 211. See also Moshe Hirsch, 'Investment Tribunals and Human Rights: Divergent Paths' in Pierre-Marie Dupuy, Francesco F Francioni, and Ernst-Ulrich Petersmann (eds), *Human Rights in International Investment Law and Arbitration* (OUP, 2008) 97.

international legal rules often involve both sociological and rational choice approaches. Following an outline of the key assumptions of the rational choice and the sociological approaches concerning compliance with international law, the chapter focuses on sociological factors influencing compliance with or deviance from international rules. It offers a broad view of the relevant rules (both formal and informal norms) and the variety of societal mechanisms involved in compliance with these rules (such as social control mechanisms). Three clusters of sociological approaches to deviance are addressed: constructionist approaches that emphasize the role of 'labelling'; social learning approaches (prominently socialization and identity); and structural-functional approaches that highlight structural patterns (such as 'anomie', and 'role-strain'). The discussion of these sociological approaches to deviance is accompanied by an examination of their application to compliance with or breach of international law.

Chapter 7 briefly assesses the contribution of sociological analysis to international law scholarship. The chapter underlines that international law operates in (and between) social groups, and that central international legal actors often constitute social groups. Thus, the point of departure of this study is that specific international legal rules emerging from and operating in these social groups reflect and affect those groups' particular features. The chapter also addresses certain limits of the sociological analysis as well as the dynamic dimension of the interactions between international law and sociological factors.

2

Sociological Theories

Regional and Global Trade Agreements

Theories seek to explain things. And thus, sociological theory attempts to explain how the social world operates. This social world consists of the behaviors, interactions, and patterns of social organization among humans... sociological theory tends to focus on interaction and organization more than behavior per se, but interactions are interpersonal behaviors, and patterns of social organization are ultimately built from interactions among individuals.

Jonathan H Turner, *Contemporary Social Theory*[1]

I. Introduction

Sociological theories seek to explain how the social world operates. Each theoretical perspective highlights a different aspect of social phenomena and presents a different explanation regarding the underlying forces that drive social events.

[1] Jonathan H Turner, *Contemporary Social Theory* (Sage, 2013) 1.

Sociological theorizing itself does not take place in a vacuum outside society.[2] Sociological theoretical approaches also offer different perspectives on international law and suggest different assumptions regarding the links between international legal relations and socio-cultural factors. Various theories cast a different light on the same international legal process and may generate different practical strategies regarding international legal dilemmas. The properties of sociological theoretical analysis are illustrated in this chapter by addressing one of the controversial dilemmas in international trade law literature: the relationship between the World Trade Organization (WTO) and regional trade agreements (RTAs).

Among the numerous sociological theories, three major perspectives are widely recognized as most influential: the structural-functional perspective, the symbolic-interactionist approach, and the social conflict perspective. Each of these core perspectives underlines different social factors and sociological investigations often employ theoretical tools borrowed from several approaches.

Contemporary literature of international trade law is considerably influenced by the rational-choice paradigm and various economic theories based on this model (e.g., public choice and game theory). This may be explained primarily by the paramount role of the rational-choice model in mainstream international economic theory, which is conventionally considered by many experts the 'natural habitat' of international economic law (IEL). Consequently, international trade law scholars and readers are often predisposed to perceive the abundant new information in this sphere (such as new treaty provisions or judicial decisions) through an economic lens. This process is particularly influential for 'newcomers' who are socialized into the international trading system. This chapter emphasizes that international economic activity is a social phenomenon and international trade should also be conceived as a specific type of social interaction.

The rapid proliferation of RTAs[3] during the two recent decades changed the landscape of the international trading system and they have become a very prominent feature of international trade relations.[4] The extensive spread of RTAs has

[2] Ibid., 1–4; Anthony Giddens and Philip Sutton, *Sociology* (7th edn, Polity, 2013) 70.

[3] The term 'regional trade agreements' refers to agreements through which the involved states grant more favourable conditions to trade than to other WTO members' trade. Mitsuo Matsushita, Thomas J Schoenbaum, and Petros C Mavroidis, *The World Trade Organization: Law, Practice and Policy* (2nd edn, OUP, 2006) 548–9; Maurice W Schiff and L Alan Winters, *Regional Integration and Development* (World Bank and OUP, 2003) 1–2. Regional trade agreements are also called 'preferential trade agreements', see, e.g., Michael J Trebilcock, Robert Howse, and Antonia Eliason, *The Regulation of International Trade* (4th edn, Routledge, 2013) 83. Though most RTAs are established between neighbouring countries, this is not universally true; see, for instance, Agreement on the Establishment of a Free Trade Area between the Government of Israel and the Government of the United States of America (signed 22 April 1984, entered into force 19 August 1985) 24 *ILM* 653, or US–Jordan: Agreement Between the United States of America and the Hashemite Kingdom of Jordan on the Establishment of a Free Trade Area (signed 24 October 2000, entered into force 17 December 2001) 41 *ILM* 63.

[4] On new trends in RTAs (including 'mega-regional' agreements), see Bernard Hoekman, 'Supply Chains, Mega-Regionals and Multilateralism: A Road Map for the WTO' (2014) Robert Schuman Centre for Advanced Studies Research Paper No RSCAS 2014/27, 5–6, 21–2 <http://papers.ssrn.com/sol3/papers.cfm?abstract_id=2406871> accessed 10 March 2015.

intensified the long-standing debate among scholars and policy-makers regarding the motives and repercussions of RTAs,[5] and whether the WTO system should promote, tolerate, or restrict the formation of new RTAs. Economic analyses of RTAs do not provide a single answer to the question regarding the desirability or undesirability of such regional agreements.

The formation and enlargement of RTAs are addressed by several WTO legal provisions—mainly, Article XXIV of the General Agreement on Tariffs and Trade[6] (GATT) and Article V of the General Agreement on Trade in Services[7] (GATS). These preferential arrangements are monitored by the WTO organs but some specialists believe that the WTO oversight mechanism suffers from an insufficient legal discipline.[8] The perceived weakness of the regulation of RTAs led the WTO members to agree, in the 2001 Doha Ministerial Declaration, to initiate negotiations aimed at clarifying and improving disciplines under the existing WTO provisions in this sphere.[9]

Contemporary international trade law literature on RTAs discusses extensively the economic motives and repercussions of RTAs (e.g., the resulting trade creation/diversion).[10] This literature is also influenced, though to a lesser extent, by studies of the political factors involved in the formation and operation of RTAs (such as the neo-functional approach).[11] The abundant legal literature pays only scant attention to socio-cultural aspects of RTAs. The economic, political, and sociological dimensions of RTAs are inextricably interlinked in the life of RTAs and cannot be properly understood in isolation. As elaborated below, sociological analysis of RTAs casts new light on this significant phenomenon and bears significant implications for the interpretation of existing legal provisions (such as Article XXIV of the GATT) and may affect the content of future rules in this controversial sphere of international trade law.

This chapter is structured as follows: Section II briefly discusses the mutual interrelationships between IEL and sociology, emphasizing that IEL rules often reflect and affect societal factors. Section III addresses the debate regarding the appropriate regulation of RTAs in the global system and outlines the legal regulation of RTAs in the WTO legal system. The section briefly discusses the relevant legal provisions (Article XXIV of the GATT, Article V of the GATS, and the

[5] See, e.g., Trebilcock, Howse, and Eliason (n 3) 83.

[6] General Agreement on Tariffs and Trade (GATT) (adopted 15 April 1994 entered into force 1 January 1995) 1867 UNTS 190; General Agreement on Tariffs and Trade, 1947 (adopted 30 October 1947, entered into force 1 January 1948) 55 UNTS 194.

[7] General Agreement on Trade in Services (GATS) (adopted 15 April 1994, entered into force 1 January 1995) 1869 UNTS 183.

[8] See Section III(b) below.

[9] 2001 Doha Ministerial Declaration, 2002, 41 *ILM* 746, para 29. See also, WTO, Rules: Regional Agreements: Building Blocks or Stumbling Blocks?' (*Hong Kong WTO Ministerial 2005: Briefing Notes*) <http://www.wto.org/english/thewto_e/minist_e/min05_e/brief_e/brief09_e.htm> accessed 13 March 2015. On the Doha round negotiations on RTAs, see Sherzod Shadikhodjaev, 'Keeping Regionalism Under "Control" of the Multilateral Trading System: State of Play and Prospects' (2013) 19 *Law and Business Review of the Americas* 327, 335–48.

[10] See Section IV(b) below.

[11] See Section IV(b) below.

'Enabling Clause'), the practice of the WTO oversight mechanism, and the major decisions of the GATT/WTO dispute settlement bodies that dealt with these provisions. Section IV presents a sociological analysis of the global/regional debate in the WTO law. The section analyses the thorny question regarding the regulation of RTAs with the most influential sociological theories: the structural-functional perspective, the symbolic-interactionist approach, and the social conflict perspective. Section V analyses the merits and limitations of each sociological perspective on RTAs, and concludes that while each of the above approaches underscores certain significant aspects of the global/regional debate, the symbolic-interactionist perspective should serve as a point of departure for legal and policy-making in this sphere. This sociological approach suggests that the relevant WTO legal rules should be interpreted liberally. Section VI briefly recaps the main conclusions drawn from the preceding sections and offers some direction regarding further research in this field.

II. The Sociology of International Economic Law

The central assumption of the sociological perspective is that social factors significantly affect (and are affected by) human behaviour.[12] The sociological core assumptions regarding the influential role of social factors on individual behaviour are extended to the economic realm by economic sociology. Well-known sociologists who explore economic behaviour attack the 'under-socialized' concept of persons that characterizes the economists' analysis. Granovetter, a leading scholar of economic sociology, argues that an adequate analysis of human behaviour requires the avoidance of theoretical extremes of 'under-socialized' and 'over-socialized' conceptions. He states that '[a]ctors do not behave or decide as atoms outside a social context, nor do they adhere slavishly to a script written for them by a particular intersection of social categories that they happen to occupy. Their attempts at purposive action are instead embedded in a concrete, ongoing system of social relations'.[13]

Under this concept, *international* economic activity does not constitute an exception, and international trade is conceived as a specific type of social interaction.[14] Statistical studies demonstrate that socio-cultural factors influence international economic relations among states, firms, and individuals. Thus, for example, Guiso, Sapienza, and Zingales show that social trust and the cultural

[12] On the central tenets of the sociological perspective, see Chapter 1, Section II.

[13] Mark Granovetter, 'Economic Action and Social Structure: The Problem of Embeddedness' in Richard Swedberg (ed), *Economic Sociology* (Edward Elgar, 1996) 239, 245. See also Frank Dobbin, 'The Sociological View of the Economy' in Frank Dobbin (ed), *The New Economic Sociology: A Reader* (Princeton University Press, 2004) 1, 5.

[14] See, e.g., Michael D Irwin and John D Kasarda, 'Trade, Transportation, and Spatial Distribution' in Neil J Smelser and Richard Swedberg (eds), *The Handbook of Economic Sociology* (Princeton University Press, 1994) 342.

features of trading countries affect the volume of trade between them.[15] And Noland's study shows that after accounting for economic factors, public attitudes are statistically correlated with trade and capital inflows, and that these attitudes are in turn correlated with indices of cultural affinity (i.e., ethnic and religious similarity) and political ideology.[16] As Ghemawat states:

> A country's cultural attributes determine how people interact with one another and with companies and institutions. Differences in religious beliefs, race, social norms, and language ... can have a huge impact on trade ... Some cultural attributes, like language, are easily perceived and understood. Others are much more subtle ... Sometimes products can touch a deeper nerve, triggering associations related to the consumer's identity as a member of a particular community.[17]

International economic relations are not only affected *by* socio-cultural factors, they often *influence* the socio-cultural features of the involved communities. Thus, for example, international trade and foreign investments are considered a source of knowledge spillovers.[18] International trade spreads knowledge, norms, and values through traders who often cross boundaries and settle in new communities, and by the content of the products or services purchased by the members of different communities. Socio-cultural factors do not necessarily support international economic relations, and resistance to the expansion of global economic integration is often based on socio-cultural concerns.[19]

In light of the mutual interrelationships between international economics and socio-cultural factors,[20] it is not surprising that IEL often reflects and affects societal factors (such as values and norms) and processes (such as socialization or identity). Alternative legal rules regulating international economic activities reflect different socio-cultural values and affect social processes. The link between international trade law and socio-cultural factors is evident in special rules for trade in cultural goods and services (such as publications, films, and television programmes),[21] which are

[15] Luigi Guiso, Paola Sapienza, and Luigi Zingales, 'Cultural Biases in Economic Exchange' (2009) 124 *Quarterly Journal of Economics* 1095. See also Gabriel Felbermayr and Farid Toubal, 'Cultural Proximity and Trade' (2010) 54 *European Economic Review* 279.

[16] Marcus Noland, 'Affinity and International Trade' (2005) Institute for International Economics Working Paper No. WP 05-3, 3, 8 <http://papers.ssrn.com/sol3/papers.cfm?abstract_id=739884> accessed 6 June 2015 and see the references therein. See also Jeffrey A Frankel, *Regional Trading Blocs in the World Economic System* (Institute for International Economics, 1997) 45–6.

[17] Pankaj Ghemawat, 'Distance Still Matters' (2001) 79 *Harvard Business Review* 137, 140–1.

[18] See, e.g., Rod Falvey, Neil Foster, and David Greenaway, 'North-South Trade, Knowledge Spillovers and Growth' (2002) 17 *Journal of Economic Integration* 650.

[19] See, e.g., Joel Richard Paul, 'Cultural Resistance to Global Governance' (2001) 22 *Michigan Journal of International Law* 1; Mark Irving Lichbach, 'Global Order and Local Resistance: Structure, Culture, and Rationality in the Battle of Seattle' (2002) Department of Government and Politics, University of Maryland <http://depts.washington.edu/wtohist/documents/Lichbach.pdf> accessed 10 March 2015.

[20] The interaction between socio-cultural factors and international *investment* is discussed in Chapter 5, Section II.

[21] For an overview of the regulation of cultural sectors in major international trade agreements and negotiations, see Jingxia Shi, *Free Trade and Cultural Diversity in International Law* (Hart,

seen as 'vehicles of social communication that promote a wider sense of belonging and cultural identity'.[22] This relationship between international trade and culture is also discernible with regard to trade in other products and services.[23]

The relationship between some socio-cultural factors and international economic relations is also explored by the proponents of the social constructivist approach in contemporary international relations literature,[24] and this chapter also draws on this literature.[25]

III. The Regulation of Regional Trade Agreements in the WTO Legal System

a. The proliferation of RTAs and the global-regional debate

The recent two decades have witnessed a rapid increase in the number of RTAs (mostly free trade areas (FTAs) and customs unions)[26] and their ever-growing number is a prominent feature of the contemporary international trading system.[27]

2013) 125 et seq.; Tania S Voon, *Cultural Products and the World Trade Organization* (CUP, 2007) 18 et seq.; Raj Bhala, *Modern GATT Law* (Sweet & Maxwell, 2005) 1179–205.

[22] Pierre Sauvé and Karsten Steinfatt, 'Towards Multilateral Rules on Trade and Culture: Protective Regulation or Efficient Protection?' (Achieving Better Regulation of Services Conference, Canberra, November 2000) 323, 327 <http://www.pc.gov.au/research/completed/better-regulation/abros.pdf> accessed 10 March 2015.

[23] See, e.g., Voon (n 21) 13 et seq.; Keith Acheson and Christopher Maule, 'Culture in International Trade' in Victor A Ginsburgh and David Throsby (eds), *Handbook of the Economics of Art and Culture* vol 1 (Elsevier, 2006) 1141; Bruce Jamieson, 'Trade Liberalization: Culture, Identity and Social Cohesion' (2001) 73 et seq., Department of Canadian Heritage: Paper prepared on behalf of the PRI-GCON Working Group on World Trade Issues <http://citeseerx.ist.psu.edu/viewdoc/download?doi=10.1.1.199.7336&rep=rep1&type=pdf> accessed 11 March 2015.

[24] For a general discussion of the social constructivist approach in international relations literature, see Chapter 1, Section IV.

[25] See Section IV(a) below.

[26] The most common RTAs are free trade areas (such as the North American Free Trade Area (NAFTA) (signed 17 December 1992, entered into force 1 January 1994) 32 *ILM* 289) and customs unions (such as the Treaty Establishing a Common Market between the Argentine Republic, the Federal Republic of Brazil, the Republic of Paraguay, the Eastern Republic of Uruguay (MERCOSUR) (signed 26 March 1991, entered into force 29 November 1991) 2145 UNTS 251). Essentially, a *free trade area* agreement is a preferential arrangement under which tariff rates among the members are eliminated, although external tariffs vis-à-vis non-members may be at different rates for different members of the agreement. *Customs union* is an arrangement under which tariffs are eliminated between members of the arrangement, and a common external tariff is applied vis-à-vis non-members. Anne O Krueger, 'Free Trade Agreements versus Customs Unions' (April 1995) NBER Working Paper No. 5084, 4–5 <http://www.nber.org/papers/w5084.pdf> accessed 11 March 2015.

[27] World Trade Organization, 'World Trade Report 2011—The WTO and preferential trade agreements: From co-existence to coherence' (WTO, Geneva, 2011), 42 <https://www.wto.org/english/res_e/booksp_e/anrep_e/world_trade_report11_e.pdf> accessed 11 March 2015; Organization of Economic Cooperation and Development, *Regionalism and the Multilateral Trading System* (OECD, 2003) 1–2; John Whalley, 'Recent Regional Agreements: Why so Many, so Fast, so Different and Where are they headed?' (2006) Centre for International Governance Innovation Working Paper 9 <https://www.cigionline.org/sites/default/files/recent_regional_agreements.pdf> accessed 11 March 2015.

As of 8 January 2015, some 604 notifications of RTAs had been received by the GATT/WTO. These WTO figures correspond to 446 physical RTAs, of which 259 are currently in force.[28] Some leading scholars consider the rapid proliferation of RTAs to be one of the major developments in international relations.[29] Though some kinds of RTAs have existed for centuries,[30] the numbers, as well as the scope of RTAs, have been steadily increasing over the last two decades. Nearly all of the WTO's members have notified participation in one or more RTAs (some members are party to numerous agreements).[31] The regulatory coverage of RTAs has become quite expansive, moving from tariffs reduction to additional issues such as the harmonization of standards, competition, and investment.[32]

Among the prominent RTAs[33] are the European Union,[34] the North American Free Trade Agreement (NAFTA),[35] the Southern Common Market (MERCOSUR),[36] the Association of Southeast Asian Nations (ASEAN) Free Trade Area (AFTA),[37] and the Common Market of Eastern and Southern Africa (COMESA).[38] Among the main characteristics of the recent wave of regionalism is not only the general increase of RTAs[39] but also the increasing participation of developing countries in such regional agreements,[40] including agreements concluded by the European Union (EU) with non-member states (such as the custom union between the EU with Turkey, and FTAs with many Mediterranean countries).[41]

28 WTO, 'Regional Trade Agreements' <http://www.wto.org/english/tratop_e/region_e/region_e.htm> accessed 11 March 2015.

29 Schiff and Winters (n 3) 1–2.

30 For a historic survey of RTAs see: Kym Anderson and Hege Norheim, 'History, Geography, and Regional Integration' in Kym Anderson and Richard Blackhurst (eds), *Regional Integration and the Global Trading System* (St. Martin's Press, 1993) 19, 26–45; Schiff and Winters (n 3) 4–6; WTO, World Trade Report 2011 (n 27) 46–54.

31 WTO, 'Regional Trade Agreements: Facts and Figures' <http://www.wto.org/english/tratop_e/region_e/regfac_e.htm> accessed 11 March 2015.

32 Claude Chase and others, 'Mapping of Dispute Settlement Mechanisms in Regional Trade Agreements—Innovative or Variations on a Theme?' (2013) WTO Staff Working Paper ERSD-2013-07 5.

33 For a list of all RTAs, see WTO, 'Regional Trade Agreements Information System' <http://rtais.wto.org/UI/PublicAllRTAList.aspx> accessed 11 March 2015.

34 See, The Consolidated Versions of the Treaty on European Union and the Treaty on the Functioning of the European Union [2010] OJ C 83/1 (hereinafter 'European Union Treaty').

35 NAFTA (n 26). 36 MERCOSUR (n 26).

37 ASEAN Free Trade Agreements <http://www.worldtradelaw.net/fta/agreements/afta.pdf> accessed 13 March 2015.

38 Agreement Establishing the Common Market for Eastern and Southern Africa <http://www.worldtradelaw.net/fta/agreements/comesafta.pdf> accessed 13 March 2015.

39 World Trade Report 2011 (n 27) 54; Philippe De Lombaerde, Antoni Estevadeordal, and Kati Souminen, 'Governing Regional Integration for Development: Introduction' in Philippe De Lombaerde, Antoni Estevadeordal, and Kati Souminen (eds) *Governing Regional Integration for Development* (Ashgate, 2008) 1.

40 World Trade Report 2011 (n 27) 56; Trebilcock, Howse, and Eliason (n 3) 86.

41 See Schiff and Winters (n 3) 2–3, 74. On the Economic Partnership Agreements between the EU and the African, Caribbean, and Pacific Group of States (ACP), see Melaku Geboye Desta, 'EC-ACP Economic Partnership Agreements and WTO Compatibility: An Experiment in North-South Inter-Regional Agreements?' (2006) 43 *Common Market Law Review* 1343.

The ongoing proliferation of RTAs intensifies the long-standing debate among scholars and policy-makers regarding the motives and repercussions of RTAs, and whether the WTO system should promote, tolerate, or restrict the formation of RTAs. The answers provided to these questions affect the interpretation of existing WTO legal provisions regarding RTAs, and affect the content of future WTO rules regarding the regulation of RTAs. While some experts are of the view that RTAs and the global WTO agreements are complementary, others emphasize their discriminatory nature and argue that they constitute a threat to the multilateral trading system. Economic analyses of RTAs do not provide a single answer to the question regarding the desirability or undesirability of such arrangements,[42] as economic literature provides support for both views.[43]

b. The regulation of RTAs in the WTO legal system

The formation and enlargement of RTAs are addressed by several WTO legal provisions—mainly, Article XXIV of the General Agreement on Tariffs and Trade[44] (GATT), Article V of the GATS,[45] and the 'Enabling Clause'[46] with regard to RTAs among developing countries. Though RTAs deviate from one of the WTO core objectives, the Most Favoured Nation (MFN) principle,[47] WTO law allows members to establish and enlarge such preferential arrangements if some conditions are fulfilled.

The most important rules are included in Article XXIV of the GATT[48] and the 1994 Understanding on the Interpretation of Article XXIV.[49] These provisions lay

[42] For a concise survey of the different economic positions on RTAs, see, e.g., Michael J Trebilcock, *Understanding Trade Law* (Elgar, 2011) 48–51; Joel Trachtman, 'Regional Trade: Regionalism' in Andrew T Guzman and Alan O Sykes (eds), *Research Handbook in International Economic Law* (Elgar, 2007) 151, 157–60; Trebilcock, Howse, and Eliason (n 3) 89 et seq.; World Trade Report 2011 (n 27) 166 et seq.

[43] On the different economic analyses of RTAs, see, e.g., Jacob Viner, *The Customs Union Issue* (Carnegie Endowment for International Peace, 1950) 3; Schiff and Winters (n 3) 46–54; Robert Z Lawrence, *Regionalism, Multilateralism, and Deeper Integration* (Brookings Institute, 1996) 44; Jagdish Bhagwati, *Termites in the Trading System: How Preferential Agreements undermine Free Trade* (OUP, 2008) 49–110; Caroline Freund, and Emanuel Ornelas, 'Regional Trade Agreements' (2010) World Bank Policy Research Working Paper 5314 <http://papers.ssrn.com/sol3/papers.cfm?abstract_id=1612091> accessed 11 March 2015; Richard Baldwin, 'Preferential Trading Arrangements' in Amrita Narlikar, Martin Daunton, and Robert Stern (eds), *The Oxford Handbook on the World Trade Organization* (OUP, 2012) 632; Peter Sutherland and others, *The Future of the WTO: Addressing Institutional Challenges in the New Millennium—Report by the Consultative Board to the Director-General Supachai Panitchpakdi* (WTO, 2004) 19–28, 79.

[44] GATT (n 6) [45] GATS (n 7).

[46] WTO, Differential and More Favourable Treatment Reciprocity and Fuller Participation of Developing Countries (28 November 1979) L/4903 <www.wto.org/english/docs_e/legal_e/enabling_e.doc> accessed 11 March 2015 [hereinafter 'The Enabling Clause'].

[47] GATT (n 6) Art1.

[48] On the legislative history of Art XXIV, see James H Mathis, *Regional Trade Agreements in the GATT/WTO* (Asser Press, 2002) 31–53.

[49] Understanding on the Interpretation of Article XXIV of The General Agreement on Tariffs and Trade 1994 (15 April 1994) <http://www.wto.org/english/docs_e/legal_e/10-24.doc> accessed 11 March 2015.

out the criteria and procedure for the assessment of new or enlarged RTAs.[50] The central requirements are as follows:

(i) '[S]ubstantially all the trade' between the RTA members is to be liberalized.[51] With respect to Customs Unions, the members are also required to apply substantially the same duties and other trade restrictions to products of third parties.[52]

(ii) The liberalization of trade among the RTA members is to be achieved 'within a reasonable length of time'.[53] The 1994 Understanding clarifies that this period 'should exceed 10 years only in exceptional cases'.[54]

(iii) Duties and other trade restrictions imposed by RTA members on products from third parties must not be higher or more restrictive than those existing prior to the formation of the RTA.[55] If the formation of a customs union leads to an increase of the bound duties (under Article II of the GATT) towards third parties, there is an obligation to provide the latter with compensatory adjustment[56] (regularly in the form of tariff concessions).[57]

(iv) RTA members must notify the WTO and provide it with the agreements and all relevant information.[58]

Article V of the GATS[59] sets out similar but somewhat weaker requirements for the formation and modifications of 'Economic Integration' agreements in *services*: [60]

[50] For a detailed analysis of the GATT Art XXIV, see Trebilcock, Howse, and Eliason (n 3) 99–117; Matsushita, Schoenbaum, and Mavroidis (n 3) 555–78; Bhala (n 21) 590–604; Nicolas JS Lockhart and Andrew D Mitchell, 'Regional Trade Agreements under GATT 1994: An Exception and its Limits' in Andrew D Mitchell (ed), *Challenges and Prospects for the WTO* (Cameron May, 2005) 217. See also Peter Van den Bossche and Werner Zdouc, *The Law and Policy of the World Trade Organization: Text, Cases and Materials* (3rd edn, CUP, 2013) 655–63; Thomas Cottier, 'The Challenge of Regionalism and Preferential Relations in World Trade Law and Policy' (1996) 1 *European Foreign Affairs Review* 149.

[51] GATT (n 6) Art XXIV(8)(b) (regarding FTAs) and Art XXIV(8)(a)(i) (regarding customs unions). This rule also requires the elimination of discriminatory standards included in RTAs. Joel P Trachtman, 'Toward Open Recognition? Standards and Regional Integration under Article XXIV of GATT' (2003) 6 *Journal of International Economic Law* 459, 485–6.

[52] GATT (n 6) Art XXIV(8)(a)(ii). This rule also requires the elimination of discriminatory standards included in customs union agreements. Trachtman (n 51) 486–7.

[53] GATT (n 6) Art XXIV(5)(c) (regarding FTAs and customs unions).

[54] Understanding on the Interpretation of Article XXIV (n 49) Art 2.

[55] GATT (n 6) Art XXIV5(b) (regarding FTAs) and Art XXIV(5)(a) (regarding customs unions). See also Understanding on the Interpretation of Article XXIV (n 49) para 2.

[56] GATT (n 6) Art XXIV(6); See also Understanding on the Interpretation of Article XXIV (n 49) paras 4–6.

[57] Sungjoon Cho, 'Breaking the Barrier between Regionalism and Multilateralism' (2001) 42 *Harvard International Law Journal* 419, 439–40.

[58] GATT (n 6) Art XXIV(7)(a). See also Understanding on the Interpretation of Article XXIV (n 49) paras 7–10. On the new transparency mechanism for RTAs (established in 2006), see further below.

[59] On Art V of the GATS, see also Van den Bossche and Zdouc (n 50) 665–8; Matsushita, Schoenbaum, and Mavroidis (n 3) 578–81.

[60] Bernard M Hoekman and Michel M Kostecki, *The Political Economy of the World Trading System* (3rd edn, OUP, 2009) 489; Lawrence (n 43) 103.

(a) The agreement must have substantial sectorial coverage (in terms of the number of sectors, volume of trade affected, and modes of supply). The agreement should not provide for the a priori exclusion of any mode of supply.[61]

(b) The agreement must provide for the absence or elimination of substantially all discrimination among the parties, in the sectors covered by the agreement. This requirement must be attained either at the entry into force of that RTA or on the basis of a reasonable time frame.[62]

(c) The agreement is to be designed to facilitate trade among the RTA parties and not raise the overall level of trade barriers towards third countries (compared to the level applicable prior to such an agreement).[63]

(d) The members must promptly notify any such agreement to the Council for Trade in Services and make available to the Council the relevant information.[64]

RTAs among developing countries that liberalize either trade in *goods or services* are subject to more lenient criteria. The 1979 Decision on Differential and More Favourable Treatment of Developing Countries ('the Enabling Clause'),[65] which has become an integral part of the GATT 1994,[66] lays out less demanding[67] requirements than those included in the GATT and GATS.[68] The Enabling Clause notes that developing countries are not required to liberalize 'substantially all of their trade' as long as FTAs between developing countries offer mutual reduction or elimination of tariffs.[69]

61 GATS (n 7) Art V(1)(a). 62 GATS (n 7) Art V(1)(b).

63 GATS (n 7) Art V(4).

64 GATS (n 7) Art V(7)(a). On the 2006 transparency mechanism, see further below.

65 'Enabling Clause' (n 46) Arts 2 and 3.

66 See, WTO, European Communities—Conditions for the Granting of Tariff Preferences to Developing Countries—Report of the Appellate Body (1 December 2003) WT/DS 246/R [90] (at note 192). See also Matsushita, Schoenbaum, and Mavroidis (n 3) 221.

67 See Hoekman and Kostecki (n 60) 488; Alberta Fabbricotti, 'The ASEAN Free Trade Area (AFTA) and its Compatibility with GATT/WTO' (2003) 8 *Asian Ybk Intl L* 37, 38; Murray Gibbs, Swarnim Wagle, and Pedro Ortega, *The Great Maze: Regional and Bilateral Free Trade Agreements in Asia* (UNDP Asia-Pacific Trade and Investment Initiative, 2005) 17.

68 The 'Enabling Clause' (n 46) Art 2(c) provides as follows: 'Regional or global arrangements entered into amongst less-developed contracting parties for the mutual reduction or elimination of tariffs and, in accordance with criteria or conditions which may be prescribed by the CONTRACTING PARTIES, for the mutual reduction or elimination of non-tariff measures, on products imported from one another.' Art 3(a) of the clause provides that: 'Any differential and more favourable treatment provided under this clause ... shall be designed to facilitate and promote the trade of developing countries and not to raise barriers to or create undue difficulties for the trade of any other contracting parties.'

69 See on this requirement, Mitsuo Matsushita and YS Lee, 'Proliferation of Free Trade Agreements and Some Systemic Issues—In Relation to the WTO Disciplines and Development Perspectives' (2008) 1 *The Law and Development Review* 23, 32–3: Hoekman and Kostecki (n 60) 488.

Agreements establishing RTAs (and interim agreements) are reviewed by the WTO organs.[70] Following the report of the Committee on Regional Trade Agreements (CRTA),[71] the Council for Trade in Goods may determine whether the particular RTA is consistent with the above criteria. If the Council finds that the RTA is not likely to comply with these conditions, it may make recommendations to the parties of the RTA. In the latter case, the RTA's members shall not put into force or maintain the regional agreement unless they are prepared to modify it in accordance with these recommendations.[72] Similar procedures apply to regional agreements on trade in services.[73] This oversight process has proven to be a weak enforcement mechanism of the conditions laid out in the WTO agreements.[74] The traditional requirement of consensus for a decision to be adopted by the Committee effectively blocked decisions disqualifying RTAs.[75]

Thus, while numerous RTAs were reviewed by the ad hoc working parties and the CRTA,[76] no RTA was condemned and only a few[77] were declared as consistent with GATT rules.[78] In addition to the examination of RTAs, the Committee devoted considerable time to debating the systemic issues surrounding RTAs.

[70] In the past, all relevant information was examined by WTO ad hoc working parties that reported to the Council for Trade in Goods. The Singapore Ministerial Meeting called for an end to the ad hoc working party review system by establishing a standing Committee on Regional Trade Agreements (CRTA). The new Committee was established in 1996 and entrusted to carry out the examination of RTAs, 'consider systematic implications of such agreements for the multilateral trading system', and make appropriate recommendations. WTO, *Decision of the General Council of 6 February 1996* (7 February 1996) WT/L/127; Mathis (n 48) 20, 306. See also Mathis (n 48) 130–1.

[71] RTAs among developing countries which are subject to the 'Enabling Clause' are reviewed by the WTO Committee on Trade and Development, Van den Bossche and Zdouc (n 50) 670.

[72] GATT (n 6) Art XXIV(7)(b); Understanding on the Interpretation of Article XXIV (n 49) Arts 7–11.

[73] GATS (n 7) Art V(7). Van den Bossche and Zdouc (n 50) 668–71.

[74] See, e.g., Petros C Mavroidis, 'Always Look at the Bright Side of Non-Delivery: WTO and Preferential Trade Agreements, Yesterday and Today' (2011) 10 *World Trade Review* 375, 376–7; Hoekman and Kostecki (n 60) 489, 509; Bhala (n 21) 604–5; Cottier (n 50) 160–1.

[75] Thus, for instance, the Panel Report, *EC—Tariff Treatment on Imports of Citrus from Certain Countries in the Mediterranean Region* (1985) (unadopted) includes the following findings: 'Given the lack of consensus among contracting parties, there had been no decision by the CONTRACTING PARTIES on the conformity with Article XXIV of the agreements … and therefore the legal status of the agreements remained open'. WTO, *Analytical Index: Guide to GATT Law and Practice* (6th edn, WTO, 1995) 761. And see Mathis's conclusion in Mathis (n 48) 83.

[76] On the practice of CRTA regarding examination of RTAs, see Moonhawk Kim, 'Inspecting the Termites: Market Structure and WTO's Consideration Process of PTAs' (APSA Annual Meeting, Chicago, August–September 2013) 3–4 <http://ssrn.com/abstract=2299655> accessed 11 March 2015; Mavroidis, 'Always Look at the Bright Side of Non-Delivery' (n 74) 376–8.

[77] See, for instance, WTO, Report of Working Party 4 on The South Africa-Southern Rhodesia Customs Union (14 May 1949) GATT/CP3/24, 9.

[78] Thus Mavroidis concludes: '[t]he numbers are there and the numbers tell one story: there is a proliferation of PTAs, the consistency of which with the multilateral rules remains unchecked'. Petros C Mavroidis, *Trade in Goods: The GATT and the Other Agreements Regulating Trade in Goods* (2nd edn, OUP, 2012) 221, 200–3. For an analysis of the practice of the GATT/ WTO ad hoc working parties, the CRTA, and WTO members in this field, see Petros C Mavroidis, 'If I Don't Do It, Somebody Else Will (or Won't)' (2006) 40 *Journal of World Trade* 187. See also Cho (n 57) 421–3; Mathis (n 48) 98.

This debate clarified members' positions regarding some key elements of the above legal provisions[79] but the CRTA was unable to make any joint recommendations to the General Council since views among members were divided.[80]

A new transparency mechanism for RTAs was established by the WTO General Council in December 2006. The new mechanism provides for early announcement of any RTA and notification to the WTO.[81] Accordingly, the WTO members participating in new negotiations that are aimed at the conclusion of an RTA shall endeavour to inform the WTO,[82] and the members' parties to a newly signed RTA shall convey to the WTO (insofar as and when it is publicly available) information regarding the RTA.[83] This information is forwarded to the WTO Secretariat, which posts it on the WTO website and periodically provides the WTO members with a synopsis of the communications received.[84] The 2006 decision also somewhat revised the CRTA procedure regarding the examination of RTAs.[85] The new transparency mechanism is implemented on a provisional basis. The WTO members will review, and if necessary modify, the decision, and replace it by a permanent mechanism adopted as part of the overall results of the Doha Round.[86]

The GATT dispute settlement bodies have relatively rarely been involved in the application and interpretation of the above legal WTO provisions and their main jurisprudence will be summarized very briefly. The 1985 GATT panel decision on the *EC Tariff Treatment of Imports of Citrus Products from the Mediterranean Region* showed a restrained approach. The panel concluded that it should abstain from examination of the relevant RTA in the context of Article XXIII (nullification and impairment).[87] The two decisions rendered by the GATT panels in the '*Bananas Case*'[88] in 1993–4 displayed a less cautious approach regarding legal

[79] See, e.g., WTO Committee on Regional Trade Agreements, *Synopsis of 'Systemic' Issues Related to Regional Trade Agreements* (Note by the Secretariat) (2 March 2000) WT/REG/W/37.

[80] Jo-Ann Crawford, 'A New Transparency Mechanism for Regional Trade Agreements' (2007) 11 *Singapore Ybk of Intl L* 133, 135. See also WTO Trade Report 2011 (n 27) 185. On the effects of the CRTA's work on regional trade, see Jason H Grant and Christopher Parmeter, 'Has the World Trade Organization Promoted Successful Regional Trade Agreements?' (BePress SelectedWorks, 2010) <http://works.bepress.com/parms/27> accessed 13 March 2015.

[81] WTO, *Transparency Mechanism for Regional Trade Agreements, Decision by the General Council* (14 December 2006) WT/L/671 (hereinafter 'General Council's Decision on Transparency'). See also WTO, *Transparency Mechanism for RTAs* <http://www.wto.org/english/tratop_e/region_e/trans_mecha_e.htm> accessed 13 March 2015; Jo-Ann Crawford and CL Lim, 'Cast Light and Evil Will Go Away: The Transparency Mechanism for Regional Trade Agreements Three Years After' (2011) 43 *Journal of World Trade* 375; Crawford (n 80).

[82] General Council's Decision on Transparency (n 81) Art 1(a). [83] Ibid., Art 1(b).

[84] Ibid., Art 2. [85] Ibid., Arts 15–17.

[86] Ibid., Art 23. On the practice of the CRTA following the 2006 Decision, see Mavroidis, 'Always Look at The Bright Side of Non-Delivery' (n 74) 377; Crawford and Lim (n 81) 375.

[87] Panel Report, European Community—Tariff Treatment on Imports of Citrus Products from Certain Countries in the Mediterranean Region (7 February 1986) GATT/ L/5776 section 4.15 (unadopted).

[88] EEC—Member States' Import Regime for Bananas (3 June 1993) DS32/R (hereinafter 'The First Bananas Case'); EEC—Member States' Import Regimes for Bananas (11 February 1994) DS38/R (hereinafter 'The Second Bananas Case'). For a detailed examination of these panels' decisions, see Mathis (n 48) 88–100.

review of RTAs under Article XXIV. These panels' decisions indicated that in the absence of an Article XXIV compatibility recommendation by the GATT working groups, RTAs could be subject to legal review by the GATT panels.[89]

The most important decision rendered by the GATT/WTO dispute settlement bodies with regard to Article XXIV[90] and the only one that directly addresses the issue of RTA compatibility with the above legal provisions is the WTO Appellate Body's decision in the *Turkey—Textile Case*.[91] A controversial question that arose in this case related to the *jurisdiction* of the WTO dispute settlement bodies to examine the legality of the WTO members' actions under Article XXIV. The Appellate Body stated that it is not called upon to address this issue in this appeal but the decision indicates that the WTO dispute settlements bodies are competent to review matters which are also referred to the evaluation of political bodies, such as the CRTA.[92]

The proper scope of the WTO judicial organs' jurisdiction regarding the formation and enlargement of RTAs, as well as the interpretation of the WTO legal provisions regarding RTAs, remain disputed between the WTO members[93] and scholars.[94] Despite the rapidly growing importance of RTAs and significant legal uncertainty regarding the relevant GATT provisions, there has been remarkably little interpretation of these provisions either by the CRTA or the GATT/WTO dispute settlement system.[95] The ongoing proliferation of RTAs and the perceived weakness of the current WTO supervisory mechanism highlight the controversy regarding the relationship between the WTO and RTAs. As Trebilcock, Howse, and Eliason note '[w]hile some analysts believe that these trading blocks and the multilateral system can be viewed as complementary and mutually reinforcing, others consider them inherently discriminatory and a major threat to the future stability and integrity of the multilateral system'.[96]

[89] The First Bananas Case (n 88) [358], [372]; The Second Bananas Case (n 88) [158].

[90] On additional decisions relating to Art XXIV, see Trebilcock, Howse, and Eliason (n 3) 117 et seq.; Mavroidis, *Trade in Goods* (n 78) 212–20.

[91] DSB, *Turkey—Restrictions on Imports of Textile and Clothing Products—Report of the Appellate Body* (AB-1995-5) (19 November 1999) WT/DS34/AB/R (hereinafter '*Turkey—Textile Case*'). For a detailed examination of this decision, see Mathis (n 48) 193–226.

[92] *Turkey—Textile Case* (n 91) [60]. For a summary of the additional findings included in this Appellate Body's decision, see Andrew T Guzman and Joost HB Pauwelyn, *International Trade Law* (Kluwer, 2012) 338–44; Joel P Trachtman, 'Decision of the Appellate Body of the World Trade Organization: Turkey–Restrictions on Import of Textile and Clothing Products' (2000) 11 *EJIL* 217; Mathis (n 48) 215–16, 255–7; Trebilcock, *Understanding Trade Law* (n 42) 46–8; Van den Bossche and Zdouc (n 50) 658–61.

[93] For a list of legal interpretative questions relating to the interpretation of the WTO rules on RTAs, see, e.g., Crawford and Lim (n 81), Section II(c).

[94] On the jurisdiction of the WTO judicial bodies under Art XXIV, see Mavroidis, 'If I Don't Do It, Somebody Else Will' (n 78); Matsushita, Schoenbaum, and Mavroidis (n 3) 555–8, 573–7; Mavroidis, *Trade in Goods* (n 78) 213–14.

[95] Trebilcock, *Understanding Trade Law* (n 42) 46. See also Trebilcock, Howse, and Eliason (n 3) 84.

[96] Trebilcock, Howse, and Eliason (n 3) 28–9.

As in other IEL areas, economic efficiency has been pervasively used as the benchmark to appraise these regional arrangements.[97] Economic studies have analysed various aspects of RTAs, including trade creation/diversion, economy of scale, transaction costs, and dynamic effects of RTAs.[98] As noted above, economic analyses of RTAs do not provide a single answer to the question regarding the desirability or undesirability of such arrangements, since economic literature provides support for both views.[99] Foreign and domestic policy factors often play a role in the formation and development of RTAs. States occasionally form or join RTAs to promote geopolitical objectives such as advancing peaceful relations, supporting political partners, or coalition building. Consequently, RTAs have also been investigated by political scientists who explored, inter alia, members' motivations,[100] the dynamics of RTAs,[101] power relations in RTAs,[102] distributive consequences of regional integration,[103] and the impact of domestic groups on RTAs (including political economy analysis).[104]

Thus, existing international trade law literature on RTAs is dominated by abundant economic and political analyses and the relevance of socio-cultural factors is under-emphasized. Current RTAs literature includes only rudimentary references to socio-cultural factors and these factors are not systematically analysed with sociological theoretical tools. The following sections focus on the sociological dimension of RTAs and sociological theoretical analysis of the regional/global debate.

[97] See, e.g., Matsushita, Schoenbaum, and Mavroidis (n 3) 552–3; Mathis (n 48) 101–15; Trebilcock, *Understanding Trade Law* (n 42) 48–51; Trebilcock, Howse, and Eliason (n 3) 89–99; Trachtman, 'Regional Trade' (n 42) 157–60; World Trade Report 2011 (n 27) 100 et seq.

[98] For a concise survey of these and additional economic analyses of RTAs, see, e.g., Trebilcock, *Understanding Trade Law* (n 42) 48–51; Viet D Do and William Watson, 'Economic Analysis of Regional Trade Agreements' in Lorand Bartel and Federico Ortino (eds), *Regional Trade Agreements and the WTO Legal System* (OUP 2006) 7, 10–20; Schiff and Winters (n 3) 13–26.

[99] See the literature cited in Section III(a) above.

[100] On foreign policy's motivation involved in the formation of RTAs, see, e.g., Schiff and Winters (n 3) 187–207; World Trade Report 2011 (n 27) 95–7; Vincent Vicard, 'Trade, Conflicts, and Political Integration: Explaining the Heterogeneity of Regional Trade Agreements' (2012) 56 *European Economic Review* 54.

[101] On the functional and the neo-functional approaches to regional economic integration, see, e.g., Arne Niemann and Philippe C Schmitter, 'Neo-functionalism' in Antje Wiener and Thomas Diez (eds), *European Integration Theory* (2nd edn, OUP, 2009) 45–65; Walter Mattli, *The Logic of Regional Integration: Europe and Beyond* (CUP, 1999) 21–8; Ben Rosamond, *Theories of European Integration* (St. Martin's Press, 2000) 31–42, 50–73.

[102] See, e.g., Robert Gilpin, *Global Political Economy* (Princeton University Press, 2001) 356–7.

[103] See, e.g., Joseph M Grieco, 'Systemic Sources of Variations in Regional Institutionalization in Western Europe, East Asia, and the Americas' in Edward D Mansfield and Helen V Milner (eds), *The Political Economy of Regionalism* (Columbia University Press, 1997) 164.

[104] See, e.g., Craig Van Grasste, 'The Political Economy of Services in Regional Trade Agreements' (2011) OECD Trade Policy Papers, No. 112, 13–16 <http://www.oecd-ilibrary.org/docserver/download/5kgdst6lc344.pdf?expires=1426232123&id=id&accname=guest&checksum=BA2ECF5DA8C111B436F5B6B6AF9E522B> accessed 13 March 2015; Julia Gray, 'Politics and Patronage: The Function of Dysfunctional Regional Trade Agreements' (Conference on 'The

IV. Sociological Analysis of RTAs

a. The sociological dimension of RTAs

Drawing on the above-discussed premises of economic sociology,[105] the sociological perspective on RTAs underscores that these agreements are embedded in socio-cultural relations among state societies. This statement implies two central arguments: (i) the formation, legal content, and implementation of RTAs *are influenced* by socio-cultural factors; (ii) the formation, legal content, and implementation of RTAs *affect* socio-cultural factors.

Regional trade agreements are significantly linked with the socio-cultural features of the RTAs' members and the relationships between them. The sociological aspects are prominent with regard to membership, level of economic integration, and the content of the RTAs' legal rules. Membership in RTAs is often influenced by socio-cultural features of the potential members and identity ties between them. State societies that share similar socio-cultural features are often more amenable to closer economic integration.[106] And vice versa, literature on RTAs reveals that significant socio-cultural dissimilarities and negative public images of other state societies impede the formation of RTAs. The impact of this factor is well documented, for instance, with regard to the formation of the NAFTA,[107] the accession of Eastern and Central European states to the EU,[108] Turkey's difficulty regarding its quest to become a full member of the EU,[109] and the relatively low level of economic integration in East Asia (compared to Western Europe).[110] In addition, the level of integration among RTA members is often influenced by the

Politics of Preferential Trade Agreements', Princeton University, 30 April to 1 May 2010), <http://www.princeton.edu/~pcglobal/conferences/ptas/Gray_pta_paper.pdf> accessed 13 March 2015.

[105] See Section II above.

[106] See, e.g., Innwon Park and Soonchan Park, 'Cultural Affinity, Political Ties, and Endogenous Regional Trade Agreements' (GEP China Conference on Structural Change and Trade Efficiency, the Nottingham Centre for Research on Globalisation and Economic Policy, November 7–8, 2013) 13–15, <http://www.nottingham.ac.uk/gep/documents/china/conferences/2013-14/ningbo/park.pdf> accessed 13 March 2015; Oli Brown and others, 'Regional Trade Agreements: Promoting Conflict or Building Peace?' (International Institute for Sustainable Development, 2005) 6 <http://www.iisd.org/pdf/2005/security_rta_conflict.pdf> accessed 13 March 2015.

[107] Amy Skonieczny, 'Constructing NAFTA' (2001) 45 *International Studies* 433. See also Guadelupe Gonzalez and Stephan Haggard, 'The United States and Mexico: A Pluralistic Security Community?' in Emanuel Adler and Michael Barnett (eds), *Security Communities* (CUP, 1998) 295, 295–8, 314–16.

[108] Frank Schimmelfennig, 'International Socialization in the New Europe' (2000) 6 *EJIR* 109, 109–10, 124.

[109] Haluk Kabaalioglu, 'The Turkish Model of Association: Customs Union before Accession' in Paul Demaret, Jean-Francois Bellis, and Gonzalo Garcia Jimenez (eds), *Regionalism and Multilateralism after The Uruguay Round* (European Interuniversity Press, 1997) 115, 116.

[110] Kong Qingjiang, 'Is the European Experience Duplicable in East Asia?' in Rüdiger Wolfrum and Volker Röben (eds), *Developments of International Law in Treaty Making* (Springer, 2005) 297, 300.

members' conception of law and their legal traditions,[111] as well as by cultural diversity among the members.[112]

RTA's legal provisions often reflect different norms and values prevailing in the involved societies or the particular region.[113] RTAs are occasionally embedded in certain identities that are manifested in their treaties.[114] Thus, for example, human rights protection is a constitutive norm of the EU[115] that significantly defines its identity.[116] This identity is manifested, inter alia, in the EU's RTAs that have included (since 1992) a clause stating that respect for human rights is an essential element of the agreements.[117] ASEAN legal rules also reflect the region's shared values and collective identity, notably with regard to the principles of non-interference in internal affairs,[118] as well as the preference of consultation and consensus as appropriate methods to settle disputes.[119] Analysing African RTAs, Gathii emphasizes the link between the relatively flexible (and less legalized) legal obligations included in these agreements and the dramatic cultural, religious, and political differences between African states.[120]

[111] See, e.g., with regard to ASEAN, Tom Ginsburg, 'Eastphalia and Asian Regionalism' (2010) 44 *University of California Davis Law Review* 859, 867–9. And with regard to MERCOSUR, see Francesco Duina, *The Social Construction of Free Trade: The European Union, NAFTA, and Mercosur* (Princeton University Press, 2006) 67–88.

[112] See, e.g., James Thuo Gathii, 'African Regional Trade Agreements as Flexible Legal Regimes' (2010) 35 *North Carolina Journal of International Law and Commercial Regulation* 571, 584–5.

[113] See, e.g., Colin B Picker, 'Regional Trade Agreements v. the WTO: A Proposal for Reform of Art XXIV to Counter this Institutional Threat' (2005) 26 *University of Pennsylvania Journal of International Economic Law* 267, 282–4. See, e.g., on the influence of cultural and historic factors on liberalization of agricultural trade in RTAs, Linda Fulponi, Matthew Shearer, and Juliana Almeida, 'Regional Trade Agreements—Treatment of Agriculture' (2011) OECD Food, Agriculture and Fisheries Working Paper 44, 24 <http://www.oecd-ilibrary.org/docserver/download/5kgg53fmnjxv.pdf?expires=1426232987&id=id&accname=guest&checksum=1F8EDE25AAF5BC4BAEDDA44E6E7C1D26> accessed 13 March 2015.

[114] On identities of international institutions (global and regional institutions), see Chapter 4, Section IV(b).

[115] See, e.g., European Union Treaty (n 34) Art 2.

[116] See, e.g., Commission, 'The European Union and the External Dimension of Human Rights Policy: From Rome to Maastricht and Beyond' (1995) COM 567, para 12. On the central role of human rights in the EU's identity and its manifestations in regional trade agreements, see Chapter 4, Section IV.

[117] See Commission, 'The inclusion of respect for democratic principles and human rights in agreements between the Community and third countries' (1995) COM 216 final. For several examples of such treaty provisions, see Marise Cremona, 'Values in the EU Constitution: The External Dimension, Centre on Democracy, Development, and the Rule of Law' (2004) 26 *Stanford Institute for International Studies* 1, 17–19.

[118] Gillian Goh, 'The ASEAN Way: Non-Intervention and ASEAN's Role in Conflict Management' (2003) 3 *Stanford Journal of East Asian Affairs* 113, 114–15; Treaty of Amity and Cooperation in Southeast Asia (adopted 24 February 1976, entered into force 21 June 1976) 1025 UNTS 15063 Art 2(1).

[119] See, e.g., Miles Kahler, 'Legalization as Strategy: The Asia-Pacific Case' (2000) 54 *International Organization* 549, 552–5. On the differences between dispute settlement procedures among South Asian countries and such procedures in agreements with non-Asian countries, see Tobias Hofmann and Soo Yeon Kim, 'Designing Reciprocity: The Politics of Dispute Settlement Mechanisms in Asia's PTAs' (Workshop on the Politics of Trade Agreements, the Niehaus Center for Globalization and Governance, Princeton University, April 30, 2010) 21 <http://www.princeton.edu/~pcglobal/conferences/ptas/KH_pta_paper.pdf> accessed 13 March 2015.

[120] Gathii (n 112) 590–1.

Even where RTAs include identical legal provisions (e.g., relating to moral or public order exceptions), the different norms and values prevailing in the distinctive regional contexts are likely to lead to different interpretations of these provisions.

As to the influence of RTAs on social factors, the formation and implementation of RTAs clearly affect socio-cultural differences. International economic integration promotes transboundary interactions among the involved states, and often reduces social dissimilarities and tensions among the involved states' societies.[121] As discussed above,[122] international trade spreads norms and values among the involved communities. For example, some scholars consider the EU enlargement process to be part of the process of international socialization[123] by which the Western community of states transmits its constitutive liberal values and norms of domestic and international conduct to the Central and Eastern European states.[124] RTAs are sometimes expressly aimed at building or fostering a sense of community among the involved peoples.[125]

The proponents of the social constructivist approach extend certain sociological insights into the sphere of international relations.[126] In accordance with this approach, states are embedded in a set of social relations, and their identity encompasses social traits defined by their interaction with other international actors.[127] Constructivist analysis of regional arrangements[128] emphasizes that developing a regional identity is an essential part of regional cooperation, and it aims to explain how cultural and normative factors contribute to the emergence of various regional arrangements. From this perspective, the formation of economic groups

[121] Moshe Hirsch, 'The Logic of North-South Economic Integration' (2005) 32 *Legal Issues of Economic Integration* 3, 14–15, 21–2. On the link between RTAs and peace/conflict, see Schiff and Winters (n 3) 187–96 and see the discussion in Section V below.

[122] See Section II above.

[123] On socialization in international institutions, see Chapter 4, Section V(b).

[124] Schimmelfennig (n 108) 109–10, 124. See also Ann Kent, 'China's International Socialization: The Role of International Organizations' (2002) 8 *Global Governance* 343; Petr Drulák and Lucie Königová, 'The Czech Republic: From Socialist Past to Socialized Future', in Trine Flockhart (ed), *Socializing Democratic Norms: The Role of International Organizations for the Construction of Europe* (Palgrave, 2005) 149.

[125] See, e.g., 'ASEAN Vision 2020' (*ASEAN*, 15 December, 1997) <http://www.asean.org/news/item/asean-vision-2020> accessed 13 March 2015. See also Kristina Jönson, 'Unity-in-Diversity: Regional Identity Building in Southeast Asia' (2010) 29 *Journal of Current Southeast Asian Affairs* 42; Michael E Jones, 'Forging an ASEAN Identity: The Challenge to Construct a Shared Destiny' (2004) 26 *Contemporary Southeast Asia* 140. See also Mark Vaile, 'APEC: Regional Markets for Prosperity' (speech at the APEC Business Forum, 2003) <http://www.trademinister.gov.au/speeches/2003/030407_apec_abac.html> accessed 13 March 2015.

[126] On the social constructivist approach in international relations literature, see Chapter 1, Section IV.

[127] See, e.g., Alexander Wendt, 'Collective Identity Formation and the International State' (1994) 88 *American Political Science Review* 385; Emanuel Adler, 'Cognitive Evolution: A Dynamic Approach for the Study of International Relations and their Progress' in Emanuel Adler and Beverly Crawford (eds), *Progress in Postwar International Relations* (CUP, 1991) 43.

[128] See, e.g., Luk Van Langenhove, *Building Regions: The Regionalization of the World Order* (Ashgate, 2011) 63–96; Sabine Saurugger and Frédéric Mérand, 'Does European Integration Theory Need Sociology?' (2010) 8 *Comparative European Politics* 1.

is affected by collective identities, a sense of common fate, and mutual trust among the potential members. Social, political, and ideological homogeneity is likely to lead to greater international interaction and association, as well as to the development of common institutions.[129]

Having noted that RTAs' rules and institutions often reflect and affect societal factors and processes, sociological inquiry emphasizes that the global/regional debate is closely related to questions regarding international social integration and coherence; that is, whether the enhancement of global or regional *social integration* is desirable, and what the likely consequences of such processes are. The corresponding debate in sociology revolves around the fundamental attitude of the larger society towards smaller communities. This debate parallels one of the most prominent theoretical divides in sociology regarding the relationship between individuals and social structures (often labelled the 'action–structure' debate).[130]

Since the ascendancy of the structural-functional perspective in the 1950s and early 1960s, no single theory has dominated the discipline. Thus, contemporary sociology and sociology of law are marked by theoretical pluralism.[131] Among the numerous sociological theories, three major perspectives are widely recognized as most influential: the structural-functional perspective, the symbolic-interactionist approach, and the social conflict perspective. Each of the core perspectives highlights a different aspect of social phenomena and sociological investigations often employ theoretical tools borrowed from several perspectives. As elaborated below, these sociological theories lead to different conceptions regarding the nature and goals of IEL, different answers to the question concerning the relationship between RTAs and the WTO, and different interpretations of existing WTO legal provisions regarding RTAs.

b. The structural-functional perspective on RTAs

Structural-functionalism was for many years the dominant sociological theory. However, in the last decades its importance has declined dramatically.[132] The two broad theories under the heading of the structural-functional approach are *structural-functionalism*, which looks at both social structures and their

[129] Emanuel Adler and Michael Barnett, 'A Framework for the Study of Security Communities' in Emanuel Adler and Michael Barnett (eds), *Security Communities* (1998) 29, 47–51; Germán Camilo Prieto, 'Constructing regionalism in South America: the Role of Ideas in the Andean Community and MERCOSUR Projects' (2003) 1 *Colombian Economic Journal* 267.

[130] On the structure–agency debate, see Chapter 1, Section II.

[131] See, e.g., Giddens and Sutton (n 2) 9, 70, 79; Ira Cohen, 'Sociological Theory' in Bryan S Turner (ed), *The Cambridge Dictionary of Sociology* (CUP, 2006) 595, 600; Craig Calhoun and others (eds), *Contemporary Sociological Theory* (Blackwell, 2002) 19. On the diversified theoretical approaches in the sociology of law, see, e.g., Reza Banakar and Max Travers (eds), *An Introductions to Law and Social Theory* (Hart, 2002) 2–3.

[132] George Ritzer and Douglas J Goodman, *Modern Sociological Theory* (6th edn, 2004) 91–2; George Ritzer and Jeffrey Stepnisky, *Sociological Theory* (9th edn, McGraw Hill, 2013) 214, 237; Turner (n 1) 49; Giddens and Sutton (n 2) 79.

functions,[133] and *structuralism*, which concerns itself with social structures. While structural-functionalism focuses on visible structures, structuralism is more focused on the social impact of hidden or underlying structures. The structural-functional perspective (sometimes labelled 'systems theory') belongs to the category of macro-sociological theories that have been developed, inter alia, by Emile Durkheim, Talcott Parsons, Robert Merton, and Niklas Luhmann. Theories belonging to the macro-sociology tradition tend to focus on large-scale groups and social patterns such as the social system as a whole and its functional elements. These approaches tend to emphasize the constraining power of social structures on individual choices. Thus, the typical units of analysis are the entire society, large groups, or certain social patterns (e.g., religion) within a society.[134]

The structural-functional perspective emphasizes the interdependence of the various components of society and the ensuing tendency of societies to enhance cooperation and integration. Consequently, this perspective attaches particular significance to social stability and equilibrium. In this perspective, social patterns (including social norms) are perceived as external constraints that are imposed on individuals. The capacity of individuals to change these 'social facts' is limited.[135]

The above features of the structural-functional perspective indicate that the general attitude of this approach to RTAs is characterized by suspicion and reluctance. The structural-functional approach to RTAs is linked to the underlying tendency of this perspective to value social integration, often through enhancing the constraining role of central institutions. Conscious that RTAs often embody values, norms, and identity, the structural-functional approach to RTAs is likely to emphasize the threatening consequences of international disintegration.

The structural-functional approach[136] views the global/regional debate from a global perspective, and the key question is often phrased from this point of view: do RTAs contribute to or undermine the achievement of global liberalization? This approach contends that RTAs undermine the integrity and underlying viability of the whole global WTO system. The frequent divergence between the legal rules included in the WTO agreements and RTAs may constitute a source for potential tensions and destructive conflicts among contracting parties of these divergent trade agreements.[137] Under the structural-functional conception, RTAs

[133] On manifest and latent functions of social structures, see Robert K Merton, *Social Theory and Social Structure* (enlarged edn, Free Press, 1968) 105, 114–23.

[134] See, e.g., Ritzer and Stepnisky (n 132) 239–46; Turner (n 1) 51, 55–8; George Ritzer, *Introduction to Sociology* (2nd edn, Sage, 2015) 49–53; Manuela Boatcă, 'Macrosociology' in George Ritzer and J Michael Ryan (eds), *The Concise Encyclopedia of Sociology* (Wiley-Blackwell, 2011) 362; John J Macionis, *Sociology* (14th edn, Pearson, 2012) 12–13; Giddens and Sutton (n 2) 18–21, 79–82; Calhoun and others (n 131) 25–6.

[135] Emile Durkheim, *The Rules of Sociological Method* (3rd edn, printing, 1962) 1–13; Ritzer and Stepnisky (n 132) 243–7; Turner (n 1) 49–63; Macionis (n 134) 12–13; Giddens and Sutton (n 2) 18–20.

[136] On the structural-functional approach to international courts, see Mikael R Madsen, 'Sociological Approaches to International Courts' in Cesare Romano, Karen Alter, and Yuval Shany (eds), *Oxford Handbook of International Adjudication* (OUP, 2014) 388, 394–7.

[137] See, e.g., Picker (n 113) 287–90.

are discriminatory not only in economic but also in political and social terms. Thus, such discriminatory arrangements often alienate non-members that are left out of the regional block. Such political and social exclusion breeds international rifts that may lead to dangerous conflicts. The structural-functional perspective on RTAs is discernible from the statements of some WTO Director Generals[138] and scholars.[139]

Thus, the structural-functional conception of the international trading system may reluctantly accept treaty provisions which allow the WTO member states to form RTAs (such as Article XXIV of the GATT), but the general inclination would be to interpret these provisions narrowly. The proponents of this approach are likely to emphasize that these provisions constitute an exception to the overarching MFN principle, and warn that liberal interpretation of these provisions may well erode the major achievements of the GATT/WTO system since 1947.

c. The symbolic-interactionist perspective on RTAs

The symbolic-interactionist perspective belongs to the category of micro-sociological theories developed, inter alia, by Max Weber, Herbert Blumer, Erwing Goffman, and Harold Garfinkel. Like other micro-sociological theories, this perspective emphasizes the role of individuals in society, and is primarily concerned with the behaviour of individuals and small groups. Micro-sociological theories regularly underline the inter-subjective aspects of individuals' interactions (i.e., the meaning that humans attribute to social phenomena).[140]

Sociology itself was perceived by Max Weber as 'a science which attempts the interpretative understanding of social action in order thereby to arrive at a causal explanation of its course and effects'.[141] From this perspective, the aim of sociology is to study social behaviour by interpreting the actions of individuals in the social world and the ways in which individuals attribute meaning to social phenomena.[142] Thus, for Weber, social action itself occurs 'when and insofar as the acting individual attaches a subjective meaning to it'.[143]

[138] 'Lamy warns rise of regional trade agreements could lead to "policy fragmentation"' WTO News (20 September 2012) <http://www.wto.org/english/news_e/sppl_e/sppl246_e.htm> accessed 13 March 2015; 'Supachai: Regional Trade Agreements Threaten WTO System' (22 December 2004) 8 (44) *Bridges Weekly Trade News Digest* 7; 'Moore Says Regional Pacts Weakening Multinational System' (16 January 2001) 5(1) *Bridges Weekly Trade News Digest* 10.

[139] See, e.g., Picker (n 113) 287–94.

[140] Ritzer and Stepnisky (n 132) 350–1.

[141] Max Weber, *The Theory of Social and Economic Organization* (OUP, 1947) 88. On Weber's concept of 'understanding', and the distinction between direct observational understanding and explanatory understanding, see John Eric Thomas Eldridge, *Max Weber: The Interpretation of Social Reality* (Nelson, 1972) 28–32.

[142] As to methodological individualism, Weber states that 'sociology itself can only proceed from the actions of one or more separate individuals and must therefore adopt strictly individualistic methods'. As cited in Eldridge (n 141) 25.

[143] Weber (n 141) 88.

According to the symbolic-interactionist approach, social structures, like society itself, are constituted and changed by interactions among individuals.[144] This perspective does not dispute the existence of the large social system, but its point of departure is that social structures emerge and are maintained 'from below', through a complex process of interaction among individuals. As people interact over time, patterns of interaction emerge, and rules governing social interaction develop.[145] The symbolic-interactionist perspective places particular stress on providing explanations of everyday social experiences, frequently from the point of view of a certain individual or types of individuals.[146]

Thus, from this perspective human beings are not viewed as the products (or victims) of the social system but rather as active agents who can resist, challenge, and change social structures.[147] The proponents of the symbolic-interactionist approach are generally critical of 'sociological determinism' in which the social action of people is treated as an outward flow or expression of forces playing on them rather than as acts which are built up by people through their interactions.[148] The social order that emerges from this approach is not accomplished by conforming to external rules. Instead, it grows out of a shared social understanding of 'taken-for-granted' social practices, and various accounting procedures underlying everyday life.[149]

The core features of the symbolic-interactionist approach[150] to *international trade law* are largely opposed to the structural-functional perspective. The point of departure of this approach is that international trade rules and institutions are not externally imposed on states and other actors but rather represent the outcome of their interactions. As the symbolic-interactionist perspective in sociology is primarily concerned with the interactive behaviour of individuals in small groups, this approach to international trade law generally prefers integration in small groups of states (rather than in large international groups). Unlike the structural-functional approach which seeks to attain global social integration through inclusive and uniform legal regimes, the symbolic-interactionist approach prefers flexible regimes that correspond to the particular social characteristics of the involved communities. This perspective views the global/regional debate from the point of view of an individual state or a region. From this viewpoint, it is often

[144] See, e.g., Herbert Blumer, *Symbolic Interactionism: Perspective and Method* (Prentice Hall, 1969) 1; Turner (n 1) 315–17; Ritzer and Stepnisky (n 132) 348–50, 352–3; Giddens and Sutton (n 2) 22–3; Macionis (n 134) 16–17; Calhoun and others (n 131) 2–4; Ritzer and Goodman (n 132) 230–3.

[145] See, e.g., Turner (n 1) 315–17; Ritzer and Stepnisky (n 132) 347–8, 352–4; Giddens and Sutton (n 2) 22–3; Macionis (n 134) 16; Calhoun and others (n 131) 26; Malcolm Waters, *Modern Sociological Theory* (Sage, 1994) 15.

[146] Ibid., 16.

[147] Ritzer and Stepnisky (n 132) 353; Turner (n 1) 315; Calhoun and others (n 131) 26; Waters (n 145) 15; Ritzer and Goodman (n 132) 217–21.

[148] Ritzer and Goodman (n 132) 230. See also Ritzer and Stepnisky (n 132) 352.

[149] See, e.g., John Heritage, *Garfinkel and Ethnomethodology* (Polity Press, 1984) 231; Tim May, *Situating Social Theory* (Open University Press, 1996) 89–90; Waters (n 145) 39.

[150] On the interpretative sociology approach to international courts, see Madsen (n 136) 391–3.

preferable to deepen economic integration among a small number of like-minded states.

The inclination of the symbolic-interactionist approach to favour regional integration also stems from the greater difficulty of creating common norms in the extremely heterogeneous WTO system (in comparison with RTAs). The ongoing expansion of the WTO membership intensifies the profound socio-cultural and ideological divisions that characterize the contemporary global economic arena. The WTO system includes 160 members (as of June 2014) from very different stages of economic development with widely differing political and cultural orientations.

The symbolic-interactionist approach argues that the need to generate shared social understandings in the international economic system cannot be effectively fulfilled by the imposition of external, global rules. Common norms that embody common understandings on the global level should emerge 'from below' (i.e., from the interaction among states societies in smaller regional groups). Different RTAs may offer more legal flexibility and are more suited to providing different trade rules to each specific region or bilateral context, in accordance with the particular socio-cultural, economic, and ideological features of the involved societies.

In sum, the ingrained aversion of sociologists employing symbolic interactionism towards integration on a large scale, and the emphasis on the need to respect the socio-cultural features of smaller communities, suggest that international trade law should allow the WTO member states wide discretion as to whether to form or join regional arrangements. Consequently, the relevant legal rules regarding RTAs (such as Article XXIV of the GATT) should be construed liberally.

d. The social conflict perspective on RTAs

The social conflict perspective belongs to the category of macro-sociological theories and has been developed, inter alia, by Karl Marx, Ralf Dahrendorf, and Emmanuel Wallerstein. For social conflict theorists, society is characterized by regular patterns of inequality regarding the allocation of essential resources among its members (e.g., wealth, authority, and political power). The uneven distribution of resources engenders social stratification and struggle among rival groups; each is interested in advancing its own interests at the direct expense of the other groups. The existing social structures are the outcome of the competition between rival groups. The dominant groups in society are interested in preserving the existing social structures that privilege them, and employ various resources to maintain the status quo. Disadvantaged groups are interested in changing the existing social order and increasing their share of social wealth and power.[151]

[151] Ritzer and Stepnisky (n 132) 267–9, 272–4; Turner (n 1) 206–19; Anthony Oberschall, 'Theories of Social Conflict' (1987) 4 *Annual Review of Sociology* 291, 291–3; Giddens and Sutton (n 2) 21–2; James Fulcher and John Scott, *Sociology* (4th edn, OUP, 2011) 53–4; Waters (n 145) 292, 321–2.

The social conflict perspective views ideologies and values as instruments that the competing groups use to advance their own goals. Thus, ideologies are often judged according to their contribution to the furtherance of the interest of a certain warring group.[152] Unlike the structural-functional perspective that emphasizes the value of social stability, the proponents of the conflict perspective view social change as inevitable and desirable.[153] The *global* social conflict perspective views the international system as stratified along several dividing lines, most prominently in accordance with economic standards (developing and developed states).[154]

The social conflict conception of IEL is conscious of economic and social stratification in the international system and is poised to unveil parallel inequalities in international economic law. Some rules (formal or informal ones) accord unequal rights to rich and poor states in some major international institutions[155] while other legal rules attach greater weight to the position of powerful states in a less distinct manner (e.g., rules applying to trade in agricultural or textile products).[156] The exposure of the international system's hidden priorities sheds light on the 'dark side' of IEL and may trigger a legal reform. Such a reform should promote equality and redistributive policies that would be implemented, inter alia, through the allocation of differential legal obligations to different states according to their level of economic development.[157]

As a macro-sociological perspective, the social conflict approach is suspicious of RTAs. Conscious of the significant power asymmetries in the global system, this perspective suggests that one of the important strategies available to developing states in their struggle against developed states is the collective act. Unification of forces enables the weaker states to strengthen their bargaining positions vis-à-vis

[152] Ritzer and Stepnisky (n 132) 274; Turner (n 1) 206.

[153] Ritzer and Stepnisky (n 132) 267, 269; Turner (n 1) 205. On the role of social change in social conflict theories, see also Oberschall (n 151) 309–14.

[154] The most famous global economic perspective is presented in Immanuel Wallerstein's world system analysis. Immanuel Wallerstein, *The Modern World System I: Capitalist Agriculture and the Origins of the European World-Economy in the Sixteenth Century* (Academic Press, 1974) 347–50, 100–3. On other global approaches in sociology, see Barry Buzan, *From International to World Society?* (CUP, 2004) 70–7.

[155] As Lowenfeld notes regarding the IMF, 'There is no provision for veto, but major decisions require super majorities, so that either the USA or the members of the European Union voting together can block approval of most important proposals'. Andreas F Lowenfeld, 'The International Monetary System: A Look Back Over Seven Decades' in Thomas Cottier and John H Jackson (eds), *International Law in Financial Regulation and Monetary Affairs* (OUP, 2012) 52, 54. On voting in the World Bank, see Sabine Schlemmer-Schulte, 'International Bank for Reconstruction and Development', *Max Planck Encyclopedia of Public International Law* (last updated October 2014) paras 17, 22 <http://opil.ouplaw.com/view/10.1093/law:epil/9780199231690/law-9780199231690-e475?rskey=YktGxt&result=1&prd=EPIL > accessed 18 March 2015.

[156] For the impact of the current WTO regime on trade in agricultural products on developing states, see, e.g., Yong-Shik Lee, *Reclaiming Development in the World Trading System* (CUP, 2006) 107–14.

[157] On the concept of 'common but differentiated responsibility' in international law, see Christopher Stone, 'Common but Differentiated Responsibility in International Law' (2004) 98 *AJIL* 276; Philippe Cullet, 'Differential treatment in International Law' (1999) 10 *EJIL* 549. And see Art 44 of the 2001 Doha Ministerial Declaration (n 9).

the stronger states in the global economic system. Regional or bilateral negotiations between a powerful trading state and developing states are inherently unequal in terms of the parties' bargaining positions, and they are likely to generate RTAs that reflect or reinforce these power asymmetries.

From this perspective, it is not surprising that some RTAs which involve developed and developing states, and particularly bilateral ones, favour the interests of the developed party and its domestic groups.[158] Certain 'North-South' RTAs[159] apply more restrictive rules to trade in agricultural products (compared to industrial goods) on the one hand, and apply liberal rules for trade in industrial goods, as well as services, on the other hand.[160] Thus, for instance, the World Bank Global Prospects Report noted that '[t]he practice of excluding many agricultural products is common, and it can limit development payoffs'.[161] Furthermore, certain trade topics that are of interest to major developed states, such as investment and competition, were not accepted by the WTO Ministerial Conference in Cancun in 2004, but are included in some RTAs concluded between some developed and developing states.[162]

From the social conflict perspective,[163] RTAs established by strong developed parties are conceived as an attempt by the powerful trading parties to shift the rule-making process from the global to the more unequal regional or bilateral level.[164] Consequently, the social conflict approach generally opposes the establishment of RTAs, which are perceived as another disguised instrument of 'divide and rule' employed by developed states to perpetuate their dominance in the world economy. Thus, this approach inclines to interpret existing WTO provisions regarding RTAs in a restrictive manner.

158 See, e.g., Rudolf Adlung Sébastien Miroudot, 'Poison in the Wine? Tracing GATS-Minus Commitments in Regional Trade Agreements' (2012) WTO Staff Working Paper ERSD-2012-04 3–4 <http://www.econstor.eu/bitstream/10419/57593/1/684915472.pdf> accessed 13 March 2015; Meridith Kolsky Lewis, 'The Politics of Indirect Effects of Asymmetrical Bargaining Power in Free Trade Agreement' in Tomer Broude and others (eds), *The Politics of International Economic Law* (CUP, 2011) 19, 19–20, 35–6.

159 For some explanations for unfavourable rules towards developing countries included in some North-South RTAs, see Moshe Hirsch, 'North-South Regional Trade Agreements: Prospects, Risks and Legal Regulation' in YS Lee and Tomer Broude (eds), *Law and Development Perspective on International Trade Law* (CUP, 2011) 225, 237–9.

160 See, e.g., Gibbs, Wagle, and Ortega (n 67) 52.

161 The World Bank, *Global Economic Prospects—Trade, Regionalism and Development* (World Bank, 2005) xiii <http://siteresources.worldbank.org/INTGEP2005/Resources/gep2005.pdf> accessed 13 March 2015. See also Matsushita and Lee (n 69) 32, and the references therein.

162 Roberto V Fiorentino, Luis Verdeja, and Christelle Toqueboeuf, 'The Changing Landscape of Regional Trade Agreements: 2006 Update' (2007) WTO Discussion Paper 12, 13 <http://www10.iadb.org/intal/intalcdi/PE/2010/05129.pdf> accessed 13 March 2015; Matsushita and Lee (n 69) 26–7. See also Bryan Mercurio, 'TRIPS-Plus Provisions in FTAs: Recent Trends' in Lorand Bartel and Federco Ortino (eds), *Regional Trade Agreements and the WTO Legal System* (OUP, 2006) 215.

163 On the social conflict approach to regional agreement between the EU and the Southern Africa Development Community, see Clair Gammage, '(Re)conceptualizing International Economic Law' in Amanda Perry-Kessaris (ed), *Socio-Legal Approaches to International Economic Law* (Routledge, 2013) 64.

164 See, e.g., Gibbs, Wagle, and Ortega (n 67) 11.

V. Symbolic Interactionism as a Point of Departure

The sociological analyses presented above reveal that the major sociological perspectives suggest different answers to the dilemma regarding the relationship between the WTO and RTAs. While the structural-functional and the social conflict perspectives favour global integration (and restriction of RTAs), the symbolic-interactionist perspective generally advocates the formation and enlargement of RTAs.

The major sociological perspectives on RTAs should not be considered exclusive but, rather, complementary. Each of the core perspectives discussed above highlights different social aspects of the WTO–RTAs relationships, and analysis of this question with several sociological lenses may meaningfully clarify the social context of this debate. I am of the view that, while each of the above sociological approaches underscores certain significant aspects of the global/regional debate, the symbolic-interactionist perspective should generally serve as a point of departure for legal and policy-making in this sphere.

The structural-functional perspective on the global/regional debate has certain virtues. Restricting the formation and enlargement of RTAs is expected to enhance global economic integration, as well as provide greater coherence and uniformity in international trade law. Increased legal coherence and uniformity are expected to decrease the likelihood of incompatible socio-legal prescriptions that may generate dilemmas for states participating in overlapping global and regional regimes. Such legal divergence may generate certain tensions among trading partners and systemic frictions. This risk is not as considerable as it might seem,[165] and some scholars emphasize the process of material convergence among global and various RTAs (and the emergence of the 'Common Law of International Trade').[166] Still, overlapping global and regional regimes are bound to generate a certain extent of legal inconsistencies and disputes. Legal coherence between global and regional regimes is likely to increase predictability and certainty in the international economic system.

Cognizing that RTAs' legal provisions often reflect and affect norms and values prevailing in the involved societies,[167] the structural-functional perspective suggests that increasing international legal coherence is likely to enhance common values in the global arena. Increasing social coherence and integration is expected to enhance stability and order, and reduce the prospects of tensions and conflicts among states that participate in overlapping regimes. As elaborated

[165] An OECD study suggests that RTAs are 'most commonly based upon underlying WTO approaches and principles', OECD, *Regionalism and the Multilateral Trading System* (n 27) 4. See also the brief comparative review of the involved trade issues 4–6.

[166] JHH Weiler, 'Cain and Abel—Convergence and Divergence in International Trade Law' in JHH Weiler (ed), *The EU, the WTO and the NAFTA: Towards a Common Law of International Trade?* (OUP, 2000) 1.

[167] See Section IV(a) above.

below, the social costs accompanying such international economic coherence are considerable.

The social conflict perspective on the global/regional debate also presents significant merits. This approach underlines the asymmetric aspects of many RTAs and the leverage of powerful trading states in negotiations leading to RTAs. Power asymmetries are particularly prominent in some bilateral RTAs that involve a large developed state and a small developing state (but not all RTAs). While the need to narrow economic gaps between developing and developed states is important, and international trade law should strive to decrease the scope of considerably unequal RTAs that favour the interests of powerful states, the abolition or imposition of substantial restrictions on RTAs is not likely to attain these aims.[168] In addition, it is noteworthy that some RTAs between developed and developing states have succeeded in narrowing the economic gaps between RTAs' members.[169]

The above goal of decreasing the detrimental repercussion of considerably asymmetric RTAs may affect the interpretation of the WTO rules (such as Article XXIV of the GATT) and the review process of such RTAs by the WTO organs. Thus, for instance, it is desirable that 'North-South' RTAs will liberalize 'substantially all trade' in agricultural and textile products (and not 'substantially all trade' in general). While these considerations should somewhat affect the interpretation and modification of the relevant GATT provisions, they do not justify the imposition of substantial restrictions on the formation of RTAs. As elaborated below, RTAs' contribution to socio-economic pluralism outweighs the undesirable impacts of some asymmetric RTAs.

The intimate link between international economic rules and social values points to the social costs of implementing the structural-functional and the social conflict approaches to RTAs. These perspectives suggest imposing greater restrictions on RTAs and increasing socio-economic integration, coherence, and equality in the global economic system. Different trade rules often reflect different social values and ideologies that prevail in different regional communities. Thus, increasing policy and legal coherence is expected to be accompanied by a process of global socio-economic integration. Such a process may certainly increase efficiency and coordination among the relevant international trade regimes, but is also expected to stifle socio-economic pluralism.

The symbolic-interactionist approach to RTAs aims to attain a lower degree of international economic order, and to promote order that grows from a less deliberate and more spontaneous interactionist process. As discussed above,[170] the symbolic-interactionist perspective favours social structures that emerge and

168 For a discussion of some mechanisms that may ameliorate the above shortcomings of certain North-South RTAs, see Hirsch, 'North-South Regional Trade Agreements' (n 159) 239–40.

169 This is the case, for instance, with regard to the accession of some Mediterranean as well as Central and Eastern states to the EU. On the potential of RTAs to attract foreign investments to developing states, see Wilfred J Ethier, 'The New Regionalism' (1998) 108 *The Economic Journal* 1149.

170 See Section IV(c) above.

are maintained 'from below', through a complex process of interactions between states and regions. This approach enhances socio-economic pluralism, which encourages various regional regimes to develop and test different legal responses to modern challenges—the 'laboratory effect'.[171] This approach also allows RTAs to address the particular socio-economic features of each region or bilateral association without excessive intervention from external global regimes.

The structural-functional and social conflict approaches to RTAs incline to undervalue the particular culture, customs, and ideology that evolved in each region or bilateral context, and apply the same (or similar) policy and legal prescription to different regions or bilateral associations. The symbolic-interactionist approach is more sensitive to the particular social features present in each particular regional or bilateral context, and more inclined to tailor-made arrangements.

The distinctive characteristics of the contemporary WTO regime lend further support to the application of the symbolic-interactionist approach to the relationship between the WTO and RTAs. The WTO regime represents a relatively 'well-ordered' sphere. It has been significantly institutionalized since the conclusion of the Uruguay Round in 1994, and is considered one of the most legalized international legal regimes; it includes numerous binding agreements that are enforced, inter alia, by effective dispute settlement bodies with compulsory jurisdiction. On the other hand, the WTO system is extremely heterogeneous and its ongoing expansion intensifies its pluralistic character.

Proponents of the structural-functional approach emphasize the undesirable results of legal incoherence, particularly leaving countries to cope with incompatible legal rules that arise from overlapping global and regional regimes. The symbolic-interactionist approach is more likely to lead to more incompatible legal rules and disputes, and this feature should not be underestimated. Still, empirical studies show that RTA parties are less likely to be engaged in political-military conflicts and that RTA membership has a stronger influence on decreasing hostilities than membership in the WTO.[172]

In addition, well-established rules of international law may alleviate the problem of legal inconsistencies. First, the basic values of the international community are embodied in peremptory norms of international law (*jus cogens*) that prevail over conflicting rules,[173] including those included in RTAs. Second, Articles 103

[171] On the 'laboratory effect' of RTAs, see Cho (n 57) 432–4, 457. See also, Trachtman, 'Regional Trade' (n 42) 160. RTAs that introduce new legal responses to modern challenges must conform to the GATT/WTO rules; i.e., rules that are included in Art XXIV (and particularly XXIV(8)) and the Understanding on Interpretation of Article XXIV as well as those included in other WTO agreements. Trachtman, 'Toward Open Recognition' (n 51).

[172] Edward D Mansfield, 'Preferential Peace: Why Preferential Trading Arrangements Inhibit Interstate Conflict' in Edward D Mansfield and Brian M Pollins (eds), *Economic Interdependence and International Conflict* (University of Michigan Press, 2003) 222, 229–31; Edward D Mansfield and Jon C Pevehouse, 'Trade Blocks, Trade Flows, and International Conflict' (2000) 54 *International Organizations* 775, 788–801. See also Philippe Martin, Thierry Mayer, and Mathias Thoenig, 'The Economics and Politics of Free Trade Agreements' (Research-based policy analysis, 2010) <http://www.voxeu.org/article/free-trade-agreements-do-they-help-keep-peace> accessed 30 March 2015.

[173] Vienna Convention on the Law of Treaties (adopted 22 May 1969, entered into force 27 January 1980) 8 *ILM* 679, Art 53.

and 25 of the UN Charter accord superior status to the Charter's fundamental provisions (including the Security Council decisions undertaken under Chapter VII) over other international treaties,[174] including the GATT[175] as well as RTAs. Third, many of the remaining questions regarding inconsistent global and regional rules may be resolved by international treaty law.[176]

Clearly, the structural-functional and social conflict approaches increase legal coherence and certainty which are significant for the expansion of international trade. Generally, the symbolic-interactionist approach strives to achieve a lesser degree of orderliness and is more amenable to tolerate some degree of legal inconsistency and instability. This approach, which emphasizes the personal and societal costs associated with social integration, is ready 'to pay the price' of lower-level order in terms of legal predictability, and prefers the above-discussed benefits of socio-economic pluralism.[177] These significant benefits justify a presumption in favour of the symbolic-interactionist approach to the regional/global debate in contemporary international trade law.

In sum, the contribution of RTAs to socio-economic pluralism in the international system, and the accompanying benefits to international trade law indicate that the WTO members should generally be accorded a significant measure of discretion in the formation and enlargement of RTAs. The above sociological analysis indicates that it is not desirable for the WTO legal regime to impose substantial restrictions on RTAs, and the relevant legal provisions should generally be interpreted in a liberal manner. Still, the desirable aim of decreasing the detrimental repercussions of considerably asymmetric RTAs should somewhat affect the interpretation of these legal rules and the operation of the WTO oversight mechanism regarding such RTAs.

[174] See, e.g., Case Concerning Questions of Interpretation and Application of the 1971 Montreal Convention (*Libya v UK*) (Order of 14 April 1992) [1992] ICJ Rep 3, [39].

[175] Art XXI(c) of the GATT explicitly states that this agreement should not be construed 'to prevent any contracting party from taking any action in pursuance of its obligations under the United Nations Charter for the maintenance of international peace and security.'

[176] See, e.g., Vienna Convention on the Law of Treaties (n 173) Art 30; Arts 1–5, ILC, 'Report of the International Law Commission on the Work of its 58th Session - Conclusions of the work of the Study Group on the Fragmentation of International Law: Difficulties arising from the Diversification and Expansion of International Law' (2006) UN Doc. A/61/10 <http://legal.un.org/ilc/texts/instruments/english/draft%20articles/1_9_2006.pdf> accessed 13 March 2015; Dinah Shelton, 'International Law and Relative Normativity' in Malcolm D Evans (ed), *International Law* (3rd edn, OUP, 2010) 141, 157–64.

[177] The concept of pluralism in moral and political philosophy is concerned with the question of what sort of restrictions central institutions may impose on people's freedom to act according to their value systems. Pluralism generally refers to the promotion of heterogeneity over homogeneity and the dispersal of power over centralism. Political pluralists advocate the desirability of a wide diffusion of sovereign power among a variety of associations and the fragmentation of governments into decentralized units. The pluralist approach views small groups as the natural form of association and suggests that the state's power should be reduced. On the pluralist approach in political philosophy, see Will Kymlicka, *Contemporary Political Philosophy* (2nd edn, 2002) 346 et seq.; Paul Hirst, 'Pluralism' in William Outhwaite (ed), *Modern Social Thought* (2006) 484; Leonard Tivey, 'Robert Dahl and American Pluralism' in Leonard James Tivey and Anthony Wright (eds), *Political Thought Since 1945* (Elgar, 1992) 91; Elinor Mason, 'Value Pluralism' in Edward N Zalta (ed), *The Stanford Encyclopedia of Philosophy* (Fall 2011 edn) <http://plato.stanford.edu/entries/value-pluralism/> accessed 13 March 2015.

VI. Concluding Remarks

This chapter focuses on sociological theories which aim to explain diverse social interactions, including international economic relations and RTAs. Each theoretical approach underlines a different aspect of social phenomena and offers different assumptions relating the links between international legal relations and socio-cultural factors. The underlying assumption that international trade law reflects and affects socio-cultural factors led me to analyse the global/regional debate from the three major sociological perspectives. The sociological analyses reveal that the principal sociological approaches suggest different answers to the question concerning the desirable relationship between the WTO and RTAs, and different interpretations of existing WTO legal provisions regarding RTAs. This sociological analysis also indicates that while each of the core sociological perspectives highlights different aspects of the WTO–RTAs relationship, the particular virtues of the symbolic-interactionist approach justify a presumption in favour of this approach to RTAs. The contribution of RTAs to socio-economic pluralism in the international system and the accompanying benefits to international trade law indicate that the relevant WTO legal rules should be interpreted in a liberal manner.

The intimate link between regional integration agreements and sociological factors offers some directions regarding future research in this field. Further studies may explore additional links between regional agreements and diverse socio-cultural factors and processes; both sociological factors relating to the members involved in RTAs (e.g., religious features or national identities) as well as socio-cultural factors and process undertaken in the regional context (e.g., socialization or the evolution of regional identity). Such works may explore, for example, the link between the particular regional agreement's institutions (not only dispute settlement mechanisms) and socio-cultural features of the members and of the region.

The fact that the same or similar legal rules are included in several regional organizations' constituent instruments invites researchers to explore the link between the different *interpretations* provided by different regional bodies and socio-cultural factors of the involved communities (including the institution's organizational culture). Similarly, future studies may examine the link between the *implementation* of the same or similar legal rules and diverse socio-cultural factors in different international groups. Finally, socio-legal works may explore dynamic aspects of socio-economic integration. Thus, for example, such studies may explore the diffusion of norms and legal rules between regional bodies (or between global and regional bodies and vice versa) and various socio-cultural processes in the particular region or in the global arena.

3

Collective Memory and International Law

Yet it is in society that people normally acquire their memories. It is also in society that they recall, recognize, and localize their memories. ... Most of the time, when I remember, it is others who spur me on; their memory comes to the aid of mine and mine relies on theirs.

Maurice Halbwachs, *On Collective Memory*[1]

[1] Maurice Halbwachs, *On Collective Memory* (Lewis A Coser tr, University of Chicago Press 1992) 38.

I. Introduction

The concept of collective memory[2] starts from the premise that social groups often influence individual memories. Society frequently reminds us that certain historical events have taken place, provides some details of the particular occurrence, and occasionally suggests certain normative lessons drawn from the event. Some other historical occurrences attract little attention or fall into oblivion. Thus the construction of collective memory is a selective process, storing and interpreting historical events according to the distinctive features of the specific contemporary society. Collective memories are significantly involved in the formation of social identity and often have an integrative effect on the social group.

International law interacts with collective memory in both directions: international law affects and is affected by collective memory. International legal mechanisms occasionally function as carriers of collective memory, most notably within expert groups. This function is prominent regarding some principles of international customary law, resolutions of certain international institutions, and judgments rendered by international courts that transmit social memories. In certain cases, international law aims to shape collective memory, prominently with regard to international criminal courts. International law's capacity to affect collective memory depends on several factors such as the rituals involved, legitimacy, and various procedural rules (e.g., those related to admissible evidence or the tribunals' jurisdiction). International law is also affected by collective memories. Memories of various social groups (including nations, and regional or professional groups) often motivate and constrain their activities in the international legal system. Consequently, collective memory occasionally influences the content, interpretation, and implementation of international law.

The impact of collective memory on international law is illustrated in this chapter by an examination of Germany's collective memory of the hyperinflation during the Weimar Republic and its impacts on European Union (EU) economic and monetary law[3] during the Eurozone debt crisis (2009–12), as well as Argentina's collective memory of past foreign interventions and its effects on the non-implementation (until 2013) of a series of international investment tribunals' awards. The discussion of the two cases highlights some common and distinctive features of collective memories and their impact on international law.

These two cases illustrate the significant influence of collective memories on international law but they also highlight their limits. In both cases, collective memory was not the sole or determinative factor, and its impact on international law declined following a certain period. In both cases, collective memories led

[2] Various terms in sociological literature refer to collective memory; prominently, 'social memory', 'cultural memory', 'popular memory', and 'group memory'.

[3] Unlike other branches of EU law, the legal rules regarding budgetary and fiscal policies (including the critical rules concerning government debt) present decentralized features of international law. These decentralized rules and procedures are addressed in Section IV(b) below.

to the formation of intermediate doctrines that affected international law. The memory of the hyperinflation in Germany led to the development of the concept of 'stability culture' and the memory of foreign interventions in Latin America led to the Calvo doctrine. The particular collective memories are embedded in these intermediate legal doctrines and in the legal principles derived from them.

Those collective memories form part of each state's identity, but while Germany's collective memory mainly emphasizes the internal dimension of its identity, Argentina's memory tends to highlight its external social boundaries vis-à-vis powerful Western states. Germany's collective memory of hyperinflation is shared by major groups in German society, while Argentina's collective memory of foreign intervention presents clear features of 'fragmented memory'—and is mainly widespread among nationalistic groups (including the ruling government during the critical period). Finally, though in both cases political parties occasionally employ collective memories, the controversial-ideological aspects are more evident in the Argentine case.

This chapter is structured as follows: Section II briefly introduces the central tenets of collective memory in sociological literature and Section III outlines the diverse interrelationships between such memories and international law, including the impact on the content, interpretation, and implementation of international legal rules. Sections IV and V address two cases that illustrate the influence of collective memory on international law and its limits. Section IV discusses Germany's collective memory of hyperinflation (1922–3), its impacts on EU economic and monetary law, and its implementation during the European debt crisis (2009–12). Section V examines Argentina's collective memory of foreign interventions and its contribution to the hostile approach of Argentina towards international investment tribunals and the non-implementation of a series of International Centre for Settlement of Investment Disputes (ICSID) awards until 2013. Section VI recaps some of the central themes of this chapter, provides some comparative remarks regarding the collective memories cited here and their influence on international law, and suggests some topics for future research in this sphere.

II. Collective Memory

The point of departure[4] of the concept of collective memory[5] is that people normally acquire their memories not only through individual (psychological

[4] I am deeply indebted to Vered Vinitzky-Seroussi and Orit Gazit (the Hebrew University Department of Sociology) and Ron Levi (University of Toronto Munk School of Global Affairs) for their helpful comments on earlier drafts of this section.

[5] Olick and Robbins define 'social memory studies' as the 'general rubric for inquiry into the varieties of forms through which we are shaped by the past, conscious and unconscious, public and private, material and communicative, consensual and challenged'. Jeffrey K Olick and Joyce Robbins, 'Social Memory Studies: From "Collective Memory" to the Historical Sociology of Mnemonic Practices' (1998) 24 *Annual Review of Sociology* 105, 112. On Assmann's definition

or physiological) means but through social processes as well. Group membership often provides materials for memory, and prods individuals into recalling particular events. Groups can produce memories of events that individuals have not directly experienced.[6] The sociological study of memory does not imply that people's recollections are unaffected by personal or biological factors, but rather highlights the social factors which influence memory (both individual and collective), emphasizing that what we remember includes more than what we have experienced personally.[7] Halbwachs, widely acknowledged as the founding father of the study of collective memory,[8] states:

> But if we examine a little more closely how we recollect things, we surely realize that the greatest number of memories come back to us when our parents, our friends, or other persons recall them to us.... Most of the time, when I remember, it is others who spur me on; their memory comes to the aid of mine and mine relies on theirs.[9]

Remembering and forgetting are closely interlinked,[10] and while some past occurrences enjoy multiple commemorations, others attract little attention or are subject to 'collective amnesia'.[11] Collective memory often affects individuals' emotions, and recollecting a particular event may generate a sense of pride or embarrassment within the community's members.[12]

The notion of collective memory is different from 'collected memory' (the sum total of personal memories) and it is clear that certain social patterns of memory cannot be reduced to individual processes.[13] The collective memory of a community is more than, and qualitatively different from, the aggregation of individual memories. A group's memory involves the integration of various personal memories into a single common past of collective stories, myths, and more.[14] Collective memory is substantiated and transmitted through a wide array of practices of commemoration, including various rituals, monument building, national

of 'cultural memory' and the distinction between communicative and cultural memory, see Jan Assmann and John Czaplicka, 'Collective Memory and Cultural Identity' (1995) 65 *New German Critique* 125, 125–6.

6 Olick and Robbins (n 5) 106; Eviatar Zerubavel, 'Social Memories: Steps to a Sociology of the Past' (1996) 19 *Qualitative Sociology* 283, 286; Jeffrey K Olick, 'Collective Memory', *International Encyclopedia of the Social Sciences* (2nd edn, Macmillan, 2008) 7–8.

7 Eviatar Zerubavel (n 6) 289. See also Ross Poole, 'Memory, History and the Claims of the Past' (2008) 1 *Memory Studies* 149, 152.

8 For a survey of the intellectual roots and the evolution of the study of collective memory, see Olick and Robbins (n 5) 106–8; Jeffrey K Olick, Vered Vinitzky-Seroussi, and Daniel Levy, 'Introduction' in Jeffrey K Olick, Vered Vinitzky-Seroussi, and Daniel Levy (eds), *The Collective Memory Reader* (OUP, 2011) 8–29; Jeffrey K Olick, 'Collective Memory: The Two Cultures' (1999) 17 *Sociological Theory* 333, 334–5.

9 Halbwachs (n 1) 38.

10 On the dynamics of remembering and forgetting, see, e.g., Alieda Assmann, 'Canon and Archive' in Astrid Erll and Ansgar Nünning (eds), *Cultural Memory Studies: An International and Interdisciplinary Handbook* (Walter de Gruyter, 2008) 97–8. See also Yael Zerubavel, *Recovered Roots* (University of Chicago Press, 1995) 8–9.

11 Ibid., 8.

12 Eviatar Zerubavel (n 6) 290.

13 Olick, 'Collective Memory: The Two Cultures' (n 8) 338, 341–2.

14 Olick, 'Collective Memory: The Two Cultures' (n 8) 342; Eviatar Zerubavel (n 6) 293–4.

holidays, museums, school textbooks, mass media, naming streets, or courts' proceedings.[15] Agents of memory include diverse state and non-state actors, as well as individuals in key positions who organize various practices which construct and preserve the particular collective memory.[16]

Collective memory is not to be equated with past historical events; though it relates to the past, it is constructed in the present and is influenced by contemporary society and its particular features. Participation in commemorations interconnects the past and the present, the individual and the community.[17] Commemoration is capable of transforming something frozen in the past into a revived presence, alive in the minds of its commemorators.[18]

Furthermore, the construction of collective memory is a selective process: not all historical events are stored in the collective memory and where a certain occurrence is remembered, the group's memory normally does not include a precise and comprehensive account of all aspects of the event.[19] Collective memory interprets historical events according to the contemporary social context of the particular society.[20] As Schwartz explains:

> Collective memory reflects reality by interpreting the past in terms of images appropriate and relevant to the present; it shapes reality by providing people with a program in terms of which their present lines of conduct can be formulated and enacted.[21]

Collective memory confers meaning to historical events,[22] and acts of commemoration occasionally produce a commemorative narrative about a particular past.[23] Such selective narratives occasionally suggest a moral message to the group and provide some normative guidelines regarding the appropriate behaviour.[24] The social context, including the political culture in which collective memories emerge, affects these social memories and commemorative practices.[25]

Sociological studies of memory[26] have expanded on the role of collective memory in the formation of social identity.[27] Individuals define themselves as belonging

[15] See, e.g., Olick and Robbins (n 5) 106; Vered Vinitzky-Seroussi, 'Commemorating a Difficult Past: Yitzhak Rabin's Memorial' (2002) 67 *American Sociological Review* 30, 51; Barbara A Misztal, *Theories of Social Remembering* (Open University Press, 2003) 19–20.

[16] On agents of memory, see Vinitzky-Seroussi (n 15) 32–3 and the references therein.

[17] Edward S Casey, *Remembering: A Phenomenological Study* (2nd edn, Indiana University Press, 2000) 250.

[18] Ibid., 256.

[19] See, e.g., Yael Zerubavel (n 10) 6–8; Vinitzky-Seroussi (n 15) 34–5.

[20] Assmann and Czaplicka (n 5) 130. See also Eviatar Zerubavel (n 6) 285; Vinitzky-Seroussi (n 15) 33; Jens Meierhenrich, 'A Question of Guilt' (2006) 19 *Ratio Juris* 314, 316–17.

[21] Barry Schwartz, *Abraham Lincoln and the Forge of National Memory* (University of Chicago Press, 2000) 18.

[22] Ibid., 17–18.

[23] Yael Zerubavel (n 10) 6; Vinitzky-Seroussi (n 15) 34–5.

[24] Assmann and Czapllicka (n 5) 131–2; Poole (n 7) 162; Eviatar Zerubavel (n 6) 6. See also Schwartz (n 21) 18.

[25] Vinitzky-Seroussi (n 15) at 45. On the interactions between political culture and collective memory, see also Jeffrey K Olick, *The Politics of Regret: On Collective Memory and Historical Responsibility* (Routledge, 2007) 21 et seq.

[26] Olick, Vinitzky-Seroussi, and Levy (n 8) 41–2. See also Pierre Nora, 'Between Memory and History: Les Lieux de Mémoire' (1989) 26 *Representations* 15; Olick and Robbins (n 5) 123.

[27] On the formation of social identities and their impacts on international law, see Chapter 4.

to some social groups, and certain aspects of their self-image derive from the social categories to which they perceive themselves as belonging.[28] Two core elements stand at the heart of social identity: similarity and difference. Individuals need a certain level of both similarity to and differentiation from others, and social identity derives from the fundamental tension between the sense of belonging (on the group's internal level) and the sense of distinctiveness (on the group's external level).[29] Some scholars emphasize the role of highlighting 'boundaries' between social groups in the process of constructing and maintaining collective identity.[30] From this perspective, group identification is constructed 'across the group boundary'.[31]

Collective memories are significantly involved in the formation of collective identity of various social groups (including nations). A group's memory preserves the store of knowledge from which the group derives awareness of its unity and peculiarity.[32] Consequently, the socialization process includes teaching the group's collective memory to new members; it constitutes an important part of a community's efforts to incorporate new members.[33]

Collective memories have an integrative influence and may also form the basis for various demands, such as taxation or sacrifice.[34] Political leaders do not ignore this force and numerous studies have explored various methods governments employ to use collective memory as an instrument for furthering their aims.[35] Occasionally, collective memories are also mobilized by subgroups (e.g., minorities) as a source of opposition. Foucault emphasized the role of developing a 'counter-memory' which challenges that narrative of the dominant group.[36] Acknowledging the political aspects of collective memory does not mean that political leaders always plan commemorative events to recruit people for their political aims. Furthermore, the exploration of the political dimension of social memories should not result in reducing the complex process of the formation of collective memory into a political analysis alone, or overlooking the socio-cultural realm in which 'the politics of memory' is situated.[37]

The fact that collective memory often contributes to collective solidarity does not imply that social groups have a single memory or that commemorative

[28] See, e.g., Henri Tajfel and John C Turner, 'The Social Identity of Intergroup Behaviour' in Stephen Worchel (ed), *Psychology of Intergroup Relations* (Nelson-Hall, 1986) 7, 12.

[29] See Chapter 4, Section II(a).

[30] Fredrik Barth, 'Introduction' in Frederick Barth (ed), *Ethnic Groups and Boundaries: The Social Organization of Culture Difference* (Little, Brown and Company, 1969) 9, 10–12, 15–16; Richard Jenkins, *Social Identity* (4th edn, Routledge, 2014) 123, 46.

[31] Ibid., 46. See also Barth (n 30) 16.

[32] Assmann and Czaplicka (n 5) 130, see also 137.

[33] Eviatar Zerubavel (n 6) 290, see also 286.

[34] Olick, Vinitzky-Seroussi, and Levy (n 8) 42.

[35] Olick and Robbins (n 5) 117; Schwartz (n 21) 14–16 and see the references therein. On limits to the malleability of the past, see Olick and Robbins (n 5) 128–9.

[36] Michel Foucault, *Language, Counter-Memory, Practice: Selected Essays and Interviews* (Cornell University Press, 1997) 160–4, 150. See also Olick and Robbins (n 5) 126; Schwartz (n 21) 17.

[37] Ibid., 14–17.

practices are uniform across all segments of society.[38] Vinitzky-Seroussi offers a model for the emergence of *fragmented* and *multivocal* commemorations, which includes three dimensions: the political culture of the commemorating society, the relevance of past to present, and the influence of agents of memory. The phenomenon of *fragmented commemoration* is defined as 'multiple commemorations in various spaces and times where diverse discourses of the past are voiced and aimed at disparate audiences'.[39] In such cases, collective memory reflects consensus but is limited to the particular group which participates in the specific commemorative practices. Such a fragmented type of commemoration is more likely to be engendered in a conflictual political culture and when a strong link exists between the past and present debates.[40] *Multivocal commemorations* take place in a shared space, a shared time, or a shared text that carries diverse meanings, thus enabling different groups with differing interpretations of the same past event to participate in these practices.[41] A multivocal type of commemoration is more likely to emerge in a consensual political culture and when the link between past events and the current agenda is not strong.[42]

III. International Law and Collective Memory

Collective memory and law, including international law, interact in both directions: law affects and is affected by collective memory.[43] A brief discussion on the impact of international law on collective memory is followed by an examination of the influence of collective memory on international law. It is noteworthy that in certain cases, the same international legal mechanism simultaneously affects and is affected by collective memory.

a. The impact of international law on collective memory

International law occasionally affects the memories of various social groups, including nations, regional groups, and global institutions. For example, some treaties or international institutions' resolutions are incorporated into national or

[38] See, e.g., Robin Wagner-Pacifici and Barry Schwartz, 'The Vietnam Veterans Memorial: Commemorating a Difficult Past' (1991) 97 *American Journal of Sociology* 376. On contested collective memories, see also Joachim J Savelsberg and Ryan D King, 'Institutionalizing Collective Memories of Hate: Law and Law Enforcement in Germany and the United States' (2005) 111 *American Journal of Sociology* 579, 589; Olick and Robbins (n 5) 126–7.

[39] Vinitzky-Seroussi (n 15) 31–2. [40] Ibid., 32. [41] Ibid., 31.

[42] Ibid., 32.

[43] For a comprehensive and perceptive discussion of the interrelationships between law and collective memory, see Joachim J Savelsberg and Ryan D King, 'Law and Collective Memory' (2007) 3 *Annual Review Law Social Science* 189. On the law and historical narratives, see Robert M Cover, 'Forward: Nomos and Narrative' (1983) 97 *Harvard Law Review* 4, 5 et seq.

regional collective memories, prominently those relating to the establishment of these groups[44] or concerning some major international conflicts.

International legal doctrines and decisions of international institutions (such as tribunals or the Security Council) occasionally function as carriers of collective memory, particularly among professional groups. Decisions of international tribunals, such as the International Court of Justice (ICJ), often influence the development or interpretation of legally binding obligations in international law. Such decisions often include a description of the relevant historical events. Students, practitioners, and scholars who study significant judgments of international tribunals often learn the specific historical events *as selected and interpreted* by those tribunals. This function of international tribunals is conspicuous with regard to the judgment of the Nuremberg tribunal (1946)[45] regarding memory of World War II and the Holocaust. A study of the customary right of self-defence necessitates learning about the Caroline Incident (1837) as presented in authoritative treatises on international law.[46] Certain resolutions of the UN Security Council (SC) also function incidentally as carriers of memories. Thus, for instance, Resolution 1368 (which is significant in the context of self-defence against terrorism) refers to the 'horrifying terrorist attacks which took place on 11 September 2001'.[47] As noted above regarding collective memory in general, the memories transmitted in these treaties, judgments, and resolutions are inherently selective.[48]

International law aims in certain cases to affect collective memory. The founders of some international tribunals aimed to influence future collective memory.[49] The founders of the Nuremberg tribunal intended to affect collective memory by assembling an archive useful also to future historians, and sought that the 'trial would also serve as a lesson in history for future generations'.[50] The selection of

44 See, e.g., on the EU constituent treaties as a constitutive element in the European collective memory; Hannes Hansen-Magnusson and Jenny Wustenberg, 'Forging a European Memory: The Treaties of Rome as a Common Tradition in the Making?' (Biennial Conference of the European Union Studies Association, Boston, 3–5 March 2011) <http://www.euce.org/eusa/2011/papers/1g_wustenberg.pdf> accessed 26 March 2015.

45 *Judgment of the Nuremberg International Military Tribunal 1946* (1947) 41 *AJIL* 172 <http://avalon.law.yale.edu/subject_menus/judcont.asp> accessed 27 March 2015.

46 See, e.g., Lori Fishler Damrosch and others, *International Law* (5th edn, West, 2009) 1134–5; Malcolm Shaw, *International Law* (7th edn, CUP, 2014) 820; Yoram Dinstein, *War, Aggression, and Self-Defence* (5th edn, CUP, 2011) 274.

47 See UNSC Res 1368 (12 September 2001) UN Doc S/RES/1368 Art 1. And regarding crimes undertaken in Bosnia and Herzegovina, see UNSC Res 771 (17 August 1992) UN Doc S/RES/771(1992) at the preamble.

48 Such decisions of international tribunals and institutions are often 'filtered' in textbooks that cite selected extracts of these decisions.

49 On the International Criminal Tribunal for Rwanda and collective memory, see Nigel Eltringham '"We are not a Truth Commission": Fragmented Narratives and the Historical Record at the International Criminal Tribunal for Rwanda' (2009) 11 *Journal of Genocide Research* 55; Irene C Lu, 'Curtain Call at Closing: The Multi-Dimensional Legacy of the International Criminal Tribunal for Rwanda' (2014) 34 *University of Pennsylvania Journal of International Law* 859, 890–4.

50 Antonio Cassese, *International Criminal Law* (3rd edn, OUP, 2013) 256. See also Savelsberg and King, 'Law and Collective Memory' (n 43) 193. Stephan Landsman, *Crimes of the Holocaust*

cases brought to international criminal tribunals (and not referred to national judiciaries) is occasionally affected by the goal of ensuring that the historical narrative emerging from the tribunal's case law will present the various aspects of the event. The 'referral' practice of the International Criminal Tribunal for the Former Yugoslavia (ICTY) shows that one of the criteria applied by the prosecutor was 'representation' and the need to set the historical record of the events.[51] The prosecutor of the International Criminal Court (ICC) adopted a similar criterion.[52] Those and additional attempts to use international criminal courts to influence future historical narratives have been criticized by some socio-legal scholars, emphasizing, inter alia, the inherent limitations of international criminal proceedings.[53]

Some international instruments explicitly aim to influence collective memories.[54] Thus, the 1972 World Heritage Convention[55] seeks to protect not only natural sites but also 'sites of memory'[56] relating, inter alia, to 'history of peoples'.[57] In addition to the 2005 Convention on the Value of Cultural Heritage,[58] the 1992 European Convention on the Protection of the Archaeological Heritage expressly

(University of Pennsylvania Press, 2005) 6–7; Ruti G Teitel, *Transitional Justice* (OUP, 2000) 73; Mark J Osiel, *Mass Atrocity, Collective Memory and the Law* (Transaction, 1997) 2.

[51] See Gilad Noam, 'Allocation of Judicial Power between Domestic and International Courts and Tribunals—Some Guidelines for the International Criminal Law System' (PhD Dissertation, Hebrew University, 2013) 156–8, 160–8, 371. See *Prosecutor v Dragomir Milosević* (Decision on Referral of Case Pursuant to Rule 11bis) ICTY IT-98-29/1-PT (8 July 2005) [11]; Luc Côté, 'Reflections on the Exercise of Prosecutorial Discretion in International Criminal Law' (2005) 3 *Journal of International Criminal Justice* 162, 176, see also 173–4.

[52] The ICC Prosecutorial Strategy for 2009–12 explained: 'While the Office's mandate does not include production of comprehensive historical records for a given conflict, incidents are selected to provide a sample that is reflective of the gravest incidents and the main types of victimization.' ICC, The Office of The Prosecutor, 'Prosecutorial Strategy: 2009–2012' (1 February 2010) para 20 <http://www.icc-cpi.int/NR/rdonlyres/66A8DCDC-3650-4514-AA62-D229D1128F65/281506/OTPProsecutorialStrategy20092013.pdf> accessed 27 March 2015.

[53] For a concise review of this criticism, see Richard Ashby Wilson, *Writing History in International Criminal Trials* (CUP, 2011) 2–4 and see the references therein. On the limitations of international tribunals in this sphere, see further below.

[54] See, e.g., Art 3 of the 'Set of principles for the protection and promotion of human rights through action to combat impunity' on the 'Duty to Preserve Memory' concerning violations of human rights and humanitarian law. Sixty-first session, Item 17 of the provisional agenda, E/CN.4/2005/102/Add.1 (Commission Decision, 8 February 2005).

[55] Convention Concerning the Protection of the World Cultural and Natural Heritage (adopted 16 November 1972, entered into force 17 December 1975) 1037 UNTS 151.

[56] UNESCO, *World Heritage at the Heart of UNESCO's Peace Mandate* <http://www.unesco.org/new/en/culture/resources/in-focus-articles/heritage-and-peace/> accessed 26 May 2015, see there the historical sites included in the World Heritage list.

[57] See the definition of 'monuments' and 'groups of buildings' at the Convention Concerning the Protection of the World Cultural and Natural Heritage (adopted 23 November 1972, entered into force 15 December 1975) 1037 UNTS 151 Art 1. And see also Art 13(4) of this Convention as well as Sections (iv) and (vi) of the UNESCO selection criteria <http://whc.unesco.org/en/criteria/> accessed 27 March 2015.

[58] See the Council of Europe Framework Convention on the Value of Cultural Heritage for Society (opened for signature 27 October 2005, entered into force 1 June 2011) CETS 199, Art 3 <http://conventions.coe.int/Treaty/EN/Treaties/Html/199.htm> accessed 27 March 2015. And the Council of Europe's Explanatory Report on this treaty's provision <http://conventions.coe.int/Treaty/EN/Reports/Html/199.htm> accessed 27 March 2015.

aims to protect the archaeological heritage 'as a source of the European collective memory'.[59] Some international institutions have designated annual memorial days to commemorate certain historical events, such as the International Holocaust Remembrance Day,[60] the International Day of Remembrance for the Victims of Slavery and the Transatlantic Slave Trade,[61] or the EU Europe Day which commemorates the 1950 Schuman Declaration.[62]

International law's capacity to function as a carrier of collective memory is influenced by several distinctive factors. As in domestic law,[63] international tribunals and the Security Council are often powerful actors in this sphere since they involve effective rituals. In addition, where historical facts or their interpretation are disputed, international bodies which are vested with legitimacy have greater capacity to affect the collective memory. Though domestic legal institutions' decisions occasionally attract much attention, international legal institutions regularly deal with issues that are more likely to attract public attention. Thus, it seems that even relatively 'uninteresting' judgments by international courts regarding boundary disputes are more likely to affect the collective memories of the involved states and regional groups.

Though international bodies enjoy certain 'comparative advantages' in transmitting collective memories, some of their distinctive features constrain that capacity. Like domestic courts,[64] international tribunals are restrained by evidentiary rules. Such rules limit the information that can be presented in legal proceedings, sometimes avoiding a significant determination regarding historical facts.[65] Similarly, unlike other carriers of collective memory (such as historians or journalists), the description of historical events by international tribunals is often limited by particular international legal rules and specific classifications,[66] for example, according to the elements of a particular legal obligation as specified in a treaty.[67] Such procedural rules do not apply to non-legal bodies like the Security

[59] See the European Convention on the Protection of the Archaeological Heritage (Revised) (opened for signature 16 January 1992, entered into force 25 May 1995) CETS 143, Art 1.

[60] See UNGA Res 60/7 (1 November 2005) UN Doc A/RES/60/7, Art 1.

[61] See UNGA Res 62/122 (17 December 2007) UN Doc A/RES/62/122, Art 3.

[62] On Europe Day, see 'Europe Day—EU Open Doors' <http://europa.eu/about-eu/basic-information/symbols/europe-day/index_en.htm> accessed 27 March 2015.

[63] On the impact of rituals with regard to domestic law, see Savelsberg and King 'Law and Collective Memory' (n 43) 190; Teitel (n 50) 75; Osiel (n 50) 15–17. On the role of ritual in court proceedings, see Oscar Chase, *Law, Culture and Ritual* (New York University Press, 2005) 114–24.

[64] Savelsberg and King, 'Law and Collective Memory' (n 43) 194; Teitel (n 50) 106; Osiel (n 50) 272; Inga Markovits, 'Selective Memory: How the Law Affects What We Remember and Forget about the Past: The Case of East Germany' (2001) 35 *Law and Society Review* 513, 514; Jody L Madeira, 'Blood Relations: Collective Memory, Cultural Trauma, and the Prosecution and Execution of Timothy McVeigh' (2008) Indiana Legal Studies Research Paper No. 102, 9 <http://ssrn.com/abstract=1007041> accessed 26 March 2015.

[65] See, e.g., regarding determination on genocide, *Case Concerning the Application of the Convention on the Prevention and Punishment of the Crime of Genocide (Bosnia and Herzegovina v Serbia and Montenegro)* (Judgment) [2007] ICJ Rep 43, [209].

[66] On this feature regarding domestic courts, see Savelsberg and King, 'Law and Collective Memory' (n 43) 194.

[67] With regard to international criminal tribunals, see Wilson (n 53) 2–3.

Council, but the latter is constrained by other rules of procedure (e.g., concerning the people entitled to present information to the Council).[68]

The most significant limitation on the capacity of international tribunals in shaping collective memories relates to their jurisdiction. Unlike domestic courts, which commonly enjoy mandatory jurisdiction concerning activities undertaken within the state's territory, the competence of international courts to render binding decisions is regularly subject to the parties' consent.[69] Thus, significant historical events are often not addressed by international tribunals. In certain (limited) cases, international tribunals may avoid the restriction of the parties' consent. This is the case, for instance, where the ICJ is authorized by the General Assembly or the SC to render an advisory opinion[70] (which though formally non-binding, is often influential in the international community) or when the Security Council refers a case to the ICC.[71]

International law may also affect the formation of collective memory by *other* agents of memory.[72] This indirect effect is prominent regarding international treaties which restrict the collection and use of data by individuals and state agencies,[73] or conventions protecting certain human rights such as the right to privacy[74] or freedom of expression.[75] Such international legal rules affect the capacity of historians, journalists, and researchers to collect and disseminate information regarding historic events.

b. The impact of collective memory on international law

Collective memories occasionally affect the content of international legal rules, their interpretation and compliance with these rules. Some collective memories are institutionalized[76] in various international legal mechanisms while others are semi-institutionalized in diverse international soft laws. Thus, for example, the

[68] See Security Council, 'Provisional Rules of Procedure', Arts 37–9 <http://www.un.org/en/sc/about/rules/chapter6.shtml> accessed 27 March 2015.

[69] See, e.g., Art 36 of the Statute of the International Court of Justice (adopted 26 June 1945, entered into force 24 October 1945) 1 UNTS XVI.

[70] See the Statute of the ICJ (n 69) Art 65; and the UN Charter Art 96.

[71] Rome Statute of the International Criminal Court (adopted 17 July 1998, entered into force 1 July 2002) 2187 UNTS 90 Art 13(b).

[72] On these indirect impacts of domestic law on collective memory, see, e.g., Savelsberg and King, 'Law and Collective Memory' (n 43) 190, 197–9. See also Markovits (n 64) 513, 530–42, 545–53.

[73] See, e.g., Convention for the Protection of Individuals with regard to Automatic Processing of Personal Data (adopted 28 January 1981, entered into force 10 January 1985) 1496 UNTS 66; Additional Protocol to the Convention for the Protection of Individuals with regard to Automatic Processing of Personal Data, regarding supervisory authorities and transborder data flows (opened for signature 8 November 2001, entered into force 1 July 2004) CETS 181.

[74] See, e.g., the International Covenant on Civil and Political Rights (adopted 16 December 1966, entered into force 23 March 1976) 999 UNTS 171 (ICCPR) Art 17.

[75] See, e.g., ICCPR Art 19.

[76] On the impact of collective memories on the differences between German and US concerning domestic hate crimes legislation and their implementation, see Savelsberg and King, 'Institutionalizing Collective Memories of Hate' (n 38) 598.

1994 Inter-American Convention on Forced Disappearance of Persons[77] and the 1973 Apartheid Convention[78] were significantly affected by collective memories of past events.

Collective memory may influence the interpretation of international treaties. Treaty interpretation often necessitates the examination of the historical background of the particular treaty. Article 32 of the 1969 Vienna Convention on the Law of Treaties invites treaty interpreters to explore (as a secondary mean of interpretation) the historical context of the particular convention as presented in the '*preparatory work*'[79] and the '*circumstances of its conclusion*'. While the treaty's preparatory work often reflects collective memories of particular events existing at the time of negotiations, the circumstances of the treaty's conclusion are more likely to be influenced by collective memory existing at the time of the interpretation.

Finally, nations' collective memories occasionally affect states' positions and conduct regarding implementation of international legal rules. Thus, for example, Japan's collective memory affects its position concerning the 1968 Non-Proliferation Treaty.[80] Collective memories influence the resort to legal remedies redressing past events,[81] such as demands for compensation for past practices known as 'comfort women' during World War II[82] or advancing territorial claims based on the memory of past events. As will be elaborated below, Argentina's collective memory regarding foreign intervention affected its approach concerning the implementation of international investment tribunals' awards.

[77] The Inter-American Convention on Forced Disappearance of Persons (entered into force 28 March 1996) 33 *ILM* 1429. On the link between the criminalization of forced disappearance on the international level (including the UN Convention) and crimes committed in Latin American during the second half of the twentieth century, see Ioanna Pervou, 'The Convention for the Protection of All Persons from Enforced Disappearance: Moving Human Rights Protection Ahead' (2012) 5 *European Journal of Legal Studies* 119, 120–2, 127.

[78] Art II of the International Convention on the Suppression and Punishment of the Crime of Apartheid (1973) explicitly links between the definition of 'apartheid' and practices undertaken by the government of South Africa during the apartheid era, International Convention on the Suppression and Punishment of the Crime of Apartheid (adopted 30 November 1973, entered into force 18 July 1976) 1015 UNTS 243 Art 2.

[79] Julian Davis Mortenson, 'Is the Vienna Convention Hostile to Drafting History?' (2013) 107 *AJIL* 780, 785–6.

[80] On the link between Japan's collective memory regarding Hiroshima and Nagasaki and its position regarding the Non-Proliferation Treaty, e.g., Emma Chanlett-Avery and Mary Beth Nikitin, 'Japan's Nuclear Future: Policy Debate, Prospects, and U.S. Interests' (2009) Congressional Research Service research paper 7-5700, 1–2, 6–7 <https://www.fas.org/sgp/crs/nuke/RL34487.pdf> accessed 26 March 2015; 'Japan's efforts in disarmament and non-proliferation Education' (submitted by Japan, 2007) Preparatory Committee for the 2010 Review Conference of the Parties to the Treaty on the Non-Proliferation of Nuclear Weapons (27 April 2007) UN Doc NPT/CONF.2010/PC.I/WP.3, para 1.

[81] See, e.g., Patrick Macklem, 'Rybná 9, Praha 1: Restitution and Memory in International Human Rights Law' (2005) 16 *EJIL* 1.

[82] See Monica E Eppinger, Karen Knop, and Annelise Riles, 'Diplomacy and Its Others: The Case of Korean Comfort Women' (18 April 2014) 2 <http://ssrn.com/abstract=2411610> accessed 26 March 2015.

The following two sections discuss the particular collective memories of Germany and Argentina and their impacts on international law. Section IV examines Germany's collective memory regarding the hyperinflation during the Weimar Republic and its impact on the content of the EU Economic and Monetary Union (EMU) law and its implementation during the Eurozone debt crisis (2009–12). Section V explores Argentina's collective memory of past foreign intervention and its contribution to the hostile approach towards international protection of foreign investors and non-implementation of a series of ICSID awards during the period from 2007 to 2013.

IV. Germany's Collective Memory, EMU Law, and the EU's Legal Response during the Debt Crisis

a. The European debt crisis (2009–2012)

The European debt crisis (2009–12) erupted with news of the deterioration of Greece's debts and that during that period four EU Members received financial assistance from the EU and the International Monetary Fund (IMF). Policy-makers encountering debt crisis may employ a variety of response measures but the controversy between proponents of the popularly called 'austerity' and 'expansionary' approaches forms the major axis of disagreement in modern economics:[83] (i) '*The austerity approach*': following the classical and new classical schools of thought in economics, this approach emphasizes the importance of fiscal discipline, prominently deficit reduction by lowering governmental spending and raising taxes, as well as the adoption of structural reforms (e.g., labour market reforms).[84] (ii) '*The expansionary approach*': following the Keynesian and new Keynesian economics, this approach emphasizes the harmful consequences of budgetary cuts and other contractionary measures during economic recession, and suggests undertaking expansionary measures (including increased government spending and expanding the money supply) to stimulate the economy.[85]

[83] On the two approaches, see Cornel Ban, 'Austerity versus Stimulus? Understanding Fiscal Policy Change at the International Monetary Fund since the Great Recession' (2014) GEGI Working Paper Series <http://www.bu.edu/pardee/files/2014/03/Austerity-vs.-Stimulus-Working-Paper.pdf> accessed 27 March 2015.

[84] For a non-technical discussion of the classical and new classical schools of thought in economics, see Marc Davis, 'Why Can't Economists Agree?' (*Investopedia*, 2011) <http://www.investopedia.com/articles/economics/09/why-economists-do-not-agree.asp> accessed 27 March 2015. On the new classical macroeconomics, see Bruce C Greenwald and Joseph E Stiglitz, 'Keynesian, New Keynesian and New Classical Economics' (1987) 39 *Oxford Economic Papers* 119; Kevin D Hoover, 'New Classical Macroeconomics', *The Concise Encyclopedia of Economics* (2nd edn, Liberty Fund Inc., 2008).

[85] For a non-technical discussion of the Keynesian and new Keynesian economics, see Greenwald and Stiglitz (n 84), 131–2; Gregory Mankiv, 'New Keynesian Economics', *The Concise Encyclopedia of Economics* (2nd edn, Liberty Fund Inc., 2008).

Economic literature remains divided regarding this controversy, and eminent economists do not share the same views regarding the desirable policy for coping with a financial crisis,[86] or concerning the impact of fiscal discipline on economic growth.[87]

The response measures undertaken by the EU bodies during the sovereign debt crisis (elaborated below) can be divided into three principal stages: (i) the EU bodies' responses during the *first stage* of the crisis (October 2009 to May 2010) are generally characterized as austerity measures. During that period, the EU bodies pressed Greece (and later other countries) to adopt painful austerity measures; (ii) during the *second stage* (May 2010 to December 2011), the EU bodies extended emergency loans to Greece and established new general rescue funds. Financial assistance was conditional on significant budgetary cuts and structural reforms that largely typify the austerity approach; (iii) during the third stage (December 2011 to September 2012) the European Central Bank (ECB) adopted new expansionary measures, prominently injecting liquidity into the Eurozone market and pledging to purchase (under certain conditions) sovereign bonds of the debt-distressed countries.

b. First and second stages of the crisis: Austerity measures, the EU pre-crisis legal regime, and conditionalities

***The first stage* of the crisis** spanned from October 2009 (the eruption of the crisis)[88] to May 2010 (the first 'bailout' to Greece). The EU's response measures, prominently regarding Greece, were generally characterized by an austerity approach. During that period, the EU bodies pressed Greece (and later other countries, such as Portugal and Ireland) to adopt austerity measures. This feature was particularly noticeable regarding various decisions and recommendations issued by the EU bodies under the Excessive Deficit Procedure (discussed below), urging Greece to take further deficit-reduction measures.[89] The EU's conservative economic

[86] See, e.g., Greenwald and Stiglitz (n 84).

[87] See, e.g., Thomas Herndon, Michael Ash, and Robert Pollin, 'Does High Public Debt Consistently Stifle Economic Growth? A Critique of Reinhart and Rogoff' (2013) Political Economy Research Institute, Working Paper 322 <http://www.peri.umass.edu/fileadmin/pdf/working_papers/working_papers_301-350/WP322.pdf> accessed 27 March 2015.

[88] See, e.g., IMF, 'IMF Country Report No. 13/156, Greece: Ex Post Evaluation of Exceptional Access under the 2010 Stand-By Arrangement' (2013) 7 <http://www.imf.org/external/pubs/ft/scr/2013/cr13156.pdf> accessed 27 March 2015.

[89] See, e.g., Council Recommendation SEC 1549 for a Council Decision establishing whether Greece has taken effective action in response to the Council recommendation of 27 April 2009. SEC(2009)1549 <http://ec.europa.eu/transparency/regdoc/rep/2/2009/EN/2-2009-1549-EN-F-0.Pdf> accessed 27 March 2015; Council Decision (EC) 2010/291 of 19 January 2010 on the existence of an excessive deficit in Slovakia [2010] *OJ L* 125/50. See also e.g., 'Greece Bailout: Athens Urged to Stick with Reforms' *BBC* (23 August 2013) <www.bbc.co.uk/news/business-19351830> accessed 27 March 2015; 'EU Tells Greece to Cut More' *Euronews* (1 March 2010) <www.euronews.com/2010/03/01/eu-tells-greece-to-cut-more/> accessed 27 March 2015.

approach followed the pre-crisis legal regime. A discussion on the socio-cultural roots of this legal regime requires a brief presentation of the EMU central principles.

A dominant feature of the EMU (and its significant weakness) relates to the asymmetry between the regulation of economic and monetary policies. The single and centralized *monetary* policy at the Union level coexists with a decentralized regime of coordination of the Members' *economic* policies.[90] The EMU drafters sought to address this gap by elaborating legal criteria regarding coordination among the EU Members' policies in the economic area and by establishing detailed surveillance and corrective procedures at the EU level. The term 'economic union' in this context generally refers to the EU Members' budgetary and fiscal policies.[91]

The Treaty on the Functioning of the EU (TFEU) sets out the basic principles for coordination among the Members' economic policies.[92] The Members and the Union are bound to comply with the guiding principles of 'stable prices', sound public finances and monetary conditions, and a sustainable balance of payments.[93] The core principle (considered by some experts as 'the cornerstone' of EMU)[94] is maintaining stable prices.

The coordination of economic policies is to be attained by establishing broad guidelines for the Members' economic policies by the Council,[95] and their implementation is monitored by the EU surveillance mechanism.[96] The principal obligations imposed on the Members concerning fiscal restraint are the prohibition of excessive budget deficit and government debt. Article 126(1) TFEU obligates the Member States to avoid excessive government deficits, and the Protocol on the Excessive Deficit Procedure further defines the 'reference values' (3% for the ratio of the government deficit to gross domestic product and 60% for the ratio of government debt to gross domestic product).[97]

These obligations regarding fiscal discipline are accompanied by rules concerning multilateral surveillance as well as those prescribed under the 'corrective mechanism'. The latter mechanism is centred on the Excessive Debt Procedure (EDP) designed to enforce the above obligation regarding budget

[90] Arts 119, 120, and 128 of The Consolidated Versions of the Treaty on European Union and the Treaty on the Functioning of the European Union [2010] OJ C 83/1 (hereinafter: TFEU). See also Rosa M Lastra and Jean-Victor Louis, 'European Economic and Monetary Union: History, Trends, and Prospects' (2013) *YB Eur L* 1, 5, 35; A Geelhoed, F Amtenbrink, and S Kingston, 'Economic, Monetary and Social Policy' in Paul JG Kapteyn and others (eds), *The Law of the European Union and the European Communities* (4th edn, Kluwer 2008) 881, 901–2; Hanspeter K Scheller, *The European Central Bank: History, Role and Functions* (2nd edn, European Central Bank, 2006) 32.

[91] See, e.g., Lastra and Louis (n 90) 35.

[92] TFEU Arts 119 and 121.

[93] TFEU Art 119(3).

[94] Dominique Servais and Rodolphe Ruggeri, 'The EU Constitution: Its Impact on Economic and Monetary Union and Economic Governance' in *Legal Aspects of the European System of Central Banks* (European Central Bank, 2005) 43, 45. See also Jean-Victor Louis, 'Monetary Policy and Central Banking in the Constitution' in *Legal Aspects of the European System of Central Banks* (European Central Bank, 2005) 27, 36.

[95] TFEU Art 121(2).

[96] TFEU Art 123(3).

[97] Protocol (No. 12) on the excessive deficit procedure, [2008] OJ C 115 (9 May 2008) 279 at Art 1.

deficit and government debt.[98] The above primary law is complemented by a secondary law elaborating and strengthening the EDP, mainly the 'Stability and Growth Pact' (SGP), essentially a series of regulations.[99] To strengthen the obligations regarding fiscal discipline and avoid an incentive for the Member States that may contemplate unsound budgetary policies, the Members and the Union are barred from assuming liability for the Members' government debt (the 'no-bailout clause').[100]

The prohibition of 'monetary financing' complements the 'no-bailout clause'; the Members' central banks as well as the ECB are forbidden to finance Members' government spending through monetary creation, including direct purchasing of debt instruments by the ECB.[101] In addition, Articles 127(1) and 282(2) TFEU emphasize that the primary objective of the European System of Central Banks (ESCB) is to maintain price stability.

***The second stage* of the crisis** started in May 2010 (the first bailout to Greece) and ended in mid-December 2011 (the new expansionary measures). During this period the EU institutions granted emergency loans to Greece (and later to Ireland[102] and Portugal).[103] The financial aid to Greece (and later to other countries) was accompanied by stringent conditionalities, especially regarding budget deficit reductions and structural reforms.

Following the first ad hoc emergency assistance to Greece, the EU bodies and Member States established rescue funds to provide financial assistance to Eurozone members[104] which experienced or were threatened by financing difficulties; the first fund was temporary (mainly the European Financial Stability

[98] In contrast to the above surveillance mechanism, the EDP is more stringent and may lead to financial sanctions. TFEU Arts 126(2)–(11). On the 'corrective mechanism', see also Kaarlo H Tuori, 'The European Financial Crisis: Constitutional Aspects and Implications' (2012) EUI Working Papers Law 2012/28 6–7 <http://cadmus.eui.eu/bitstream/handle/1814/24301/LAW_2012_28_Tuori.pdf?sequence=1> accessed 27 March 2015; Lastra and Louis (n 89) 51–4.

[99] Council Regulation (EC) 1466/97 of 7 July 1997 on the strengthening of the surveillance of budgetary positions and the surveillance and coordination of economic policies [2007] *OJ L* 209; Council Regulation (EC) 1467/97 of 7 July 1997 on speeding up and clarifying the implementation of the excessive deficit procedure [1997] *OJ L* 209. On these regulations, see Geelhoed, Amtenbrink, and Kingston (n 90) 910–28; Lastra and Louis (n 90) 55–6. These Regulations had been amended in 2005: Council Regulation 1005/2005 of 30 June 2005 fixing the derived intervention prices for white sugar for the 2005/6 marketing year [2005] *OJ L* 174; Council Regulation 1056/2005 of 27 June 2005 amending Regulation (EC) No. 1467/97 on speeding up and clarifying the implementation of the excessive deficit procedure [2005] *OJ L* 174/5.

[100] TFEU Art 125. On the objective of Art 125, see Case C-370/12, *Pringle v Government of Ireland*, Judgment of 27 November 2012 [135].

[101] TFEU Art 123(1).

[102] Ireland—Memorandum of Understanding on Specific Economic Policy Conditionality, 3 December 2010.

[103] Portugal—Memorandum of Understanding on Specific Economic Policy Conditionality, 17 May 2011.

[104] On European Financial Stabilization Mechanism, available to euro area members and non-euro area members, see Council Regulation (EU) 407/2010 of 11 May 2010 establishing a European financial stabilisation mechanism [2010] *OJ L* 118/1; European Financial Stabilisation Mechanism <http://ec.europa.eu/economy_finance/eu_borrower/efsm/> accessed 27 May 2015.

Facility (EFSF))[105] and was followed by the permanent European Stability Mechanism (ESM).[106] The establishment of the ESM was accompanied by an amendment to Article 136 of the TFEU, which conditioned a resort to these general funds by meeting 'strict'[107] conditionalities (also sanctioned in the ESM treaty)[108] which largely characterize the austerity approach.[109] The EDP was strengthened in December 2011 by a series of legislative acts (the 'six pack')[110] and further reinforced by additional regulations (the 'two pack'),[111] as well as by a new international treaty (the 'Fiscal Compact') that also aims to strengthen fiscal discipline through the 'balanced budget rule' and the automatic correction mechanism.[112]

The conditionalities: The Greek Economic Adjustment Programme prescribes significant conditionalities[113] which essentially characterize the austerity approach. The Greek Memorandum of Understanding (MoU) elaborated detailed measures to be undertaken by Greece within specified time frames. These conditionalities include requirements regarding significant debt reduction and cuts in the public sector,[114] budget discipline,[115] increasing various taxes, and abrogating certain tax exemptions;[116] and labour market reforms (including and amending employment protection legislation).[117]

105 Council Regulation 407/2010 (n 104). On the EFSF, see Boris Ryvkin, 'Saving the Euro: Tensions with European Treaty Law in the European Union's Efforts to Protect the Common Currency' (2012) 45 *Cornell International Law Journal* 227, 240–5.

106 Treaty Establishing the European Stability Mechanism. The euro area Member States signed the treaty on 2 February 2012 and the ESM was inaugurated on 8 October 2012. European Stability Mechanism <www.esm.europa.eu/> accessed 26 March 2015.

107 See European Council Decision of 25 March 2011 amending Art 136 of the Treaty on the Functioning of the European Union with regard to a stability mechanism for Member States whose currency is the euro [2011] *OJ L* 91/1.

108 ESM Treaty (n 106) Arts 3 and 12.

109 As stated by the ECB, '(d) the ESM has to observe the principles of cautious and sound financial management' Opinion of the ECB on a draft European Council Decision amending Art 136 of the TFEU with regard to the ESM [2011] OJ C 140/8.

110 On the 'six-pack' (five regulations and one directive), see Council Regulation (EC) 1466/97 (n 99).

111 Commission, '"Two-Pack" enters into force, completing budgetary surveillance cycle and further improving economic governance for the euro area' MEMO/13/457.

112 Treaty on Stability, Coordination and Governance in the Economic and Monetary Union (signed 1 February 2012) <http://europa.eu/rapid/press-release_DOC-12-2_en.htm> accessed 27 March 2015.

113 The Economic Adjustment Programme for Greece is elaborated in a series of key documents: (1) Council decision; (2) Memorandum of Understanding (MoU), and (3) Memorandum of Economic and Financial Policies (MEFP). The MoU and MEFP were drafted jointly by the EC, ECB, IMF, and the Greek authorities, and were subsequently transformed into EU law. 'The Second Economic Adjustment Programme for Greece First Review—December 2012' (2012) 123 European Economy Occasional paper 123, 7 <http://ec.europa.eu/economy_finance/publications/occasional_paper/2012/pdf/ocp123_en.pdf> accessed 27 March 2015.

114 Greece: Memorandum of Understanding on Specific Economic Policy Conditionality, May 3 2010 [Hereinafter 'the Greek MoU'], 4, 8, 14, 15.

115 Ibid., 4. 116 Ibid., 1, 4–5. 117 Ibid., 2, 9.

c. Germany's collective memory and the EU's response measures during the crisis (2009–2012)

(i) Germany and the Economic and Monetary Union: The EU austerity approach during the first stage of the crisis generally followed the pre-crisis EMU rules. As noted, this feature was particularly prominent regarding various decisions and recommendations issued by the EU bodies under the Excessive Deficit Procedure.[118] The Treaty provisions on EMU concerning 'no-bailout', fiscal discipline, and price stability constituted the basis for the EU's measures undertaken towards Greece and underpinned the disinclination to extend financial aid during the first stage of the crisis.

The central EMU's rules were considerably influenced by Germany and its central bank,[119] particularly the provisions concerning price stability,[120] excessive deficits,[121] and 'no-bailout'.[122] The ECB is considered a conservative central bank which prioritizes price stability and fiscal discipline.[123] The ECB was shaped according to the German model, and the inflation-fighting Bundesbank.[124]

The measures undertaken during the *second stage* of the crisis, though deviating from the 'no-bailout' principle, also significantly reflect the austerity approach. As discussed previously, this approach is manifested in the conditionalities attached to the assistance programme to Greece and other countries, as well as the requirement that resorting to the general bailout funds would be contingent on compliance with strict conditionalities.

Germany's conservative financial policy, and particularly its ingrained aversion to expansionary measures, is affected not only by economic factors but significantly also by fears that such measures may lead to higher inflation rates.[125] These inflation fears[126] are particularly associated with the collective memory of

[118] See Section IV(b)(b) above.

[119] See, e.g., Lucia Quaglia, *Central Banking Governance in the European Union: A Comparative Analysis* (Routledge, 2007) 62–3; Kenneth Dyson, *The Politics of the Euro-Zone* (OUP, 2000) 115; Lastra and Louis (n 90) 39.

[120] See, e.g., Geelhoed, Amtenbrink, and Kingston (n 90) 905.

[121] See, e.g., Lastra and Louis (n 90) 39; see Geelhoed, Amtenbrink, and Kingston (n 90) 912; Tuori (n 98) 8.

[122] Kevin Featherstone, 'The Greek Sovereign Debt Crisis and EMU' (2011) 49 *Journal of Common Market Studies* 193, 201–2.

[123] See, e.g., Michael Steen, 'ECB sticks to its monetary guns' *Financial Times Online* (Frankfurt, 7 March 2013) <http://www.ft.com/intl/cms/s/0/3dad09ea-871a-11e2-bde6-00144feabdc0.html#axzz3VUDl9IC3> accessed 27 March 2015. See also Gavyn Davies, 'ECB Eschews Global Monetary Stampede' (*Financial Times Blog*, 7 February 2013) <http://blogs.ft.com/gavyndavies/2013/02/07/ecb-eschews-global-monetary-stampede/> accessed 27 March 2015.

[124] David Howarth and Peter Loedel, *The European Central Bank: The New European Leviathan?* (Palgrave Macmillan, 2003) 52, 147; Tuori (n 98) 8; Philipp Maier and Thijs Knaap, 'Who supported the Deutsche Bundesbank?: An Empirical Investigation' (2002) 24 *Journal of Policy Modeling* 831, 831–2.

[125] See, e.g., Patrick O'Callaghan, 'Collective Memory in Law and Policy: The Problem of the Sovereign Debt Crisis' (2012) 32 *Legal Studies* 642, 657–9.

[126] On the results of a poll held in Germany regarding fear of inflation, see Section IV(c)(iii) below.

the hyperinflation during the Weimar Republic (1922–3).[127] As elaborated below, hyperinflation is connected in the German collective memory not only to the loss of millions of Germans' savings but also to the breakdown of democracy and the Nazis' rise to power.[128]

(ii) Agents of collective memory: As already noted, agents of memory include diverse state and non-state actors actively taking part in various practices which form or preserve a particular collective memory.[129] Though numerous agents are involved in the formation and maintenance of the German collective memory regarding hyperinflation and its normative lessons, this section briefly addresses four significant agents: political actors, the German central bank, the mass media, and the German Historical Museum. As discussed below, these agents interact with one another.

Many agents of the German collective memory often use the term 'stability' (Stabilität), 'stability culture' (Stabilitätskultur) and related words. The concept of 'stability culture' (and related notions) mediates between the collective memory of the hyperinflation and specific normative rules emanating from this concept. These stability terms are linked in Germany to several economic principles, prominently the fight against inflation and stable prices.[130] Thus, for example, Howarth and Rommerskirchen use the priority given to the fight against inflation as the proxy for 'stability culture'.[131] As to the European economic and monetary regime, the German 'stability culture' includes elements of the overriding objective of price stability, strict government deficits and public debts, central bank independence, prohibition of monetizing public debt and no-bailout.[132] Various terms related to stability and inflation aversion are used interchangeably in the German literature,[133] by political leaders, and the mass media (see further below).[134]

[127] On the hyperinflation during that period, see, e.g., Frank D Graham, *Exchange, Prices, and Production in Hyper-Inflation: Germany, 1920–1923* (Russell and Russell, 1967); Niall Ferguson, *The Ascent of Money: A Financial History of the World* (Penguin Books, 2009) 102–7.

[128] See, e.g., Peter Henning Loedel, *Deutsche Mark Politics* (Boulder, 1999) 37–8, 5; Alexander Jung, 'Millions, Billions, Trillions: Germany in the Era of Hyperinflation' *Spiegel Online* (14 August 2009) <http://www.spiegel.de/international/germany/millions-billions-trillions-germany-in-the-era-of-hyperinflation-a-641758.html> accessed 27 March 2015.

[129] See Section II above.

[130] David Howarth and Charlotte Rommerskirchen, 'A Panacea for all Times? The German Stability Culture as Strategic Political Resource' (2013) 36 *West European Politics* 750, 752–3. See also, Maier and Knaap (n 124) 831; Michael Mertes, 'Germany's Social and Political Culture: Change through Consensus?' (1994) 123 *Daedalus* 1, 6.

[131] Howarth and Rommerskirchen (n 130) 753–4.

[132] See, e.g., Peter Praet, 'Sound money, sound finances, a competitive economy—principles of a European culture of stability' (Symposium on 'Perspectives for a common stability culture in Europe', Berlin, 27 February 2012, 14–19, <http://www.bis.org/review/r120228d.pdf> accessed 27 March 2015.

[133] Dieter Lindenlaub, 'Deutsches Stabilitätsbewusstsein' (2010) 50 Die Kulturelle Seite der Währung, *Historische Zeitschrift* 63. See also Howarth and Loedel (n 124) 54.

[134] See, e.g., 'New Culture of Stability: Germany Forges Ahead on Reforming the Euro' *Spiegel Online* (19 May 2010) <http://www.spiegel.de/international/europe/new-culture-of-stability-germany-forges-ahead-on-reforming-the-euro-a-695679.html> accessed 27 March 2015; 'German Parliamentary Vote: Merkel Says Future Peace and Prosperity At Stake in Crisis Talks' *Spiegel Online* (26 October 2011) <http://www.spiegel.de/international/europe/german-parliamentary-vote-merkel-says-future-peace-and-prosperity-at-stake-in-crisis-talks-a-794141.html> accessed 27 March 2015.

Political parties and leaders have significantly contributed to the formation and preservation of the German collective memory and its normative lessons. An empirical study shows that support for the stability culture and the fight against inflation cuts across party lines and that there is no marked difference between voters of the main parties concerning inflation aversion.[135] The main German political parties generally agree on the need for tight limits on government debt and applying measures to avert breaches of this principle.[136] Notwithstanding that the objective of price stability is shared by all major parties, the memory of the hyperinflation of 1922–3 has been used during election campaigns,[137] and occasionally also by parties' leaders in the political debates held during the European debt crisis.[138]

The significance of the 'stability culture' in the German political system is manifested, for example, in speeches delivered by the German Chancellor, Angela Dorothea Merkel, addressing various issues relating to the Eurozone financial crisis during a critical period of the crisis.[139] An examination[140] of her speeches delivered before Germany's Federal parliament from 1 November 2011 to 31 December 2012[141] shows that they all contain references to terms relating to anti-inflation and price stability ('stability culture', 'stability union', 'financial stability', 'stability policy', and equivalent terms).[142] The then Minister of Economy and Technology in Merkel's coalition, Brüderle, delivered a speech discussing the proposal to issue 'Eurobonds' and highlighted the link between the German stability culture and Germans' fears of inflation:

> While the Americans are concerned about deflation, the fear of hyperinflation is imprinted in the genetic code of the German population. This explains the different practices on either side of the Atlantic.[143]

[135] Howarth and Rommerskirchen (n 130) 754–6.

[136] Sebastian Dullien and Ulrike Guérot, 'The Long Shadow of Ordoliberalism: Germany's Approach to the Euro Crisis' (2012) European Council on Foreign Relations Policy Brief, 8 <http://ecfr.eu/page/-/ECFR49_GERMANY_BRIEF.pdf> accessed 27 March 2015. On the positions of the German parties on this topic (and the variation among them), see 5–8.

[137] See, e.g., Eric E Rowley, *Hyperinflation in Germany: Perceptions of a Process* (Scholar Press, 1994).

[138] Howarth and Rommerskirchen (n 130) 759–61.

[139] Various proposals to address the financial crisis were discussed during this period, prominently issuing 'Eurobonds', the ECB low-interest loans (longer-term refinancing operation 'LTRO') and the 'bond-buying programme'. These latter two ECB programmes are discussed in Section IV(d) below.

[140] I am grateful to Ms Anna Lechermann (Hebrew University and Ruprecht-Karls University Heidelberg) who carried out this survey.

[141] During this period Chancellor Merkel delivered thirteen speeches before the General Federal parliament.

[142] Thus, e.g., Merkel's speech on 27 June 2012 includes a statement that the causes of the crisis lie in fundamental errors in the foundation of the economic and monetary union and the *horrendous state debt*, and that '[t]he economic and monetary union must become a stability union' (translated). Chancellor Angela Merkel, 'Government Statement on the European Council before the German Parliament', Plenarprotokoll 17/186 (Berlin, 27 June 2012) 22221 and 22224 (translated) <http://dipbt.bundestag.de/dip21/btp/17/17186.pdf> accessed 27 March 2015.

[143] Speech of Rainer Brüderle (of the FDP party) (translated), General debate on the federal budget 2012 in the German Parliament, Plenary Protocol 17/142 (17th Legislative Period, 142nd

The German central bank has been a central agent of the German memory regarding the hyperinflation and the normative lessons regarding financial behaviour. The term 'stability culture' was coined by the former Bundesbank President, Schlesinger, who argued that 'sound money needs not only a stability oriented policy by central bankers and the government … it needs a stability culture in the public and in politics'.[144] The Bundesbank perceived its role as the guardian of monetary stability[145] and its influence as a significant agent of memory relates to its independent status[146] under the German legislation,[147] and the broad public support it enjoys in German society as the guarantor of stable currency and political order.[148] The Bundesbank's officials have published their views regarding sound economic monetary policy, stability culture, and the importance of price stability in the Eurozone.[149]

Public speeches delivered by the President of the German Central Bank, Jens Weidmann, well illustrate the Bundesbank's role as an agent of collective memory. They emphasize the importance of financial stability and often refer to historical events (in Germany and elsewhere). Thus, for example, Weidmann's speech on 8 November 2011 linked the EU's monetary regime and the lessons drawn from hyperinflation in Germany.[150] And Weidmann explained in another speech the link between Germany's emphasis on monetary stability and its past experience: '[a]dmittedly, this experience [the hyperinflation during the 1920s'] may have contributed to the fact that monetary stability is of particular importance to us Germans. The positive experiences that we have made with regard to the D-Mark however play an equally important role'.[151]

Session) (23 November 2011) 16926 <http://dipbt.bundestag.de/dip21/btp/17/17142.pdf> accessed 27 March 2015.

144 As cited in Howarth and Rommerskirchen (n 130) 752.

145 Quaglia (n 119) 65. See also Loedel (n 128) 38, 40.

146 On the link between the independence of the German central bank and memories of the hyperinflation, see Rowley (n 137) 176; Quaglia (n 119) 48.

147 See Art 12 of the Bundesbank Act (22 October 1992) 1 *Federal Law Gazette* 1782 (English) <http://www.bundesbank.de/Redaktion/EN/Downloads/Bundesbank/Tasks_and_organisation/bundesbank_act.pdf?__blob=publicationFile> accessed 27 March 2015. See also Loedel (n 128) 39–40.

148 Howarth and Loedel (n 124) 54–5; Quaglia (n 119) 61–2; Philip Maier, *Political Pressure, Rhetoric and Monetary Policy* (Elgar, 2002) 109–10; Maier and Knaap (n 124) 831; Loedel (n 128) 3.

149 See, e.g., on public statements by the Bundesbank officials regarding the dangers of harming the 'stability culture', Howarth and Rommerskirchen (n 130) 761. On the link between European debt crisis and the lessons to be learnt from history, see Bundesbank, 'Inflation—lessons learnt from history' (15 October 2012) <http://www.bundesbank.de/Redaktion/EN/Topics/2012/2012_10_15_inflation_lessons_learnt_from_history.html> accessed 27 March 2015.

150 Jens Weidmann, 'Managing Macroprudential and Monetary Policy—A Challenge for Central Banks' (8 November 2011) 8 <http://www.bundesbank.de/Redaktion/EN/Downloads/Press/Reden/2011/2011_11_08_weidmann_macroprudential_and_monetary_policy.pdf?__blob=publicationFile> accessed 27 March 2015 (in English).

151 Jens Weidmann, 'To Safeguard the Stability Union' (5 July 2012) <http://www.bundesbank.de/Redaktion/DE/Reden/2012/2012_07_05_weidmann_stabilitaetsunion.html> accessed 27 March 2015 (translated).

Though *the mass media* is usually associated with reporting on current events, it is considered as a significant vehicle of collective memory in modern societies.[152] The significance of this agent lies in its ability to reach huge communities simultaneously and its influence on public opinion.[153] The media's capacity to affect collective memory is also linked to *repeated* reports and the creation of an *association* between current and historic events. Pedemonte considers the repetition of similar content in the media as being a decisive factor in the 'entrance into the long-term memory of audiences'.[154] No less important, the media often creates an association between current and past events (e.g., by inviting a comparison or by an analogy), and takes part in the interpretation of the new information.[155]

A brief examination of articles published in *The Spiegel* confirms the role of the German press in maintaining the association between the Eurozone debt crisis and the issue of inflation. A brief survey[156] examined articles published in the *Spiegel Online* (the German edition)[157] which addressed various aspects of the crisis during two significant periods in which the ECB announced two financial programmes[158] (discussed below). This examination reveals that most of the articles (addressing the crisis) published in the above two periods mentioned the words inflation/stability or equivalent terms.[159] Thus, for example, *The Spiegel* warned in November 2011: 'History of economy teaches, once inflation commenced, it is difficult to get it under control'.[160] And later this newspaper explained: Germans have always been concerned about their savings. Today, the fear of a massive devaluation of money is higher than it has ever been.[161]

Historical museums also play a role in constructing and preserving collective memories. The permanent exhibition on the Weimar Republic in Berlin's German Historical Museum[162] emphasizes the traumatic experience of hyperinflation. The

152 Barbie Zelizer, 'Why Memory's Work on Journalism Does not Reflect Journalism's Work on Memory' (2008) 1 *Memory Studies* 79–81; Janice Hume, 'Memory Matters: The Evolution of Scholarship in Collective Memory and Mass Communication' (2010) 10 *Review of Communication* 181, 181–2.

153 Damián Fernández Pedemonte, 'Media Cases and Social Memory in Argentina post 2001' (2012) 5 *Journal for Communication Studies* 61, 67–8; Hume (n 152) 187.

154 Pedemonte (n 153) 68, 72.

155 Zelizer (n 152) 83–5; Pedemonte (n 153) 72.

156 I am grateful to Mr Oscar Weller (Hebrew University and Law Graduate of the Humboldt-University Berlin) who carried out this examination.

157 See <http://www.spiegel.de>.

158 The first period spans from 1 November 2011 until 31 December 2011 (during which the ECB adopted the 'low-interest loans programme') and the second period spans from 1 July 2012 until 31 August 2012 (during which the ECB adopted the 'bond-buying programme').

159 Out of 59 articles published during both periods, 38 articles mentioned the above terms. During the first period (November to December 2011) 62.5% of the articles (25 out of 40) mentioned these terms. During the second period (July to August 2012) 68.4% of the articles (13 out of 19) referred to these terms.

160 'Am Abgrund' *Spiegel Online* (28 November 2011) <http://www.spiegel.de/spiegel/print/d-82244908.html> accessed 27 March 2015 (translated).

161 'Umfrage: Fast Jeder Zweite Deutsche Hat Angst vor Inflation' *Spiegel Online* (8 December 2011) <http://www.spiegel.de/wirtschaft/service/umfrage-fast-jeder-zweite-deutsche-hat-angst-vor-inflation-a-802430.html> accessed 27 March 2015 (translated).

162 The author visited this exhibition on 19 December 2013.

exhibition clearly illustrates the link created in the German collective memory between the hyperinflation and various events, particularly the suffering of the German people and the rise of the Nazis to power. Thus, for example, Plaque No. 6.2.15 on 'The beginning of National Socialism' states: 'At the high-water mark of inflation in November 1923 the Hitler Movement could count almost 55,000 members.'[163] And another plaque explains the exhibit 'NSDP membership booklet, München, 16 Oktober 1923: '[h]yperinflation, social destitution, and political discontent led to an influx of members for the NSDAP. Between the start of 1922 and the end of 1923, the number of members increased from 6,000 to 55,000'.[164]

The above discussion indicates that unlike other cases of 'fragmented memories',[165] the memory of the hyperinflation and its normative lessons transcend political lines in German society. This essentially consensual memory of the hyperinflation is apparently linked to the consensual political culture that generally prevails in Germany.[166]

(iii) Collective memories, inflation fears, and the EU economic and monetary law: In light of the above discussion on German collective memory of hyperinflation and its agents, the results of a poll held in September 2012 come as no surprise. According to this poll published in the German newspaper Frankfurter Allgemeine Zeitung regarding Germans' biggest anxieties: 63% of Germans were worried about inflation, 52% about natural disaster, 46% about illness, and 39% about terrorism. As noted in this article, the inflation rate in Germany at that time was 2.1%, only 0.1% higher than the official inflation target (2%).[167]

The above-discussed German collective memory and the normative lesson regarding anti-inflationary policy, as well as Germany's considerable influence on EU economic and monetary law and policy[168] shed light on the austerity approach adopted by EU law and the assistance programmes. The language of EU monetary and economic law reconfirms the impact of the German collective memory. The EMU legal regime is infused with the language of the German stability culture.[169] The terms 'stability' or 'stable prices' are mentioned five times in TFEU's

[163] Original text in English and German. And Plaque No. 6.2 on 'The Early Years of the Weimar Republic' explains: 'The social misery and political instability of the Republic were the perfect breeding-ground for radical parties and extremist groups in the early 1920s' (original text in English and German).

[164] Original text in English and German. This plaque bears no number.

[165] See Section II above and Section V(e) below.

[166] On the German political culture and striving for the broadest social and political culture, see Michael Mertes, 'Germany's Social and Political Culture: Change through Consensus?' (1994) 123(1) *Daedalus* 1, 6. On the significance of political culture (particularly relating to consensual or dissensual features) for collective fragmented memory, see Vinitzky-Seroussi (n 15) 44–5.

[167] Christian Siedenbiedel, 'Die Angst vor der Inflation' *Frankfurter Allgemeine Zeitung* (23 September 2012) <http://www.faz.net/aktuell/wirtschaft/eurokrise/schuldenkrise-die-angst-vor-der-inflation-11899733.html> accessed 27 March 2015. See also Joe Weisenthal, 'Germans Are REALLY Worried About Inflation' *Business Insider* (23 September 2012) <http://www.businessinsider.com/german-fear-of-inflation-2012-9> accessed 27 March 2015.

[168] See Section IV(c)(1) above.

[169] On the link between terms relating to 'stability' and anti-inflationary policies, see Section IV(c)(2) above.

EMU chapter (Title VII); the ESM Treaty refers to 'stability' forty times,[170] and this term is mentioned fifteen times in the new Treaty on Stability, Coordination and Governance (the 'Fiscal Compact').[171] As to secondary law, the term 'stability' was mentioned thirty-nine times in the two regulations that essentially constituted the SGP,[172] and the words 'stability' or 'stabilisation' were mentioned seven times in the EFSF regulation.[173] Thus, maintaining price stability (under Article 119 (3) TFEU) is considered as 'the cornerstone' of EMU,[174] the primary objective of the ECSB,[175] and the latter's '*raison d'être*'.[176]

Collective memory (like other sociological factors) makes some strategies more likely to be activated but is not determinative.[177] As discussed below, the pro-austerity approach which the EU applied during the first and second stages of the crisis was changed during the third stage of the sovereign debt crisis.

(d) Third stage of the crisis: Expansionary measures and additional social factors

The third stage of the crisis (December 2011 to September 2012) is characterized by a change in the EU's policy and the adoption of certain expansionary measures. The significant financial measures were the Long-term Refinancing Operation (LTRO), which unfolded in December 2011 and February 2012, and more importantly, the Outright Monetary Transactions (OMT) established in early September 2012. The ECB applied these milestone measures when uncertainty about the sustainability of public finance, which had been largely confined to Greece, Ireland, and Portugal, spread increasingly to Italy and Spain (and their borrowing costs soared),[178] and the ECB faced widespread fears that the Eurozone was heading for a break-up.[179]

[170] The ESM Treaty (n 106).

[171] The 'Fiscal Compact' (Treaty on Stability, Coordination and Governance in the Economic and Monetary Union) also aims to strengthen fiscal discipline in the euro area through the 'balanced budget rule' and the automatic correction mechanism <http://europa.eu/rapid/press-release_DOC-12-2_en.htm> accessed 27 March 2015. Council Regulation 407/2010 of 11 May 2010 establishing a European financial stabilization mechanism [2010] *OJ L* 118/1.

[172] This term is mentioned 32 times in the Council Regulation (EU) 1466/97 of 7 July 1997 on the strengthening of the surveillance of budgetary positions and the surveillance and coordination of economic policies [1997] *OJ L* 209, and seven times in Council Regulation (EC) 1467/97 of 7 July 1997 on speeding up and clarifying the implementation of the excessive deficit procedure [1997] *OJ L* 209.

[173] Council Regulation 407/ 2010 (n 104).

[174] Servais and Ruggeri (n 94) 45; Louis (n 94) 36. [175] TFEU Arts 127(1) 282(2).

[176] René Smits, *The European Central Bank: Institutional Aspects* (Kluwer, 1997) 184.

[177] See, e.g., Joachim Savelsberg and Ryan King, *American Memories: Atrocities and the Law* (Sage Foundation, 2011) 150. And with regard to other socio-cultural factors, see, e.g., Ann Swidler, *Talk of Love: How Culture Matters* (University of Chicago Press, 2001) 105, 117.

[178] 'Economic and Monetary Developments' (2011) *ECB Monthly Bulletin* 48.

[179] On these fears, see, e.g., Jörg Asmussen, 'Introductory Statement by the ECB in the Proceedings before the Federal Constitutional Court' (11 June 2013) <http://www.ecb.europa.eu/press/key/date/2013/html/sp130611.en.html> accessed 27 March 2015.

The LTRO was announced on 8 December 2011;[180] under the programme the ECB offered low-interest loans with a term of three years and 1% interest to banks in the euro area.[181] Though the loans were not offered to European governments, the banks appeared to have used a sizable share of the cash received from the ECB to buy the European government bonds so desperately in need of customers at that time. By providing liquidity for up to three years, the ECB assisted in depressing spreads in the sovereign and credit derivative markets.[182] The OMT ('bond-buying programme') was announced in early August 2012,[183] and under it the ECB pledged to purchase *unlimited* quantities of debt-distressed countries' sovereign bonds in the secondary markets. Countries resorting to the OMT programme must apply to the above-discussed Eurozone assistance funds (EFSF or ESM programmes) and accept the fiscal conditionalities.[184] The OMT programme's signalling effect constituted a turning point in the financial crisis—followed by a dramatic fall in borrowing costs for Italy and Spain (the two countries most at risk of contagion from the Greek crisis).[185]

Though the above-described measures of the ECB deviated from the previous orthodox policy, compared to the policies of other active central banks, they

[180] The LTRO was lodged again in February 2012. On previous LTRO operations, see Nautz Linzert and Ulrich Bindseil, 'The Longer Term Refinancing Operations of the ECB' (2004) ECB Working Papers Series No. 359 <http://www.ecb.europa.eu/pub/pdf/scpwps/ecbwp359.pdf> accessed 27 March 2015.

[181] Mario Draghi and Vítor Constâncio, 'Introductory Statement to the Press Conference' (8 December 2011) <http://www.ecb.int/press/pressconf/2011/html/is111208.en.html> accessed 27 March 2015.

[182] Lionel Barber and Michael Steen, 'Person of the Year: Mario Draghi' *Financial Times Online* (13 December 2012) <http://www.ft.com/cms/s/0/8fca75b8-4535-11e2-838f-00144feabdc0.html#axzz3VUQnaWaM> accessed 27 March 2015. See also, Nicholas Kulish, 'Central Bank Becomes an Unlikely Hero in Euro Crisis' *NY Times* (20 January 2012) <http://www.nytimes.com/2012/01/21/world/european-central-bank-eases-euro-crisis-a-bit.html?_r=0> accessed 27 March 2015.

[183] The technical features of the OMT were published on 6 September 2012, ECB, 'Technical Features of Outright Monetary Transactions' (6 September 2012) <http://www.ecb.int/press/pr/date/2012/html/pr120906_1.en.html> accessed 27 March 2015.

[184] Ibid.

[185] See, e.g., 'Draghi—Word to the Wise' *Financial Times Online* (30 December 2012) <http://www.ft.com/intl/cms/s/2748fbc6-4879-11e2-a1c0-00144feab49a,Authorised=false.html?_i_location=http%3A%2F%2Fwww.ft.com%2Fcms%2Fs%2F3%2F2748fbc6-4879-11e2-a1c0-00144feab49a.html%3Fsiteedition%3Dintl&siteedition=intl&_i_referer=http%3A%2F%2Fsearch.ft.com%2Fsearch%3Fq%3Dstandby%26t%3Dall%26fa%3Dpeople%252Corganisations%252Cregions%252Csections%252Ctopics%252Ccategory%252Cbrand%26s%3D-initialPublishDateTime%26f%3Dorganisations%255B%2522European%2BCentral%2BBank%2522%255D%255B%2522European%2BCentral%2BBank%2522%255D%26curations%3DARTICLES%252CBLOGS%252CVIDEOS%252CPODCASTS%26highlight%3Dtrue#axzz3VUQnaWaM> accessed 27 March 2015; Jeff Black and Jana Randow, 'Draghi Relegating Rates Makes OMT Policy Weapon of Choice' *Bloomberg* (9 November 2012) <http://www.bloomberg.com/news/2012-11-09/draghi-makes-omt-policy-weapon-of-choice-as-ecb-relegates-rates.html> accessed 27 March 2015.

are still restricted measures (regarding conditionalities and 'sterilization').[186] Nonetheless, in light of the German central bank's long-standing attitude towards prioritizing price stability, and Germany's fears of inflation, it was unsurprising that the Bundesbank vigorously opposed the OMT programme.[187]

In view of Germany's collective memory regarding inflation and its substantial influence in the European monetary system, the question arises why Germany accepted (albeit reluctantly) the OMT. As noted above, collective memory is often a significant factor but not a determinative one, and other factors are also relevant to such complex developments. A comprehensive answer to the above question regarding the factors motivating Germany to accept the OMT necessitates a comprehensive discussion of economic, sociological, and political factors involved in the crisis; this section, however, very briefly addresses sociological factors relating to the external social pressure exerted on Germany and its collective identity.

Every society deploys diverse social control mechanisms (i.e., the means to encourage and enforce conformity to societal expectations and norms). Social control involves a myriad of measures, involving both formal and informal mechanisms. The latter include expressions of praise or social disapproval, contempt, and particularly threats of social isolation.[188] Many states and international institutions exerted considerable pressure on Germany to drop its opposition to expansionary measures; including the USA, the G-20 countries, the Organisation for Economic Co-operation and Development (OECD), the IMF, and the World Bank.[189] Germany felt isolated in this debate,[190] and this time it was not a controversy between the Eurozone northern and southern countries but rather between Germany 'and the rest'.[191]

186 The OMT is conditioned by compliance with conditionalities, and in order to reduce the risk of inflation, the programme is to be accompanied by 'sterilization' (i.e. removing the additional cash through the system). ECB, 'Technical features of Outright Monetary Transactions' (n 183).

187 See, e.g., Michael Steen, James Fontanella-Khan, and Michael Stothard, 'ECB Signals Resolve to Save Euro' *Financial Times Online* (6 September 2006) <http://www.ft.com/cms/s/0/b70ff9a8-f84c-11e1-b0e1-00144feabdc0.html> accessed 27 March 2015; Henrik Böhme, 'Opinion: ECB Becomes Europe's Politburo' *Die Welt* (7 September 2012) <http://www.dw.de/opinion-ecb-becomes-europes-politburo/a-16225255> accessed 27 March 2015; 'Mario Draghi's Audacious Gamble' *Financial Times Online* (6 September 2012) <http://www.ft.com/intl/cms/s/0/43ef8050-f820-11e1-828f-00144feabdc0.html#axzz3VUaKlRwZ> accessed 27 March 2015.

188 On social control mechanisms, see Chapter 6, Section III.

189 See, e.g., 'The World from Berlin: 'Germany as Isolated on Euro as US Was On Iraq' *Spiegel Online* (29 November 2011) <http://www.spiegel.de/international/europe/the-world-from-berlin-germany-as-isolated-on-euro-as-us-was-on-iraq-a-800618.html> accessed 27 March 2015; 'Merkel's International Isolation' *Spiegel Online* (18 June 2012) <http://www.spiegel.de/international/europe/g-20-pressure-mounting-on-merkel-for-quick-solution-to-the-euro-crisis-a-839481-2.html> accessed 27 March 2015; Quentin Peel, 'Schäuble View on Eurozone at odds with US' *Financial Times Online* (29 July 2012) <http://www.ft.com/intl/cms/s/0/bb93774e-d97e-11e1-8529-00144feab49a.html#axzz3VZo7WQmJ> accessed 27 March 2015; Robert Zoellick, 'Europe Must Prepare an Emergency Plan' *Financial Times Online* (31 May 2012) <http://www.ft.com/intl/cms/s/0/c3200410-aa6b-11e1-899d-00144feabdc0.html#axzz3VUaKlRwZ> accessed 27 March 2015.

190 'See, e.g., 'Germany as Isolated on Euro as US Was on Iraq' (n 189).

191 See, e.g., Wolfgang Münchau, 'Weidmann is Winning the Debate on Policy' *Financial Times Online* (9 September 2012) <http://www.ft.com/intl/cms/s/0/130ad186-f82c-11e1-bec8-00144feabdc0.html#axzz3VUaKlRwZ> accessed 27 March 2015.

The second factor motivating Germany to accept (grudgingly) the ECB expansionary measures relates to its collective identity and the symbolic value of the euro. Money has long been related to national identity, and images on bills and coins are regularly selected in order to connect with historical and national symbols of nation states.[192] Similarly, the euro is clearly not only a currency but also a symbol of collective identity.[193] Germany's acceptance of the OMT programme is also significantly linked to German post-war identity. Risse explains that for post-war Germany '[t]o be a "good German" meant to be a "good European" and to wholeheartedly support European integration efforts. Being a "good European German" also implied finally having overcome the country's militarist and nationalist past and having learned the lessons from history'.[194] The links between the threats to the European currency, lessons gained from European history, and the German sense of obligation towards European integration process were emphasized also in a speech delivered by the German Chancellor in the German parliament.[195]

In sum, Germany's European identity and the considerable international social pressure exerted on Germany cast light on the latter's acceptance of the ECB's OMT programme, which deviates from the rules emanating from the German collective memory regarding hyperinflation.

V. Argentina's Collective Memory, the Calvo Doctrine, and Compliance with ICSID Awards

The largest wave of claims[196] lodged against a single state in investment tribunals involved over forty claims submitted by foreign investors against Argentina following the economic crisis (2001–2). Most of these claims were submitted to the tribunals of the International Centre for Settlement of Investment Disputes (ICSID). As elaborated below, the government of Argentina declined to implement a series of ICSID damage awards during a period of about six years (2007–13). This section examines Argentina's collective memory of past foreign interventions

[192] Thomas Risse, 'The Euro Between National and European Identity' (2003) 10 *Journal of European Public Policy* 487, 487–8.

[193] See, e.g., Jean Pisani-Ferry and Adam S Posen, *The Euro at Ten: The Next Global Currency?* (Institute for International Economics, 2009) 1; Giles Bootheway, 'The Symbolic Value of the Euro in the Eurozone Crisis' (2012) 19 Proceedings of ASBBS 77 et seq. <http://asbbs.org/files/ASBBS2012V1/PDF/B/BoothewayG.pdf> accessed 27 March 2015.

[194] Risse, 'The Euro between National and European Identity' (n 192) 498.

[195] Chancellor Angela Merkel, 'Government Statement on the European Council before the German Parliament on 27 June 2012', Plenary Protocol 17/135, 15955 <http://dipbt.bundestag.de/dip21/btp/17/17135.pdf> accessed 27 March 2015.

[196] I am indebted to Oscar Garibaldi (arbitrator, and a retired partner of Covington & Burling LLP) and Jorge Viñuales (of the University of Cambridge Faculty of Law) who were kind enough to provide very helpful comments on earlier drafts of this section.

and its contribution to its hostile approach towards ICSID tribunals, as well as to the non-implementation of those investment awards during this period.

a. The economic crisis in Argentina and ICSID proceedings

The government of Argentina adopted a new economic plan in 1989, which included the privatization of government-owned industries and public utilities (such as gas and water distribution services). The new legislation also effectively pegged the Argentine currency to the US dollar. Accordingly, gas and water tariffs were to be calculated in US dollars and expressed in pesos at the exchange rate existing at the time of billing, and they were to be adjusted periodically according to the US Producer Price Index (PPI). The economic crisis which unfolded from the late 1990s led, inter alia, to a dramatic increase in unemployment and poverty. The crisis worsened significantly in 2001 and the government responded with serious legislative and administrative measures, including the *Corralito Decree* (December 2001) which significantly restricted the withdrawal of money from bank accounts, the transfer of funds abroad, and the currency exchange. A state of public emergency was declared on 6 January 2002, and later the right of licensees of the public utilities to adjust tariffs according to the US PPI was terminated, as well as the calculation of tariffs in dollars. Thus, the convertibility regime, which had pegged the peso to the US dollar, was effectively abolished, the peso was devalued, and different exchange rates were introduced for transactions.[197]

These and other governmental measures were challenged in numerous claims lodged by foreign investors against Argentina, most of them were registered with ICSID and a few were filed under the United Nations Commission on International Trade Law (UNCITRAL) Arbitration Rules.[198] The following discussion focuses on ICSID claims, and particularly four disputes that were finally resolved in the 2013 settlement agreement. In the case of *CMS v Argentina*, a US firm dealing with gas transportation in Argentina argued that the termination of the calculation of tariffs in US dollars and of the tariff adjustment in accordance with PPI violated Argentina's commitments made to foreign

[197] This brief survey of the crisis and the government's response measures is based on the following decisions of ICSID tribunals: *CMS Gas Transmission Company v Argentina* (*CMS v Argentina*), Decision of the Ad Hoc Committee on the Application for Annulment of the Argentine Republic (25 September 2007) ICSID Case No. ARB/01/8, [30]–[31]; *CMS Gas Transmission Company v Argentina (CMS v Argentina)*, Decision of the Tribunal on Objections to Jurisdiction (17 July 2003) ICSID Case No. ARB/01/8, [18]–[20]; *CMS Gas Transmission Company v Argentina* (*CMS v Argentina*), Award (12 May 2005) ICSID Case No. ARB/01/8, [59]–[66]; *Vivendi v Argentina* (*Vivendi v Argentina*), Award (20 August 2007) ICSID Case No. ARB/97/3, [8.4.2]; *Continental Casualty Company v Argentina* (Continental Casualty), Award (5 September 2008) ICSID Case No. ARB/03/9, [100]–[126], [137]–[151].

[198] For a list of these claims submitted against Argentina (updated to March 2009), see, Lucy Reed, 'Scorecard of Investment Treaty Cases Against Argentina Since 2001' (*Kluwer Arbitration Blog*, 2 March 2009) <http://kluwerarbitrationblog.com/blog/2009/03/02/scorecard-of-investment-treaty-cases-against-argentina-since-2001/> accessed 27 March 2015.

investors.[199] In *Continental Casualty v Argentina*, a US insurance company that had administered a privatized workers' compensation insurance scheme in Argentina argued that Argentina failed to adopt policies to support its currency and that its emergency measures (such as the restrictions on the transfer of funds abroad and the 'pesification' of US denominated contracts) were in violation of the 1991 US–Argentina bilateral investment treaty (BIT).[200] In *Azurix v Argentina,* a US company which had been granted a 30-year concession to operate a water and sewage utility, argued that Argentina's measures resulted in the non-application of the concession's tariff regime and breached the 1991 BIT's provisions.[201] In the *Vivendi* case, a French corporation had entered into a concession contract with Argentina to operate a water and sewage system in the province of Tucumán. The firm contended that it had to terminate the agreement due to public attacks by officials of the government of Tucumán, and that it was forced to provide services for another 10 months.[202] The claimant argued that these measures violated the 1991 BIT between Argentina and France, and sought damages.[203] The claimants' arguments in these cases related to numerous provisions included in these BITs, prominently relating to the questions of whether the measures undertaken by the government of Argentina constituted 'indirect expropriation'; whether these measures breached the relevant BITs' provisions regarding 'fair and equitable treatment', 'full protection and security', as well as the 'umbrella clauses'; and whether the government was exempted from its liability due to a state of 'necessity'.

(i) Expropriation: The investors' arguments regarding indirect expropriation were rejected in three awards (*CMS, Azurix,* and *Continental*) and these tribunals found that there was no substantial deprivation of the investment.[204] The *Vivendi* tribunal accepted this contention and ruled that the claimant was radically deprived of the economic use and enjoyment of its concessionary rights.[205]

(ii) 'Fair and equitable treatment' (FET): The primary question was whether the above Argentine measures breached the obligation to respect the investor's 'legitimate expectations'. The *Vivendi* tribunal accepted the claimant's main argument[206] that the breach of contractual provisions by Argentina undermined the investor's legitimate expectations.[207] The *Azurix* tribunal also recognized that 'legitimate expectations' constitutes an element of the obligation regarding

199 *CMS v Argentina*, Award (n 197) [85]–[86].

200 *Continental Casualty* (n 197) [62]–[64].

201 *Azurix Corp. v Argentina (Azurix)*, Award (14 July 2006) ICSID Case No. ARB/01/12, [41]–[43].

202 *Vivendi v Argentina* (n 197) [3.2.1]–[3.2.2].

203 *Vivendi v Argentina* (n 197) [3.2.3]–[3.2.4].

204 *CMS v Argentina*, Award (n 197) [263]–[264]; *Azurix* (n 201) [321]–[322]. The Continental Casualty tribunal rejected this argument regarding expropriation, on the grounds that the defense of 'necessity' was available to Argentina, *Continental Casualty* (n 197) [275].

205 *Vivendi v Argentina* (n 197) [7.2.29] and [7.5.30].

206 See, e.g., *Vivendi v Argentina* (n 197) [5.2.15].

207 *Vivendi v Argentina* (n 197) [7.4.42].

FET,[208] and found that it was breached by Argentina.[209] The tribunal in *CMS* did not explicitly refer to 'legitimate expectations' but ruled that the requirement regarding 'stable legal and business environment' constituted an essential element of FET, and that this principle was violated by Argentina in the particular case.[210] In *Continental Casualty*, the tribunal rejected the argument that Argentina frustrated the claimant's legitimate expectations, noting that there were no specific undertakings by Argentina in the particular case.[211]

(iii) 'Full protection and security': A breach of 'full protection and security' was claimed in all the above cases but was addressed significantly in the *Azurix* and *Vivendi* awards. In both cases the tribunals discussed whether 'full protection and security' clauses were limited to physical detrimental activities or also included obligations regarding 'stable business environment'. The *Vivendi* tribunal preferred the broader interpretation and rejected the argument that this clause should be limited to physical security of foreign investors and their property.[212] The *Azurix* tribunal also accepted the broader interpretation of this provision, recognizing that stability of the investment's environment is as important to foreign investors as physical protection.[213]

(iv) 'Umbrella clause': Three of the four tribunals (*CMS, Continental*, and *Azurix*) addressed investors' argument that a breach of contractual arrangements or governmental measures inconsistent with the host state's legislation amounted to a breach of the 'umbrella clause' included in the relevant BITs. In the *CMS* Award, the tribunal seemed to accept this argument,[214] but this finding was later annulled for failure 'to state reasons'.[215] The Annulment Committee concluded that the 'umbrella clause' would only entail obligations arising independently of the BIT and only relating to specific obligations concerning the investment (not general obligations imposed by the law of the host state).[216] The latter interpretation was reaffirmed by the tribunal in the *Continental* tribunal, which ruled that the provisions of the legislative regime in Argentina (which were changed) did not constitute a source of obligations Argentina had assumed specifically towards the claimant.[217] In *Azurix*, the tribunal rejected the argument regarding the 'umbrella clause' since the contractual claims did not refer to a contract concluded between the specific parties to the dispute.[218]

208 *Azurix v Argentina* (n 201) [372].
209 *Azurix v Argentina* (n 201) [374].
210 *CMS v Argentina*, Award (n 197) [274]–[275]. On 'stable legal environment' and ICSID awards regarding Argentina, see Moshe Hirsch, 'Between Fair and Equitable Treatment and Stabilization Clause' (2011) 12 *Journal of World Investment and Trade* 783, at Section III.
211 *Continental Casualty* (n 197) [259], [261]. The remaining arguments regarding FET were rejected (save for one based on the defense of 'necessity'), *Continental Casualty* (n 197) [262].
212 *Vivendi v Argentina* (n 197) [7.4.17].
213 *Azurix* (n 201) [406], [408]. The tribunal noted however, that this obligation can be limited to physical protection, if the word 'full' is not included in the BIT, see *Azurix* (n 201) [408].
214 *CMS v Argentina* (n 197) Award [303].
215 *CMS v Argentina*, Decision on Annulment (n 197) [97].
216 *CMS v Argentina*, Decision on Annulment (n 197) [95a].
217 *Continental Casualty* (n 197) [300]–[302].
218 *Azurix* (n 201) [384].

(v) 'Necessity': Two of the four tribunals examined whether the doctrine of 'necessity' (or rules regarding 'non-precluded measures') might exempt the government of Argentina from its liability for certain response measures (which prima facie breached foreign investors' rights). Whereas the *CMS* tribunal rejected Argentina's necessity argument,[219] the tribunal in *Continental Casualty* accepted the necessity defence with regard to most claims.[220] Both tribunals, however, rejected Argentina's contention that the relevant clause was of a 'self-judging' nature.[221]

Following numerous arbitral proceedings, a series of (at least four)[222] final damage awards were rendered against Argentina by ICSID tribunals.[223] For about six years (2007–13), Argentina declined to compensate these ICSID award creditors.[224] One of the significant factors affecting Argentina's decision not to comply with these ICSID awards during this period relates to collective memory existing among nationalist groups (including the governing Peronist party at that time, Front for Victory) regarding foreign interventions in Argentina and Latin America. As elaborated below, this collective memory is interwoven with the Calvo doctrine and certain ideologies emphasizing the utmost importance of sovereignty and independence from foreign powers.

b. Colonialist interventions and legal responses

The early evolution of the law of diplomatic protection of aliens (including foreign investors) took place in the historical context of colonialism.[225] During the nineteenth and early twentieth centuries, the exercise of diplomatic protection by powerful states was often accompanied by the threat or use of force against developing countries ('gunboat diplomacy').[226] Arbitral proceedings in this

[219] *CMS v Argentina*, Award (n 197) [355].

[220] *Continental Casualty* (n 197) [170] et seq.

[221] See *CMS v Argentina*, Award (n 197) [366] et seq.; *Continental Casualty* (n 197) [183].

[222] The 2013 settlement agreement (discussed below) related also to a non-ICSID award in favour of foreign investor (*National Grid v Argentina*). This tribunal was established under the UNCITRAL Rules. Luke Eric Peterson 'After settling some Awards, Argentina takes a more Fractious Path in Bond-Holder Case, with New Bid to Disqualify Arbitrators' (December 30, 2013) 6(24) *Investment Arbitration Reporter*.

[223] For the outcomes of numerous ICSID proceeding (based on Argentine sources), see Cecilia María Minaverry, 'International arbitration as a dispute resolution mechanism: The Argentine case in ICSID' (*Observatory on Latin America*, 2013) Section 4 and Annex 1 <http://www.observatorylatinamerica.org/en/programs/pnk/334-international-arbitration-as-a-dispute-resolution-mechanism-the-argentine-case-in-icsid> accessed 27 March 2015. See also Luke Eric Peterson, 'Argentina by the Numbers: Where Things Stand with Investment Treaty Claims Arising Out of the Argentine Financial Crisis' *Investment Arbitration Reporter* (1 February 2011).

[224] On Argentina's argument regarding the non-implementation of these awards, see Section V(c) below.

[225] See, e.g., Andrew Newcombe and Lluis Paradell, *Law and Practice of Investment Treaties* (Kluwer Law International, 2009) 8; Kate Miles, *The Origins of International Investment Law* (CUP, 2013) 19–32.

[226] See, e.g., Newcombe and Paradell (n 225) 8-9; Miles (n 225) 47–8, 59; Mary H Mourra, 'The Conflicts and Controversies in Latin American Treaty-Based Disputes', in Mary H Mourra (ed), *Latin American Investment Treaty Arbitration* (Kluwer, 2008) 5, 7.

sphere were often undertaken under the pressure of actual or threatened military force.[227] Latin American states particularly suffered from numerous armed interventions during their formative years, often aimed at protecting foreign nationals engaged in commercial activities and their property.[228] Such practices led many Latin American states to resent diplomatic protection and restrict foreign investors that were viewed as instruments of neo-colonialism or foreign dominance.[229]

Latin American countries adopted various response measures to those foreign interventions, including attempts to employ military force, developing international legal doctrines, and cultural resistance.[230] In the battle of *Vuelta de Obligado*, one of the memorable battles in Argentina's history, the Argentine army, under the leadership of Juan Manuel de Rosas,[231] fought to block the Anglo-French fleet in the Paraná River on 20 November 1845.[232] Though the Anglo-French fleet succeeded in entering the Paraná River, the battle became a symbol of the defence of national sovereignty, and 'endeared him [Rosas] forever in the hearts of Argentinian nationalists'.[233]

In light of the abuse (real or perceived) of diplomatic protection, Latin American countries, and particularly Argentine diplomats and jurists, sought to develop international legal doctrines to resist the international protection of foreign investors' rights, whether through diplomatic or military intervention.[234] The Drago Doctrine was developed in 1902 in light of various instances of 'gunboat diplomacy' carried out by European powers, in particular with regard to Latin American states which were unable or unwilling to honour their financial obligations. In reaction to the blockade and bombardment of Venezuelan ports by

[227] See, e.g., Newcombe and Paradell (n 225) 8.

[228] See, e.g., Donald R Shea, *The Calvo Clause: A Problem of Inter-American and International Law Diplomacy* (University of Minnesota Press, 1955) 12–14; Miles (n 225) 28, 56–8, 67–9; Magnus Jesko Langer and Jorge E Viñuales, 'Foreign Investment in Latin-America: Between Love and Hatred' (2010), 4–5, <http://ssrn.com/abstract=1652736> accessed 27 March 2015; John Dugard, 'Diplomatic Protection' in R Wolfrum (ed), *Max Planck Encyclopedia of Public International Law* (OUP, 2012) <http://opil.ouplaw.com/home/EPIL> accessed 28 May 2015, para 3; Patrick Juillard, 'Calvo Doctrine/Calvo Clause' in R Wolfrum (ed), *Max Planck Encyclopedia of Public International Law* (OUP, 2012) <opil.ouplaw.com/home/EPIL> para 2; Charles Lipson, *Standing Guard: Protecting Foreign Capital in the Nineteenth and Twentieth Centuries (*University of California Press, 1985) 14, 18, 40, 53–4, 187.

[229] See, e.g., Omar E Garcia-Bolivar, 'The Latin American Struggle With the International Law of Foreign Investment: Is It A Demand for A More Balanced System?' (December 2009) 6 *Transnational Dispute Management* 1–2; Shea (n 228) 13.

[230] For a discussion on these (and other) response strategies, see Peter H Smith, *Talons of the Eagle* (4th edn, OUP, 2013) 64–91.

[231] On the controversy among historians regarding Rosas, see further below.

[232] Rosas was the Governor of Buenos Aires Province and the leader of the Argentine Confederation from 1829 until his overthrow in 1852 (with a brief interruption in the 1830s). Jeffrey M Shumway, 'Sometimes Knowing How to Forget is Also Having Memory: The Repatriation of Juan Manuel de Rosas and the Healing of Argentina', in Lyman L Johnson (ed), *Death, Dismemberment, and Memory: Body Politics in Latin America* (University of New Mexico Press, 2004) 105, 110–11.

[233] Shumway (n 232) 111. See also Daniel K Lewis, *The History of Argentina* (Palgrave Macmillan, 2001) 43; Arthur P Whitaker, *The United States and Argentina* (Harvard University Press, 1954) 52–3.

[234] Newcombe and Paradell (n 225) 9; Lipson (n 228) 111, 18, 74–5, 80–2; Smith (n 230) 77–80.

the warships of Great Britain, Germany, and Italy in 1902–3, Argentina's Minister of Foreign Affairs, Luís María Drago, argued that public debts cannot justify armed intervention or occupation of territory of American states by a European power.[235]

The opposition to international legal rules concerning the external protection of foreign investors in the nineteenth century, and particularly the right of the investor's home state to intervene in disputes between the host state and the investor, was manifested in the Calvo doctrine.[236] This legal doctrine was articulated by Argentine jurist and diplomat Carlos Calvo; and was developed in reaction to the threat of European intervention in the Argentine confederation in 1834–50 and other Latin American states.[237] It emphasized the host state's sovereignty and the preclusion of other states from extending protection to their nationals abroad. Accordingly,[238] host states' courts should have exclusive jurisdiction over disputes involving foreign states' nationals, other states' nationals should not be entitled to better treatment than that accorded to nationals, and foreign nationals' rights are to be regulated by the host state's law.[239]

The Calvo doctrine was considered by Argentine and other Latin American lawyers as a legal instrument necessary to defend their political and economic independence.[240] Discussing the Vuelta de Obligado battle and the Calvo doctrine, Garibaldi explains: '[w]hat is certain is that those episodes, and Calvo's reaction to them, earned both Rosas and Calvo the status of icons of later Argentine nationalist politics.'[241]

Indeed, Rosas became a hero to some Peronist and other nationalist groups (of both the right and the left).[242] His memory was recurrently revived and nurtured (including in popular literature and radio programmes) by nationalist groups in Argentina, emphasizing anti-imperialist sentiments.[243] Though Rosas has remained a controversial figure, his name was revived during the Peron period,

[235] Wolfgang Benedek, 'Drago-Porter Convention' (1907), in R Wolfrum (ed), *Max Planck Encyclopedia of Public International Law* (OUP, 2007) opil.ouplaw.com/home/EPIL, paras 1–2; Shea (n 228) 14–15.

[236] See, e.g., Langer and Viñuales (n 228) 6–7.

[237] Oscar M Garibaldi, 'Carlos Calvo Redivivus: The Rediscovery of the Calvo Doctrine in the Era of Investment Treaties' (December 2006) 3(5) 3 *Transnational Dispute Management* 14–16; Bernardo Cremades, 'The Resurgence of the Calvo Doctrine in Latin America' (November 2005) 2(5) *Transnational Dispute Management* 2. See also; ILC, 'Report of the International Law Commission on the Work of its 54th Session' (29 April to 7 June and 22 July to 16 August 2002) UN Doc A/57/10, para 257; Shea (n 228) 5.

[238] On 'Calvo clause' in contractual arrangements, see, e.g., Dugard, 'Diplomatic Protection' (n 228) para 65. See also Newcombe and Paradell (n 225) 9–10.

[239] See, e.g., Newcombe and Paradell (n 225) 13; Miles (n 225), 50; Juillard (n 228) para 3; Shea (n 228) 17–19. See also Cremades (n 237) 2–3.

[240] As Miles noted: 'In essence, the goal of the Calvo Doctrine was to eradicate the ever-present threat of foreign state intervention triggered by trader, or settler disputes'. Miles (n 225) 51. See also Langer and Viñuales (n 228) 1, 5–6.

[241] Garibaldi (n 237) 15.

[242] Shumway (n 232) 117.

[243] Louis Alberto Romero, *A History of Argentina in the Twentieth Century* (Pennsylvania State University Press, 2002) 72–3, 88–9; Shumway (n 232) 115–19. See also Whitaker (n 233) 76–8, 120.

and Juan Peron himself made his admiration for Rosas clear in his writings.[244] As in other cases of collective memory,[245] the memory of Rosas has been nurtured selectively; emphasizing activities relating to fighting powerful foreign powers while neglecting others (such as dictatorial policies).[246]

c. Calvo's legacy and ICSID

Though the Calvo doctrine has not been substantially incorporated into general international law,[247] some of its elements contributed to the development of the principle regarding the exhaustion of local remedies,[248] and influenced some clauses in BITs[249] and the legislation of some Latin American countries.[250] By the end of the 1970s, the Calvo doctrine was firmly entrenched in Latin American thinking and was taught in law schools 'as an article of faith, a matter of national and regional identity.'[251] In light of the conspicuous inconsistency between the Calvo doctrine and the ICSID arbitration mechanism under the auspices of the World Bank (allowing foreign investors to sue host states in international arbitral tribunals),[252] it came as no surprise that Latin American countries opposed the establishment of ICSID, associated it with foreign intervention, and perceived it 'as sort of a war machine against the Calvo Doctrine.'[253]

The collective memory of foreign interventions in Argentina during its formative period enhanced its vigilance regarding foreign interference. The vigorous attack lodged by the US Ambassador to Argentina against Juan Peron during the 1946 election campaign[254] and the US interventions in Latin American countries

[244] Shumway (n 232) 114–15. See also William Dusenberry, 'Juan Manuel de Rosas as Viewed by Contemporary American Diplomats' (1961) 41 *The Hispanic American Historical Review* 495, 495–6, 514; Lewis (n 233) 45.

[245] See Section II above.

[246] See, e.g., Dusenberry (n 244) 495–6; Joseph R Barager, 'The Historiography of the Rio de la Plata Area Since 1830' (1959) 39 *The Hispanic American Historical Review* 588, 590–1.

[247] See, e.g., Rudolph Dolzer and Christoph Schreuer, *Principles of International Investment Law* (2nd edn, OUP, 2012) 2; Juillard (n 228) para 13; Miles (n 225) 51; Newcombe and Paradell (n 225) 13.

[248] See, e.g., ILC, 'Report of the International Law Commission Fifty-fourth session' (n 237) para 313; Juillard (n 228) para 26–7.

[249] See, e.g., Cremades (n 237) 4–5.

[250] see, e.g., Juillard (n 228) para 5–6; Langer and Viñuales (n 228) 10–12; Cremades (n 237) 3–4; Garibaldi (n 237) 22–3.

[251] Garibaldi (n 237) 29. And Mourra explains: 'The doctrine would prove to become the single most influential legal doctrine affecting the development of Latin American laws pertaining to foreign investors in the twentieth century. Mourra (n 226) 9.

[252] The ICSID is not an arbitral tribunal but it provides a legal and organizational framework for the arbitration of disputes between foreign investors and host states. It allows disputes between these parties to be arbitrated without interference from domestic courts of the host state. Thus, domestic courts have no power to stay, to compel, or to otherwise influence ICSID arbitral proceedings. Newcombe and Paradell (n 225) 29; Dolzer and Schreuer (n 247) 239.

[253] Juillard (n 228) para 18. See also Paul C Szasz, 'The Investment Disputes Convention and Latin America' (1970–1) 11 *Virginia Journal of International Law* 256, 259–60; Langer and Viñuales (n 228) 23–5; Alden F Abbott, 'Latin America and International Arbitration Conventions: The Quandary of Non-Ratification' (1976) 17 *Harvard International Law Journal* 131, 135, 138–9.

[254] See, e.g., Romero (n 243) 98, 99.

during the Cold War[255] further intensified anti-imperialist sentiments and sovereignty concerns among nationalistic groups in Argentina (including Peronist groups).

Opposition to ICSID changed during the 1980s and 1990s, when many Latin American countries adopted liberal economic reforms, acceded to the ICSID Convention and concluded BITs.[256] Significant elements of BITs and the ICSID arbitral mechanism are incompatible with the Calvo doctrine and that divergence was highlighted by the *CMS v Argentina* tribunal:

> Had the Claimant renounced recourse to arbitration, for example by resorting to the courts of Argentina, this would have been a binding selection under the BIT. In that case, the Tribunal would agree with Counsel for the Republic of Argentina that although *Carlos Calvo*, a distinguished Argentine international jurist who fathered the Calvo Doctrine and Clause, *will not become an honorary citizen of countries having entered into bilateral investment treaties*, this would still be a binding decision. However, as no such renunciation took place, the Calvo Clause will not resuscitate in this context.[257]

Though significant elements of the ICSID and BITs are inconsistent with the Calvo doctrine, it still constitutes a part of the legal heritage and identity of Argentina and other Latin American states.[258] As Garibaldi (himself a critic of the Calvo doctrine) explains, the doctrine 'has the romantic appeal of history and tradition and shared experience deeply ingrained in Latin American culture. It has the heroic mantle of a theory believed to have preserved Latin American dignity in the face of abusive claims of capital-exporting countries.'[259]

Arguments inspired by the Calvo doctrine were raised[260] by Argentina in ICSID proceedings related to the 2001 financial crisis,[261] and the legal justification presented by Argentina for the non-payment of compensation according to ICSID awards resonate with this doctrine. Argentine officials explained that

[255] On these US interventions, see, e.g., Daniel C Hellinger, *Comparative Politics of Latin America* (Routledge, 2011) 514–47; Smith (n 230) 151 et seq.

[256] See, e.g., Cremades (n 237) 5–6; Garibaldi (n 237) 32–5; Langer and Viñuales (n 228) 25–6. As noted by Titi, four-fifths of all Argentinean BITs in force were signed between 1991 and 1996. Catharine Titi, 'Investment Arbitration in Latin America: The Uncertain Veracity of Preconceived Ideas' (2014) 30 *Arbitration International* 357, 361.

[257] *CMS v Argentina*, Decision of the Tribunal on Objections to Jurisdiction (17 July 2003) [emphasis added, footnote omitted] [81]. See also [82].

[258] See, e.g., Draft Articles on Diplomatic Protection with commentaries (2006) 72–3 <http://legal.un.org/ilc/texts/instruments/english/commentaries/9_8_2006.pdf> accessed 27 March 2015; Julliard (n 228) paras 13, 17; Garibaldi (n 237) 29.

[259] Garibaldi (n 237) 57.

[260] On the link between the Calvo and Drago doctrines, past foreign invasions, and legal proceedings abroad relating to the restructuring of Argentina's public debt, see Por Mario Rapoport, 'Deuda, Soberanía y Crecimiento' (*Página/12 Online*, 24 August 2014) <http://www.pagina12.com.ar/diario/elpais/1-253717-2014-08-24.html> accessed 27 March 2015.

[261] See, e.g., *Azurix v Argentina*, Decision on Jurisdiction (8 December 2003) ICSID Case No. ARB/01/12, [29]; *AES v Argentina*, Decision on Jurisdiction (26 April 2005) ICSID Case No. ARB/02/17, [97]. See also Garibaldi (n 237) 38–9 and the references therein; Carlos E Alfaro, 'Argentina: ICSID Arbitration and BITs Challenged by the Argentine Government' *Mondaq* (21 December 2004) <http://www.mondaq.com/article.asp?articleid=30151&searchresults=1&login=true> accessed 27 March 2015.

those damage awards were not paid because the award creditors had not complied with the procedure required by the ICSID Convention. Though this interpretation was contested by leading scholars[262] and certain ICSID decisions,[263] Argentine officials argued that under Article 54(1) of the ICSID Convention, foreign investors had to enforce these awards as final judgment of a *local court*: 'The ICSID mechanism ... does not provide ICSID's award holders with a super-right that renders meaningless all administrative requirements under the local law of the recipient country.'[264] From this perspective, the non-payment of those damage awards did not constitute a breach of the ICSID Convention.[265] ICSID award creditors, however, were advised not to apply to Argentine courts, inter alia, because of the 'Rosatti Doctrine'[266] (developed by Argentina's former Solicitor General) which refers to the Calvo doctrine, according to which ICSID arbitration and investment treaties violate basic Argentinian constitutional principles.[267]

d. Sovereignty concerns, collective memory, and ICSID

ICSID arbitration and concerns relating to loss of sovereignty are often linked in the Argentine press. The daily *Página/12* (which generally supports the Peronist left-wing government of President Cristina Fernández de Kirchner) frequently associates ICSID proceedings with loss of sovereignty,[268] supremacy of

[262] Dolzer and Schreuer explain in their book that though the procedure for the enforcement of ICSID awards is governed by the law on the execution of judgments in each country, the domestic court or authority is limited to verifying that the award is authentic. Accordingly, there is no review of ICSID awards by domestic courts in the course of proceedings for recognition and enforcement. Dolzer and Schreuer (n 247) 310–11. See also Christoph Schreuer and others, *The ICSID Convention: A Commentary* (2nd edn, CUP, 2009) 1141, at para 87. See also Titi (n 256) at 373 and the references therein.

[263] See, e.g., Charles B Rosenberg, 'The Intersection of International Trade and International Arbitration: The Use of Trade Benefits to Secure Compliance with Arbitral Awards' (2013) 44 *Georgetown Journal of International Law* 503, 512–15 and see the references therein.

[264] Embassy of Argentina (Washington DC), Hearings of the International Monetary Policy and Trade Subcommittee of the House Financial Services Committee: The Role of the United States in The World Bank and Multilateral Development Banks (2011) (the section on 'Issues before the International Centre for Settlement of Investment Disputes ("ICSID")' at para 2) <http://embassyofargentina.us/embassyofargentina.us/files/110729tohousefinancialservicesandforeignaffairscommittees.pdf> accessed 27 March 2015.

[265] Ibid., para 3. See also Embassy of Argentina (Washington DC), Inaccurate Statements in H.R. 5564 that Argentina is Compelled to Rebut (3 June 2011) para 4 <http://embassyofargentina.us/embassyofargentina.us/files/letterambchiaradia06032011.pdf> accessed 27 March 2015; 'Argentina—position on ICSID' (22 February 2011) <http://embassyofargentina.us/embassyofargentina.us/files/responsetoalecinrelationtotheresolutionsupportingthereevaluationofargentinasgeneralsystemofpreferencesgspbenefitsbytheustra.pdf> accessed 27 March 2015.

[266] Luke Eric Peterson, 'Argentine Crisis Arbitration Awards Pile Up, but Investors Still Wait for a Payout' *International News* (25 June 2009) <http://justinvestment.org/2009/07/argentine-crisis-arbitration-awards-pile-up-but-investors-still-wait-for-a-payout/> accessed 27 March 2015.

[267] On the 'Rosatti Doctrine' see Charity L Goodman, 'Uncharted Waters: Financial Crisis and Enforcement of ICSID Awards in Argentina' (2007) 28 *University of Pennsylvania Journal of International Economic Law* 452–3; Garibaldi (n 237) 41–3.

[268] See, e.g., 'Ejerceremos un Control de Constitucionalidad', Interview with Horacio Rosatti, Argentine Minister of Justice (*Página 12 Online*, 30 April 2005) <http://www.pagina12.com.ar/

international judicial procedures,[269] and pressure exerted by international agencies and/or foreign investors.[270] This link is highlighted, for example, in the interview with the winner of the 2012–13 President Néstor Kirchner's Fellowship awarded for research devoted to ICSID and BITs.[271] The expropriation of the Spanish Repsol's property rights in YPF (the Argentine energy corporation) in 2012[272] was presented by the Argentine President as a 'recovery of sovereignty'[273] and the title of the presidential decree that implemented the expropriation was 'Hydrocarbon Sovereignty'.[274]

The link between the importance of national sovereignty for the government and Argentina's collective memory of past foreign intervention is exemplified in the decision of Cristina Kirchner's government in 2010 to turn the Day of National Sovereignty into a national holiday. Under the President's decree, this event is to be observed every year on 20 November and it commemorates Rosas' Battle of Vuelta de Obligado against the Anglo-French fleet.[275] The presidential decree emphasizes that this event is one of the nation's most important historical landmarks and mentioned that France and England attempted to colonize parts of Argentina.[276] In a statement submitted to the Chamber of Deputies, Deputy German Enrique (from the ruling coalition) emphasized the current need

diario/suplementos/cash/subnotas/1849-530-2005-05-07.html> accessed 27 March 2015; Javier Lewkowicz, '"No es Necesario Entregar la Soberanía"' (*Página 12 Online*, 21 August 2012) <http://www.pagina12.com.ar/diario/economia/2-201463-2012-08-21.html> accessed 27 March 2015; Roberto Briscioli, 'Pérdida de soberanía'(*Página 12 Online*, 25 November 2012) <http://www.pagina12.com.ar/diario/suplementos/cash/17-6429-2012-11-25.html> accessed 27 March 2015.

269 See, e.g., 'Tribunal con Fallo Cantado' (*Página 12 Online*, 12 April 2005) http://www.pagina12.com.ar/diario/economia/2-49644-2005-04-12.html> accessed 27 March 2015; 'Qué Reclaman y Quién lo Resuelve' (*Página 12 Online*. 27 March 2012) <http://www.pagina12.com.ar/diario/economia/subnotas/2-58392-2012-03-27.html> accessed 27 March 2015.

270 See, e.g., Javier Lewkowicz, 'Los Abogados le Sacan Punta al Lápiz' (*Página 12 Online*, 14 April 2012) <http://www.pagina12.com.ar/diario/economia/2-191870-2012-04-14.html> accessed 27 March 2015; David Cufré, 'La que Rompe no Sería Argentina, sino Ellos' (*Página 12 Online*, 26 April 2005) <http://www.pagina12.com.ar/diario/elpais/1-50265.html> accessed 27 March 2015.

271 Javier Lewkowizc, 'No es Necesario Entregar la Soberanía' (*Página 12*, 21 August 2012) <http://www.pagina12.com.ar/diario/economia/2-201463-2012-08-21.html> accessed 27 March 2015.

272 On this expropriation and the involved international legal rules, see Stephen Pelliccia, 'Repsol, YPF, and Argentina: A Hypothetical Look at the Pending ICSID Arbitration over YPF' (2013) ExpressO: <http://works.bepress.com/stephen_pelliccia/1> accessed 27 March 2015.

273 See, e.g., Simon Romero and Raphael Minder, 'Argentina to Seize Control of Oil Company' *NY Times online* (16 April 2012) <http://www.nytimes.com/2012/04/17/business/global/argentine-president-to-nationalize-oil-company.html?_r=0> accessed 27 March 2015.

274 Decreto 1227/ 2012, Sobernania Hidrocarburifera, Boletin Offical de la Republica Argentina, 27 July 2012 <http://www.boletinoficial.gov.ar/Avisos/VerPDF.castle?f=20120727&s=01&pd=1&ph=0> accessed 27 March 2015. See also Ricardo W Beller and María Lorena Schiariti, 'Argentina: Regulation of The New Hydrocarbons Sovereignty Regime' *Mondaq* (7 August 2012) <http://www.mondaq.com/x/190692/Energy+Law/Regulation+Of+The+New+Hydrocarbons+Sovereignty+Regime> accessed 27 March 2015.

275 On this battle and its historical context, see Section V(a) above.

276 Feriados Nacionales, Decreto 1584/2010, Establécense Feriados Nacionales y días no laborables. Bs. As., 2/11/2010 <http://www.infoleg.gov.ar/infolegInternet/anexos/170000-174999/174389/norma.htm> accessed 27 March 2015.

to defend Argentine identity against foreign invaders.[277] As noted below, Kirchner's Day of Sovereignty speeches referred to the Drago doctrine and the ongoing need for fighting to protect economic and political independence.

e. Collective memory, political ideology, and agents of memory

The collective memory of foreign powers' interventions in Argentina and Latin America, and the resultant Calvo doctrine, have significantly contributed to sovereignty concerns, the association of ICSID[278] with loss of sovereignty, and to a hostile attitude towards ICSID. During the ICSID proceedings, Argentina raised legal arguments inspired by the Calvo doctrine as justification for non-payment of ICSID damage awards until October 2013.[279] The memories of the historical context in which the Calvo doctrine emerged still reverberate among large groups in the Argentine society. 'For a Latin American, invoking the Calvo Doctrine amounts to going back to one's roots.'[280]

The Calvo doctrine constitutes an intermediary concept linking the collective memory of foreign intervention with specific legal rules emanating from this legal doctrine. The historical context of foreign intervention that led to the formation of the Calvo doctrine, it is submitted, is embedded in the doctrine and legal principles derived from this doctrine. Like other cases discussed above, it seems that the legal doctrine effectively functions here as a 'carrier' of the particular collective memory.[281]

This collective memory and the ensuing attentiveness to external threats to sovereignty that accompany the international protection of foreign investors are profoundly intertwined with political ideology.[282] The Calvo doctrine has become intertwined with nationalist ideology in Argentina, emphasizing the state's right to make economic policy decisions unconstrained by foreign factors.[283] The memory of various foreign interventions in Argentina and other Latin American states is one of the significant factors that has nourished nationalist ideology, adopted by nationalist groups (of the right and the left) in Argentina,[284] including President

[277] H. Cámara de Diputados de la Nación, Proyecto de resolucion, 8165-D-2010, 171 (11/11/2010) <http://www1.hcdn.gov.ar/proyxml/expediente.asp?fundamentos=si&numexp=8165-D-2010> accessed 27 March 2015.

[278] On foreign intervention in Latin America in the last 150 years, the Calvo doctrine, and the Argentine resistance to ICSID, see, e.g., Liliana Constante, 'El CIADI y la Constitución Nacional' (*Aldorso*, 5 May 2012) 5 <http://www.aldorso.com.ar/05-MAY-12/COSTANTE%20-%20EL%20CIADI%20%20es%20inconstitucional.pdf> accessed 27 March 2015.

[279] See Section V(b) above.

[280] Garibaldi (n 237) 57.

[281] See Section III(a) above.

[282] For an insightful analysis of the link between the collective memory and Zionist ideology, see Yael Zerubavel (n 10) 13–36. See also Vasile Docea, 'History, Ideology and Collective Memory' (2010) 1 *Acta Universitatis Sapientiae—European and Regional Studies* 83.

[283] On this ideology, see, e.g., Garibaldi (n 237) 23.

[284] On the link between the Calvo clause and left-wing parties in Latin America, see, e.g., Garibaldi (n 237) 57, 23. See also, Wenhua Shan, 'From North-South Divide to Private-Public Debate: Revival of the Calvo Doctrine and the Changing Landscape in International Investment Law' (2007) 27 *Northwestern Journal of International Law and Business* 631, 632, 649, 654 (and see the references therein).

Cristina Fernández de Kirchner's Peronist party (Front for Victory). These memories, occasionally cultivated by political groups,[285] have contributed to a hostile approach vis-à-vis ICSID as a mechanism that protects foreign investors.

Sociological literature on collective memory reveals that although collective memory often contributes to collective solidarity, this does not imply that it is shared by all segments of society.[286] The previous discussion and personal interviews with experts on Argentina indicate that the collective memory relating to foreign interventions and ensuing sovereignty concerns are not shared by all major segments of the Argentine population. This memory is widespread among nationalist groups (including Kirchner's Peronist party) but not necessarily in other circles. This fragmented memory appears to parallel social and ideological divisions within Argentine society.[287]

Agents of memory include various state and non-state actors taking an active part in diverse practices which form or preserve the collective memory.[288] Among the agents that are involved in the preservation of collective memories regarding foreign intervention (and the ensuing normative lessons regarding defending sovereignty) are political parties and leaders, diverse public bodies, and the mass media. *Nationalist parties* revived several times the memory of Rosas and the Vuelta de Obligado battle as symbols of heroic struggle against foreign powers' intervention.[289] And President Cristina Kirchner decided to commemorate that battle annually in a national holiday (Day of Sovereignty).[290] Christina Kirchner's Day of Sovereignty speeches drew parallel lines between Argentina's external debt restructuring and the 1845 battle,[291] and referred to the Drago doctrine, new forms of domination, and the ongoing need to fight great powers for protecting economic and political independence.[292] The

[285] See Section V(a) above.

[286] See Section II above.

[287] On the fragmented nature of Argentine society, see, e.g., Yves Dezalay and Bryant G Garth, *The Internationalization of Palace Wars: Lawyers, Economists, and the Contest to Transform Latin American States* (University of Chicago Press, 2002) 37–41; Michiel Baud, 'State and Society in Argentina: Change and Continuity under the Kirchners' (2013) 95 *European Review of Latin American and Caribbean Studies* 114, 121; Félix E Martín and Marvin L Astrada, 'Argentine Strategic Culture' (Florida International University, Applied Research Center, Miami, 2010) 5, 12, 26 44; Martín Becerra, Santiago Marino, and Guillermo Mastrini, *Mapping Digital Media: Argentina* (Open Society Foundation. 2012), 8, 91–2.

[288] See Section II above.

[289] Romero (n 243) 72–3, 88–9; Shumway (n 232) 115–19.

[290] See Section V(c) above.

[291] CFK: 'No Hablemos de Piquete, Hablemos de Aprietes y Amenazas' (*Página/12 Online*, 20 November 2012) <http://www.pagina12.com.ar/diario/ultimas/20-208205-2012-11-20.html> accessed 27 March 2015.

[292] Cristina Fernández de Kirchner, 20 de NOV. Acto por el Día de la Soberanía Nacional, 20 November 2012 <https://www.youtube.com/watch?v=H9g4nFKIBNg> accessed 27 March 2015; Cristina Fernández de Kirchner, 18 de NOV. Día de la Soberania Nacional. Cristina Fernández, 18 November 2011 <https://www.youtube.com/watch?v=XFCWSRQALn4> accessed 27 March 2015; Acto por el 166° Aniversario de la Vuelta de Obligado: Palabras de la Presidenta de la Nación, 18 de Noviembre de 2011 <http://presidencia.gob.ar/discursos/25549-acto-por-el-166o-aniversario-de-la-vuelta-de-obligado-palabras-de-la-presidenta-de-la-nacion> accessed 27 March 2015; Discurso de Cristina Fernández de Kirchner en el Acto por el Día de la Soberanía Nacional, en el Paraje Vuelta de Obligado, 20 de noviembre de 2010, Archivo digital de Presidencia de la Nación <http://archivohistorico.educ.ar/sites/default/files/x_13.pdf> accessed 27 March 2015.

Vice-President's (Boudou) speech commemorating the battle in 2013 linked the iconic Argentine leaders San Martin and Peron with Rosas and Néstor Kirchner,[293] and the Chief of Staff's (Capitanich) speech in 2014 linked the battle with the opposition of the previous government to demands by the IMF.[294]

Diverse public bodies have also been active in commemorative practices aimed at preserving the collective memory of the Vuelta de Obligado battle and its ensuing normative lessons regarding economic independence from foreign powers. Thus, for instance, a thermal power plant,[295] a street in Buenos Aires,[296] and schools[297] have been named after the 1845 battle. The official website of the historical site of the battle (of the San Pedro municipality) presents this battle as the first defence of the national economic interests, which protected the nation from economic imperialistic activities.[298] The battle is presented in the website of Telam (a state enterprise) as a victory in the struggle for national sovereignty and it observes that the reason for the invasion was an economic one.[299]

A hall in the National Historical Museum in Buenos Aires is devoted to this battle; it displays items and testimonies about the battle, and emphasizes its importance for the defence of Argentine sovereignty.[300] And at the particular site, the historical museum Museo de Sitio Batalla de Obligado was established by the Department of Culture, the Municipality of San Pedro, and a local conservative group.[301]

As noted previously, the capacity of the mass media to reach huge communities simultaneously and its influence on public opinion explain the significant role of this vehicle of collective memory. The media's capacity to affect collective memory is also linked to *repeated* reports and the creation of an *association* between current

[293] 'Vamos a Redoblar Nuestro Compromiso' (*Página/12 Online*, 21 November 2013) <http://www.pagina12.com.ar/diario/elpais/1-234053-2013-11-21.html> accessed 27 March 2015.

[294] 'Soberanía es no a los Buitres' (*Página/12 Online*, 21 November 2014) <http://www.pagina12.com.ar/diario/elpais/1-260332-2014-11-21.html> accessed 27 March 2015.

[295] 'Argentina Awards Turnkey Contract for Combined-cycle Power Plant' (*Power Engineering*, 9 July 2012) <http://www.power-eng.com/articles/2012/07/argentina-awards-turnkey-contract-for-combined-cycle-power-plant.html> accessed 27 March 2015.

[296] Plaza General Manuel Belgrano <http://www.turismo.buenosaires.gob.ar/es/atractivo/plaza-general-manuel-belgrano> accessed 27 March 2015.

[297] See, e.g., Dirección General de Información y Evaluación Educativa, *Establecimientos de Nivel Primario, Provincia de Santa Fe, Año 2010* <https://www.santafe.gov.ar/index.php/educacion/content/download/104897/516408/file/Primario.pdf> accessed 27 March 2015; Información Mundial sobre Educación <http://worldinfo.co/es/edu/?s=vuelta+de+obligado> accessed 27 March 2015.

[298] Municipalidad de San Pedro, El Valor de la Historia (vuelta de obligado) <http://www.sanpedro.gov.ar/turismo.obligado.php> accessed 27 March 2015.

[299] Pacho O'Donnell, Un combate por la soberanía <http://www.elortiba.org/obligado.html> accessed 27 March 2015. See also the interactive website of the Advisory Council of Education (province of Entre Rios), Batalla La Vuelta de Obligado <http://entrerios.gov.ar/CGE/recursosaprender/vuelta_de_obligado/> accessed 27 March 2015.

[300] Muestras permanentes y nuevas salas de exposición, en el Museo Histórico Nacional <http://www.cultura.gob.ar/agenda/muestras-permanentes-y-nuevas-salas-de-exposicion-en-el-museo-historico-nacional/> accessed 27 March 2015.

[301] Museo de Sitio 'Batalla de Obligado'<http://sanpedro.gov.ar/turismo/?p=1023> accessed 27 March 2015 [San Pedro province].

and historic events.[302] As to the Argentine press, the daily *Página/12* (which generally supports Kirchner's Peronist government) occasionally associates the battle of Vuelta de Obligado with national struggles for independence and sovereignty, resisting foreign domination,[303] colonialism[304] (including the struggle on the Falkland/Malvinas islands),[305] the expropriation of the Spanish Repsol's property rights in YPF,[306] and the government's legal battles against foreign firms relating to the restructuring of Argentina's public debt.[307] As noted above, this newspaper frequently associates ICSID proceedings with loss of sovereignty and pressure exerted by international agencies and/or foreign investors.

In conclusion, the collective memory of past foreign interventions (often relating to foreign nationals' property rights) during Argentina's formative period led directly to the development of the Calvo doctrine as a defence instrument against such abused and perceived practices. This legal doctrine and its embedded collective memories have become firmly entrenched in Argentine legal thinking (occasionally cultivated by ideological groups and media), and have significantly contributed to sovereignty concerns and associated hostile approach towards international mechanisms aimed at protecting foreign investors (prominently ICSID). The underlying conception of the Calvo doctrine and the associated memories of foreign intervention were intertwined among large groups in the Argentine society, and constituted one of the significant factors affecting the government's decision not to implement the above series of ICSID awards until October 2013.

In addition to the above-discussed role of collective memory, other factors influenced the hostile approach undertaken by the government of Argentina vis-à-vis ICSID, prominently those relating to the 'legitimacy deficit' of ICSID tribunals in Argentina. Legitimacy affects the prospects of compliance with international

[302] See Section IV(c)(ii) above.

[303] See, e.g., Norberto Alayón, 'Carta a los Ingleses Progresistas' (*Página/12 Online*, 21 February 2012) <http://www.pagina12.com.ar/diario/elpais/1-187999-2012-02-21.html> accessed 27 March 2015.

[304] See, e.g., José Pablo Feinman, 'Colonialismo Ayer y Hoy', *Página/12 Online*, 17 June 2012) <http://www.pagina12.com.ar/diario/contratapa/13-196557-2012-06-17.html> accessed 27 March 2015.

[305] See, e.g., 'Otra Mirada Sobre las Islas' (*Página/12 Online*, 16 June 2014) <http://www.pagina12.com.ar/diario/elpais/1-248697-2014-06-16.html> accessed 27 March 2015; Julián Andrés Domínguez, 'Las Malvinas y una Fecha Histórica' (*Página/12 Online*, 3 January 2013) <http://www.pagina12.com.ar/diario/elpais/subnotas/211116-61820-2013-01-03.html> accessed 27 March 2015; Raúl Kollmann, 'Ningún país del mundo acepta la soberanía inglesa en Malvinas' (*Página/12 Online*, 3 February 2013) <http://www.pagina12.com.ar/diario/elpais/1-213145-2013-02-03.html> accessed 27 March 2015.

[306] Julián Domínguez, 'Las vueltas de Obligado' (*Página/12 Online*, 21 November 2014) <http://www.pagina12.com.ar/diario/elpais/1-260333-2014-11-21.html> accessed 27 March 2015.

[307] For an article associating foreign creditors' litigation against Argentina in US courts, national sovereignty, and economic colonialism and the 1845 Rosas' battle, see Julián Domínguez, Por Más Soberanía (*Página/12 Online*, 7 July 2014) <http://www.pagina12.com.ar/diario/elpais/1-250230-2014-07-07.html> accessed 27 March 2015. See also 'Recalde le Apuntó a Héctor Méndez' (*Página/12 Online*, 26 July 2014) <http://www.pagina12.com.ar/diario/economia/2-251582-2014-07-26.html> accessed 27 March 2015.

law.[308] The government of Argentina (at that time) and social groups supporting it raised significant doubts regarding the legitimacy of ICSID tribunals, particularly pertaining to their independence and impartial attitude. Argentine newspapers, and particularly the daily *Página/12*, frequently emphasized that ICSID depended on the World Bank[309] and was generally biased in favour of foreign investors.[310]

f. The 2013 settlement agreement and additional factors

The government of Argentina reached a settlement agreement with five award creditors in mid-October 2013; four of them relate to ICSID awards. According to this agreement, the award creditors would be paid in Argentine bonds.[311] The settlement agreement shows that though collective memory has influenced the Argentine approach vis-à-vis ICSID, it is not a determinative factor. A comprehensive discussion of the various factors (sociological, economic, and political ones) influencing Argentina to reach this settlement agreement exceeds the limits of this chapter and this section refers very briefly to the influence of economic sanctions as well as some features of the Argentine collective identity.

The economic pressure exerted on Argentina to comply with ICSID awards included the US decision to suspend Argentina's preferential trade status (under the US General System of Preferences legislation) as well US's vote against extending certain loans to Argentina by the World Bank and Inter-American Development Bank.[312] Sociological factors also seem to have contributed to the decision to

[308] On the impact of legitimacy on compliance with international law, see, e.g., Chris A Thomas, 'The Concept of Legitimacy and International Law' (December 2013) LSE Law, Society and Economy Working Papers 14–16 and see the references therein <http://eprints.lse.ac.uk/51746/1/__libfile_repository_Content_Law,%20society%20and%20economics%20working%20papers_2013_WPS2013-12_Thomas.pdf> accessed 27 March 2015; Thomas M Franck, *The Power Of Legitimacy Among Nations* (OUP, 1990) 3; Beth A Simmons, 'Compliance with International Agreements' (1998) 1 *The Annual Review of Political Science* 75, 87–9.

[309] See, e.g., Mario Wainfeld, 'Qué Difícil es Ser Normal' (*Página/12 Online*, 3 April 2005) <http://www.pagina12.com.ar/diario/elpais/1-49263.html> accessed 27 March 2015; 'La que Rompe no Sería Argentina, sino Ellos' (*Página/12 Online*, 26 April 2005) <http://www.pagina12.com.ar/diario/elpais/1-50265.html> accessed 27 March 2015; Fernando Krakowiak, 'Arbitro Bombero' (*Página/12 Online*, 2 May 2005) <http://www.pagina12.com.ar/diario/suplementos/cash/35-1898-2005-05-29.html> accessed 27 March 2015; 'Qué Reclaman y Quién lo Resuelve' (*Página/12 Online*, 27 March 2012) <http://www.pagina12.com.ar/diario/economia/subnotas/2-58392-2012-03-27.html> accessed 27 March 2015.

[310] See, e.g., Fernando Krakowiak, 'Arbitro Bombero' (n 309); Javier Lewkowicz, 'Los Abogados le Sacan Punta al Lápiz' (n 270); Modesto Emilio Guerrero, 'Venezuela se Fue del Ciadi' (*Página/12 Online*, 25 July 2012) <http://www.pagina12.com.ar/diario/elmundo/4-199469> accessed 27 March 2015.

[311] Luke Eric Peterson, 'After Settling some Awards' (n 22); Reuters, 'Argentina to pay $500 million to resolve disputes with foreign firms' (19 October 2013) <http://uk.reuters.com/article/2013/10/18/uk-argentina-worldbank-payment-idUKBRE99H16X20131018> accessed 27 March 2015.

[312] See, e.g., Rosenberg (n 263) 504, 517; Roger Alford, 'Using Trade Remedies to Enforce Arbitration Awards' (*Kluwer Arbitration Blog*, 22 March 2014) http://kluwerarbitrationblog.com/blog/2014/03/22/using-trade-remedies-to-enforce-arbitration-awards/ accessed 27 March 2015.

reach this settlement agreement, prominently those relating to the stigmatizing effects of economic sanctions,[313] and certain tendencies in the Argentine collective identity aspiring to avoid isolation in the international community.[314] It is noteworthy that unlike certain other Latin American countries which withdrew from the ICSID Convention, and notwithstanding some calls to follow these countries,[315] the government of Argentina decided not to disengage with this (and other) international economic institutions.

VI. Concluding Remarks

Collective memory and international law interact in both directions: international law affects and is affected by collective memories of diverse social groups. As discussed here, international legal concepts and institutions occasionally function as carriers of collective memories (including ICJ decisions and the Calvo doctrine). In some cases, international law directly aims to shape the collective memory of future generations, prominently in the sphere of international criminal law. The capacity of such international legal mechanisms to influence the collective memory of social groups is influenced by the particular features of the international legal system (and of the specific international legal mechanism), including evidentiary rules and the jurisdiction of international bodies.

The analysis of the collective memories of Germany and Argentina in Sections IV and V reveals the significant impact—and the limits—of collective memory on international law. These two cases also present some substantial differences regarding the particular collective memories and their influence on international law. While the German collective memory regarding hyperinflation considerably influenced *the content* of the EU's economic and monetary law (particularly during the first and the second stages of the Eurozone debt crisis), the Argentine collective memory of foreign powers intervention constituted one of the major factors affecting the decision *not to implement* ICSID awards until October 2013. Unlike the crucial influence of the collective memory of hyperinflation on the content of EMU provisions, Argentina's collective memory and the ensuing Calvo doctrine were not substantially incorporated into general international law. This memory and the resultant doctrine rather substantially contributed to the resistant approach adopted by Argentina towards ICSID tribunals. The latter case is somewhat similar to Foucault's conception of 'counter-memory'—collective memory which is developed as a source of opposition to the dominant narrative regarding

[313] On the stigmatizing effects of economic sanctions, see Chapter 4, Section IV(b).

[314] On recurring tendencies in the Argentine national identity aspiring to integrate with other countries in the international system, see, e.g., Carlos H Waisman, 'The Dynamics of National Identity Frames: The Case of Argentina in the Twentieth Century' in Louis Roniger and Mario Sznajder (eds), *Constructing Collective Identities and Shaping Public Spheres: Latin American Paths* (Sussex Academic Press, 1998) 149, 153–6; Martín and Astrada (n 287) 9–11, 22.

[315] See, e.g., Titi (n 256) at 361, 364.

the evolution of law concerning diplomatic protection and the protection of foreign investors. This historical narrative presents the host states as the weak parties, vulnerable to foreign interference by powerful powers, and hints that they should be protected by international law.

As noted in Section II, collective memories are involved in the formation of social identity and a social group's memory preserves the knowledge from which the group derives its unity and peculiarity. The collective memories of Germany and Argentina constitute a significant element of their identities but they differ regarding their emphasis on the two core elements of social identity. While Germany's collective memory of hyperinflation primarily relates to the internal aspect of national identity, Argentina's collective memory of foreign intervention highlights the external dimension of collective identity, thus emphasizing the social boundaries between Argentina (and other Latin American states) vis-à-vis powerful Western powers. Generally, underlining the external aspects of collective identity tends to foster internal similarity among group members.[316]

The two collective memories are also markedly different regarding their composition and modus of influence on international law. While Germany's collective memory of the hyperinflation is mainly linked to an economic approach (the classical or new classical schools of thought), Argentina's collective memory is profoundly intertwined with a political ideology (mainly nationalistic). As noted here, the memory of foreign intervention in Argentina and Latin America is one of the significant factors that have nourished nationalist ideology, which, in turn, influenced Argentina's approach to foreign investors and the international mechanism aiming to protect them.

The two collective memories led to the formation of an intermediate concept that affected international law. Germany's collective memory of the hyperinflation led to the concept of 'stability culture' that considerably affected the EMU's legal rules, and Argentina's memory of foreign intervention generated the Calvo doctrine that substantially influenced the government's approach towards ICSID tribunals. The memories of the historical context of these two intermediate doctrines are embedded in the legal principles derived from these doctrines. In both cases, the intermediate legal doctrines—'stability culture' and Calvo doctrine—function as carriers of collective memory.

Collective memories often have an integrative effect on a social group but this does not imply that such memories are always shared by all segments of the given society.[317] The collective memories of Germany and Argentina described here are very different in that regard. While Germany's collective memory of the hyperinflation and the ensuing normative lesson regarding fighting inflation are shared by the major political groups, Argentina's collective memory of foreign intervention and the accompanying need to defend national sovereignty vigilantly are mainly widespread among nationalistic groups (including Cristina Kirchner's Peronist

[316] Jenkins (n 30) 13. And see Chapter 5 on Social Identity and International Law.
[317] See Section II above.

government). This integrative feature of Germany's collective memory relates to the consensual character of the German political system, while Argentina's fragmented memory corresponds with social divisions in Argentine society.

Collective memories are often promoted by political groups.[318] The occasional employment of collective memories by political parties is noticeable in both the German and Argentine cases but it is more conspicuous in Argentina. The political aspects of the collective memory of foreign intervention are manifested regarding the government's decision to commemorate Rosas' Battle of Vuelta de Obligado in a national holiday. As noted, the political employment of collective memories is widespread but it should not lead to a reduction of the process of forming and preserving those memories to the political realm (and overlooking the socio-cultural factors involved in this process). Political leaders occasionally refer to past events but they do not always do so in order to further political aims; and their capacity to shape collective memories is not unlimited (and is often related to the socio-cultural features of the particular society).

The two cases illustrate not only the significant impact of collective memory on international law but also its limits. In both cases, collective memories significantly influenced international law but they were not the sole or determinative factor. EMU legal rules and the implementation of ICSID awards were influenced by the collective memories described here, but in both cases, the impact of these memories declined. The ECB significantly deviated from the pro-austerity approach in September 2012 and the government of Argentina agreed to provide some compensation to ICSID award creditors in October 2013. Additional factors (both socio-cultural and economic ones) led to these deviations from legal policies derived from these collective memories.

This chapter has discussed the interaction between collective memory and international law, and examined two cases illustrating the impact of such memories on international law. Further international socio-legal studies can explore additional spheres of international law that are influenced by collective memories and identify common variables affecting their impact on international law. And vice versa, future studies could examine the influence of diverse international legal mechanisms on collective memories of social groups. Such studies may systematically analyse what kinds of international agents of memory—and under what circumstances—are more likely to influence national, regional, or global memories. The selective employment of international criminal tribunals as an instrument to shape collective memory[319] invites an in-depth discussion on the suitability of using such legal mechanisms to affect collective memories.[320] Such a study may involve a discussion on whether international legal mechanisms should promote single or multivocal memories in national and transnational societies. Different theoretical approaches in sociological literature may suggest different answers to this question.

318 See Section II above. 319 See Section III(a) above.
320 On such questions, see, e.g., Teitel (n 50) 40; Wilson (n 53).

4

Social Identity, International Groups, and International Law

Who I am is closely interwoven with ideas about the society in which I live and the views of others who also inhabit that same social context ... Identity involves personal investment, often on a massive scale, to the extent that people are willing to die to claim or protect their own identities, but it is always socially located.

Kath Woodward, *Understanding Identity*[1]

I. Introduction

International law is infused with social identities. States and other international actors operate in multilayer maps, and factors located on their identity maps often motivate and constrain their activities in the international legal

[1] Kath Woodward, *Understanding Identity* (Hodder Education 2002) vii.

system. Collective entities (such as states and international institutions) hold multiple identities; some are institutionalized in various legal rules, while others are semi-institutionalized in diverse soft laws or informal international groups. These identities often affect the perception, judgment, and behaviour of international actors, including their positions and the behaviour they undertake regarding international legal rules. Thus, for example, national identities influence states' decisions to develop or employ certain weapons of mass destruction, and international institutions' identities motivate certain international actors to promote compliance with international human rights treaties. Economic and political dimensions of international law are often overlain with a social identity dimension. While, in reality, these dimensions are inseparable, this chapter is devoted to a social identity analysis of international law.

Identity is a central concept in the sociology's established conceptual toolbox.[2] The term 'identity' has become central to many fields of sociology and social science over recent years.[3] Identity matters in our daily life and affects people's perceptions and attitudes towards other people, as well as their own behaviour. As Jenkins explains: 'one of the first things that we do on meeting a stranger is attempt to identify them, to locate them on our "mindscapes"'.[4] Prominent identities include ethnicity, nationality, geographical location, gender, religion, occupation, and historical roots.

Section II exposes the basic tenets of social identity and Section III briefly examines the role of identity in international relations literature (according to the constructivist approach). Section IV(a) discusses certain links between international law and social identity (including rules regarding the use and production of weapons of mass destruction (WMD)). Section IV(b) analyses the links between the European Union's (EU) identity and its external trade policy aimed at the promotion of compliance with international human rights law. Section IV(c) explores the employment of social identity tools as a complementary interpretative instrument to clarify the content of certain international legal provisions (such as those relating to minority groups and disqualification of adjudicators). Section V provides a summary of our conclusions and suggests some topics for future research.

[2] Richard Jenkins, *Social Identity* (4th edn, Routledge, 2014) 15. On the various streams in sociological identity theory, see Jan E Stets and Peter J Burke, 'A Sociological Approach to Self and Identity' in Mark Leary and June Tangney (eds), *Handbook of Self and Identity* (Guilford Press, 2002) 9–10.

[3] Anthony Giddens and Philip Sutton, *Sociology* (7th edn, Polity, 2013) 307.

[4] Jenkins (n 2) 27.

II. Social Identity

a. Key issues in social identity

Social identity[5] has been explored in the sociological literature and in the social psychological literature.[6] Though the two perspectives on identity present some differences regarding their origin, orientation, and language,[7] there are also substantial similarities and overlap. In most cases, the differences are a matter of emphasis.[8] As Stets and Burke note, concepts developed in both spheres always and simultaneously influence perception, affective relations, and behaviour.[9] This chapter combines theoretical tools and empirical findings drawn from both sociological and social psychological scholarship.

The concept of identity is closely associated with the symbolic-interactionist approach in sociological literature.[10] As discussed in Chapter 2, this micro-sociological approach analyses social behaviour in terms of daily interactions between people, as well as between the individual and the wider social structure.[11] From this perspective, identity is a pivotal concept which mediates the relationships between individuals and the social group.[12] Individuals hold multiple identities that vary in their relative overall importance, and each one is represented in the individual's mind.[13] Jenkins defines identity as follows:

> As a very basic starting point, identity is the human capacity—rooted in language—to know 'who's' and 'who' ... This involves knowing who we are, knowing who others are,

[5] I am deeply indebted to Orit Gazit of the Hebrew University Department of Sociology for helpful comments on an earlier draft of this section.

[6] The common term employed in sociological literature is 'identity theory' and the common term used in social psychological literature is 'social identity theory'. Jan E Stets and Peter J Burke, 'Identity, Theory and Social Identity Theory' (2000) 63 *Social Psychology Quarterly* 224.

[7] Sociological literature on identity emphasizes social roles, self-meaning and shared meanings, interactions, and 'identity salience'. Social psychological literature on identity emphasizes inter-group relations and group behaviour (and is often labelled as 'group-based identity'), cognitive processes, evaluative consequences, conformist behaviour, and certain personal motivational underpinning identification. On the common and different aspects of these two approaches to social identity, see Stets and Burke, 'Identity, Theory and Social Identity Theory' (n 6) 224–33; Michael A Hogg, Deborah J Terry, and Katherine M White, 'A Tale of Two Theories: A Critical Comparison of Identity Theory with Social Identity Theory' (1995) 58 *Social Psychology Quarterly* 255, 262–5.

[8] Stets and Burke, 'Identity, Theory and Social Identity Theory' (n 6) 223–4. See also ibid., 255.

[9] Stets and Burke 'Identity, Theory and Social Identity Theory' (n 6) 228.

[10] Hogg, Terry, and White (n 7) 255. On streams of identity approaches in the symbolic interactionist doctrine, see Stets and Burke 'Identity, Theory and Social Identity Theory' (n 6) 10–11.

[11] See Chapter 2, Section IV(c). On the link between social identity and the symbolic-interactionist approach, see, e.g., Hogg, Terry, and White (n 7) 256.

[12] Hogg, Terry, and White (n 7) 255, 257; Marilynn B Brewer, 'The Many Faces of Social Identity: Implications for Political Psychology' (2001) 22 *Political Psychology* 155.

[13] Hogg, Terry, and White (n 7) 259; Sheldon Stryker and Peter J Burke, 'The Past, Present, and Future of an Identity Theory' (2000) 63 *Social Psychology Quarterly* 284, 286; Walter G Stephan and Cookie White Stephan, *Intergroup Relations* (Westview Press, 1996) 90. Richard J Crisp, 'Prejudice

them knowing who we are, us knowing who they think we are, and so on. *This is a multi-dimensional classification or mapping of the human world and our places in it, as individuals and as members of collectives.*[14]

People have individual and collective identities, and these aspects of social identity are tightly bound together within the embodied self.[15] *Personal* identity differentiates one's self from other individuals and includes personal traits and the self's social categorization into social groups (e.g., by membership in certain groups).[16] In addition to personal identity, people identify themselves collectively; *collective identification* evokes imagery of people who resemble one another and share inter-subjective characteristics.[17] Despite this analytical distinction between personal and collective identities, it is often impossible in reality to disentangle group identity from personal identity.[18]

Two dynamic elements stand at the heart of social identity (both personal and collective): similarity and difference. Individuals and groups need a certain level of both similarity to and differentiation from others, and social identity derives from the fundamental tension between the sense of belonging and the sense of distinctiveness.[19]

Generally, social psychological scholarship tends to emphasize that identity and its cognitive consequences deriving from group membership. Sociological literature inclines to underline the dynamic and interpretative aspects of identity, and particularly its link to the 'social role',[20] underscoring that having a particular identity often pressures individuals to behave according to social expectations related to the particular role (such as 'parent' or 'teacher').[21] Where people identify with a group or social role, they tend to adopt the meaning that accompanies the

and Perceiving Multiple Identities' in John F Dovidio and others (eds), *Prejudice, Stereotyping And Discrimination* (Sage, 2010) 508.

[14] Jenkins (n 2) [emphasis added] 6. From a social psychological perspective, Tajfel defines social identity as 'that part of the individual's self concept which derives from his knowledge of his membership of a asocial group (or groups) together with the values and emotional significance attached to that membership', Henri Tajfel, *Human Groups and Social Categories: Studies in Social Psychology* (CUP, 1981) 254–5.

[15] Giddens and Sutton (n 3) 309; John C Turner and Rina S Onorato, 'Social Identity, Personality, and the Self-Concept: A Self-Categorization Perspective' in Tom R Tyler, Roderick M Kramer, and Oliver P John (eds), *The Psychology of the Social Self* (Erlbaum Publishers, 1990) 38; see also Jenkins (n 2) 39–41.

[16] Stephen Worchel, 'A Developmental View of the Search for Group Identity' in Stephen Worchel and others (eds) *Social Identity: International Perspectives* (Sage, 1998) 53, 55; Turner and Onorato (n 15) 13; Jenkins (n 2) 112–13; Marilynn B Brewer, 'The Social Self: On Being the Same and Different at the Same Time' (1991) 17 *Personality and Social Psychology Bulletin* 475, 475–6.

[17] Jenkins (n 2) 104.

[18] Stets and Burke, 'Identity, Theory and Social Identity Theory' (n 6) 228. On the relationships between personal and collective identity, see John C Turner and others, 'Self and Collective: Cognition and Social Context' (1994) 20 *Personality and Social Psychology Bulletin* 454.

[19] Brewer, 'The Social Self' (n 16) 475–7.

[20] The term 'role' refers in sociological literature to socially defined expectations that a person in a given social position follows. On the concept of role in sociology, see Chapter 1, Section II.

[21] On the importance of 'role' in sociological identity theory, see also Hogg, Terry, and White (n 7) 264. See also Giddens and Sutton (n 3) 307–8.

particular identity, and act accordingly to represent that meaning.[22] In this sense, identity is the set of meanings that are tied to the self, and those meanings often operate across various social roles and situations.[23]

Social groups, like individuals, strive to establish their identity and this group identity often outlives its members.[24] Groups interact with other groups and their individual members to construct a group identity. This collective identity has two dimensions: the identity of the particular group vis-à-vis its members, and the group's identity as it relates to other groups.[25] Groups and individuals identified with the group maintain reciprocal relationships; individuals affect the development of the group identity, and the group guides the actions of its members.[26] Groups strive to establish an independent identity from other groups, and also struggle with group members to maintain the group's identity equal to, if not more important than, the individual members' identity.[27]

b. The construction of social identity

Social identity is formed in a dialectic process between internal and external categorizations. Human beings have the propensity to categorize individuals into groups,[28] and social categorizations—both internal and external—are cognitive tools that segment, classify, and order the social environment. These categorizations do not merely organize the social world, they also provide a system of orientation for self-reference: they define the individual's place in society.[29] Individuals define themselves as belonging to some social groups, and certain aspects of their self-image are derived from the social categories to which they perceive themselves as belonging. Individuals self-categorize themselves differently according to the contexts in which they find themselves and the contingencies with which they are faced.[30] Thus, individuals always act in the context of a complex social structure out of which multiple identities emerge.[31]

[22] Stets and Burke, 'Identity, Theory and Social Identity Theory' (n 6) 227; see also Hogg, Terry, and White (n 7) 256; Stets and Burke, 'A Sociological Approach to Self and Identity' (n 2) 11 et seq.

[23] Stets and Burke, 'Identity, Theory and Social Identity Theory' (n 6) 229.

[24] Worchel (n 16) 65.

[25] Ibid., 65, 72–3. See also Alberto Melucci, 'The Process of Collective Identity' in Hank Johnston and Bert Klandermans (eds), *Social Movements and Culture* (University of Minnesota Press 1995) vol 4, 41, 47–8.

[26] Worchel (n 16) 66; Melucci (n 25) 47.

[27] Worchel (n 16) 65. On the various stages in the development of group identity, see Worchel 56–62.

[28] See, e.g. Tajfel (n 14) 255–9; Phyllis Anastasio, Betty Bachman, Samuel Gaertner, and John Dovidio, 'Categorization, Recategorization and Common Ingroup Identity' in Russell Spears and others (eds), *The Social Psychology of Stereotyping and Group Life* (Blackwell, 1997).

[29] Henri Tajfel and John C Turner, 'The Social Identity of Intergroup Behaviour' in Stephen Worchel and William G Austin (eds), *Psychology of Intergroup relations* (2nd edn, Nelson Hall, 1986) 7.

[30] Ibid., 12. See also Stets and Burke, 'Identity, Theory and Social Identity Theory' (n 6) 225; Jenkins (n 2) 114–15.

[31] Stets and Burke, 'A Sociological Approach to Self and Identity' (n 2).

Social categorization: The identity formation process begins with categorization undertaken by an external collective group or categorization that is done internally by the individual.[32] In both cases, identity emerges (and is maintained) within a two-way relationship between self-categorization and collective categorization. Thus, individuals present themselves in a particular way and that presentation is accepted or contested by significant others, and others' responses feed back to the presenter. Similarly, individuals may internalize collective identity into their self-identity and that internalization is likely to modify the way they present themselves to others.[33] Consequently, some scholars view the identity construction process as 'negotiations' between individuals and the collective.[34] Internal or external aspects of identity may be dominant at different stages of identity formation and often interact simultaneously.[35]

Boundaries: As discussed above, identity consists of two core elements of similarity and difference. Some scholars emphasize the role of highlighting the differences ('boundaries') between social groups in the process of constructing and maintaining *collective identity*.[36] Barth explains (in the context of ethnic groups) that 'groups only persist as significant units if they imply marked difference in behaviour, i.e., persisting cultural differences.'[37] From this perspective, group identification is constructed 'across the group boundary';[38] highlighting difference vis-à-vis other groups generates internal similarity among the group members.[39]

Symbols and rituals are often part of the formation and maintenance of group identity.[40] Symbols and community rituals often generate or reinforce a sense of shared belonging.[41] These symbols spawn an image of group homogeneity and often mask diversity among members of the identity group. Thus, symbols allow individual diversity and collective similarity to co-exist within social groups.[42]

[32] Jenkins (n 2) 13, 111.

[33] Jenkins (n 2) 46, 73, 95.

[34] See, e.g., Stets and Burke, 'Identity, Theory and Social Identity Theory' (n 6) 227.

[35] Jenkins (n 2) 73, 80, 83, 86, 113. See also Stets and Burke, 'A Sociological Approach to Self and Identity' (n 2) 225; Hogg, Terry, and White (n 7) 257.

[36] Fredrick Barth, 'Introduction' in Frederick Barth (ed), *Ethnic Groups and Boundaries: The Social Organization of Culture Difference* (Little Brown & Company, 1969) 9, 10–12; Jenkins (n 2) 123, 46.

[37] Barth (n 36) 15–16.

[38] Jenkins (n 2) 46. As Barth explains, even where persons of different identity groups interact with each other, the persistence of ethnic groups 'implies not only criteria and signals of identification, but also a structuring of interaction which allows the persistence of cultural differences'. Barth (n 36) 16.

[39] Jenkins (n 2) 13.

[40] Morita Hodaka and Servátka Maroš, *Symbols, Group Identity and the Hold-Up Problem* (30 November 2011) 1. <http://ssrn.com/abstract=1966354> accessed 20 March 2015; Jenkins (n 2) 146–7.

[41] Morita and Servátka (n 40) 1; Randall Collins, *Interaction Ritual Chains* (Princeton University Press, 2004) 95, 98; Jenkins (n 2) 137–9.

[42] Jenkins (n 2) 139–40, 145; Collins (n 41) 81–3.

Language (including dialect) and the construction of social identity are inextricably linked.[43] Language indicates how societies classify their environment (both physical and social) and each social group has its own distinctive system of classification, which, in part, maintains boundaries between insiders and outsiders.[44] Thus, '[t]o choose one language over another provides an immediate and universally recognized badge of identity'.[45] Language often reflects distinctive regional, ethnic, religious, or historical backgrounds. Ethnic groups may utilize language as a symbolic means of fostering or developing identity, or as a means of defence against encroachment by outsiders.[46]

Collective narratives and memories often contribute to the emergence and maintenance of social identities.[47] Collective narratives place an identity group within a historically constituted world, and they render the world intelligible and coherent to their members.[48] Such stories[49] 'constitute narrative bonds' that frequently delineate the social groups' boundaries.[50] Collective memories[51] occasionally produce a commemorative narrative about a particular past.[52] Such social memories often suggest a moral message and provide some normative guidelines regarding the appropriate behaviour.[53] Collective memories preserve the store of knowledge from which the group derives awareness of its unity and peculiarity.[54]

Institutions often reflect and reinforce identities.[55] Most collective identities are institutionalized to a certain degree, and the prominent examples are ethnic[56]

[43] Bonny Norton, 'Language, Identity, and the Ownership of English' (1997) 31 *TESOL Quarterly* 419.

[44] John Scott and Gordon Marshall, 'Language', *Oxford Dictionary of Sociology* (3rd edn, OUP, 2009) 406.

[45] David Crystal, *How Language Works* (Penguin Books, 2006) 303.

[46] Scott and Marshall (n 44) 406–7; Crystal (n 45) 303. See also Woodward (n 1) 79; Rawi Abdelal, Yoshiko M Herrera, and Alastair Iain Johnston, 'Identity as a Variable' (2006) 4 *Perspectives on Politics* 699; Jenkins (n 2) 145.

[47] See, e.g., Francesca Polletta, '"It Was like a Fever ..." Narrative and Identity in Social Protest' (1998) 45 *Social Problems* 137; Klaus Eder, 'A Theory of Collective Identity' (2009) 12 *European Journal of Social Theory* 427; Woodward (n 1) 28.

[48] Woodward (n 1) 28.

[49] On the particular influence of 'ontological narratives' and identity, see Margaret R Somers, 'Narrative, Narrative Identity, and Social Action: Rethinking English Working-Class Formation' (1992) 16 *Social Science History* 591. See also Woodward (n 1) 29.

[50] Eder (n 47) 428–31.

[51] On the concept of collective memory in sociological literature and its interaction with identity as well as international law, see Chapter 3, Sections II (on collective memory and its interaction with social identity) and III (on interactions between collective memories and international law).

[52] Yael Zerubavel, *Recovered Roots* (University of Chicago Press, 1995) 6.

[53] Ross Poole, 'Memory, History and the Claims of the Past' (2008) 1 *Memory Studies* 149, 162.

[54] Jan Assmann, 'Collective Memory and Cultural Identity' (1995) 65 *New German Critique* 125, 130, see also 137.

[55] Jenkins (n 2) 47, 166.

[56] On the institutionalization of ethnic identities in Africa during the colonization period, see Mahmood Mamdani, 'Race and Ethnicity as Political Identities in the African Context' in Mahmood Mamdani and others (eds), *Keywords: Identity* (Other Press, 2004) 4–8.

or gender identities.[57] Organizations[58] (such as nation states) are occasionally involved in shaping social identities,[59] and particularly in collective identification. Organizational memberships are aspects of individual identity.[60] People join organizations, *inter alia*, to acquire a new identity or validate an existing one.[61] The organizational identity of individuals also depends on other members' recognition and may involve negotiations with the organization's 'gate-keepers'.[62] The acceptance of new members to the organization is frequently accompanied by certain 'rites of passage' that invest collective identities, thus 'making' the new members feel that they belong to the group.[63] Some organizations (like criminal courts) possess the capacity to authoritatively identify people (individually or collectively) as belonging to a certain group and thus may stigmatize their incumbents.[64]

Social identities are fluid and the identity formation process is never final; not even death freezes the picture.[65] Identity may well change at different stages of socialization,[66] due to a change in the relevant comparison (the 'Other'), or in response to the changing societal context.[67]

c. The consequences of social identity

'A change in identity is a stick poked into a pond; ripples spread in all directions'.[68] Identities often generate significant practical consequences. The impact of identity is particularly evident regarding people's perception, evaluation, and behaviour. It is noteworthy that the link between identity and behaviour is neither straightforward nor always predictable. Identity is likely to have a certain impact but does not determine everything.[69] 'Identity salience' is a major factor that affects the activation of identity in a particular situation.

Identity salience: As noted above, each person and each group have multiple identities and it is not certain which identity is more likely to influence individuals or groups in a particular context. Even in the absence of multiple identities, a similar question arises regarding the factors affecting the likelihood of activating

[57] Jenkins (n 2) 166.

[58] For a sociological definition of 'organizations', see, e.g., Jenkins (n 2) 147, 170.

[59] On the role of states in shaping identity, see Kwame Anthony Appiah, 'The State and the Shaping of Identity' (Tanner Lectures on Human Values, Cambridge, 30 April 2001), <http://tannerlectures.utah.edu/_documents/a-to-z/a/Appiah_02.pdf> accessed 20 March 2015.

[60] Michael A Hogg and Deborah J Terry, 'Social Identity Theory and Organizational Process' in Michael A Hogg and Deborah J Terry (eds), *Social Identity Process in Organizational Context* (Psychology Press, 2001) 1. See also Michael G Pratt, 'Social Identity Dynamics in Modern Organizations' in Michael A Hogg and Deborah J Terry (eds) *Social Identity Process in Organizational Context* (Psychology Press, 2001) 13.

[61] Jenkins (n 2) 183. [62] Ibid., 187. [63] Ibid., 177–8.

[64] Ibid., 188, 201, 47. On international labelling agencies, see Chapter 6, Section IV(a).

[65] Giddens and Sutton (n 3) 307; Hogg, Terry, and White (n 7) 255; Jenkins (n 2) 10, 18; Stets and Burke 'Identity, Theory and Social Identity Theory' (n 6) 233.

[66] Jenkins (n 2) 90. [67] Hogg, Terry, and White (n 7) 261, 265.

[68] Jenkins (n 2) 189. [69] Ibid., 6–8, 10.

a single identity. 'Identity salience' refers to the probability that an identity will be invoked and form the basis for action in diverse situations.[70] Identity salience includes quantitative and qualitative components. The quantitative element relates to the number of people or groups to whom a person or group is tied through identity. Generally, the more people or groups are tied to a particular identity, the more likely it is that a specific identity will be activated. The qualitative aspect relates to the relative strength of identity ties with other people or groups which are associated with the particular identity. Generally, stronger identity ties are more likely to lead to a more salient identity.[71]

Depersonalization: Once an identity is activated, the core process underlying many consequences relates to depersonalization (i.e., viewing people as a function of their respective group membership, rather than in terms of their individual characteristics or interpersonal relationships).[72] Depersonalization effectively brings self-perception and behaviour into line with the relevant in-group prototype, thus transforming the self from being a unique individual into a member of the group[73] and transforming individuality into group behaviour.[74] Once identity is activated, the main impact relates to people's perception (including self-perception), evaluations (including self-evaluation), and behaviour towards other people.[75]

Perception: At the cognitive level, the activation of social identity leads individuals identified with a group to accentuate perceived similarities between the self and other in-group members, and people tend to perceive *themselves* as more similar to other group members.[76] Individuals also tend to emphasize perceived similarities among the group members[77] and this stereotyped perception enhances the sense of group homogeneity.[78] On the other side of the identity boundary,

[70] Hogg, Terry, and White (n 7) 257; Stets and Burke, 'Identity, Theory and Social Identity Theory'(n 6) 229.

[71] Stets and Burke, 'Identity, Theory and Social Identity Theory' (n 6) 230; Hogg, Terry, and White (n 7) 258. On additional factors affecting identity salience (relating to the immediate social context and the individual's own interpretation of the context), see Stets and Burke, 'Identity, Theory and Social Identity Theory' (n 6) 230–1; Worchel (n 16) 55. For a more nuanced explanation of the influence of identity on behaviour (particularly its role in *facilitating* action), see Ann Swidler, *Talk of Love: How Culture Matters* (University of Chicago Press, 2001) 87.

[72] On the interpersonal—intergroup continuum, see Tajfel and Turner (n 29) 8–10. See also Hogg, Terry, and White (n 7) 261; Stets and Burke, 'Identity, Theory and Social Identity Theory' (n 6) 231–2; Turner and others (n 18) 455.

[73] The sociological approach to identity emphasizes that the transformation to group member is undertaken when one incorporates group membership (including the meaning and expectations associated with that role) into the self; Stets and Burke, 'Identity, Theory and Social Identity Theory' (n 6) 225.

[74] Dominic Abrams and Michael A Hogg, 'Social Identity and Self-Categorization' in John F Dovidio and others (eds), *Prejudice, Stereotyping And Discrimination* (Sage, 2010) 177, 187; Hogg, Terry, and White (n 7) 261.

[75] On the impact of identity on emotions, see Stets and Burke, 'A Sociological Approach to Self and Identity' (n 2) 21–3; Jenkins (n 2) 6–7.

[76] Stets and Burke, 'Identity, Theory and Social Identity Theory' (n 6) 225, 233; Hogg, Terry, and White (n 7) 260.

[77] Jenkins (n 2) 114–15; Hogg, Terry, and White (n 7) 260.

[78] Stets and Burke, 'Identity, Theory and Social Identity Theory' (n 6) 226; Hogg, Terry, and White (n 7) 260; Stephan and Stephan explain that one way of increasing self-esteem is to exaggerate

identification with a group tends to sharpen the perceived differences between group members and out-group members;[79] out-group members are more likely to be perceived as undifferentiated.[80]

Evaluation: Identification with a group tends to enhance self-evaluation which constitutes a motivation for social identification.[81] The enhanced self-worth that accompanies group identity does not regularly accompany unilateral identification with a group but it rather derives from the group's acceptance of the individual as a member.[82] People identified with a particular group tend to evaluate members of the group positively[83] and to evaluate people belonging to other groups negatively (the latter attitude tends to further enhance their own self-esteem as group members).[84] Perceived similarity within the group tends to promote greater liking, trust, and solidarity with in-group members.[85] Group identity is often accompanied by stereotyping, (i.e., attributing specific personal traits to people based on their membership in a social group).[86]

Behaviour: Identification with a group demands some loyalty and behavioural conformity, and group members orient their behaviour towards other members.[87] From a social psychological perspective, conformist behaviour is a natural corollary of the group members' similar perceptions.[88] As discussed above, the sociological analysis of identity emphasizes the important function of 'social role',[89] and 'enacting' the role according to the group's expectations is likely to enhance self-esteem. A perception of poor role performance may engender doubts about self-worth, and produce symptoms of distress.[90]

between-group differences and minimize within-group differences on positively evaluated dimensions. Stephan and Stephan (n 13) 100.

79 Jenkins (n 2) 154; Hogg, Terry, and White (n 7) 260. See also Stets and Burke, 'Identity, Theory and Social Identity Theory' (n 6) 225.

80 Stephan and Stephan (n 13) 94.

81 Stets and Burke, 'Identity, Theory and Social Identity Theory' (n 6) 225, 232; Hogg, Terry, and White (n 7) 260; Barbara-Ann Mullin and Michael A Hogg, 'Motivations for Group Membership: The Role of Subjective Importance and Uncertainty Reduction' (1999) 21 *Basic and Applied Social Psychology* 91, 91–2; Henri Tajfel, *Human Groups and Social categories: Studies in Social Psychology* (CUP, 1981) 254.

82 Stets and Burke, 'Identity, Theory and Social Identity Theory' (n 6) 233.

83 Ibid., 226; Tajfel and Turner (n 29) 13.

84 Stets and Burke, 'Identity, Theory and Social Identity Theory' (n 6) 232. On self-esteem and identity, see also Stets and Burke, 'A Sociological Approach to Self and Identity' (n 2) 6–7.

85 Abrams and Hogg (n 74) 182. The general tendency of in-group members to favour members of their own group over other groups has some exceptions (prominently regarding groups that are low in status, power and prestige). Charles Stangor and John T Jost, 'Commentary: Individual, Group and System Levels of Analysis and their Relevance to Stereotyping and Intergroup Relations' in Russell Spears and others (eds), *Social Psychology of Stereotyping and Group Life* (Blackwell, 1997) 346.

86 Stephen Worchel and Hank Rothgerber, 'Changing the Stereotype of the Stereotype' in Russell Spears and others (eds), *The Social Psychology of Stereotyping and Group Life* (Blackwell, 1997) 72, 74–8. See also Section IV(c)(ii) below.

87 See, e.g., Jenkins (n 2) 157–8, 152.

88 Stets and Burke, 'Identity, Theory and Social Identity Theory' (n 6) 227.

89 Giddens and Sutton (n 3) 307–8; Stets and Burke, 'Identity, Theory and Social Identity Theory' (n 6) 227.

90 Hogg, Terry, and White (n 7) 257–8.

From a legal perspective, the most undesirable impacts of social identity relate to behaviour towards non-members. Identification with a group is very often accompanied by the tendency to provide in-group members better treatment ('favouritism') and discriminatory treatment towards out-group members.[91] Tajfel and Turner, after surveying empirical studies, conclude:

> All this evidence implies that in-group bias is a remarkably omnipresent feature of inter-group relations ... results of relevant studies ... all showing that the mere perception of belonging to two distinct groups—that is, social categorization per se—is sufficient to trigger inter-group discrimination favouring the in-group. In other words, the mere awareness of the presence of an out-group is sufficient to provoke inter-group competitive or discriminatory responses on the part of the in-group.[92]

Furthermore, empirical evidence suggests that undertaking a behaviour that creates a difference between two groups is more important to a group's members than following an efficient economic strategy which increases the gains for in-group members.[93]

Favouritism and discriminatory treatment towards out-group members enhance group identification and collective self-esteem of in-group members.[94] Perceived discrimination, however, also tends to increase group identification among members of the discriminated group.[95] Group identification often leads to competitive or hostile behaviour towards out-group members but it depends on various factors,[96] such as subjective beliefs about the nature of relations with the out-group.[97]

Thus, social identity affects people's perceptions and attitudes towards others, as well as their own behaviour. In addition to sociological and social psychological literature, social identity analysis of international law also draws on the social constructivist approach in international relations literature.

[91] Hogg, Terry, and White (n 7) 260; Stets and Burke, 'Identity, Theory and Social Identity Theory' (n 6) 232; Jenkins (n 2) 8; Stephan and Stephan (n 13) 92–3. On certain factors that increase and decrease the likelihood of inter-group discrimination, see Richard Y Bourhis, John C Turner, and André Gagnon, 'Interdependence, Social Identity and Discrimination' in Russell Spears and others (eds), *The Social Psychology of Stereotyping and Group Life* (Blackwell, 1997) 273, 276.

[92] Tajfel and Turner (n 29) 13.

[93] Tajfel and Turner (n 29) 14; Stephan and Stephan (n 13) 92–3.

[94] Tajfel and Turner (n 29) 19; Stets and Burke, 'Identity, Theory and Social Identity Theory' (n 6) 232; Hogg, Terry, and White (n 7) 260. On additional group motivations for stereotyping, prejudice and discrimination, see Stangor and Jost (n 85) 338–52. On additional motives directing inter-group behaviour, see Stephan and Stephan (n 13) 101.

[95] Jolanda Jetten and others, 'Rebels with a Cause: Group Identification as a Response to Perceived Discrimination from the Mainstream' (2001) 27 *Personality and Social Psychology Bulletin* 1204.

[96] Additional factors affecting inter-group discrimination include the degree to which individuals identified with the group, the salience of the relevant categorization, the degree to which the groups are comparable, the in-group relative status and the perceived status differences between the groups. Bourhis, Turner and Gagnon (n 91) 273, 276.

[97] Hogg, Terry, and White note that these beliefs are not necessarily accurate reflections of reality because they can be, and often are, ideological constructs. Hogg, Terry, and White (n 7) 260. On the interactions between social identity and collective action, see also Abrams and Hogg (n 74) 179, 187.

III. Identity in International Relations

Social identity (and particularly collective identity) is a core concept of the social constructivist approach in contemporary international relations literature;[98] sociological scholarship has significantly influenced the development of this perspective on international politics.[99] According to the constructivist approach, the international system and states are not exogenously given and do not exist independently of the thoughts and ideas of the people involved.[100] International politics and related concepts are human creations and exist as inter-subjective beliefs that are widely shared among people.[101] Thus the social world is a world of human conscious that includes language, signals, and understanding among human beings, and especially groups such as states.[102]

Identity (and particularly collective identity) is one of the key concepts in the constructivist scholarship,[103] and Hopf states that 'identities are the most proximate causes of choices, preferences, and action.'[104] Certain constructivist writings on identity draw on sociological (and particularly on symbolic-interactionist) literature as well as social psychological literature.[105] States' identities are constructed by their interaction with other international actors, domestic societies, and international social structures.[106] The role of collective identities (including

[98] On the social constructivist approach in international relations literature, see Chapter 1, Section IV.

[99] On the links between the constructivist approach and sociology (and particularly the symbolic-interactionist approach) see, e.g., Alexander Wendt, 'Collective Identity Formation and the International State' (1994) 88 *American Political Science Review* 385, 386, 394. See also Jutta Brunnee and Stephen J Toope, 'International Law and Constructivism: Elements of an International Law Theory of International Law' (2000) 20 *Columbia Journal of Transnational Law* 27.

[100] Wendt, 'Collective Identity Formation' (n 99) 386; Peter J Katzenstein, 'Introduction: Alternative Perspectives on National Security' in Peter J Katzenstein (ed), *The Culture of National Security: Norms and Identity in World Politics* (Columbia University Press, 1996) 1, 22; Bahar Rumelili, 'Constructing Identity and Relating to Difference: Understanding the EUs' (2004) 30 *Review of International Studies* 27, 30–1; Robert Jackson and Georg Sørensen, *Introduction to International Relations: Theories and Approaches* (4th edn, OUP, 2010) 164, 172.

[101] Ibid., 162, 166. [102] See, e.g., ibid., 165.

[103] See, e.g., Wendt, 'Collective Identity Formation' (n 99) 385; James D Fearon, 'What is Identity (As We Now Use the Word)?' (1999) 3 <http://web.stanford.edu/group/fearon-research/cgi-bin/wordpress/wp-content/uploads/2013/10/What-is-Identity-as-we-now-use-the-word-.pdf> accessed 21 March 2015; Thomas Risse, *A Community of Europeans? Transnational Identities and Public Spheres* (Cornell University Press, 2010) 20.

[104] Ted Hopf, 'The Promise of Constructivism in International Relations Theory' (1998) 23 *International Security* 171, 174.

[105] See, e.g., Wendt, 'Collective Identity Formation' (n 99) 386, 394; Jackson and Sørensen (n 100) 163; Hopf (n 104) 175; Rumelili (n 100) 30–1.

[106] Wendt, 'Collective Identity Formation' (n 99) 387; Peter J Katzenstein, Ronald L Lepperson, and Alexander Wendt, 'Norms, Identity, and Culture in National Security' in Peter J Katzenstein (ed), *The Culture of National Security: Norms and Identities in World Politics* (Columbia University Press, 1996) 11, 35–6. On variations in the constructivist literature regarding emphasis on domestic or international factors see, e.g., Jackson and Sørensen (n 100) 170–2 and the references therein; Emanuel Adler, 'Cognitive Evolution: A Dynamic Approach for the Study of International Relations and their Progress' in Emanuel Adler and Beverly Crawford (eds), *Progress in Postwar International*

corporate identities like states)[107] is particularly underlined in that literature.[108] Wendt argues that collective identities (bilateral, regional, or global) vary by issue, time, and place.[109] Thus, a state may have multiple identities, such as 'sovereign', 'leader of the free world' or 'imperial power'.[110]

The social constructivist perspective seeks to clarify the links between state interests, norms, and identity. Constructivists argue that identity formation occurs before, or at least concurrently with, interest formation.[111] Collective identity strongly implies a particular set of interests. Hopf presents the example *of the identity of a 'great power' which implies specific interests differing from those implied by the identity of a 'European Union member'*.[112] From this perspective, interests are dependent on identities,[113] and Wendt states: '[h]ow a state satisfies its corporate interests depends on how it defines the self in relation to the other, which is a function of social identities at both domestic and systemic levels of analysis.'[114] Consequently, changes in state identity also affect national security interests and policies of states,[115] and call for taking particular actions.[116]

Norms either affect the formation of identities in the first place (generating expectations of new particular identities in a given context) or prescribe behaviours for already constituted identities (generating expectations about how a particular identity will influence behaviour in varying circumstances).[117] The link between norms and identity is particularly strong with regard to 'constitutive norms' that define group membership.[118] The above links between identity and norms indicate that identities and the norms associated with them ensure a

Relations (Columbia University Press, 1991) 43, 257; John Ruggie, *Constructing the World Polity* (Routledge, 1998) 11–14; Richard Steinberg and Jonathan Zasloff, 'Power and International Law' (2006) 100 *AJIL* 64, 82–5.

107 Wendt defines corporate identity as the intrinsic, self-organizing qualities that constitute actor individuality. For organizations, it means their constituent individuals, physical resources, and the shared beliefs and institutions in virtue of which individuals function as a 'we'. Wendt, 'Collective Identity Formation' (n 99) 386.

108 See, e.g., Wendt, 'Collective Identity Formation' (n 99) 386; Fearon (n 103) 33.

109 Wendt, 'Collective Identity Formation' (n 99) 390.

110 Alexander Wendt, 'Anarchy is What States Make of It' (1992) 46 *International Organization* 391, 398.

111 Brunne and Toope (n 99) 4; Christian Reus-Smit, *The Moral Purpose of the State* (Princeton University Press, 1999) 29; Ian Hurd, 'Constructivism' in Christian Reus-Smit (ed), *The Oxford Handbook of International Relations* (OUP, 2008) 298, 303.

112 Hopf (n 104) 176.

113 Wendt, 'Collective Identity Formation' (n 99) 386, 390; Hopf (n 104) 176.

114 Wendt, 'Collective Identity Formation' (n 99) 386.

115 Lepperson, Wendt, and Katzenstein (n 106) 52.

116 Wendt, 'Collective Identity Formation' (n 99) at 387. See also Martha Finnemore, 'Constructing Norms of Humanitarian Intervention' in Peter J. Katzenstein (ed), *The Culture of National Security: Norms and Identity in World Politics* (Columbia University Press 1996) 153, 159, 169, 184.

117 Lepperson, Wendt, and Katzenstein (n 106) 54. See also Jackson and Sørensen (n 100) 169; Audie Klotz, *Norms in International Relations: The Struggle Against Apartheid* (Cornell University Press, 1995) 56, 168–71; Audie Klotz, 'Norms Reconstituting Interests: Global Racial Equality and U.S. Sanctions Against South Africa' (1995) 49 *International Organization* 451, 461–2, 472.

118 Abdelal, Herrera, and Johnston (n 46) 697–8. For Reus-Smit, state societies have been based on fundamental moral purposes derived from their identity. Reus-Smit (n 111) 156.

minimal level of predictability. Thus, durable expectations between international actors require inter-subjective identities that are sufficiently stable to ensure a predictable pattern of behaviour in the international system.[119]

Social identity analysis of international law is often associated with the constructivist approach in international relations literature. As elaborated below, collective identity often facilitates, motivates, and constrains activities of collective actors in the international legal system.

IV. Social Identity and International Law

a. Identity matters

Numerous international legal rules and concepts are infused with social identity. International law often institutionalizes (to various degrees) identities that are encoded into diverse international instruments. Thus, international legal rules and concepts often reflect and affect identities of major collective groups in the international community, including states, regional groups (such as the MERCOSUR[120] or the EU)[121] or semi-institutionalized groups (such as the G-20).[122]

Exploring international law from a social identity perspective enables an understanding of significant processes involved in the evolution of international law and its implementation in reality. As elaborated below, social identity analysis may not only shed light on past and present trends in international law, but also bear significant implications for the *interpretation* of existing legal provisions, as well as offering some suggestions regarding practical measures to enhance the effectiveness of certain international legal mechanisms.

States and other international groups have multiple identities and often present different identities in various subsets of the international system (in regional and global arenas or in different sectors of international law). Thus, a state may be identified with its role as a 'leader' in a particular sector of international law while not purporting to lead in other spheres. These different identities affect the behaviour of states in negotiations leading to international treaties (such as climate change agreements)[123] or their responses to violation of human rights treaties.[124]

[119] Hopf (n 104) 174–5.

[120] See, e.g., Andrea Oelsner, 'The Institutional Identity of Regional Organizations, or Mercosur's Identity Crisis' (2013) 57 *International Studies Quarterly* 115.

[121] On the EU's identity, see Section IV(b) below.

[122] See, e.g., John J Kirton, *G20 Governance for a Globalized World* (Ashgate, 2013) 34.

[123] On the leadership identities of the USA and the EU in the climate change negotiations (and their impact on the negotiation process), see Jutta Brunnée, 'Europe, The United States, and the Global Climate Regime: All Together Now?' (2008) 24(1) *Journal of Land Use and Environmental Law* 1, 28–30. See also Daniela Sicurelli, *The European Union's Africa Policies* (Ashgate, 2010) 135. On the identities of the EU and the USA after the Cold War, see Sonia Lucarellia, 'Values, Identity and Ideational Shocks in the Transatlantic Rift' (2006) 9 *Journal of International Relations and Development* 304.

[124] See Section IV(b) below.

The identity of international actors is frequently influenced by physical factors, such as the geographical region, but this is not necessarily the crucial factor. Some states located in Asia or Oceania may, for instance, belong to an international identity group outside their geographical region.[125] National identities often relate to the ethnic or religious composition of the state's population, its historical roots (e.g., colonial ties), and other socio-cultural traits. Collective identities are occasionally linked to international networks in which states and international institutions are embedded (formal regional institutions or various informal groups like the G-20).[126] As elaborated below, collective identities are often involved in the formation of international institutions, frequently relating to the national identity of their members or other international institutions with which they are affiliated.[127]

Weapons of mass destruction: The production and use of WMD are occasionally related to the collective identity of international actors. The impact of national identity is notable on the employment of chemical weapons. Price and Tannenwald emphasize the link between the legal prohibition against using chemical weapons and the identity of a 'civilized nation'. Their study reveals that the origins of the chemical weapons 'taboo' were implicated in exclusionary practices that distinguished between civilized and uncivilized areas of the globe.[128] The breaches of this legal prohibition and their justification (e.g., by Italy against Ethiopia in 1935–6,[129] and by Iraq in 1998) reflect the understanding that modern warfare between industrialized states is qualitatively different from war involving an 'uncivilized nation'.[130] They explain that '[t]he symbolic connection of CW [chemical weapons] with standards of civilized conduct has made it more difficult for advanced nations to employ these weapons against each other'.[131] Thus, compliance with the legal prohibition to employ chemical weapons is occasionally tied to the identity of 'civilized nation'.

[125] Thus, e.g., regarding the UN electoral ('regional') groups, certain non-Western European countries like Greece, Australia, New Zealand, Canada, and Israel are members of the *Western European and Others Group*. On the UN regional groups and the element of identification with a group of states, see, Sam Daws, 'The Origins and Development of UN Electoral Groups' in Ramesh Thakur (ed), *What is Equitable Geographic Representation in the 21st Century?* (United Nations University, 1999) 11, 15. On the factor of image in New Zealand's policy regarding UN groups, see Daws, at 16. On the historic evolution of the Western European and Others group and its links with European identity, see Norbert Gotz, 'Western Europeans and Others: the making of Europe at the United Nations' (2008) 33 *Alternatives: Global, Local, Political* 366, 372–3.

[126] See, e.g., Kirton (n 122) 34.

[127] See Section IV(b) below.

[128] Richard Price and Nina Tannenwald, 'Norms and Deterrence: The Nuclear and Chemical Weapons Taboos' in Peter Katzenstein (ed), *The Culture of National Security: Norms and Identity in World Politics* (Columbia University Press, 1996) 114, 130–1.

[129] Italy contended that the 'Ethiopians have repeatedly shown she [*sic!*] is not worthy of the rank of a civilized nation'; Price and Tannenwald (n 128) 132. In a letter to the League of Nations, Italy accused Ethiopian forces of violating several articles of the 1925 Geneva Protocol and 'savage' aggression. Lina Grip and John Hart, 'The Use of Chemical Weapons in the 1935–36 Italo-Ethiopian War' (October 2009) SIPRI Arms Control and Non-proliferation Programme 6 <http://www.sipri.org/research/disarmament/chemical/publications/ethiopiapaper> accessed 21 March 2015. See also Richard M Price, *The Chemical Weapons Taboo* (Cornell University Press, 1997) 108.

[130] In 1998, the Iraqi foreign minister defended the use of chemical weapon and argued: 'There are different views on this matter from different angles. You are living on a civilized continent.' Price and Tannenwald (n 128) 132.

[131] Ibid., 131.

Collective identities are occasionally involved in the production of nuclear weapons. In a well-known article published in *International Security*, Sagan presents three states' motivations for developing nuclear weapons: increasing national security against foreign threats; advancing domestic and bureaucratic interests; and providing an important normative symbol of a state's modernity and identity.[132] Regarding the link between this powerful weapon and national identity,[133] Sagan presents some nuclear decisions as serving important symbolic functions—shaping and reflecting a state's identity.[134] The significant link between decisions to build nuclear weapons and national identity[135] was evident, for example,[136] in France's development of nuclear weapons in the 1950s[137] and its reluctance to stop nuclear testing in the mid-1990s.[138] The influence of national identity on nuclear weapon's policy is explicit in Japan's policy after World War II. As Mochizuki explains, Japan's decision not to build nuclear weapons relates not only to 'pragmatic pacifism' but also to the central motive relating to its national identity as a 'peace state'.[139]

The following sections elaborate on the impact of the EU's collective identity on promoting the enforcement of human rights treaties, as well as the employment of theoretical tools and empirical evidence drawn from social identity literature as an interpretative instrument to clarify the content of certain international legal rules.

b. International institutions' identity and the enforcement of human rights treaties by EU trade measures

International institutions' identity: The formation and activities of international institutions often reflect collective identities. Membership in these organizations often represents various identity ties, such as regional (e.g., Organization for American States that also represent certain ideological traits);[140] religious (e.g.,

[132] Scott D Sagan, 'Why Do States Build Nuclear Weapons? Three Models in Search of a Bomb' (1996) 21 *International Security* 54, 54–5. On these factors, see also Mike M Mochizuki, 'Japan Tests the Nuclear Taboo' (2007) 14 *Non-proliferation Review* 306.

[133] On the importance of national identity and prestige for developing nuclear weapons, see also Barry O'Neill, 'Nuclear Weapons and National Prestige' (February 2006) Cowles Foundation Discussion Paper No. 1560 <http://ssrn.com/abstract=887333> accessed 21 March 2015.

[134] Sagan (n 132) 73.

[135] For additional examples, see O'Neill (n 133) 4. On the link between nuclear policy and national identity, see also Maria Rost Rublee, *Non-Proliferation Norms: Why States Choose Nuclear Restraint?* (University of Georgia Press, 2009) 13–15.

[136] With regard to Pakistan, see Feroz Hassan Khan, *Eating Grass: The Making of the Pakistani Bomb* (Stanford University Press, 2012) 9–11. See also 7.

[137] On the link between the development of nuclear weapons by France during the 1950s and national identity, see, e.g., Jacques EC Hymans, *The Psychology of Nuclear Proliferation: Identity, Emotions, and Foreign Policy* (CUP, 2006) 85. See also Gabrielle Hecht, *The Radiance of France: Nuclear Power and National Identity After World War II* (MIT Press, 2009) 28, 56, 89.

[138] Sagan (n 132) 79–80.

[139] Mochizuki (n 132) 306–7. See also Satake Tomohiko, 'Japan's Nuclear Policy: Between Non-Nuclear Identity and US Extended Deterrence' (May 2009) Austral Policy Forum, 3–4 <http://nautilus.org/wp-content/uploads/2009/12/Tomohiko-PDF.pdf> accessed 21 March 2015.

[140] See, e.g., the website of the Organization of American States, 'Who We are', <http://www.oas.org/en/about/who_we_are.asp> accessed 21 March 2015.

Organization for the Islamic Conference);[141] historical (e.g., the Commonwealth of Nations);[142] or ideological (e.g., NATO).[143]

The identity of an international institution[144] regularly co-exists with (and is often related to) its members' national identities, as well as with the identities of other international institutions with whom it is affiliated. The latter identity link is prominent concerning the ties between Islamic Conference, the Arab League, and the African Union,[145] or between the EU and the Council of Europe.[146]

Like other identity groups, international institutions often construct common symbols, including flags, anthems, a special memorial day (e.g. to celebrate the establishment of the organization),[147] and, occasionally, collective narratives as well.[148] The identities of international organizations may be discerned from their constituent documents,[149] and particularly provisions regarding the admission of new members[150] and exclusion/suspension of existing members[151] which highlight the 'boundaries' between them and other international groups.[152]

[141] Said Mahmoudi, 'Organization of the Islamic Conference', in R Wolfrum (ed), *Max Planck Encyclopedia of Public International Law* (OUP, 2009) <http://opil.ouplaw.com/home/EPIL> accessed 30 May 2015.

[142] On the Commonwealth of Nations and its links to the British Empire, see Laurie Fransman, 'Commonwealth Subjects and Nationality Rules', in R Wolfrum (ed), Max Planck Encyclopedia of Public International Law (OUP, 2009) <http://opil.ouplaw.com/home/EPIL>.

[143] On the collective identity and the ideology of NATO, see, e.g., Christopher Hemmer and Peter J Katzenstein, 'Why is There No NATO in Asia? Collective Identity, Regionalism, and the Origins of Multilateralism' (2002) 56 *International Organization* 575, 587–8.

[144] On the stages of development of international organizations' identity in light of developmental psychological literature, see Sungjoon Cho, 'An International Organization's Identity Crisis' (2014) 34 *Northwestern Journal of International Law and Business* 359, 373–83.

[145] See, e.g., Mahmoudi (n 141) para 5.

[146] The Council of Europe quotes Juncker in its official website: 'the Council of Europe and the European Union were products of the same idea, the same spirit and the same ambition. They mobilised the energy and commitment of the same founding fathers of Europe'. *The Council of Europe's Relations with the European Union* <http://www.coe.int/t/der/eu_EN.asp> accessed 21 March 2015.

[147] See, e.g., on the Pan American Day and the Organization of American States, Columbus Memorial Library, Pan-American Day April 14<http://www.oas.org/columbus/PanAmericanDay.asp> accessed 21 March 2015. On the ASEAN Day, see Charter of the Association of Southeast Nations (adopted 20 November 2007, entered into force 15 December 2008) 2624 UNTS 223 (ASEAN Charter) Art 39.

[148] On the EU's 'narratives of projection' (and specifically regarding the WTO), see the insightful essay by Kalypos Nicolaidis and Robert Howse, 'This is my EUtopia ... : Narrative as Power' (2002) 40 *Journal of Common Market Studies* 767. See also, Organization of American States 'Our History' <http://www.oas.org/en/about/our_history.asp> accessed 21 March 2015.

[149] Mahmoudi notes that the Charter of the 1972 Charter of the Organization of the Islamic Conference was inspired by the Charter of the Arab League and the Charter of the Organization of African Union. See, e.g., Mahmoudi (n 141) para 5.

[150] See, e.g., Art 3 of the Statute of the Council of Europe (signed 5 May 1949, entered into force 3 August 1949) 87 UNTS 103 Art 3. On the EU's admission requirements regarding human rights protection, see Section IV(b) below.

[151] See, e.g., the 1992 OAS Protocol of Washington (which amended the OAS Charter by adding a new Art 9) stipulating the suspension of any member whose democratically elected government has been overthrown by force. On this amendment and the practice of OAS in that regard, see Konstantinos D Magliveras, *Exclusion from Participation in International Organisations* (Kluwer, 1999) 165, 171–4.

[152] On international organizations' common political identity and possible expulsion, see Henry G Schermers and Niels M Blokker, *International Institutional Law* (5th edn, Martinus Nijhoff Publishers, 2011) 113.

Similarly, the practice of international institutions in other spheres (such as sanctions imposed on non-members or decisions adopted by their judicial organs), also contribute to the formation or change of their identity. Occasionally, the basic instruments of international institutions expressly aim to construct common identity.[153] Thus, for example, the Constitutive Treaty of the Union of South American Nations affirms the member's 'determination to build a South American identity'.[154]

States occasionally join international institutions to reaffirm their identity, and many states are interested in admission to an organization like the OECD that projects an image of a 'prestigious club'[155] or the 'rich man's club.'[156] International institutions also affect the international identity of states (including *non*-members) by classifying them according to level of 'development' (e.g. 'least developed states'[157] or 'developed states')[158] or the quality of their governance.[159] Decisions by international organizations (including their tribunals) which label[160]

[153] Art 35 of the Charter of the Association of Southeast Asian Nations (ASEAN) provides as follow: 'ASEAN Identity: ASEAN shall promote its common ASEAN identity and a sense of belonging among its peoples in order to achieve its shared destiny, goals and values'. See also ASEAN Charter (n 147) Art 1(14). See also Michael E Jones, 'Forging an ASEAN Identity: The Challenge to Construct a Shared Destiny' (2004) 26 *Contemporary Southeast Asia* 140. See also on the Organization of the Islamic Conference, Mahmoudi (n 141) para 5.

[154] Third recital to the Preamble of the South American Union of Nations Constitutive Treaty (signed 23 May 2008, entered into force 11 March 2011) 2742 UNTS, at the Preamble <http://treaties.un.org/doc/Publication/UNTS/No%20Volume/48456/Part/I-48456-08000002802d4c72.pdf> accessed 22 March 2015.

[155] See, e.g., regarding South Korean membership in the OECD, Dong Chon Suh, 'Trade and Financial Liberalization in South Asia' in Daljit Singh and Reza Y Siregar (eds), *ASEAN and Korea* (Institute for Southeast Asian Studies, Singapore 1997) 19, 68. See regarding Slovenia's membership <http://www.svrez.gov.si/en/areas_of_work/slovenia_member_of_the_oecd/organisation_for_economic_co_operation_and_development_oecd/> accessed 22 March 2015. And see regarding Israel's membership, 'Israel to join prestigious OECD economic club' *France 24—International News* (27 May 2010) <http://www.france24.com/en/20100527-israel-join-prestigious-oecd-economic-club-netanyahu-sarkozy-paris/> accessed 22 March 2015.

[156] On the OECD as the 'rich man club', see, e.g., Thalif Deen, 'Chile to Join the "Rich Man's Club"' *Inter Press Service* (21 December 2009) <http://ipsnews.net/news.asp?idnews=49777> accessed 22 March 2015; '50 Years of the OECD: An Exclusive Club with Global Goals' *Deutsche Welle* (30 September 2011) <http://www.dw-world.de/dw/article/0,,15099080,00.html> accessed 22 March 2015.

[157] See UN-OHRLLS, 'The Criteria for Identification and Graduation of the LDCs' <http://www.un.org/special-rep/ohrlls/ldc/ldc%20criteria.htm> accessed 22 March 2015.

[158] On the classification of states accordance to their level of economic development, see, e.g., the Human Development Index (HDI) developed by the UN Development Programme (UNDP) <http://hdr.undp.org/en/statistics/> accessed 24 March 2015; The World Bank, Country and Lending Groups <http://data.worldbank.org/about/country-classifications> accessed 24 March 2015.

[159] See World Bank, *Worldwide Governance Indicators* (WGI) <http://info.worldbank.org/governance/wgi/index.asp> accessed 24 March 2015; Daniel Kaufmann, Aart Kraay and Massimo Mastruzzi, 'The Worldwide Governance Indicators: Methodology and Analytical Issues' (2010) Policy Research Working Paper 5430, 4 <http://elibrary.worldbank.org/doi/pdf/10.1596/1813-9450-5430> accessed 24 March 2015.

[160] On international labelling and international institutions, see also Chapter 6, Section IV(a).

a particular state 'aggressive'[161] or impose sanctions on another, may contribute to the preservation or modification of state identity (e.g. as a 'pariah state').

EU identity and human rights protection: EU institutions are involved in the formation of European identity[162] and they have constructed (occasionally together with the Council of Europe) various symbols of collective identity.[163] As discussed above, symbols and rituals are often part of the development and maintenance of group identity. Symbols and community rituals often generate or reinforce a sense of shared belonging.[164] Thus, for example, in 1983 the EU parliament adopted the European flag (previously adopted by the Council of Europe);[165] the EU leaders officially adopted the European anthem in 1985 (formerly adopted by the Council of Europe),[166] and the EU institutions annually celebrate Europe Day (9 May) in which the collective memory of the 1950 Schuman declaration and the ensuing moral lessons are reinforced.[167] As noted below, the EU members also published a formal decision on the European Identity in 1973.

Norms often constitute a significant element of collective identity and this is particularly remarkable with regard to 'constitutive norms' that define group membership.[168] International human rights norms have a particular status in that regard and they occasionally play a significant role in defining the identity of democratic and liberal states.[169] The EU bodies have repeatedly stated that human rights protection constitutes a constitutive norm.[170] Thus, for example, Article 2 of the Treaty on European Union (TEU) solemnly states:

161 See the UN Charter Art 39.

162 For a survey of political science literature on European identity and the European Union, see Erik Jones, 'Identity and Solidarity' in Erik Jones, Anand Menon, and Stephen Weatherill (eds), *The Oxford Handbook of the European Union* (OUP, 2012) 690. See also Jeffrey Checkel and Peter Katzenstein, *European Identity* (CUP, 2009) 1.

163 On the impacts of symbols on European identity, see Michael Bruter, 'Winning Hearts and Minds for Europe: The Impact of News and Symbols on Civic and Cultural European Identity' (2003) 36 *Comparative Political Studies* 1148, 1165–7.

164 See Section II above.

165 European Union, *The European Flag*, <http://europa.eu/about-eu/basic-information/symbols/flag/index_en.htm> accessed 24 March 2015.

166 European Union, *The European Anthem*, <http://europa.eu/about-eu/basic-information/symbols/anthem/index_en.htm> accessed 24 March 2015.

167 European Union, *Europe Day—EU Open Doors*, <http://europa.eu/about-eu/basic-information/symbols/europe-day/index_en.htm#why_europe_day> accessed 24 March 2015; European Union, *The Schuman Declaration—9 May 1950*, <http://europa.eu/about-eu/basic-information/symbols/europe-day/schuman-declaration/> accessed 24 March 2015. On the commemorative rituals that have developed since 1957 to mark the anniversaries of signing of the Rome Treaty, see Hannes Hansen-Magnusson and Jenny Wustenberg, 'Forging European Memory: The Treaties of Rome as a Common Tradition in the Making?' (European Union Studies Association Conference, Boston, 3–5 March 2011).

168 On the role of 'constituent norms' in the formation of international identity, see Section III above.

169 See, e.g., Thomas Risse and Kathryn Sikkink, 'The Socialization of International Human Rights Norms into Domestic Practices: Introduction' in Thomas Risse, Stephen C Ropp, and Kathryn Sikkink (eds), *The Power of Human Rights* (CUP, 1999) 1, 12.

170 On human rights as 'core values' of the EU, see also European Union, *The EU and Human Rights*, <http://eeas.europa.eu/human_rights/index_en.htm> accessed 24 March 2015.

The Union is founded on the values of respect for human dignity, freedom, democracy, equality, the rule of law and respect for human rights, including the rights of persons belonging to minorities.[171]

The central role of human rights protection in the *EU identity*[172] was explicitly emphasized by the EU's bodies. Thus, for example,[173] the EU Commission states: 'the European Union has gradually come to define itself in terms of the promotion of those [human] rights and democratic freedoms.'[174] And in the 'Document on The European Identity' (1973), the EU foreign ministers clarified that:

Sharing as they do the same attitudes to life, ... they are determined to defend the principles of representative democracy, of the rule of law, of social justice—which is the ultimate goal of economic progress—and of *respect for human rights. All of these are fundamental elements of the European Identity.*[175]

The EU's institutions are legally committed to comply with fundamental human rights[176] and may suspend certain membership rights of members which seriously and persistently breach these norms.[177] As noted above, identities of international institutions may particularly be discerned from provisions regarding the admission of new members which highlight the boundaries between them and other international groups. Any European country which wishes to become a member of the EU must satisfy the existing members and the EU's institutions

[171] The Consolidated Versions of the Treaty on European Union and the Treaty on the Functioning of the European Union [2010] OJ C 83/1 (hereinafter 'European Union Treaty'). And the Preamble to the Charter of Fundamental Rights of the European Union underlines that: 'The peoples of Europe, ... are resolved to share a peaceful future based on common values. Conscious of its spiritual and moral heritage, the Union is founded on the indivisible, universal values of human dignity, freedom, equality and solidarity; it is based on the principles of democracy and the rule of law.' Charter of Fundamental Rights of the European Union [2010] OJ C 83/2.

[172] On the central role of human rights in the EU's identity, see also Marise Cremona, 'Values in the EU Foreign Policy' in Malcolm Evans and Panos Koutrakos (eds), *Beyond the Established Legal Orders: Policy Interconnections between the EU and the Rest of the World* (Hart, 2011) 307. See also Ian Manners, 'The Constitutive Nature of Values, Images, and Principles in the European Union' in Sonia Lucarelli and Ian Manners (eds), *Values and Principles in European Union Foreign Policy* (Routledge, 2006) 19, 31–4, 38–41.

[173] See also, Commission, 'The European Union and the External Dimension of Human Rights Policy: From Rome to Maastricht and Beyond' (Communication) COM (1995) 567 final, 5.

[174] Ibid., para. 12. See also Marise Cremona, 'Values in the EU Constitution: the External Dimension, Centre on Democracy, Development, and the Rule of Law' (November 2004) 26 Stanford Institute for International Studies 2.

[175] Declaration on The European Identity published by the Nine Foreign Ministers on 14 December 1973, Copenhagen [emphasis added] <http://www.cvce.eu/content/publication/1999/1/1/02798dc9-9c69-4b7d-b2c9-f03a8db7da32/publishable_en.pdf> accessed 24 March 2015.

[176] See Art 3(1) TEU (n 171); EU Charter of Fundamental Rights (n 171) Art 51.

[177] Art 7 TEU (n 171). See also Manfred Nowak, 'Human Rights 'Conditionality' in Relation to Entry to, and Full Participation in, the EU' in Philip Alston (ed), *The EU and Human Rights* (OUP, 1999) 687, 690. On the link between certain sanctions operated by the EU members against another member and the EU identity, see Stefan Seidendorf, 'Defining Europe Against its Past?—Memory Politics and the Sanctions Against Austria in France and Germany' (2005) 6 *German Law Journal* 439, 443 et seq.

that it respects human rights and is committed to applying them.[178] In addition, accession to the European Convention on Human Rights (ECHR) constitutes a de facto condition for EU membership[179] and the EU shall accede to the Convention.[180]

The EU's human rights policies are particularly pronounced in its external relations with other international actors. The EU often presents itself as a human rights promoter in the international arena.[181] This external feature of the EU's identity arises, for example, from Articles 3(5)[182] and 21(1)[183] of the TEU,[184] as well as diverse public documents of the EU bodies. Thus, for instance,[185] the EU Council stated in a 'strategic' document (2012):

> The European Union is founded on a shared determination to promote peace and stability and *to build a world founded on respect for human rights*, democracy and the rule of law. *These principles underpin all aspects of the internal and external policies of the European Union* ... The EU will continue to throw its full weight behind advocates of liberty, democracy and human rights the world.... *The EU will speak out against any attempt to undermine respect for universality of human rights.*[186]

[178] Art 49 TEU (n 171); European Council in Copenhagen: Conclusions of the Presidency (22 June 1993) DOC/93/3 ('Copenhagen Criteria') Art 7(A)(iii). On the link between this condition to become a member of the EU and the underlying identity of the EU, see Helene Sjursen, 'Why Expand? The Question of Legitimacy and Justification in the EU's Enlargement Policy' (2002) 40 *Journal of Common Market Studies* 491, 508.

[179] See, e.g., Gwendolyn Sasse, 'EU conditionality and minority rights', EUI Working Papers 2005/16, 1 <http://cadmus.eui.eu/bitstream/handle/1814/3365/05_16.pdf?sequence=1> accessed 24 March 2015.

[180] Art 6 TEU (n 171). On the state of the negotiation process between the Council of Europe and the European Union regarding the EU's accession to the European Convention on Human Rights, see http://www.coe.int/t/dghl/standardsetting/hrpolicy/Accession/default_en.asp accessed 30 March 2015.

[181] See, e.g., Giuseppe Balducci, 'The study of the EU promotion of human rights: the importance of international and internal factors' (2008) GARNET Working Paper No. 61/08, 3, 16. See also Cremona, 'Values in the EU Constitution' (n 174) 7 et seq. See also Gráinne de Búrca, 'The European Courts and the Security Council: Between Dédoublement Fonctionnel and Balancing of Values: Three Replies to Pasquale De Sena and Maria Chiara Vitucci' (2009) 20 *EJIL* 853.

[182] Art 3(5) of the TEU provides as follows: '5. *In its relations with the wider world*, the Union shall uphold and promote its values and interests and contribute to the protection of its citizens. It shall contribute to peace, security, the sustainable development of the Earth, solidarity and mutual respect among peoples, free and fair trade, eradication of poverty and the *protection of human rights*, in particular the rights of the child, as well as to the strict observance and the development of international law, including respect for the principles of the United Nations Charter' [emphasis added].

[183] Art 21(1) of the TEU provides that '1. *The Union's action on the international scene shall be guided by the principles* which have inspired its own creation, development and enlargement, and which it seeks to advance in the wider world: democracy, the rule of law, the universality and *indivisibility of human rights and fundamental freedoms*, respect for human dignity, the principles of equality and solidarity, and respect for the principles of the United Nations Charter and international law' [emphasis added].

[184] On Arts 3(5) and 21 of the TEU, see Lorand Bartels, 'The EU's Human Rights Obligations in Relation to Policies with Extraterritorial Effects' (2014) 25 *EJIL* 1071, 1073–5.

[185] See also Parliament, 'Joint Communication to the European Parliament and the Council, Human Rights and Democracy at the Heart of EU external action—towards a more effective approach' (12 December 2011) COM(2011) 886 final, 4.

[186] Council of the European Union, 'EU Strategic Framework and Action Plan on Human Rights and Democracy' (25 June 2012) 11855/12 [emphasis added] 1–2 <http://www.consilium.

As noted previously, social identity consists of two core elements of similarity (mainly on the internal level, among the group's members) and difference (mainly on the external level, vis-à-vis non-members). Groups need a certain level of both similarity and differentiation from others, and social identity derives from the tension between the sense of belonging and the sense of distinctiveness.[187] An analysis of the current EU constitutional framework for human rights protection reveals rather a clear difference between the importance accorded to human rights in EU external relations as compared to internal relations.[188] The existing constitutional framework (with the exception of anti-discrimination law) assigns a more circumscribed role to human rights within the context of internally focused EU policies, and the dominant focus is external, empowering, and even obliging the EU to promote human rights actively in its international policies.[189]

This EU bifurcated approach may be explained by some sociological literature which emphasizes the role of highlighting social differences between the particular social group and other groups in the process of constructing and maintaining collective identity. Emphasizing differences vis-à-vis other groups tends to foster internal similarity among group members.[190] The EU's emphasis on external human rights policies underlines its identity as a liberal-democratic group[191] towards other international groups.

The EU's social role as human rights promoter and external trade instruments: Sociological literature underlines the link between social identity and social role, underscoring that having a particular identity often pressures individuals and groups to behave according to social expectations related to their particular role. Where people identify with a group, they tend to adopt the meaning that accompanies the particular identity, and act accordingly to represent that meaning.[192] The self-representation of the EU as a promoter of human rights worldwide[193] has been significantly accepted in the international community, and has led to the construction of the EU's social role regarding protecting human rights in the international system. Recognition of the EU's role is discernible, for instance, from literature,[194]

europa.eu/uedocs/cms_data/docs/pressdata/EN/foraff/131181.pdf> accessed 30 March 2015. This role of the EU in the international community is also emphasized in the EU's official website: 'The European Union sees human rights as universal and indivisible. It actively promotes and defends them both within its borders and when engaging in relations with non-EU countries.' European Union, *The EU and Human Rights*, <http://eeas.europa.eu/human_rights/index_en.htm> accessed 24 March 2015.

187 See Section II above.

188 Gráinne de Búrca, 'The Evolution of EU Human Rights Law' in Paul Craig and Grainne de Burca (eds), *The Evolution of EU Law* (2nd edn, OUP, 2011) 465, at 491, see also 492–4.

189 Ibid., 467 and see the references therein. See also 494.

190 See Section II above.

191 On the role of human rights norms in defining identities of liberal states, see Risse and Sikkink (n 169) 1–2, 8–9.

192 See Section II above.

193 See, e.g., the EU statements cited above in this section (such as the 2012 'strategic paper'). On the EU self-representation regarding the emphasis of values in its foreign policy, see also, Sonia Lucarelli, 'Introduction: Values, Principles, Identity and European Union Foreign Policy' in Sonia Lucarelli and Ian Manners (eds), *Values and Principles in European Union Foreign Policy* (Routledge, 2006) 1, 2–4.

194 See, e.g., Balducci (n 181) 1–3, 16–21; Joseph S Nye, *Soft Power* (Public Affairs, 2004) 76, 80; Richard Gowan and Franziska Brantner, 'A Global Force for Human Rights? An Audit

and the awarding of the Nobel Prize for contribution to advancement of peace, democracy, and human rights.[195]

This social role of the EU in the international community influences the behaviour of EU institutions and other international actors in this field. For example, if a certain state commits flagrant and extensive violations of human rights, expectations are likely to arise that the EU will react and adopt some measures against that state. Such expectations create social pressure on the EU and affect its behaviour in the international system.

The EU's identity as human rights promoter is projected out through a variety of frameworks,[196] and this section focuses on trade measures. The two principal trade instruments in this sphere are conditioned preferences for developing countries and human rights clauses in trade agreements with non-members. Trade preferences granted to developing countries (in addition to those prescribed under the World Trade Organization (WTO) law) are regulated by the EU's 'Generalized System of Preferences' (GSP) legislation, and such preferences are conditioned by compliance with certain requirements relating to human rights.[197] The 2012 GSP Regulation elaborates the conditions that beneficiary countries must comply with, including the ratification of a series of international human rights conventions (listed in Annex VIII);[198] the absence of unlawful reservations to these conventions;[199] and lack of rulings regarding serious failure to effectively implement any of those conventions (as determined by the relevant conventions' monitoring bodies).[200] These trade preferences are to be temporarily withdrawn if the beneficiary country does not fulfil the above requirements or does not cooperate with the Union's monitoring procedures (set out in this Regulation).[201]

Since 1992,[202] the EU's trade agreements with third parties have included a 'human rights clause' requiring the parties to respect human rights and democratic

of European Power at the UN' (2008) European Council on Foreign Relations Policy Paper, 1, 8 <http://kms2.isn.ethz.ch/serviceengine/Files/RESSpecNet/91657/ipublicationdocument_singledocument/12CA5C36-C4CC-46BD-B38F-B1CB7717F217/en/Global_Force_Human_Rights_EU_0908.pdf> accessed 24 March 2015.

195 'European Union (EU)—Facts' (21 May 2014) <http://www.nobelprize.org/nobel_prizes/peace/laureates/2012/eu-facts.html> accessed 24 March 2015.

196 See, e.g., European Commission, *Furthering Human Rights and Democracy Across the Globe* (2007) <http://eeas.europa.eu/human_rights/docs/brochure07_en.pdf> accessed 24 March 2015; European Union, *EU Strategic Framework on Human Rights and Democracy* (25 June 2012) <http://www.consilium.europa.eu/uedocs/cms_data/docs/pressdata/EN/foraff/131169.pdf> accessed 24 March 2015.

197 Lorand Bartels, *Human Rights Conditionality in the EU's International Agreements* (OUP, 2005) 7–12, 68–70.

198 'Regulation (EU) No 978/2012 of The European Parliament and of the Council of 25 October 2012, applying a scheme of generalized tariff preferences and repealing Council Regulation (EC) 732/2008' [2012] *OJ L* 303/1, Art 9(1)(b) [hereafter 'EU GSP Regulation'].

199 EU GSP Regulation (n 198) Art 9(1)(c).

200 Art 9(1)(b) of the EU GSP Regulation (n 198) Art 9(1)(b).

201 Section of the Preamble of the EU GSP Regulation (n 198).

202 On the evolution of such human rights provisions in the EU treaties, see Bartels, *Human Rights Conditionality* (n 197) 12 et seq.

principles.[203] The EU Council adopted in 1995 a formal policy of including such clauses in all future cooperation and trade agreements,[204] and today they are contained in agreements with more than 120 countries.[205] The recent human rights provisions present a similar structure: (i) a basic obligation to comply with human rights;[206] (ii) a provision allowing a party to undertake appropriate measures in case of breach of the above 'essential clause';[207] and (iii) monitoring and implementation provisions.[208]

Identity motivated compliance and international social labelling: Sociological deviance literature discusses a variety of societal factors involved in compliance and breach of norms, including external motivations (such as 'social control') and internal motivations (such as identity).[209] As noted above, social identity often constitutes an influential factor that promotes compliance with a group's norms, and particularly with its 'constitutive norms'.[210] Since human rights constitute a constitutive element in the EU's identity as a Western-liberal community, and EU membership signals acquiring or validating existing international identity, these factors exert significant influence on the twenty-eight members of this prestigious group (new and older ones) to comply with international human rights law.

The EU's legal rules regarding conditioned accession to the EU and suspension of membership rights reflect and reinforce this important feature of the EU group membership. The EU's identity, however, does not ensure that all members will comply with its human rights norms. Generally, a member whose bond with the group is weak (or socially alienated from the group) is less likely to be committed to the group's norms.[211] From this perspective, if an EU member is significantly

[203] Lorand Bartels, 'Human Rights and Sustainable Development Obligations in EU Free Trade Agreements' (September 2012) Legal Studies Research Paper Series University of Cambridge Faculty of Law 1; Communication from the Commission to the Council and the European Parliament, 'The European Union's role in promoting human rights and democratisation in third countries' COM (2001) 252 final.

[204] Bartels, *The European Parliament's Role in Relation to Human Rights in Trade and Investment agreements* (February 2014) <http://www.europarl.europa.eu/RegData/etudes/etudes/join/2014/433751/EXPO-JOIN_ET(2014)433751_EN.pdf> accessed 24 March 2015, 3.

[205] Bartels, 6.

[206] See, e.g., Art 2 of the 2002 Euro-Mediterranean Agreement establishing an Association between the European Communities and their Member States, of the one part, and the Hashemite Kingdom of Jordan, of the other part, [2002] *OJ L* 129/3 (15.5.2002).

[207] On the EU Commission's discretionary powers under such a provision (Article 86 of the 2006 EU—Lebanon Association Agreement) and its non-binding nature, see Case C-581/11 P *Mugraby v Council of the European Union*, judgment of 12 July 2012 [69]–[71]; Lorand Bartels, 'A Model Human Rights Clause for the EU's International Trade Agreements' 17–18 (February 2014) German Institute for Human Rights and MISEREOR 10,<http://ssrn.com/abstract=2405852> accessed 24 March 2015.

[208] Bartels, *The European Parliament's Role in Relation to Human Rights* (n 204), 8. Regarding the above second element ('non-execution clause'), these measures must be taken in accordance with the relevant rules of international law, see Bartels, *Human Rights Conditionality* (n 197) 7.

[209] See Chapter 6, Section IV(b).

[210] See Sections II(c) and III above.

[211] On the link between a weak bond to society and non-compliance, see Paul Rock, 'Sociological theories of crime', in Mike Maguire, Rod Morgan, and Robert Reiner (eds), *The Oxford Handbook of Criminology* (OUP, 2012) 57; John J Macionis, *Sociology* (14th edn, Pearson 2012) 202.

less identified with the group or perceives itself as socially marginalized in the European Community, it is more likely to breach the group's norms, including those relating to human rights.

As already noted, certain international institutions possess the capacity to authoritatively identify people or groups as belonging to a certain category and thus may stigmatize their incumbents. The suspension of trade benefits by the EU (e.g., under the GSP programme) carries not only certain economic consequences, but it also conveys a signal by a significant human rights actor classifying that particular country as a serious violator of international human rights norms. This aspect of international labelling is significant to the targeted states, occasionally not of lesser importance than the economic consequences of trade sanctions. Social identity, however, is regularly constructed in a dialectic process between a particular state and other actors in the international community, and the latter state is not necessarily a passive object in this process. Thus, the targeted state may challenge and try to reject such stigmas relating to breaching human rights.[212]

Out-group actors and compliance with the group's norms: While a group's constitutive norms are expected to significantly influence in-group members, they are less likely to have the same impact on out-group actors. Non-member states which are targeted by EU trade measures relating to allegations of breach of human rights often experience a sense of social exclusion and discrimination.[213] The suspension of trade benefits by the EU in this context also conveys a moral judgement, often relating to the legitimacy of the particular government.[214] Thus, while the EU's employment of trade measures in this context may intensify external social pressure on the particular state, it may also increase a sense of alienation and exclusion within the particular society, and diminish the prospects of compliance.

The above-noted distinctive out-group/in-group effects on compliance with international norms suggest that the employment of EU trade measures in this sphere should be undertaken in an inclusive context which downplays the social boundaries between the EU and non-members. From this perspective, it is

[212] See, e.g., with regard to the EU human rights policy, Rebecca Adler-Nissen, 'Stigma Management in International Relations: Transgressive Identities, Norms, and Order in International Society' (2014) 68 *International Organization* 143, 160–5.

[213] Inconsistent trade measures towards non-members in this sphere seem to erode the legitimacy of the EU's human rights policy towards non-member states. On the incoherent application of such trade measures towards non-members suspected for breaching human rights, see, e.g., Armin Paasch, 'Human Rights in EU Trade Policy—Between Ambition and Reality' (December, 2011) *Ecofair Trade Dialogue Discussion Paper* 3, 12–13; Nivedita Sen and Balu G Nair, 'Human Rights Provisions in the forthcoming Indian-EU Free Trade Agreement' (2011) 4 *National University for Juridical Science Law Review* 417, 423, 430; Guy Harpaz and Eyal Rubinson, 'The Interface between Trade, Law and Politics and the Erosion of Normative Power Europe' (2010) 35 *European Law Review* 551, 566–70.

[214] On the link between the conception of international human rights and international legitimacy, see, e.g., Balducci (n 181) 4; Michael Joseph Smith, 'Sovereignty, Human Rights and Legitimacy in the Post-Cold War World' (2001) <http://faculty.virginia.edu/irandhumanrights/mjsonsovty.htm> accessed 24 March 2015. On international human rights protection and standard of legitimacy (and 'standard of civilization'), see Jack Donnelly, 'Human Rights: A New Standard of Civilization?' (1998) 74 *International Affairs* 1, 14.

desirable that such an inclusive framework (which includes the link between trade measures and human rights performance) highlights features shared by both parties (such as common heritage, ideological ties etc.). A comprehensive framework that emphasizes common identity, if meaningful for the particular non-member state, is expected to decrease the sense of exclusion and enhance the prospects of compliance with the specific human rights. And if a non-member breaches human rights in this context, the social identity perspective does not suggest drastic exclusionary measures (such as expulsion from the socio-economic group) but rather accompanying trade sanctions with signals regarding potential partnership in the future.

Identity-driven measures and considerations of efficiency: The above EU trade provisions have been implemented in only a small subset of potential cases (usually in response to coups d'état or significant deteriorations in a political situation)[215] and their effect on compliance with international human rights law is not clear.[216] These facts should not lead to the conclusion that the EU is likely to discard the inclusion of such provisions in its GSP programme and trade agreements, or not apply such trade measures following a breach of international human rights. Considerations of efficiency do not constitute the crucial factor in this sphere. The 'logic of identity' is different from (and occasionally inconsistent with) the 'logic of efficiency'. The central motivation leading to the adoption of these legal provisions and trade measures relates to the self-image of the EU and its aspiration to project this identity. Considerations of efficiency apparently affect this EU policy but they do not constitute the predominant factor in this sphere. The underlying link between the EU trade-human rights policy and its collective identity indicates that this policy is relatively durable and not likely to be radically changed within a short period.

c. Social identity as an interpretative tool

Theoretical tools and empirical evidence drawn from social identity literature may assist legal decision-makers in interpreting certain international legal rules. The resort to such complementary interpretative tools is desirable where legal instruments refer to entities which significantly involve social groups. This potential practical value of social identity analysis is illustrated below with regard to

[215] Bartels, 'A Model Human Rights Clause for the EU's International Trade Agreements' (n 207) 10; Bartels, *The European Parliament's Role in Relation to Human Rights* (n 204) 12; Bartels, *Human Rights Conditionality* (n 197) 9; Sen and Nair (n 213) 427.

[216] See, e.g., Fabienne Zwagemakers, 'The EU's Conditionality Policy: A New Strategy to Achieve Compliance' (January 2012) IAI Working Papers 12/03, 5–6 <http://www10.iadb.org/intal/intalcdi/PE/2012/09808.pdf> accessed 24 March 2015; Daniela Donno, 'Legalization and Leverage: Human Rights Conditionality in the European Union's Economic Agreements' (American Political Science Association Annual Meeting, New Orleans, September 2012) 7–9, 19–24, and see the references therein; Bartels, *Human Rights Conditionality* (n 197) 17–19; Paasch (n 213) 14–15. See also Hadewych Hazelzet, 'Suspension of Development Cooperation: An Instrument to Promote Human Rights and Democracy?' (August 2005), European Centre for Development Policy Management, 12–13.

interpretation of legal rules relating to state succession, impartiality of international adjudicators, and some social groups protected by diverse international instruments.

(i) Succession of states: Legal rules regarding state succession are regarded as one of the most complex spheres in international law;[217] this difficulty particularly applies to the questions of whether and to what extent a new state ('successor') remains bound by the treaties of the former sovereign.[218] State practice does little to substantiate either of the competing principles; the continuity of rights and obligations from the old to the incoming authority and the 'clean slate theory' under which the incoming sovereign is freed from rights and obligations.[219] In light of the ambiguous legal situation, Craven suggests focusing on whether the state concerned retains its previous personality, and specifically its identity.[220] Consequently, it is suggested that '[t]he task for the future, therefore, is to map out some of the characteristics and determinants of state identity in a way that takes into account not merely the formal properties of statehood, but also the sense of 'self, 'singularity', and 'community', that justifies the attachment of international legal obligations to particular territories and social groups.'[221] This approach[222] offers a sound legal policy for guiding legal decision-makers in this particularly complex sphere of international law.

Social identities are dynamic and the process of identity construction is never final.[223] Similarly, national identities gradually change in response to various developments, including change in the environment or the relevant out-group.[224] Only a radical change in national identity justifies the discontinuation of treaty rights and obligations. This approach suggests analysing whether the change in government has led to such a fundamental change in national identity. Theoretical tools and empirical evidence drawn from social identity literature may assist legal decision-makers to examine whether the particular state's identity has changed dramatically.

The examination of certain socio-legal features may indicate whether a radical identity change has taken place. Dramatic changes in national identity are often reflected in significant changes in national legislation (particularly constitutional documents), and are occasionally accompanied by a change in the name[225] of

217 See, e.g., Malcolm Shaw, *International Law* (7th edn, CUP, 2014) 694; Matthew CR Craven, 'The Problem of State Succession and the Identity of States under International Law' (1998) 9 *EJIL* 142–3.

218 Issues regarding the succession of territorial treaties (e.g., boundary treaties) have been clarified in practice and international tribunals' jurisprudence. See, e.g., Shaw (n 217) 702–3.

219 Craven (n 217) 144. See also Shaw (n 217) 695.

220 Craven states in that regard: 'Identity, therefore, provides the key to determining the proper set of norms that are to be applied in a given case'. Craven (n 217) 152.

221 Craven (n 217) 162.

222 Fitzmaurice apparently supports this principle; Malgosia Fitzmaurice, 'Treaties' in R Wolfrum (ed), *Max Planck Encyclopedia of Public International Law* (OUP, 2010) <http://opil.ouplaw.com/home/EPIL> para 118.

223 See Section II(b) above.

224 See, e.g., Riccarda Torriani, 'The Dynamics of National Identity' (2002) 37 *Journal of Contemporary History* 559.

225 On the links between names and social identity, see Woodward (n 1) 25–6. For a sociological discussion of names, see Thomas Molnar, 'A Sociology of Names' (1999) 34 *The Intercollegiate Review* 39.

the state.[226] Exceptional changes in national identity are also often reflected in the state's sense of belonging and manifested in accession to new international groups (e.g., joining significantly different international institutions). Withdrawal from some international groups (either institutionalized or not) may also accompany such fundamental changes in national identity.

Social identity is not a unilateral process and new identity emerges within a two-way relationships between self-identity and external (group) acceptance.[227] Thus, unilateral statements by the new government regarding dramatic changes in national identity are insufficient to support discontinuation of treaty rights and obligations. The international community's acceptance of the new identity is significant for establishing a radically new national identity. Thus, the responses of other states and/or international (regional or global) institutions to the particular state's new self-representation are significant for accepting such a contention regarding new national identity.

(ii) Impartiality of adjudicators and disqualification criteria: Social identity influences individuals' perceptions and evaluation.[228] Attributing personality traits to people belonging to social groups ('stereotyping')[229] systematically affects how individuals perceive and process new information, as well as respond to members of social groups.[230] Such attribution of personality characteristics is prevalent in daily life[231] and frequently useful in everyday social interaction.[232] The ascription of such traits to individuals is rooted in the social group and represents the attitude of the in-group members towards other groups.[233]

Empirical studies indicate that we often have distorted perceptions and evaluations of traits of group members. Two principal mechanisms tend to reinforce stereotyped traits associated with social groups. The first mechanism concerns

226 On the symbolic, political, and legal implications of changing the name of a state, see Michael Ioannidis, 'Naming a State: Disputing over Symbols of Statehood at the Example of Macedonia' (2010) *14 Max Planck Yearbook of United Nations Law* 507. For a list of countries which changed their names, see 'Historical Country Names' (*Nations Online*) <http://www.nationsonline.org/oneworld/hist_country_names.htm> accessed 24 March 2015.

227 See Section II(b) above.

228 See Section II(c) above.

229 John F Dovidio and others, 'Prejudice, Stereotyping and Discrimination: Theoretical and Empirical Overview' in John F Dovidio and others (eds), *Prejudice, Stereotyping and Discrimination* (Sage, 2010) 5–8; Gregory R Maio and others 'Attitude and Intergroup Relations' in John F Dovidio and others (eds), *Prejudice, Stereotyping and Discrimination* 261, 265; Stephan and Stephan (n 13) 7.

230 Dovidio and others (n 229).

231 On the omnipresence of stereotypes and the natural inclination to categorize the world (including regarding inter-group relations), see, e.g., Carl L Palmer, 'Which Cues Matter? The Implications of Stereotype Appeals and Explicit Predispositions for Group-Centric Issue Opinion' (August 2010) 2–3 <http://ssrn.com/abstract=1664772> accessed 24 March 2015. Stephan and Stephan state in that regard: 'In fact, stereotypes, as defined here, are an almost inevitable consequence of categorization'. Stephan and Stephan (n 13) 7. See also Patricia G Devine and Lindsay B Sharp, 'Automaticity and Control in Stereotyping and Prejudice' in Todd D Nelson (ed), *Handbook of Prejudice, Stereotyping, and Discrimination* (Taylor & Francis, 2009) 61.

232 Stephan and Stephan (n 13) 4. Anastasio and others explain that one reason why such stereotypes are resistant to change is that they are functional in reducing the complexity of the social environment. Anastasio and others (n 28) 236.

233 Worchel and Rothgerber (n 86) 77–8. See also Dovidio and others (n 229) 6.

the *collection of information*, and empirical studies indicate that people often solicit information which confirms their hypotheses (rather than pursuing evidence that could disconfirm their hypotheses).[234] Stephan and Stephan emphasize that '[i]t is important to note that people are probably unaware that they are gathering information in a biased manner. Even when people are offered a reward for gathering unbiased information, they still tend not to do so.'[235] The second mechanism relates to *processing information*; empirical studies reveal that 'expectancy-confirming information' is generally better remembered than 'expectancy-disconfirming information'.[236] Even when disconfirming information is being encoded, people tend to process information in ways that support pre-existing stereotypes.[237]

The above mechanisms of collecting and processing information are occasionally relevant to international adjudication. International adjudicators are frequently required to process volumes of information, evaluate the reliability of evidence submitted by the parties, ascertain trustworthiness of witnesses belonging to different social groups, and apply vague legal concepts (e.g., 'good faith'[238] or 'fair and equitable treatment').[239] Adjudicators' identification with a social group involved in or affected by the legal proceedings may lead to arguments regarding biased adjudicatory process and the 'impartiality'[240] of adjudicators.

The link between the mental attitude towards the parties and the legal concept of 'impartiality' clearly arises from the Supreme Court of Canada's decision in the Valente case:

> Impartiality refers to a state of mind or attitude of the tribunal in relation to the issues and the parties in a particular case. The word 'impartial', , , connotes absence of bias, actual or perceived.[241]

[234] Stephan and Stephan (n 13) 21 and see the empirical studies cited therein.

[235] Stephan and Stephan (n 13) 21. On the activation of stereotypical consideration without awareness, see also Palmer (n 231) 3.

[236] Stephan and Stephan (n 13) 22; See also Dovidio and others (n 229) 8.

[237] Stephan and Stephan (n 13) 25 and the see the empirical studies cited therein. See also Anastasio and others (n 28) 238.

[238] See, e.g., Vienna Convention on the Law of Treaties (adopted 23 May 1969, entered into force 27 January 1980) 1155 UNTS 331 Arts 26, 31(1), 46(2), 69(2)(b).

[239] On the increasing importance of the principle of 'fair and equitable treatment' in international investment law, see, e.g., Rudolf Dolzer and Christoph Schreuer, *Principles of International Investment Law* (2nd edn, OUP, 2012) 130; Moshe Hirsch, 'Between Fair and Equitable Treatment and Stabilization Clause' (2011) 12 *Journal of World Investment and Trade* 783.

[240] As Malintoppi explains, the terms 'independence' and 'impartiality' are often used interchangeably but they must be distinguished. The term 'independence' refers to the absence of connection, financial or otherwise, with a party to the proceedings. The term 'impartiality' refers to the absence of prejudice or bias. Loretta Malintoppi, 'Independence, Impartiality, and Duty of Disclosure of Arbitrators' in Peter Muchlinski, Federico Ortino, and Christoph Schreuer (eds), *Oxford Handbook of International Investment law* (OUP, 2008) 789, 807. See also the jurisprudence of the European Court on Human Rights cited in *Mehmet Ali Yilmaz v Turkey* App no. 29286/95 (EctHR, 25 September 2001) [35].

[241] *Valente v The Queen*, [1985] 2 SCR 673, [15].

And the Human Rights Committee stated that 'impartiality' (under article 14(1) of the International Covenant on Civil and Political Rights (ICCPR))[242] 'implies that judges must not harbour preconceptions about the matter put before them, and that they must not act in ways that promote the interests of one of the parties'.[243]

Diverse international tribunals have various rules as to the required qualifications and different criteria regarding disqualification of adjudicators. The International Court of Justice (ICJ) Statute prohibits judges from acting in cases where they have previously acted in that capacity.[244] Judge Buergenthal's proposal to interpret this standard broadly and adopt a lower threshold of 'appearance of bias'[245] was not accepted by the Court.[246] The International Criminal Tribunal for the Former Yugoslavia (ICTY) Rules of Procedure focus on whether the judge has any personal interest or association that might affect her/his impartiality.[247] The ICTY examined the question of impartiality from the perspective of judges in national courts and the Appeals Chamber ruled in the famous Furundzija case that proof of either actual bias or an appearance of bias is sufficient to disqualify ICTY judges.[248] The ECHR aims to guarantee 'an independent and impartial tribunal'[249] and the European Court of Human Rights (ECtHR) has developed a two-prong test for judicial bias that includes both an *objective test* (examining whether the adjudicator offered guarantees sufficient to exclude any legitimate doubt in this respect) as well as a *subjective test* (examining the personal conviction and behaviour of a particular judge in a given case).[250] Similarly, the American Convention on Human Rights aims to guarantee an

[242] Art 14(1) of the ICCPR provides as follows: 'All persons shall be equal before the courts and tribunals. In the determination of any criminal charge against him, or of his rights and obligations in a suit at law, everyone shall be entitled to a fair and public hearing by a competent, independent and impartial tribunal established by law', ICCPR (adopted 16 December 1966, entered into force 23 March 1976) 999 UNTS 171 Art 14(1).

[243] HRC. *Arvo O Karttunen v Finland*, Communication No. 387/1989 (views adopted on 23 October 1992) UN Doc CCPR/C/46/D/387/1989 [7.2].

[244] See Statute of the International Criminal Court (adopted 17 July 1998, entered into force 1 July 2002) 33 UNTS 993 Art 17(2).

[245] *Legal Consequences of the Construction of the Wall* (Order of 30 January 2004) [2004] ICJ Rep 3, [10]–[11], [14] (dissenting opinion of Judge Buergenthal).

[246] *Legal Consequences of the Construction of the Wall* (Order of 30 January 2004) [2004] ICJ Rep 3, [8].

[247] See ICTY, 'Rules of Procedure and Evidence' (10 December 2009) UN Doc IT/32/Rev.44, rules 15 and 34 <http://www.icty.org/x/file/Legal%20Library/Rules_procedure_evidence/IT032_rev44_en.pdf> accessed 24 March 2015. And see also the Statute of the International Criminal Court (n 244) Art 41.

[248] *Prosecutor v Furundzija* (Judgment) IT-95-17/1A (July 21, 2000) [179]. Consequently, the Appeals Chamber ruled that a judge should be considered impartial if 'the circumstances would lead a reasonable observer, properly informed, to reasonably apprehend bias', see [189]. On this decision, see also, Theodor Meron, 'Judicial Independence and Impartiality in International Criminal Tribunals' (2005) 99 *AJIL* 359, 366–7.

[249] See the European Convention on Human Rights (adopted 4 November 1950, entered into force 3 September 1953) 213 UNTS 222 (ECHR) Art 6(1).

[250] *Ali Yilmaz v. Turkey* (n 240) [36]. See also *Piersack v Belgium* (1982) Series A No. 53, [30(a)].

'independent, and impartial tribunal'[251] and the Inter-American Court stated that 'impartiality demands that the judge ... approaches the facts of the case *subjectively free of all prejudice* and also offers sufficient objective guarantees to exclude any doubt the parties or the community might entertain as to his or her lack of impartiality'.[252]

As to arbitral proceedings between sovereign states and foreign investors, Article 57 of the Convention on the Settlement of Investment Disputes between States and Nationals of other States (ICSID Convention) provides that a proposal to disqualify an arbitrator should indicate 'a manifest lack of' some qualities,[253] inter alia, that the particular adjudicator may not 'be relied upon to exercise independent judgment'.[254] As noted in the Commentary on ICSID Convention '[t]he requirement that the lack of qualities must be "manifest" imposes a relatively heavy burden of proof on the party making the proposal'.[255] This test was reaffirmed by a series of ICSID tribunals[256] and the test of 'appearance of impartiality' was rejected in the *Amco v Indonesia* tribunal.[257]

An adequate criterion regarding disqualification of adjudicators aims to balance between the need to ensure impartial proceedings and the reality of existing links between adjudicators and other professionals (e.g. lawyers, counsels, or diplomats).[258] The above-noted common tendency to attribute personality traits to members of social groups suggests that more weight be granted to the first factor in legal disputes characterized by a higher likelihood for biased perception and evaluation.

[251] See American Convention on Human Rights (adopted 21 November 1969, entered into force 18 July 1978) 1144 UNTS 143 Art 8(1).

[252] *Barbera et al. v Venezuela,* Judgment, Inter-American Court of Human Rights Series C No 182 (5 August 2008) [56] [emphasis added]. See also *Palamara-Iribarne v Chile,* Judgment, Inter-American Court of Human Rights Series C No. 135 (22 November 2005) [146].

[253] See the Convention on the Settlement of Investment Disputes between States and Nationals of other States (adopted 18 March 1965, entered into force 14 October 1966) 575 UNTS 159 Arts 14(1) and 57.

[254] Art 14(1) of the ICSID Convention (n 253) Art 14(1) and see also Art 40(2).

[255] Christoph H Schreuer, Loretta Malintoppi, August Reinisch, and Anthony Sinclair, *The ICSID Convention: A Commentary* (CUP, 2009) 1202; See also *Suez and Vivendi v Argentina* (Decision on a Second Proposal for the Disqualification of a Member of the Arbitral Tribunal) ICSID Case No. ARB/03/19 (12 May 2008), 17.

[256] See, e.g., *Abaclat v Argentina* (Request for the Disqualification of President Pierre Tercier and Arbitrator Albert Jan van den Berg) ICSID Case No. ARB/07/5 (15 September 2011) [6]; *Burlington v Ecuador* (Decision on the Proposal for Disqualification of Professor Francisco Orrego Vicuña) ICSID Case No. ARB/08/5 (13 December 2013) [68], [80]. See also Schreuer and others (n 255) 1201–8.

[257] *Amco Asia Corporation and others v Republic of Indonesia* (Decision on the Proposal to Disqualify an Arbitrator) ICSID Case ARB/81/1 (24 June 1982) (unreported), referred to in Schreuer and others (n 255) 1203. For several recent decisions that may indicate a different trend in that regard, see Chiara Giorgetti, 'Towards a Revised Threshold for Arbitrators' Challenges Under ICSID?' (*Kluwer Arbitration Blog*, 2 July 2014) <http://kluwerarbitrationblog.com/blog/2014/07/03/towards-a-revised-threshold-for-arbitrators-challenges-under-icsid/> accessed 24 March 2015.

[258] See, e.g., Ruth Mackenzie and Philippe Sands, 'International Courts and Tribunals and the Independence of the International Judge' (2003) 44 *HJIL* 271, 280. On the relations between arbitrators and advocates in investment proceedings, see Malintoppi (n 240) 792.

Social identity literature indicates that where adjudicators identify with a social group substantially involved in the dispute (formally or informally), their perceptions and evaluations of evidence submitted by the parties are susceptible to bias. It is noteworthy that most people are not aware of their bias. In light of the higher probability of biased perceptions and evaluation in such legal disputes, social identity analysis suggests setting a lower threshold for proving 'impartiality' under international tribunals' procedural rules. Thus, where such circumstances exist, the heavy burden imposed by ICSID rules and jurisprudence on a party seeking to disqualify an arbitrator—and the demand 'to establish facts that make it obvious and highly probable, not just possible'[259]—seem excessively heavy. From this perspective, where there is reasonable evidence that the adjudicator has identified with one of the social groups involved, it is desirable to set a less demanding standard (such as the above-discussed 'appearance of bias' standards adopted by the ICTY), or to interpret accordingly existing rules by the ICSID tribunals.[260]

This proposal requires adjudicators to ascertain whether a particular judge or arbitrator has identified with a social group substantially involved in the dispute. To assess this issue, adjudicators may employ tools and empirical studies regarding the construction of social identity.[261] Evidence regarding the above-discussed factors of 'identity salience' (quantitative and qualitative)[262] of the specific adjudicator is particularly relevant to an evaluation of the probability of biased perception and evaluation. In such cases, it is desirable to assess both the number of persons to whom the particular adjudicator is connected through identity links as well as the strength of the identity ties with the relevant social group. Where this analysis indicates that the likelihood of activating a particular identity is significant, the grounds for setting a lower burden of proof for disqualifying the particular adjudicator are even more compelling. In such cases, the legal presumption of impartiality attached to adjudicators[263] is unwarranted.

(iii) Defining social groups under international instruments: Certain international legal rules aim to protect various social groups, such as '*peoples*' (under the rules regarding self-determination[264] and the First Protocol to the Geneva

[259] *Suez and Vivendi v Argentina* (n 255) 17.

[260] Similarly, in such cases, the above-discussed proposal tabled by Judge Buergenthal seems more desirable than the existing standard under the ICJ jurisprudence. For a possible different interpretation of the above ICSID provisions, see, e.g., James Crawford, 'Challenges to Arbitrators in ICSID Arbitrations' (PCA Peace Palace Centenary Seminar, October 2013) <http://pca-cpa.org/shownews.asp?ac=view&nws_id=398&pag_id=1261> accessed 24 March 2015.

[261] See Section II(b) above.

[262] See Section II(c) above.

[263] On the presumption of impartiality, see, e.g., *Prosecutor v Furundzija* (n 248) [182]; Schreuer and others (n 255) 1201–2.

[264] See ICCPR (n 242) Art 1; Declaration on Friendly Relations between States, UNGA Res 2625 (XXV) (24 October 1970) UN Doc A/RES/2625(XXV).

Convention),[265] 'minority groups' (under the ICCPR),[266] '*indigenous peoples*' (under the Convention concerning Indigenous Peoples),[267] '*group or collectivity*' (under the International Criminal Court (ICC) Statute),[268] and '*social groups*' (under the Refugees Convention).[269] Various international treaties grant these groups diverse legal rights and impose corresponding obligations on other parties. The relevant legal instruments do not provide a definition of the relevant social group and generally, there is no consensus on the elements of this concept.[270]

As discussed above, social identity constitutes a critical link between the individual and social groups, and a social group cannot exist without some measure of common identity among the group's members.[271] Thus, the employment of theoretical tools and empirical evidence drawn from social identity literature may

[265] Art 96(3) of the First Protocol Additional to the Geneva Conventions. And see the definition in Art 1(4) of this Protocol. Protocol Additional to the Geneva Conventions of 12 August 1949, and relating to the Protection of Victims of International Armed Conflict (Protocol I) (adopted 8 June 1977, entered into force 7 December 1979) 1125 UNTS 3.

[266] ICCPR (n 242) Art 27; See also the UNGA, 'Declaration on the Rights of Persons belonging to National or Ethnic, Religious and Linguistic Minorities' (18 December 1992) UN Doc A/RES/47/135.

[267] ILO Convention concerning Indigenous and Tribal Peoples in Independent Countries (adopted 27 June 1989, entered into force 5 September 1991) 28 *ILM* 1382.

[268] One of the central elements of 'crimes against humanity' is that the perpetrators target the relevant persons by reason of their membership in a group rather than their individual characteristics. Art 7(1)(h) of the Statute of the International Criminal Court provides: '(h) *Persecution against any identifiable group or collectivity* on political, racial, national, ethnic, cultural, religious, gender' [emphasis added]. Statute of the International Criminal Court (n 244) Art 7(1)(h); the interpretation of Art 7(1)(h) above in *The Elements of the Crime* clarifies that: '2. The perpetrator targeted such person or persons by reason of the identity of a group or collectivity or targeted the group or collectivity as such.' Report of the Preparatory Commission for the International Criminal Court on the Elements of Crimes' (2 November 2000) UN Doc PCNICC/2000/1/Add.2. On this feature of crimes against humanity, see David Luban, 'A Theory of Crimes Against Humanity' (2004) 29 *Yale Journal of International Law* 85, 103, 107–8.

[269] Art 1A(2) of the Refugees Convention provides as follows: 'As a result of events ... and owing to well founded fear of being *persecuted for reasons of* race, religion, nationality, *membership of a particular social group* or political opinion' [emphasis added]. Convention relating to the Status of Refugees, (adopted 28 July 1951, entered into force 22 April 1954) 189 UNTS 150.

[270] The ICCPR and GA Resolution 2625 do not provide a definition of 'people', and similarly the First Protocol to the Geneva Convention. And see International Covenant on Economic, Social and Cultural Rights, (adopted 16 December 1966, entered into force 3 January 1976) 993 UNTS 3. See also Yves Sandoz and others (eds), *Commentary on the Additional Protocols of 8 June 1977 to the Geneva Conventions of 12 August 1949* (Martinus Nijhoff Publishers, 1987) 52. On the lack of an internationally agreed definition of 'minorities', see, e.g., Kristin Henrard, 'Minorities, International Protection' in *R Wolfrum (ed), Max Planck Encyclopedia of Public International Law* (OUP, 2008), <http://opil.ouplaw.com/home/EPIL> para 2. The ILO Convention on Indigenous Peoples does not define who indigenous and tribal peoples are. ILO, *Manual: ILO Convention on Indigenous and Tribal Peoples, 1989 (No. 169)* (rev. edn, ILO, 2003). On the lack of generally accepted definition of the concept of 'indigenous people', see also Henrard, para 17. The term 'crime against humanity' is defined in Art 7 of the ICC Statute but the term 'identifiable group or collectivity' is not defined in the Statute or in the Elements of Crime. The term 'refugee' is defined in Art 1 of the Refugee Convention but the Convention does not define the term 'membership of a particular social group' under Art 1A(2) of the Convention.

[271] See, e.g., Christine M Von Der Haar, *Social Psychology: A Sociological Perspective* (Pearson 2005) 370; Brewer, 'The Many Faces of Social Identity' (n 12); Barth (n 36) 10–11; Jarlah Benson, *Working More Creatively with Groups* (Routledge 2000) 5.

assist legal decision-makers in ascertaining the definition of social groups under the particular international instrument.

A review of international legal literature reveals that it is generally agreed that the definition of the above social groups includes two essential elements: (i) common features that are shared by the members of the group (the 'objective element');[272] and (ii) group consciousness (the 'subjective element').[273] An additional, external component, mentioned in social identity literature (recognition by wider society),[274] is included in certain definitions cited in legal literature,[275] but does not usually constitute a mandatory requirement according to that literature.[276] Social identity literature suggests that the elements of common traits ('boundaries') and group consciousness ('self-identity') constitute mandatory elements in virtually all cases.[277]

As discussed in social identity literature, identity emerges and is maintained within a two-way relationship between self-identification (by individuals or groups that present their identity) and collective identification (acceptance or

[272] On the objective element in the definition of 'people' under the principle of self-determination, see UNESCO, 'Final Report and Recommendations of the International Meeting of Experts on further study of the concept of the rights of peoples UNESCO', UNESCO (Paris, 27–30 November 1989) (22 February 1990) UN Doc SHS-89/CONF.602/7, 7–8 <http://www.burmalibrary.org/docs18/Rights_of_Peoples-report-UNESCO-red.pdf> accessed 23 March 2015. And regarding this element in the definition of 'people' under the 1977 First Protocol, see Yves Sandoz and others (eds) *Commentary on the Additional Protocols* (n 270) 53. On this element in the definition of the term 'identifiable group or collectivity' under the ICC Statute, see, e.g., Elements of the Crime, Art 7(1)(h)(3) (n 268). On this element in the definition of 'social group' under Art 1 of the Refugees Convention, see Refugee and Humanitarian Division, Department of Immigration and Multicultural and Indigenous Affairs, *Particular social group: An Australian Perspective* (2007) 65, 71, 81 <http://www.immi.gov.au/media/publications/refugee/convention2002/07_social_group.pdf> accessed 23 March 2015; Henrard (n 270) para 4; OHCHR, 'Minority Rights: International Standards and Guidance for Implementation' (2010) 2. On this element in the definition 'indigenous people', under Convention on Indigenous Peoples, see *Manual: ILO Convention on Indigenous and Tribal Peoples* (n 270) 7.

[273] On the subjective element in the definition of 'people' under the rules regarding self-determination, see UNESCO Expert Group (n 272) 7–8. Regarding this element in the definition of 'people' under the First Protocol, see Yves Sandoz and others (eds) Commentary on the Additional Protocols (n 270) 52. On this element in the definition of 'social group' under Art (1) of the Refugees Convention see Refugee and Humanitarian Division, *Particular social group: An Australian Perspective* (n 272) 67, 71; Dieter Kugelmann, 'Refugees' in R Wolfrum (ed), *Max Planck Encyclopedia of Public International Law* (OUP, 2010), <http://opil.ouplaw.com/home/EPIL> para 11. On this element in the definition of 'minority' under Art 27 of the ICCPR, see Henrard (n 270) para 13; OHCHR, Minority Rights (n 272) 3. On this element in the definition of 'indigenous people' under the Convention on Indigenous Peoples, see Art 1(2) of the Convention on Indigenous Peoples; Henrard (n 270) para 17; *Manual: ILO Convention on Indigenous and Tribal Peoples* (n 270) 8.

The subjective element is not included in the above-mentioned Art 7(1)(h) of The Elements of the Crime of the ICC. On the exceptional nature of this provision (and other provisions aiming to protect social groups from persecution), see further below.

[274] See Section II(b) above.

[275] See, e.g., regarding the definition of 'people' under the First Protocol, Yves Sandoz and others (eds) Commentary on the Additional Protocols (n 270) 53.

[276] See, e.g., regarding 'minority groups', Henrard (n 270) paras 14–16, and the authorities cited therein; see in that regard on the definition of 'social group' under the Refugees Convention, OHCHR, Minority Rights (n 272).

[277] On the exceptional nature of legal rules aiming to protect social groups from persecution or discrimination, see further below.

dismissal by the wider society).[278] From this perspective, unilateral identification by the relevant social group is not sufficient to lead to the formation of a protected social group under international law. As elaborated below, some external acceptance of the particular group by the international community is needed for the group's legal protection.

The relative weight assigned to the respective elements of self-identity and external acceptance should vary according to the aim of the particular legal regime. Where the specific legal instrument aims at *granting certain benefits* to the members of a group (e.g., rights concerning ancestral lands),[279] both elements should be carefully examined. From this perspective, Article 1(2) of the Convention on Indigenous Peoples which provides that self-identification is the 'fundamental criterion'[280] should not be interpreted as determining that the internal element is the crucial element in the concept of social identity. On the other hand, it should be noteworthy that the needed 'external' recognition does not imply that recognition by the particular party which is bound to respect the group's rights (and often to assume the corresponding burden) is a prerequisite for legal recognition of the social group.[281] In such cases, recognition by groups of states, international institutions, or international tribunals may fulfil the element of external recognition.

Where the specific legal regime is *designed to protect a group's members* from discrimination or persecution, identification of the persecuted persons is often undertaken by members of the persecuting group (even where the persecuted individuals do not identify with the persecuted group). In such cases, it is suggested that both internal and external recognition be examined; but the centre of gravity should certainly be shifted to external identification by the persecuting group. The absence of self-identification by the persecuted individuals should not bar their protection under the relevant international instrument.

In addition to the elements of the 'social group', it is desirable that legal decision-makers take into account additional elements of social identity. Since the closely connected concepts of 'social group' and 'social identity' are elusive, it is neither desirable nor possible to define them in a precise and rigid fashion. Consequently, it is suggested to interpret these concepts in a flexible manner. It is desirable that legal decision-makers who are called upon to apply this concept broaden their scope of examination and examine evidence regarding additional factors discussed above, including symbols and rituals, language (including dialect), and collective narratives. Beside the essential elements of common objective

[278] See Section II(b) above.

[279] See, e.g., Arts 13–16 of the Convention on Indigenous Peoples; Henrard (n 270) para 18.

[280] Art 1(2) of the Indigenous Convention provides as follows: 'Self-identification as indigenous or tribal shall be regarded as a fundamental criterion for determining the groups to which the provisions of this Convention apply'. The *Manual: ILO Convention on Indigenous and Tribal Peoples* explains that 'Convention No. 169 is the first international instrument which recognizes self-identification of indigenous and tribal peoples as a fundamental criterion'. *Manual: ILO Convention on Indigenous and Tribal Peoples* (n 270) 8.

[281] The absence of governmental recognition of a *minority group* is not considered as a determinant fact. Henrard (n 270) paras 14, 16; OHCHR, Minority Rights (n 272).

features, self-identification[282] and some external recognition, the absence of any of the additional elements should not bar recognition of a particular social group under international law.

Finally, the nature of the above-discussed 'objective' element of social groups is worth clarifying. The common features that mark the boundaries of a particular group are widely labelled 'the objective element' in legal literature, mainly in contrast to the 'subjective element' of group identity (or 'group consciousness'). From a sociological perspective, these common features are not necessarily strictly objective, and often present significant subjective aspects. Some of the common features, like religious or other beliefs, are not always objectively discerned by members of other groups. Still, these features are very 'real' for the members of the particular group. As Jenkins states: '[g]roups may be imagined, but this does not mean that they are imaginary. They are experientially real in everyday life.'[283] Consequently, an examination of the 'objective' elements of a social group may require evidence as to the inter-subjective meanings shared by the members of the particular group's members.

V. Concluding Remarks

States and other international actors operate in complex identity networks that often affect their positions and activities in the international legal system. International legal rules and social identities interact in various manners, and diverse international identities (e.g., local, ethnic, and historical) are occasionally encoded into international legal rules. Social identity constitutes a conceptual bridge between individuals and collective groups (like 'peoples' or 'minority groups') or between collective groups (such as states or international institutions). Consequently, the impact of social identities on international law is particularly noticeable regarding legal rules regulating various links between individuals and social groups (e.g., affiliation with in a minority group), ties between states and a variety of international groups, and links between international groups (e.g., among regional groups). From this perspective, parallel to the central notion of 'inter-group relations' in social identity literature, it is possible to explore numerous international law rules as regulating diverse aspects of 'inter-*national*-group relations'.

As discussed above, international institutions often present significant aspects of identity groups (such as symbols, rituals, and collective narratives). International organizations' rules regarding accession of new members and suspension of existing ones often reflect the social boundaries that distinguish between the relevant international identity group and other international groups. Occasionally the

[282] As discussed above, the internal element of self-identity should not constitute an essential element with regard to legal rules that aim to protect persecuted groups.

[283] Jenkins (n 2) 12, see also 11–13.

basic instruments of international institutions expressly aim to construct a common identity.[284]

Social identities often affect international law-making. National identities occasionally influence state decisions to join or withdraw from international treaties that symbolize certain international identities. International institutions' identity also lead certain organizations to pre-condition the accession of new members by ratifying treaties that represent the group's identity; occasionally they aim to project their identities via trade treaties with non-member states.[285]

Social identity literature may not only shed new light on the content and form of international legal rules; it may also provide a complementary interpretative tool to clarify the content of legal provisions in international instruments. The interpretative contribution of tools and empirical knowledge drawn from social identity studies has been illustrated here with regard to the concepts of 'social groups' (which underlies diverse collective groups in the international system), 'impartiality' of adjudicators, and states succession.[286] While such an interpretation is expected to improve the quality of interpretation of various international legal rules, social identity analysis does not imply that additional methods of interpretation (including the conventional tools of legal interpretation) should not be considered.

This chapter discusses several prominent examples illustrating the mutual links between social identity and international law. Further socio-legal studies may explore additional domains of international law that reflect and affect social identities. Future work may examine substantive rules regarding the scope of the 'right to identity' of various groups (such as minority groups under international law[287] or national identities under EU law).[288] Social identity literature may assist legal decision-makers in interpreting various questions regarding the link between trade and culture, such as the 'cultural exception' included in some international trade treaties (like the NAFTA)[289] or provisions included in the General Agreement on Tariffs and Trade (GATT) (such as Article XX(f)).[290]

[284] See Section IV(b) above. [285] See Section IV(b) above.

[286] See Section IV(c) above.

[287] On the right of minority groups to maintain their identity, see, e.g., Henrard (n 270) para 23–4.

[288] Art 4(2) of the Treaty on European (consolidated version) provides that: 'The Union shall respect the equality of Member States before the Treaties as well as their national identities' [2012] OJ C 326.

[289] See, e.g., the North American Free Trade Agreement (signed 17 December 1992, entered into force 1 January 1994) (1993) 32 *ILM* 289 (NAFTA) Art 2106 and annex 2106. On the application of this provision to investment disputes, see, e.g., *UPS v Canada* (Award on the Merit) UNCITRAL (24 May 2007) [166], [169]. On cultural exception in NAFTA, see Jingxia Shi, *Free Trade and Cultural Diversity in International Law* (Hart Publishing, 2013) 232–9.

[290] For an analysis of cultural exception in the GATT and GATS (including aspects of national identity), see, e.g., Sandrine Cahn and Daniel Schimmel, 'The Cultural Exception: Does It Exist in GATT and GATS Frameworks' (1997) 15 *Cardozo Arts and Entertainment Law Journal* 281.

5

Diffusion of Norms and its Limits

Socio-Legal Fragmentation, Investment Tribunals, and Human Rights Law

We argue that where actors are seen as falling into the same category, diffusion should be rapid. Such effects may operate via perceptions built into the actors involved. The individual or organization's cognitive map identifies reference groups that bound social comparison processes. Rational mimicking requires prior and potential adopters be understood as fundamentally similar, at least with respect to the practices at issue.

David Strang and John W Meyer 'Institutional Conditions for Diffusion'[1]

[1] David Strang and John W Meyer 'Institutional Conditions for Diffusion' (1993) 22 *Theory and Society* 487, 490–1.

I. Introduction

The interactions between various branches of international law have attracted considerable attention from public international law scholars,[2] and this chapter aims to analyse a particular case of legal fragmentation from a sociological perspective: the interactions between international investment law and human rights law. While investment tribunals often incorporate rules of general international law, they adopt a consistent approach with regard to the *non*-significant role of international human rights law in investment disputes. Informed by sociological and sociology of law literature concerning diffusion of cultural traits (including laws), this chapter seeks to shed light on the socio-cultural dimension of the interactions between these two branches of international law.

The following analysis is premised on two (related) arguments: first, international investment law is significantly being developed and interpreted in the investment arbitration community, and the particular features of this social group influence the content of this law (including tribunals' jurisprudence). Second, legal interactions between various branches of international law (either integration or fragmentation) may be analysed as a social interaction between the relevant communities. More specifically, it is argued that the *socio-cultural distance* between the particular international legal settings affects the prospects of diffusion of norms across different branches of international law.

Section II discusses the influence of socio-cultural factors on various aspects of foreign investments, as well as the interaction between these factors and international investment law. Section III(a) briefly reviews sociological and sociology of law literature concerning the diffusion of cultural traits; Section III(b) sketches some lines regarding the mutual interrelationships between foreign investments and human rights protection; and Section III(c) elaborates on the limited diffusion of human rights norms in the investment arbitration community. Section IV(a) explores the investment arbitration community as a social group and examines the impact of the particular features of this group on investment tribunals' jurisprudence regarding human rights instruments. Section IV(b) considers the interactions between human rights and investment laws as a social interaction, analyses the socio-cultural distance between the two social groups, and discusses the impact of this distance on the attitude adopted by investment arbitrators towards resorting to human rights instruments. Section V addresses the dynamic aspect of the relationship between the two branches of international law and presents some factors which may enhance the prospects of diffusion of human rights

[2] See ILC, 'Report of the International Law Commission on the Work of its 58th Session, Part XII/D—Conclusions of the work of the Study Group on the Fragmentation of International Law: Difficulties Arising from the Diversification and Expansion of International Law' (1 May to 9 June and 3 July to 11 August 2006) UN Doc A/61/10 para 251. See also Section III below.

norms within the investment arbitration community. Section VI provides a brief summary of the main conclusions arising from the previous sections.

II. Socio-Cultural Factors, Foreign Investment, and International Investment Law

The sociological core assumptions regarding the influential role of social factors on individual behaviour are extended to the economic realm by economic sociology.[3] From this perspective, international economic activity does not constitute an exception, and foreign investment is also conceived of as a specific type of social interaction. Empirical studies show that socio-cultural factors affect foreign investment flows,[4] preferred investment location, and the measure of control sought by investors over foreign partners. Business management literature reveals that firms are less likely to invest in culturally distant[5] countries.[6] Thus, firms are more likely to launch foreign investment in markets relatively similar to their own.[7] The correlation between volumes of foreign investment and cultural distance is associated with the uncertainty that affects transaction costs. Where investment involves significant cultural distance, firms are less capable of specifying transaction contingencies and are concerned that their agents in the foreign territory take advantage of the principals' limited knowledge.[8]

Foreign investments are also influenced by the 'social capital' (the level of trust and set of values facilitating cooperation among the community's members) in the potential location.[9] Economic literature has established that trust is not only affected by the characteristics of the particular country but also by cultural aspects of the match between the two countries; and lower bilateral trust is likely to lead to less investment flow between two countries.[10] Thus, for example, Cheng and Wu's study reveals that

[3] See Chapter 2, Section II.

[4] Thus, for example, Siegel, Licht and Schwartz found that cultural distance concerning egalitarianism is a robust and economically significant obstacle to foreign investment flows. They define egalitarianism as 'the belief that all people are of equal worth and should be treated equally in society'. Jordan I Siegel, Amir N Licht, and Shalom H Schwartz, 'Egalitarianism, Cultural Distance, and FDI: A New Approach' (2013) 24 *Organization Science* 1174, 1174–5.

[5] On the roots and evolution of the concept of 'cultural distance' see Oded Shenkar, Yadong Luo, and Orly Yeheskel, 'From "Distance" to "Friction": Substituting Metaphors and Redirecting Intercultural Research' (2008) 33 *Academy of Management Review* 905, 907–9.

[6] See, e.g., Seung-Hyun Lee, Oded Shenkar, and Jiatao Li, 'Cultural Distance, Investment Flow, and Control in Cross-border Cooperation' (2008) 29 *Strategic Management Journal* 1117, 1117–19 and see references therein.

[7] See, e.g., Shenkar, Luo, and Yeheskel (n 5) 907 and the reference therein.

[8] Ibid., 907–8.

[9] On the economic impacts of 'social capital' and its definition, see Rafael La Porta and others 'Trust in Large Organizations' (1997) 87 *American Economic Review* 333.

[10] Luigi Guiso, Paola Sapienza, and Luigi Zingales, 'Cultural Biases in Economic Exchange?' (2009) 124 *The Quarterly Journal of Economics* 1095.

foreign companies prefer to locate their new affiliates in provinces (in China) with higher social capital.[11]

Socio-cultural features do not only affect the volume and location of foreign investments but also investors' entry mode decisions regarding level of control sought by the foreign firm vis-à-vis its partners in the foreign country. Empirical studies indicate that low control modes are often selected in situations characterized by greater cultural distance. Thus, significant cultural distance leads firms to reduce the risk of cooperating with culturally different partners by choosing a lower control investment mode.[12]

Intercultural differences often influence negotiations and the likelihood of concluding a transnational investment agreement. Since culture influences how people think, communicate, and behave, it also affects how they negotiate. Negotiations involving business executives from dissimilar cultures—having different goals and different perceptions of fair outcomes[13]—are often impeded by cultural barriers.[14] Similarly, communication patterns during negotiations vary across cultures and this difference occasionally constitutes an additional hurdle to the conclusion of investment agreements.[15]

International investments are not only *affected by* socio-cultural factors, they often *influence* the socio-cultural features of the involved communities. Managerial literature emphasizes the importance of foreign investment as a channel for the diffusion of knowledge, technology, and management practices.[16] Thus, individuals, groups, and organizations involved in foreign investments are viewed in this literature as 'cultural carriers' which transmit cultural content and signals from one state to another.[17]

In light of the mutual interrelationships between foreign investment and socio-cultural factors, it is not surprising that international *legal rules* in this sphere[18] often reflect and affect societal factors and processes. Alternative legal

[11] James S Ang, Yingmei Cheng, and Chaopeng Wu, 'The Role of Social Capital and Cultural Biases in the Investment Behaviour of Foreign High-Tech Firms' (2011) <http://ssrn.com/abstract=1786535> accessed 2 March 2015.

[12] The level of control is defined in this study as the extent of ownership involvement in a cooperative relationship. Lee, Shenkar, and Li (n 6) 1118–19, and see the references therein.

[13] See, e.g. Rajesh Kumar, 'Culture and Emotions in Intercultural Negotiations', in Michele J Gelfand and Jeanne M Brett (eds), *The Handbook of Negotiation and Culture* (Stanford University Press, 2004) 13; Kwok Leung and Kwok-Kit Tong, 'Justice Across Cultures: A Three-Stage Model for Intercultural Negotiation', in Michèle J Gelfand and Jeanne M Brett (eds), *The Handbook of Negotiation and Culture* (Stanford University Press, 2004) 313.

[14] Jeswald W Salacuse, 'Negotiating: The Top Ten Ways That Culture Can Affect Your Negotiation' (September/October 2004) *Ivey Business Journal* <http://iveybusinessjournal.com/publication/negotiating-the-top-ten-ways-that-culture-can-affect-your-negotiation/> accessed 2 March 2015.

[15] Wendi Lyn Adair and Jeanne M Brett, 'Culture and Negotiation Processes' in Michele J Gelfand and Jeanne M Brett (eds), *The Handbook of Negotiation and Culture* (Stanford University Press, 2004) 158, 161–3.

[16] See, e.g., Lee Branstetter, 'Is Foreign Direct Investment a Channel of Knowledge Spillovers? Evidence from Japan's FDI in the United States', (2006) 68 *Journal of International Economics* 325.

[17] Shenkar, Luo, and Yeheskel (n 5) 914.

[18] The link between international investment law and socio-cultural factors is evident in special rules regarding cultural sectors which are included in certain investment treaties. See, e.g., The North

rules regulating international investments reflect different socio-cultural values of the involved communities and affect social processes[19] in these communities. Some legal rules applied in international investment law originated in other branches of international law; as elaborated below, the prospects of such diffusion of non-investment legal rules to investment law are affected by the particular features of the investment arbitration community as well as the socio-cultural distance between the relevant international legal settings.

III. International Legal Diffusion and Fragmentation: Investment Law and Human Rights Law

a. Diffusion and fragmentation in international law

The interactions between various branches of international law (and among tribunals)[20] have attracted vast attention from public international law scholars.[21] The International Law Commission explained this phenomenon with the example of the 'exotic' investment law:

> One of the features of late international modernity has been what sociologists have called 'functional differentiation', the increasing specialization of parts of society and the related autonomization of those parts.... *The fragmentation of the international social world has attained legal significance especially as it has been accompanied by the emergence of specialized and (relatively) autonomous rules or rule-complexes, legal institutions* and spheres of legal practice. What once appeared to be governed by 'general international law' has become the field of operation for such specialist systems as 'trade law', 'human rights

America Free Trade Agreement (adopted 8 December 1992, entered into force 1 January 1994) 32 *ILM* 289 (NAFTA) Art 2005 and annex 2106; Agreement Between Canada and—for the Promotion and Protection of Investments <http://italaw.com/documents/Canadian2004-FIPA-model-en.pdf> accessed 03 March 2015, Art 10(6) (Canada's Model Bilateral Investment Treaty). For an application of the above NAFTA's cultural exception, see, e.g., *United Parcel Service v Canada* (Award on the Merit of 24 May 2007) UNCITRAL <http://italaw.com/sites/default/files/case-documents/ita0885.pdf> accessed 6 March 2015 [167]–[172].

[19] On cultural aspects of some investment relations and disputes, see Annette Froehlich, 'Cultural Matters in Investment Agreements and Decisions' in August Reinisch and Christina Knahr (eds), *International Investment Law in Context* (Eleven, 2007) 141.

[20] On judicial borrowing among international courts and particularly, of the EFTA, MERCUSOR, and the European Court of Justice, see Benedikt Pirker, 'Interpreting Multi-Sourced Equivalent Norms: Judicial Borrowing in International Courts', in Yuval Shany and Tomer Broude (eds), *Multi-Sourced Equivalent Norms in International Law* (Hart, 2011) 93.

[21] See ILC, 'Report of the International Law Commission', (n 2); Andreas Fischer-Lescano and Gunther Teubner, 'Diversity or Cacophony?: New Sources of Norms in International Law Symposium', (2004) 25 *Michigan Journal of International Law* 999; Dirk Pulkowski, 'Narratives of Fragmentation: International Law between Unity and Multiplicity' (Founding Conference of the European Society of International Law, Florence, 2004) <http://www.esil-sedi.eu/fichiers/en/Pulkowski_670.pdf> accessed 5 March 2015. On the influence of 'interpretative communities' on fragmentation of international law, see Michael Waibel, 'Interpretive Communities in International Law' (2014) University of Cambridge Faculty of Law Research Paper No. 62/2014. <http://ssrn.com/abstract=2513411> accessed 5 March 2015.

law', 'environmental law', 'law of the sea', 'European law' and even such *exotic and highly specialized knowledges as 'investment law' or 'international refugee law' etc.—each possessing their own principles and institutions.*[22]

The ongoing proliferation of international investment agreements, increasing number of treaties in other branches of international law, and the considerable growth of investor–state arbitration[23] enhance the prospects for overlaps between obligations included in investment and non-investment instruments. Consequently, arguments regarding the relationships between rules arising from investment and non-investment instruments (e.g., environmental treaties)[24] are brought at the different stages of international investment litigation (including during discussions on liability[25] and on remedies).[26]

The discussion on factors affecting legal decision-makers to apply rules developed in other branches of international law is resonated with sociological literature regarding the diffusion of cultural traits.[27] Sociologists (as well as scholars from additional disciplines) seek to explain the process through which cultural features of one social group are transmitted to another one,[28] and discuss conditions and mechanisms affecting the spread of socio-cultural patterns (or the lack thereof).[29] These transmitted cultural patterns include religions, languages,

[22] ILC, 'Fragmentation of International Law: Difficulties Arising from the Diversification and Expansion of International Law—Report of the Study Group of the International Law Commission finalized by Martti Koskenniemi' (13 April 2006) UN Doc A/CN.4/L.682, [emphasis added, footnotes omitted] paras 7–8.

[23] For quantitative data on investor–state cases, see UNCTAD, 'IIA Issue Note 1—Recent Trends in IIAS and ISDS' (19 February 2015) UNCTAD/WEB/DIAE/PCB/2015/1 <http://unctad.org/en/PublicationsLibrary/webdiaepcb2015d1_en.pdf> accessed 5 March 2015.

[24] For a comprehensive analysis of the interactions between environmental protection and international investment law, see Jorge E. Viñuales, *Foreign Investment and the Environment in International Law* (CUP, 2012) 18–22, 83 et seq.

[25] See, e.g., *S.D. Myers v Canada* (Partial Award of 13 November 2000) UNCITRAL <http://italaw.com/sites/default/files/case-documents/ita0747.pdf> accessed 5 March 2015 [150] (with regard to the interaction between the NAFTA's investment obligations and the Basel Convention on the Control of Transboundary Movement of Hazardous Wastes and their Disposal). See also *SPP (ME) v Egypt* (Award on the merits of 20 May 1992), ICSID Case No. ARB/84/3 <https://icsid.worldbank.org/ICSID/FrontServlet?requestType=CasesRH&actionVal=showDoc&docId=DC671_En&caseId=C135> accessed 5 March 2015 [78] (with regard to the relationship between the UNESCO World Heritage Convention and investment obligations).

[26] See, e.g., *Santa Elena v Costa Rica* (Final Award of 17 February 2000) ICSID Case No. ARB/96/1 <http://italaw.com/documents/santaelena_award.pdf> accessed 5 March 2015 [71] (with regard to the interaction between international environmental law and investment obligations).

[27] For a concise survey of sociological literature on cultural diffusion, see Elihu Katz, 'Cultural Diffusion' in John R Hall, Laura Grindstaff, and Ming-Cheng Lo (eds), *Handbook of Cultural Sociology* (Routledge, 2010) 668–9 et seq.

[28] On the diffusion of *world* cultural models to states, see John W Meyer and others, 'World Society and the Nation-State' (1997) 103 *American Journal of Sociology* 144.

[29] Katz defines the elements of the study of cultural diffusions as follows: 'the study of cultural diffusion may be characterized as (1) the reception, or adoption, (2) of some idea or innovation, (3) over time, (4) by units of adoption—individuals, groups, organizations, nations—linked by: (5) channels of communication, internal and external; (6) social structures; and (7) systems of norms and values' Katz (n 27) 670. According to Roger's widely cited definition of 'diffusion of innovations', diffusion is a process by which an innovation is communicated through certain

technical changes, political ideologies, and norms. When cultural traits traverse from one community to another, they may constitute an engine of social change within the receiving community.[30] Social traits may be spread through diverse channels, including trade, investment, colonisation, migration, and the mass media; but it is clear that such interactions between communities (even intensified ones) do not always lead to a successful diffusion.[31]

In addition to the interaction between the two social groups, an essential factor standing out in the sociological diffusion literature relates to 'cultural fit'[32] between the involved communities.[33] Thus, Strang and Meyer emphasize that perceived similarity may enhance the rate of diffusion and where actors are seen as falling into the same category, diffusion should be more rapid.[34]

International relations literature, and particularly the social constructivist approach,[35] also emphasizes that shared collective understandings and socio-cultural linkages facilitate the diffusion of norms among nations (e.g., norms relating to economic liberalism[36] and political liberalism).[37] Checkel thus underlines that diffusion of norms is more rapid when a 'cultural match' exists between the systemic norms of the involved groups. Exploring the diffusion of international norms to domestic societies, he defines cultural match 'as a situation where the prescriptions embodied in an international norm are convergent with domestic norms, as reflected in discourse, the legal system (constitutions, judicial codes, laws), and bureaucratic agencies (organizational ethos and administrative

channels over time among the members of the social system. Everett M Rogers, *Diffusion of Innovations* (5th edn, Free Press, 2003) 11–35.

[30] See, e.g., Katz (n 27) 669.

[31] For a discussion on non-diffusion of norms, see, e.g., Sebastian Heilmann and Nicole Schulte-Kulkmann, 'The Limits of Policy Diffusion: Introducing International Norms of Anti-Money Laundering into China's Legal System' (2011) 24 *Governance* 639; Diarmuid Torney, 'Assessing EU Leadership on Climate Change: The Limits of Diffusion in EU Relations with China and India' (2012) KFG Working Paper Series <http://userpage.fu-berlin.de/kfgeu/kfgwp/wpseries/WorkingPaperKFG_46.pdf> accessed 5 March 2015.

[32] See, e.g., Strang and Meyer (n 1) 489; Katz (n 27) 678, 670–1. On the importance of organizational cultural fit for the internalization of external human rights norms, see Galit A Sarfaty, 'Why Culture Matters in International Institutions: The Marginality of Human Rights at the World Bank' (2009) 103 *AJIL* 647, 649, 654. See also Galit A Sarfaty, *Values in Translation: Human Rights and the Culture of the World Bank* (Stanford University Press, 2012) 75–105.

[33] On additional elements affecting the process of diffusion, see Katz (n 27) 671–3; Strang and Meyer (n 1) 488–90.

[34] Strang and Mayer (n 1) 490–2. On the significance of states' institutional models and close ties between them (regarding the diffusion of mass education), see John W Meyer, Francisco O Ramirez, and Yasemin Nuhoglu Soysal, 'World Expansion of Mass Education, 1870–1980' (1992) 65 *Sociology of Education* 128, 135, 146.

[35] On the social constructivist approach in international relations literature, see Chapter 1, Section IV.

[36] Beth A Simmons and Zachary Elkins, 'The Globalization of Liberalization: Policy Diffusion in the International Political Economy' (2004) 98 *American Political Science Review* 171, 175–6, 185–7.

[37] Beth A Simmons, Frank Dobbin, and Geoffrey Garret, 'Introduction: The International Diffusion of Liberalism' (2006) 60 *International Organization* 781, 789–801. For a survey of international relations literature on this issue, see also Amy Gurowitz, 'The Diffusion of International Norms: Why Identity Matters' (2006) 43 *International Politics* 305, 307–10.

procedures).'[38] Some international law literature addresses certain aspects of international diffusion of norms,[39] generally focused on states and how international law shapes states' behaviour.[40]

Sociology of law literature on 'legal transplants'[41] explores various sociological issues affecting the diffusion of laws, primarily among national legal systems. This literature ('legal adaptation') emphasizes the importance of 'legal cultures'[42] of the involved nations, contacts between them, and similarity or complementarity between the 'exporting' and 'importing' societies.[43] Socio-legal scholars also underline the key role of the legal professional community in the process of legal borrowing.[44]

Drawing on the above sociological, sociology of law, and social constructivist literature on diffusion of norms, the following sections analyse the *lack* of meaningful diffusion of international human rights norms within the investment arbitration community.

b. Foreign investments and international human rights

'Fragmentation' issues are particularly controversial with regard to the links between international investment law and human rights instruments, and investment scholars are increasingly studying the interactions between these two spheres of international law.[45] The relationships between foreign investment and human

[38] Jeffrey T Checkel, 'Norms, Institutions and National Identity in Contemporary Europe' (1999) 43 *International Studies Quarterly* 83, 87.

[39] See, e.g., Ryan Goodman and Derek Jinks, 'Toward an Institutional Theory of Sovereignty' (2003) 55 *Stanford Law Review* 1749 (on the influence of *global* cultural patterns on states' behaviour). For a sociological exploration of the impact of interactions between states' interpretations of an international treaty and their diffusion to international law, see Nitsan Chorev, 'Changing Global Norms through Reactive Diffusion: The Case of Intellectual Property Protection of AIDS Drugs' (2012) 77 *American Sociological Review* 831, 834.

[40] Galit A Sarfaty, 'International Norm Diffusion in the Pimicikamak Cree Nation: A Model of Legal Mediation' (2007) 48 *Harvard International Law Journal* 441, 445 and see the references therein.

[41] For a concise and perceptive discussion of socio-legal studies in comparative law, see Annelise Riles, 'Comparative Law and Socio-Legal Studies' in Mathias Reimann and Reinhard Zimmermann (eds), *Oxford Handbook of Comparative Law* (OUP, 2006) 775.

[42] On legal cultures, see Section IV(b) below.

[43] David Nelken, 'Towards a Sociology of Legal Adaptation' in David Nelken and Johannes Feest (eds), *Adapting Legal Cultures* (Hart, 2001) 3, 42–3. On the significance of 'complementarity' between the involved legal systems, see Pitman B Potter, 'Legal Reform in China: Institutions, Culture, and Selective Adaptation' (2004) 29 *Law & Social Inquiry* 465, 478–9; Otto Kahn-Freund, 'On Uses and Misuses of Comparative Law' (1974) 37 *Modern Law Review* 1, 12–13. On the influence of deeply held values, common sense assumptions, and cultural role of legal proceedings on the prospects of successful legal borrowing, see Lawrence Rosen, *Law as Culture* (Princeton University Press, 2006) 43; Oscar G Chase, *Law, Culture and Ritual: Disputing Systems in Cross-Cultural Context* (New York University Press, 2005) 48.

[44] See, e.g., Lawrence Friedman, 'Some Comments on Cottorrell and Legal Transplants' in David Nelken and Johannes Feest (eds), *Adapting Legal Cultures* (Hart, 2001) 93, 96.

[45] See, e.g., Pierre-Marie Dupuy, Francesco Francioni, and Ernst-Ulrich Petersmann (eds), *Human Rights, International Investment Law and Investor-State Arbitration* (OUP, 2009); Eric De Brabandere, 'Human Rights Considerations in International Investment Arbitration' in Malgosia Fitzmaurice and Panos Merkouris (eds), *The Interpretation and Application of the European*

rights protection are mixed: foreign investment may promote human rights in some cases, and decrease their protection in others.[46] Thus, for instance, where foreign investors establish basic services which allow poor populations access to water or electricity, these investments may further the protection of certain social and economic rights.[47] In contrast, the implementation of some projects by foreign investors may involve human rights violations. This may be the case, for example, where foreign investors breach their employees' basic workers' rights in the host state (and in the absence of host governmental intervention to protect the workers).[48] In other cases, the execution of an investment contract may involve a breach of human rights of the local population residing in the area. This type of argument was raised during the North American Free Trade Agreement (NAFTA) litigation between Glamis and the United States. The Quechan people contended that their indigenous rights—which were threatened by approval of the Glamis claim—were protected, inter alia, by the International Covenant on Civil and Political Rights (ICCPR), the International Labour Organization (ILO) Convention concerning Indigenous and Tribal Peoples, and the Inter-American Convention on Human Rights.[49]

These two branches of international law address an asymmetric legal structure between sovereign states and individuals or companies. States are generally in a superior legal position vis-à-vis individuals and foreign investors. Thus, for example, states may unilaterally change the domestic law applicable to these

Convention of Human Rights: Legal and Practical Implications (Martinus Nijhoff Publishers, 2013) 183; Luke Eric Peterson, 'Human Rights and Bilateral Investment Treaties: Mapping the Role of Human Rights Law within Investor-State Arbitration' (2009) *Rights and Democracy* <http://publications.gc.ca/collections/collection_2012/dd-rd/E84-36-2009-eng.pdf> accessed 5 March 2015; UNCTAD, 'Selected Recent Developments in IIA Arbitration and Human Rights: International Investment Agreements—IIA Monitor No. 2' (10 June 2009) UNCTAD/WEB/DIAE/IA/2009/7; Todd Weiler, 'Balancing Human Rights and Investor Protection: A New Approach for a Different Legal Order' (2004) 27 *Boston College International and Comparative Law Review* 429; Cordula A Meckenstock, *Investment Protection and Human Rights Regulation* (Nomos, 2010); Bruno Simma, 'Foreign Investment Arbitration: A Place for Human Rights?' (2011) 60 *International & Comparative Law Quarterly* 573.

46 On the diverse links between human rights and investments see, e.g., UNHCR, 'Economic, Social and Cultural Rights: Human Rights, Trade and Investment—Report of the High Commissioner for Human Rights' (2 July 2003) UN Doc E/CN.4/Sub.2/2003/9, 8–13; Kevin Kolben, 'Foreign Investment and Human Rights Link' in *Human Rights, Trade and Investment Matters* (*Amnesty International*, May 2006) <http://www.amnestyusa.org/sites/default/files/pdfs/hrtradeinvestmentmatters.pdf> accessed 5 March 2015; David L Richards, Ronald D Gelleny, and David H Sacko 'Money with a Mean Streak? Foreign Economic Penetration and Government Respect for Human Rights in Developing Countries' (2011) 45 *International Studies Quarterly* 219; Debora Spar, 'Foreign Investment and Human Rights' (1999) 42 *Challenge* 55.

47 See, e.g., Ursula Kriebaum, 'Privatizing Human Rights: The Interface between International Investment Protection and Human Rights' (2006) 5 *Transnational Dispute Management* 1.

48 See, e.g., Sandra Polaski, 'Linking Trade and Investment Agreements to Improvements in Labor Rights' in *Human Rights, Trade and Investment Matters* (Amnesty International, May 2006). <http://www.amnestyusa.org/sites/default/files/pdfs/hrtradeinvestmentmatters.pdf> accessed 5 March 2015.

49 *Glamis Gold Ltd. v United States of America* (Non-Party Supplemental Submission, Submission of the Quechan Indian Nation of 16 October 2006) UNCITRAL <http://www.state.gov/documents/organization/75016.pdf> accessed 5 March 2015.

non-state actors, and are in a better position to influence changes in international law (e.g., through concluding international treaties).[50] Consequently, legal rules and institutions developed in these spheres strive to compensate the inferior legal position of individuals and investors under the domestic law by enhancing their legal protection at the international level.

Both international investment law and human rights law grew out from law of state responsibility for injuries to aliens.[51] While individuals and foreign investors were primarily protected in the past by their states of nationality (in accordance with the rules on diplomatic protection),[52] their protection is increasingly facilitated by various international mechanisms to which they gain direct access.[53]

Questions regarding the diffusion of international human rights norms to international investment law have attracted the attention of international law scholars, and arguments regarding inconsistent obligations deriving from human rights and investment treaties are increasingly brought by different parties to investment disputes.[54] Thus, in the recent decade, investment tribunals encountered diverse arguments raised by host states,[55] foreign investors,[56] and non-state parties (in amicus briefs),[57] regarding the application of international human rights norms in investment law.

[50] See, e.g., Moshe Hirsch, 'Interactions between Investment and Non-Investment Obligations' in Peter Muchlinski, Federico Ortino, and Christoph Schreuer (eds), *The Oxford Handbook of International Law on Foreign Investment* (OUP, 2008) 154, 179.

[51] On state responsibility for injuries to aliens and human rights, see, e.g., Henry J Steiner and Philip Alston, *International Human Rights in Context: Law, Politics and Morals* (3rd edn OUP, 2008) 85–9. On state responsibility for injuries to aliens and the protection of foreign investors, see M Sornarajah *The International Law on Foreign Investment* (2nd edn, CUP, 2004) 89, 104–5.

[52] See, e.g., Rudolph Dolzer and Christoph Schreuer, *Principles of International Investment Law* (2nd edn, OUP, 2012) 1–6, 232–4; R Doak Bishop, James Crawford, and William Michael Reisman *Foreign Investment Disputes: Cases, Materials and Commentary* (Kluwer, 2005) 3–4; Kenneth J Vandevelde, *United States Investment Treaties: Policy and Practice* (Kluwer, 1992) 7–8; Andrew Paul Newcombe and Lluis Paradell, *Law and Practice of Investment Treaties* (Kluwer, 2009) 8 et seq.

[53] Though diplomatic protection is no longer the main instrument for protecting the rights of foreign investors, states of nationality sometimes extend diplomatic protection to their investors. See, e.g., *Ahmadou Sadio Diallo (Republic of Guinea v Democratic Republic of The Congo)* (Judgment) [2010] ICJ Rep 639.

[54] For a detailed analysis of such arguments see Moshe Hirsch, 'Investment Tribunals and Human Rights: Divergent Paths' in Pierre-Marie Dupuy, Francesco Francioni, and Ernst-Ulrich Petersmann (eds), *Human Rights in International Investment Law and Arbitration* (OUP, 2008) 97, 99–107; Clara Reiner and Christoph Schreuer, 'Human Rights and International Investment Arbitration' in Pierre-Marie Dupuy, Francesco Francioni, and Ernst-Ulrich Petersmann (eds), *Human Rights in International Investment Law and Arbitration* (OUP, 2008) 82. See also Peterson, (n 45) 22–31.

[55] See, e.g., regarding the Inter-American Convention on Human Rights, *Sempra Energy International v Argentine Republic* (Award of 28 September 2007) ICSID Case No. ARB./02/16 <http://italaw.com/sites/default/files/case-documents/ita0770.pdf> accessed 6 March 2015 [98]; and regarding the jurisprudence of the European Court of Human Rights, see *Siemens AG v Argentine Republic* (Award of 6 February 2007) ICSID Case No. ARB./02/08 <http://italaw.com/sites/default/files/case-documents/ita0790.pdf> accessed 6 March 2015 [346].

[56] See, e.g., regarding the application of international customary law, *Biloune v Ghana* (1993) 95 ILR 184 (1993) 202–3.

[57] See, e.g., regarding the application of various instruments regarding rights of indigenous peoples, *Glamis Gold Ltd. v United States of America* (Non-Party Supplemental Submission) (n 49).

c. Investment tribunals' approach to human rights law

An analysis of the investment awards reveals that while these tribunals often incorporate rules of general international law[58] (particularly the Vienna Convention on the Law of Treaties[59] and the International Law Commission (ILC) Rules on State Responsibility),[60] they adopt a quite consistent approach with regard to the *non*-significant role of international human rights law in investment disputes.[61] With few exceptions (such as the *Mondev* and al-Warraq awards),[62] investment tribunals have declined to examine thoroughly the specific provisions of international human rights instruments invoked by the parties.

Two decisions well illustrate the investment tribunals' reserved approach regarding the application of human rights law in investment disputes. The dispute in the *Von Pezhold v Zimbabwe* conjoined cases relates to properties in Zimbabwe on which the foreign investors operate timber plantations. The disputed properties were acquired by the government of Zimbabwe as part of its land reform programme.[63] The European Center for Constitutional and Human Rights (ECCHR) and four indigenous communities in Zimbabwe filed a petition to make submissions as amicus curiae in the arbitral proceedings.[64] The ECCHR asserted that the cases 'raise critical questions of international human rights law, which engage both the duty of the Zimbabwean state and the responsibility of

[58] For an application of postal treaties in investment proceedings, see *United Parcel Service v Canada* (n 18) [118]–[119]. For an application of general international law regarding bribery in investment proceedings, see *World Duty Free v Kenya* (Award of 4 October 2006) ICSID Case No. ARB/00/7 <http://italaw.com/documents/WDFv.KenyaAward.pdf> accessed 6 March 2015 (invoking international public policy); *Inceysa Vallisoletana SL v Republic of El Salvador* (Award of 2 August 2006) ICSID Case No. ARB/03/26 <http://italaw.com/sites/default/files/case-documents/ita0424_0.pdf> accessed 6 March 2015 (invoking general principles of law).

[59] The Vienna Convention on the Law of Treaties (adopted 23 May 1969, entered into force 27 January 1980) 1155 UNTS 331.

[60] ILC, 'Responsibility of States for Internationally Wrongful Acts 2001', annexed to UNGA Res 56/83 (28 January 2002) UN Doc A/RES/56/83 <http://www.un.org/en/ga/search/view_doc.asp?symbol=A/RES/56/83&referer=http://www.un.org/en/documents/&Lang=E> accessed 6 March 2015.

[61] See, e.g., Hirsch, 'Investment Tribunals and Human Rights: Divergent Paths' (n 54) 106–7; Reiner and Schreuer (n 54) 90; Barnaly Choudhury, 'Democratic Implications arising from the Intersection of Investment Arbitration and Human Rights' (2009) 46 *Alberta Law Review* 983, 988–90. See also Brabandere (n 45) 191, 208; Tamar Meshel, 'Human Rights in Investor-State Arbitration: The Human Right to Water and Beyond' (2015) 6 *Journal of International Dispute Settlement* 277.

[62] *Mondev International Ltd. v United States of America* (Award of 11 October 2002) ICSID Case No. ARB(AF)/99/2 <http://italaw.com/sites/default/files/case-documents/ita1076.pdf> accessed 6 March 2015 [143]–[144]; al-Warraq v Indonesia (Award of 15 December 2014) <http://www.italaw.com/sites/default/files/case-documents/italaw4164.pdf> accessed 28 August 2015, [240]–[251], [521]–[522], [556]–[580].

[63] European Center for Constitutional and Human Rights (ECCHR), *Human Rights Inapplicable in International Investment Arbitration? A Commentary on the Non-Admission of ECCHR and Indigenous Communities as Amici Curiae before the ICSID Tribunal* (July, 2012) <http://www.ecchr.de/worldbank.html?file=tl_files/Dokumente/Wirtschaft%20und%20Menschenrechte/ICSID%20tribunal%20-%20Human%20Rights%20Inapplicable_A%20Commentary.pdf> accessed 6 March 2015, 2.

[64] *Von Pezold and others v Zimbabwe,* (Procedural Order No. 2 of 26 June 2012) ICSID Case No. ARB/10/15 http://italaw.com/sites/default/files/case-documents/ita1044.pdf accessed 6 March 2015 [1].

the investor company, with regard to the affected indigenous peoples.'[65] The tribunals explained in an interim decision that they had the discretion to allow non-disputing parties to make a submission[66] but ruled that '[t]he Petitioners provided no evidence or support for their assertion that international investment law and international human rights law are interdependent such that any decision of these Arbitral Tribunals which did not consider the content of international human rights norms would be legally incomplete.'[67] Furthermore, the arbitrators stated that:

> [I]n order for the Arbitral Tribunals to consider [the ECCHR's] ... submission, they would need to consider and decide whether the indigenous communities constitute 'indigenous peoples' for the purposes of grounding any rights under international human rights law. *Setting aside whether or not the Arbitral Tribunals are the appropriate arbiters of this decision, the decision itself is clearly outside of the scope of the dispute before the Tribunals.*[68]

Consequently, the Arbitral Tribunals denied the ECCHR's application to submit amicus curie.[69]

The *Azurix* award also typifies the generally unenthusiastic attitude of investment tribunals towards the application of international human rights law. Azurix, a corporation established in the USA, invested in a utility that distributed drinking water and treated sewage water in Argentina's Province of Buenos Aires. Azurix alleged that Argentina violated its obligations under the 1991 bilateral investment treaty (BIT) between the US and Argentina, international law, and Argentine law.[70] One of the arguments raised by Argentina related to the consistency between the BIT provisions and international human rights law. The government of Argentina argued that its measures leading to the termination of the investment agreement were justified by the need to protect consumers' rights. 'According to Argentina's expert, a conflict between a BIT and human rights treaties must be resolved in favour of human rights because the consumers' public interest must prevail over the private interest of a service provider.'[71] The tribunal addressed this argument briefly and noted that the matter had not been fully argued, and 'failed to understand the incompatibility in the specifics of the instance case'.[72]

Thus far, notwithstanding numerous arguments raised by various parties, and a few tribunals' general statements regarding the superior status of peremptory

[65] Ibid., [2]. [66] Ibid., [48]. [67] Ibid., [58].

[68] Ibid., [emphasis added] [60]. See also [61].

[69] Ibid., [64]. For a criticism of this decision, see ECCHR (n 63).

[70] *Azurix Corporation v Argentine Republic* (Award of 14 July 2006) ICSID Case No. ARB/01/12 (14 July 2006) http://italaw.com/sites/default/files/case-documents/ita0061.pdf accessed 6 March 2015 [3].

[71] Ibid., [254].

[72] Ibid., [261]. The Azurix tribunal also addressed the links between investment tribunals and the jurisprudence of the European Court of Human Rights (at [311]–[312]).

human rights,[73] no investment tribunal has discharged a party from its investment obligations or reduced the amount of compensation due to the injured party.

Investment tribunals which encountered such arguments presented diverse explanations for their *un*enthusiastic attitude towards resorting to human rights instruments. These reasons included lack of sufficiently elaborated arguments by the parties (the *Azurix*[74] and *Siemens*[75] cases), lack of jurisdiction (the *Biloune,*[76] *Euro-Tunnel,*[77] and *Aguas del Tunari*[78] cases), the limited reach of the particular treaty provisions (the *Grand River* case),[79] and different features of the two branches of international law (the *Siemens*[80] and the *Valores*[81] awards, as well as the *Azurix* Annulment award).[82] Some tribunals concluded, after analysing the relevant circumstances, that the specific issues disputed by the parties did not involve inconsistent investment and human rights obligations (the *Suez,*[83]

[73] The Methanex tribunal stated as follows: 'as a matter of international constitutional law a tribunal has an independent duty to apply imperative principles of law or jus cogens and not to give effect to parties' choices of law that are inconsistent with such principles.' *Methanex v USA* (Final Award of the Tribunal on Jurisdiction and Merits of 3 August 2005) UNCITRAL <http://italaw.com/sites/default/files/case-documents/ita0529.pdf> accessed 6 March 2015, at Part IV, Chapter C [24]. In addition, the Phoenix tribunal explained: 'To take an extreme example, nobody would suggest that ICSID protection should be granted to investments made in violation of the most fundamental rules of protection of human rights, like investments made in pursuance of torture or genocide or in support of slavery or trafficking of human organs.' *Phoenix Action Ltd. v Czech Republic* (Award of 15 April 2009) ICSID Case No. ARB/06/5 <http://italaw.com/sites/default/files/case-documents/ita0668.pdf> accessed 6 March 2015 [78]. See also *EDF International v Argentine Republic* (Award of 11 June 2012) ICSID Case No. ARB/03/23 <http://italaw.com/sites/default/files/case-documents/ita1069.pdf> accessed 6 March 2015 [912]–[914].

[74] *Azurix v Argentina* (n 70) [3].

[75] *Siemens AG v Argentine Republic* (n 55) [79].

[76] *Biloune v Ghana* (n 56) 202–3.

[77] *Channel Tunnel Group v Governments of the United Kingdom and France*, (Partial Arbitral Award of 30 January 2007) <http://www.pca-cpa.org/upload/files/ET_PAen.pdf> accessed 6 March 2015 [148].

[78] *Aguas del Tunari SA v Bolivia* (Petition by NGOs and people to participate as an intervening party or amici curiae of 29 August 2002) ICSID Case No. ARB/02/3 <http://italaw.com/sites/default/files/case-documents/ita0018.pdf> accessed 6 March 2015 [47]–[48].

[79] Encountering arguments regarding international instruments on rights of indigenous peoples, the Grand River tribunal ruled that the fair and equitable treatment standard (under Art 1105 of the NAFTA) 'does not incorporate other legal protections that may be provided investors or classes of investors under other sources of law. To hold otherwise would make Article 1105 a vehicle for generally litigating claims based on alleged infractions of domestic and international law and thereby unduly circumvent the limited reach of Article 1105 as determined by the Free Trade Commission in its binding directive.' *Grand River v USA* (Award of 12 January, 2011) UNCITRAL <http://italaw.com/sites/default/files/case-documents/ita0384.pdf> accessed 6 March 2015 [219].

[80] *Siemens AG v Argentine Republic* (n 55) [354].

[81] *Quasar de Valores v Russia* (Award of 20 July 2012) SCC Case No. 24/2007 <http://www.italaw.com/sites/default/files/case-documents/ita1075.pdf> accessed 6 March 2015 [22].

[82] *Azurix v Argentina* (Decision on the Application for Annulment of the Argentine Republic of 1 September 2009) ICSID Case No. ARB/01/12 Annulment Proceeding <http://italaw.com/sites/default/files/case-documents/ita0065.pdf> accessed 6 March 2015 [128].

[83] The Suez tribunal stated as follows: 'Argentina is subject to both international obligations, *i.e.* human rights *and* treaty obligations, and must respect both of them. Under the circumstances of this case, Argentina's human rights obligations and its investment treaty obligations are not inconsistent, contradictory, or mutually exclusive.' *Suez v Argentina* (Decision on Liability of 30 July 2010) ICSID Case No. ARB/03/17 <http://italaw.com/sites/default/files/case-documents/ita0813.pdf> accessed 6 March 2015 [240].

CMS,[84] *Saur*,[85] *EDF*,[86] and *Sempra*[87] cases) and some tribunals did not elaborate the reasons for this approach.

Several investment tribunals were ready to examine the impact of the European human rights law on investment disputes. Thus, for instance, the *Tecmed* and *Azurix* tribunals cited the case law of the European Court of Human Rights (ECtHR) (the *James* case)[88] in order to emphasize the vulnerability of investors in foreign countries.[89] A later attempt by Argentina to apply the same ECtHR judgment was dismissed by the *Siemens* tribunal, emphasizing the inconsistency between the European Convention's rules regarding the 'margin of appreciation' and international investment law.[90] A more balanced analysis of the case law of this European Court was undertaken by the *Mondev* tribunal.[91]

In all the above cases dealing with the interaction between investment and human rights instruments, no investment tribunal has absolved a party from its investment obligations or reduced the amount of compensation due to human rights instruments. The non-diffusion of international human rights norms to international investment law may be explained by various factors, but informed by the above sociological and sociology of law literature on diffusion, the following section focuses on the particular features of the investment arbitration community and the socio-cultural distance between the two relevant communities.

IV. Communities, Socio-Cultural Distance, and Legal Fragmentation

Sociologists of law have long emphasized that law is rooted in communities; laws have always been considered by these scholars as expressive types of these

[84] The CMS tribunal concluded, after analysing the relevant circumstances, that the issues disputed by the parties did not raise the 'question of affecting fundamental human rights'; *CMS Gas Transmission v Argentina* (Award of 12 May 2005) ICSID Case No. ARB/01/08 <http://italaw.com/sites/default/files/case-documents/ita0184.pdf> accessed 6 March 2015 [121]. For Argentina's argument in this regard see [114].

[85] *Saur International v Argentina* (Decision on Jurisdiction and Liability of 6 June 2012) ICSID Case No. ARB/04/4 <http://italaw.com/sites/default/files/case-documents/ita1016.pdf> accessed 6 March 2015 [330]–[332] (in Spanish).

[86] *EDF International v Argentine Republic* (n 73) [912]–[914].

[87] *Sempra Energy International v Argentine Republic* (n 55) [332].

[88] *James and Others v The United Kingdom* App no. 8793/79 (ECtHR, 21 February 1986) [50].

[89] *Técnicas Medioambientales Tecmed SA v United Mexican States* (Award of 29 May 2003) ICSID Case No. ARB(AF)/00/2 <http://italaw.com/sites/default/files/case-documents/ita0854.pdf> accessed 7 March 2015 [122]; *Azurix v Argentina* (n 70) [311].

[90] *Siemens AG v Argentine Republic* above (n 55) [354].

[91] *Mondev International Ltd. v United States of America* (n 62) [143]–[144]. See also *Saipem SpA v Bangladesh* (Decision on Jurisdiction and Recommendation on Provisional Measures of 21 March 2007) ICSID Case No. ARB/05/07 <http://italaw.com/sites/default/files/case-documents/ita0733.pdf> accessed 7 March 2015 [130], [132].

communities.[92] International investment law is significantly being developed and interpreted in the investment arbitration community, and the particular features of this community influence the content of this law (including investment tribunals' jurisprudence). Informed by the above sociological diffusion literature, it is submitted that the *socio-cultural distance* between the particular international legal settings affects the prospects of diffusion of norms across different branches of international law. Generally, greater socio-cultural distance between the involved social settings and groups tends to decrease the prospects for successful diffusion of norms. Thus, the propensity of investment tribunals to accord a significant role to human rights treaties is influenced not only by the particular features of the investment arbitration community but also by the socio-cultural distance between these two branches of international law.[93]

a. The investment arbitration community

The investment arbitration community[94] is a social group that primarily includes lawyers, arbitrators, scholars, and other experts specializing in investment arbitration.[95] This community shares some basic norms, including the principal duties of arbitrators (such as neutrality, fairness, confidentiality, expertise, and efficiency).[96] Community members are concerned about the opinions and respect of their colleagues, and peer pressure[97] exerted by other members operates to enforce the group's norms.[98] Unlike judges in permanent international courts, many members of the community have mixed roles, and many arbitrators contemporaneously

[92] Roger Cotterrell, *Law, Culture and Society: Legal Ideas in the Perspective of Social Theory* (Ashgate, 2006) 117, 161. See also Reza Banakar and Max Travers, 'Classical Sociology and Law' in Reza Banakar and Max Travers (eds), *An Introduction to Law and Social Theory* (Hart, 2002) 9, 10; Rosen (n 43) 2–9; Paul Schiff Berman, 'The Enduring Connections between Law and Culture' (2009) 57 *American Journal of Comparative Law* 101 and see the references therein.

[93] This contention does not aim to downplay other factors influencing interactions among various branches of international law.

[94] This section does not aim to provide a comprehensive analysis of the investment arbitration community. For a comprehensive (and insightful) sociological analysis of the international commercial arbitration community (until 1996), see Yves Dezalay and Bryant G Garth, *Dealing in Virtue: International Commercial Arbitration and the Construction of a Transnational Legal Order* (University of Chicago Press, 1996).

[95] On the important role of legal professionals in the process of legal borrowing, see Section III(a) above. On the 'epistemic community' of international investment lawyers and scholars, see Jeswald W Salacuse, 'The Emerging Global Regime for Investment' (2010) 51 *Harvard International Law Journal* 427, 465–6.

[96] See, e.g., William W Park, 'Arbitration in Autumn' (2011) 2 *Journal of International Dispute Settlement* 287; Joshua Karton, *The Culture of International Arbitration and the Evolution of Contract Law* (OUP, 2013) 85–90, 96–9, 115–16; Catherine A Rogers, *Ethics in International Arbitration* (OUP, 2014) 240 et seq.; Dezalay and Garth (n 94) 8.

[97] On the role of informal social control mechanisms in the implementation of norms, see Chapter 6, Section III(c).

[98] See, e.g., William W Park, 'Arbitrator Integrity: The Transient and the Permanent' (2009) 46 *San Diego Law Review* 629, 653, 658.

work as lawyers.[99] In addition, much of the writing is done by authors involved in investment treaty arbitrations.[100]

Notwithstanding certain divisions and stratification (addressed further below), the members of this social group constitute a fairly close-knit community.[101] The members of the group often use the term 'investment arbitration community' in investment arbitration discussion lists (see further below), international legal blogs,[102] conferences,[103] investment awards,[104] and literature.[105]

Investment arbitrators have a privileged status in the investment arbitration community. Empirical studies[106] reveal that most arbitrators originate from Europe and North America, and approximately 75% come from OECD countries.[107] The lack of gender balance among investment arbitrators is striking: 95% of International Centre for Settlement of Investment Disputes (ICSID) arbitrators have been male.[108] According to Harten, women have been much

[99] On the 'mixing of roles' of arbitrators and lawyers, see Dezalay and Garth (n 94) 49–51; Rogers, *Ethics in International Arbitration* (n 96) 318–19. See also Karton (n 96) 49–51.

On the important role of large law firms in international arbitration, see Dezalay and Garth (n 94) 8, 37–8, 48, 53.

[100] Stephan W Schill, 'W(h)ither Fragmentation? On the Literature and Sociology of International Investment Law' (2011) 22 *EJIL* 875, 893–4.

[101] Ibid., 866, 877; Karton (n 96) 2; Michael Waibel and Yanjui Wu, 'Are Arbitrators Political?' (2001) ASIL Research Forum Working Paper, 18; Daphna Kapeliuk, 'The Repeat Appointment Factor—Exploring Decision Patterns of Elite Investment Arbitrators' (2010) 96 *Cornell Law Review* 47, 77–8; Sergio Puig, 'Social Capital in the Arbitration Market' (2014) 25 *EJIL* 387, 400.

[102] See, e.g., Mike McClure, 'Most Favoured Nation Clauses—No Favoured View on How They Should Be Interpreted' (*Kluwer Arbitration Blog*, 25 July 2011) <http://kluwerarbitrationblog.com/blog/2011/07/25/most-favoured-nation-clauses-%E2%80%93-no-favoured-view-on-how-they-should-be-interpreted/> accessed 7 March 2015.

[103] See, e.g., Yas Banifatemi, 'Modern Law for Global Commerce' (Congress to celebrate the fortieth annual session of UNCITRAL Vienna, 9–12 July 2007) <http://www.uncitral.org/pdf/english/congress/Banifatemi.pdf> accessed 7 March 2015, 4.

[104] See, e.g., *Phoenix Action Ltd. v Czech Republic* (n 73) [34].

[105] See, e.g., August Reinisch, 'The Proliferation of International Dispute Settlement Mechanisms: The Threat of Fragmentation vs. the Promise of a More Effective System?' in Isabelle Buffard and others (eds), *International Law between Universalism and Fragmentation: Festschrift in Honour of Gerhard Hafner* (Martinus Nijhoff Publishers, 2008) 107, 119.

[106] These studies (mentioned below) have largely examined ICSID investment arbitrators. ICSID is the most important forum in international investment arbitration.

[107] David Gaukrodger and Kathryn Gordon (2012), 'Investor-State Dispute Settlement: A Scoping Paper for the Investment Policy Community' (2012) OECD Working Papers on International Investment 2012/03, 44 <http://www.oecd-ilibrary.org/docserver/download/5k46b1r85j6f.pdf?expires=1425725077&id=id&accname=guest&checksum=06EAC135D4DEA10B912459D398F8F6DA> accessed 7 March 2015; OECD, 'Investment Division Investor-State Dispute Settlement' (Public Consultation, 16 May to 9 July 2012), para 119 <http://www.oecd.org/dataoecd/61/29/50291642.pdf> accessed 7 March 2015; See also *The ICSID Caseload Statistics* (Issue 2014-2), 18–19 <https://icsid.worldbank.org/ICSID/FrontServlet?requestType=ICSIDDocRH&actionVal=ShowDocument&CaseLoadStatistics=True&language=English52> accessed 7 March 2015; Bianco Rogerio Carmona, 'The International Centre for Settlement of Investment Disputes (ICSID): An Empirical Research on the Voting Behaviour of Arbitrators' (28 November 2009), 24–5 <http://ssrn.com/abstract=1514882> accessed 7 March 2015. See also Puig (n 101) 405, 419.

[108] OECD, 'Investor-State Dispute Settlement' (Public Consultation) (n 107) para 119; Gaukrodger and Gordon (n 107) 44. See also Puig (n 101) 403–4, 419. In contrast, three of the seven members of the WTO Appellate Body are female; Kapeliuk (n 101) 78–9.

better represented among international judiciaries (women have comprised 32% of ECtHR appointees since 1995 and 19% of Appellate Body members in World Trade Organization (WTO) history).[109]

A relatively small group of frequently appointed arbitrators constitutes the core group which exerts significant influence in the investment arbitration community. The repeated nomination of the same person to serve as arbitrator is widespread in investment tribunals[110] (far more common than among WTO panels).[111] Thus, an OECD study notes that 'a group of only 12 arbitrators have been involved (typically as one or more of three arbitrators) in 60% of a large sample of ICSID cases'.[112] This elite group exercises a considerable influence in the legal profession,[113] and since they are present in 60% of the tribunals, they 'spread their influence not only on a quarter of tribunals, but well over half of them.'[114] Kapeliuk observes in her study on frequent arbitrators that: 'arbitrators appointed at least four times represent 14.9% of the arbitrator population. While this percentage seems low, these arbitrators' presence in the total number of concluded cases is impressive: at least one elite arbitrator was present in 80.2% of the concluded cases.'[115]

The investment arbitration community[116] is composed of two subgroups of specialists with commercial law and public international law background. These two sub-legal cultures present several (occasionally significant) different characteristics.[117] Thus, for example, Wälde emphasized the difference between these

[109] Gus Van Harten, 'The (lack of) women arbitrators in investment treaty arbitration' (2012) 59 *Columbia FDI Perspectives* <http://ccsi.columbia.edu/files/2014/01/FDI_59.pdf> accessed 7 March 2015.

[110] See, e.g., Puig (n 101) 407, 418.

[111] Jose Augusto Fontoura Costa, 'Comparing WTO Panelists and ICSID Arbitrators: The Creation of International Legal Fields' (2011) 1(4) *Oñati Socio-Legal Series* 1 <http://www.opo.iisj.net/index.php/osls/article/viewFile/63/207> accessed 7 March 2015. Joost Pauwelyn, 'WTO Panelists Are From Mars, ICSID Arbitrators Are From Venus: Why? And Does it Matter?' (1 January 2015), 7–10 <http://ssrn.com/abstract=2549050> accessed 7 March 2015.

[112] OECD, 'Investor-State Dispute Settlement' (Public Consultation) (n 107) para 120. For additional data on the most frequent arbitrators, see, e.g., Kapeliuk (n 101) 78; Jeffery Commission, 'A Snapshot of ICSID Arbitrators in Pending Cases' (*Kluwer Arbitration Blog*, 4 September 2009) <http://kluwerarbitrationblog.com/blog/2009/09/04/a-snapshot-of-icsid-arbitrators-in-pending-cases/> accessed 7 March 2015.

[113] See Kapeliuk (n 101) 68–9; Catherine A Rogers, 'Emerging Dilemmas in International Economic Arbitration: The Vocation of the International Arbitrator' (2005) 20 *American University International Law Review* 957, 967. See also Dezalay and Garth (n 94) 8.

[114] Costa (n 111) 12. See also Gaukrodger and Gordon (n 107) 45.

[115] Kapeliuk (n 101) 73.

[116] On the ideological division in the investment arbitration community between those having a 'pro-investor' or 'pro-state' reputation, see Pauwelyn (n 111) 13 and the references therein.

[117] On the differences between the approaches of these two groups, see Thomas W Wälde, 'The Present State of Research Carried Out by the English-Speaking Section of the Centre for Studies and Research' in *Hague Academy Report on International Investment Law* (2007) 68 et seq; Thomas W Wälde, 'Procedural Challenges in Investment Arbitration under the Shadow of the Dual Role of the State: Asymmetries and Tribunals Duty to Ensure, Pro-actively, the Equality of Arms' (2010) 26 *Arbitration International* 3, 4–5. See also Schill (n 100) 887–9; Anthea Roberts, 'Clash of Paradigms: Actors and Analogies Shaping the Investment Treaty System' (2013) 107 *AJIL* 45, 54–5; Karl-Heinz Böckstiegel, 'Commercial and Investment Arbitration: How Different are they Today?: The Lalive Lecture 2012 (2012) 28 *Arbitration International* 577.

approaches regarding the underlying relationships between the parties to investment arbitration. While the commercial arbitration tradition tends to underline the principle of 'equality of arms' and not granting states certain privileges, the public international law tradition is marked by pervasive deference to the state.[118] The present-day investment arbitration community (including investment tribunals) is dominated by the commercial arbitration paradigm.[119]

Members of the investment arbitration community are connected by various channels of communication that facilitate transmission of information and exchange. In addition to numerous professional conferences and meetings which provide a means of socializing new members into the existing legal culture,[120] the community is significantly influenced by electronic methods of communication.[121] The relatively new electronic means include the Investment Treaty News,[122] Investment Arbitration Reporter,[123] Kluwer Arbitration Blog,[124] and United Nations Conference on Trade and Development (UNCTAD) reports as well as its Investment Policy Blog.[125] Prominently, the OGEMID[126] discussion list includes virtually everybody in the community of investment lawyers, hosting frequent discussions on new developments in investment law and practice.[127] As Schill notes: 'OGEMID created a community sense among lawyers who often enough had never met in person. It thereby helped to forge the emergence of one global discourse on investment law'.[128] This discussion group annually publishes the OGEMID Awards which are granted (following votes by members of the OGEMID community) to, inter alia, the most influential award of the year as well as the most controversial or surprising arbitration decision of the year.[129]

[118] Wälde, 'Procedural Challenges' (n 117) 5–8. See also Roberts (n 117) 55.

[119] Wälde, 'Procedural Challenges' (n 117) 5. See also Wälde, 'The Present State of Research' (n 117) 75–6; Schill (n 100) 888; Roberts (n 117) 87; Gus Van Harten, *Investment Treaty Arbitration and Public Law* (OUP, 2007) 5–6, 58; Julie A Maupin, 'Public and Private in International Investment Law: An Integrated Systems Approach' (2014) 54 *Virginia Journal of International Law* 367, 394. On the importance of the equality of the parties in investment arbitration, see, e.g., *Malicorp v Egypt* (Decision on the Application for Annulment of Malicorp Limited of 3 July 2013) ICSID Case No. ARB/08/18 <http://italaw.com/sites/default/files/case-documents/italaw5000.pdf> accessed 7 March 2015 [36].

[120] See, e.g., Schill (n 100) 886; Karton (n 96) 7. On the importance of certain meetings, see also Dezalay and Garth (n 94) 50.

[121] Schill (n 100) 886.

[122] *Investment Treaty News* <http://www.iisd.org/itn/> accessed 7 March 2015.

[123] *Investment Arbitration Reporter* <http://www.iareporter.com/> accessed 7 March 2015.

[124] *Kluwer Arbitration Blog* <http://kluwerarbitrationblog.com/> accessed 7 March 2015.

[125] On UNCTAD various reports and publications, see International Investment Agreements (IIAs) Division on Investment and Enterprise <http://unctad.org/sections/diae_dir/docs/diae_sectiondescription_en.pdf> accessed 7 March 2015.

[126] Oil, Gas, Energy, Mining, and Investment Disputes. On the aims of this electronic discussion forum see also <http://www.transnational-dispute-management.com/news.asp?key=4> accessed 7 March 2015.

[127] Schill (n 100) 886–7. See also Campbell McLachlan, Laurence Shore, and Matthew Weiniger, *International Investment Arbitration: Substantive Principles* (OUP, 2007) 19.

[128] Schill (n 100) 887.

[129] As the editors explain: 'It is not designed to be a contest, does not purport to be scientific. This is just informal recognition among colleagues and a little bit of fun to start the new

The above features of the investment arbitration community (and additional ones addressed below) affect investment tribunals' approach[130] towards human rights law. This is particularly prominent with regard to the dominant commercial arbitration mindset and the private law culture that infuses investment tribunals' jurisprudence, as well as the ensuing ingrained tendency to downplay the role of public interests involved in investment disputes. And as argued above, the *socio-cultural distance* between the particular international legal settings as well as the interrelationships between the involved communities affect the prospect of diffusion of norms from one branch of international law to another.

b. The socio-cultural distance between investment and human rights laws

The social settings in which international investment and human rights laws emerge and are interpreted are very different. The members of the two communities pursue extremely different career paths.[131] While most human rights lawyers work in legal divisions of non-governemntal organizations (NGOs),[132] investment lawyers and arbitrators are predominantly lawyers-practitioners, legal scholars, or former judges affiliated with commercial law firms.[133] As Waibel and Wu state in that regard:

> Arbitrators are typically recruited from the pool of individuals with substantial experience in advising clients on international investment law. *There is thus little prospect for recruitment for lawyers working outside the large and well-known European and US law firms.*[134]

These divergent career paths indicate that the members of the two communities undergo starkly different socialization processes. Thus, for instance, while investment lawyers are inclined to emphasize the importance of unimpeded flow of capital, legal predictability,[135] and market economy ideology,[136] human rights lawyers are

year'. OGEMID Awards <http://www.transnational-dispute-management.com/ogemidawards/> accessed 7 March 2015.

[130] On the impact of the investment community's sociological features on the practice of de facto precedence in international investment jurisprudence, see Moshe Hirsch, 'The Sociology of International Investment Law' in Zachary Douglas, Joost Pauwelyn, and Jorge E Viñuales (eds), *The Foundations of International Investment Law: Bringing Theory into Practice* (OUP, 2014) 143, 162 et seq.

[131] On the influence of judges' professional background on judicial behaviour, see Erik Voeten, 'International Judicial Behaviour' in Cesare P Romano, Karen J Alter, and Yuval Shany (eds), *Oxford Handbook of International Adjudication* (OUP , 2014) 550, 565.

[132] On the role of NGOs in the human rights community, see, e.g., George E Edwards, 'Assessing the Effectiveness of Human Rights Non-Governmental Organizations (NGOs) from the Birth of the United Nations to the 21st Century' (2009) 18 *Michigan State Journal of International Law* 165.

[133] Waibel and Wu observe that more than 60% of arbitrators are in full-time private practice. Waibel and Wu (n 101) 28. See also Pauwelyn (n 111) 4–5.

[134] Waibel and Wu (n 101) [emphasis added] 28.

[135] On the importance of legal predictability in international investment law (and Max Weber's theoretical writing) see, e.g., *Suez v Argentina* (n 83) [203]. On the protection of legal predictability in the context of the fair and equitable clause in international investment law, see Moshe Hirsch 'Between Fair and Equitable Treatment and Stabilization Clause' (2011) 12 *Journal of World Investment and Trade* 783.

[136] On the close links between liberal economic ideology and international investment law see, e.g., Kenneth J Vandevelde, 'Sustainable Liberalism and the International Investment Regime'

more concerned with universal values and underline the primacy of human rights over other international legal rules[137] (including international investment law).[138]

While human rights lawyers are often linked to a certain social movement and determined to take sides in political or moral struggles,[139] most investment lawyers are anxious to maintain a neutral position.[140] Each community has a distinct heritage and collective narratives.[141] For example, while 'the great petroleum arbitrations' during the 1960s and 1970s 'occupy a quasi-mythical position' in international investment law,[142] the adoption of the Universal Declaration of Human Rights constitutes a central collective narrative for human rights lawyers.[143] Human Rights Day is annually observed worldwide on 10 December, marking the anniversary of the UN General Assembly's proclamation of the Universal Declaration.[144]

The members of the two communities employ different terminologies. Thus, while human rights lawyers frequently refer to 'the Covenants', 'CAT', or 'CERD', many of them hardly recognize terms like 'FET', 'umbrella' clause, or 'fork in the road' clause. Similarly, most investment lawyers are not familiar with the above human rights jargon. While these different vocabularies do not constitute an insurmountable language barrier, they point out the fundamental conceptual differences between these spheres of international law. On the significance of language of law, Lawrence Friedman noted:

> Any occupational group will make use of verbal shorthand: indeed, any group with shared experiences will do so. Lawyers share a common training, in law schools and universities. This gives them a common culture ... Words, phrases, and memories, drilled into lawyers'

(1997) 19 *Michigan Journal of International Law* 373, 395; Suzanne A Spears, 'The Quest for Policy Space in a New Generation of International Investment Agreements' (2010) 13 *Journal of International Economic Law* 1037, 1045–7.

137 On the peremptory nature of fundamental human rights, see, e.g., Teraya Koji, 'Emerging Hierarchy in International Human Rights and Beyond' (2001) 12 *EJIL* 917.

138 See, e.g., ECCHR (n 63) 4.

139 On the opposition of human rights activists to 'the image of the traditional scales of justice—calm, detached, neutral—in favour of a more prophetic image of law as a turbulent struggle' Deena R Hurwitz, 'Lawyering for Justice and the Inevitability of International Human Rights Clinics' (2003) 28 *YJIL* 505, 512. On 'cause lawyers' (or 'public interest') and their determination to take sides in political and moral struggles, see Corey S Shdaima, 'What's in a Name?: Cause Lawyers as Conceptual Category' (2006) Bepress Legal Series Paper 903 <http://law.bepress.com/cgi/viewcontent.cgi?article=4436&context=expresso> accessed 7 March 2015.

140 On the importance of neutrality as an element of the 'virtue' of arbitrators, see Dezalay and Garth (n 94) 8, 83; Karton (n 96) 114–17. See also Section IV(a) of this chapter. On the significance of being distant from politics, see Dezalay and Garth (n 94) 45, 98.

141 On the role of collective narratives in developing group identity, see Chapter 4, Section (II)(b).

142 See, e.g., Dezalay and Garth (n 94) 74.

143 Joseph Slaughter, *Human Rights, Inc: The World Novel, Narrative Form, and International Law* (Fordham University Press, 2007) 1–2, 15, 64, 70, 81. On the importance of collective narratives in the sphere of human rights, see Audrey Osler and Juanjuan Zhu, 'Narratives in Teaching and Research for Justice and Human Rights' (2011) 6 *Education, Citizenship and Social Justice* 223.

144 See UNGA Res 423 (V) (4 December 1950) inviting all states and international organizations to observe this day to celebrate the proclamation of the Universal Declaration on 10 December 1948.

heads during training, unite the profession, link it to a shared tradition, mark it as a kind of brotherhood, separated from the layman's world.[145]

The human rights and investment communities have developed dissimilar legal cultures. 'Legal culture' is a method of describing relatively stable patterns of legally oriented social behaviour and attitudes. The identifying elements of legal culture range from facts about institutions such as the role of lawyers and adjudicators, to various forms of behaviour such as litigation and aspects of legal ideas, values, aspirations, and mentalities. Though numerous studies identify legal culture with the nation state, patterns of legal culture can and must also be sought at both the sub-national and the transnational level.[146] The members of the investment and human rights communities have different legal cultures and different views regarding the role of law and tribunals.[147]

The different legal cultures prevailing in human rights and investment laws assign different social roles[148] to adjudicators. Generally, international tribunals fulfil two principal functions in the international legal system: settling disputes between the particular rival parties and developing legal rules to guide future behaviour. Tribunals' inclinations in that regard often influence the normative content of their decisions. Tribunals which give significant weight to their law-making role are more likely to take into account wider public policy considerations and seek a due balance between the competing interests. On the other hand, tribunals which emphasize their role in settling the dispute between the specific parties are less prone to grant significant weight to the broader policy issues involved in the disputes. Most investment tribunals incline to adopt the *inter partes* model (which is prevalent in commercial arbitration) and grant precedence to their role as settlers of disputes between the particular parties.[149] This role perception of investment adjudicators[150] and the link to the commercial arbitration tradition is well illustrated by the statement of the *Glamis* tribunal:

This Tribunal was constituted to address a particular dispute between Glamis and the United States of America. In this sense, *the Tribunal sees its mandate* under Chapter 11 of

[145] Lawrence Meir Friedman, *Law and Society: An Introduction* (Prentice Hall, 1977) 89.

[146] David Nelken, 'Using the Concept of Legal Culture' (2004) 29 *Australian Journal of Legal Philosophy* 1, 3. On the concept of legal culture, see also Cotterrell (n 92) 81–96. On the elements of legal culture, see David Nelken, 'Towards a Sociology of Legal Adaptation' (n 43) 25–6.

On legal culture as a methodological approach in international economic law scholarship, see Colin B Picker, 'Comparative Legal Cultural Analyses of International Economic Law: A New Methodological Approach' (2013) 1 *Chinese Journal of Comparative Law* 21

[147] On legal culture of arbitration, see, e.g., Tom Ginsburg, 'The Culture of Arbitration' (2003) 36 *Vanderbilt Journal of Transnational Law* 1335; On legal traditions in international commercial arbitration, see Leon Trakman, 'Legal Traditions and International Commercial Arbitration' (2006) 17 *American Review of International Arbitration* 1.

[148] Social role is defined in sociology as 'bundles of socially defined attributes and expectations associated with social position', *Penguin Dictionary of Sociology* (13th edn, Penguin Books, 2000) 301.

[149] See, e.g., Wälde, 'The Present State of Research' (n 117) 75–6; Choudhury (n 61) 988–99; Van Harten (n 119) 5–6, 58.

[150] The Romak tribunal stated as follows:

Ultimately, the Arbitral Tribunal has not been entrusted, by the Parties or otherwise, with a mission to ensure the coherence or development of 'arbitral jurisprudence.' *The*

the NAFTA *as similar to the case-specific mandate ordinarily found in international commercial arbitration. In the normal contractual setting, a tribunal is a creature of contract, tasked with resolving a particular dispute arising under a particular contract.* In all likelihood, a particular contract gives rises to only one arbitration.[151]

Generally, international commercial arbitrators perceive their primary role as providers of services to the parties[152] and their managerial skills in settling such disputes are of major importance for business people and arbitrators.[153] In light of the above prevalent role perception, most investment arbitrators are inclined to focus on the particular facts of the dispute and downplay the weight of public interest issues, including human rights protection.

On the substantive level, these two settings diverge along the private/public divide. Generally, international human rights law has evolved within the public law[154] sphere, and various freedoms, rights, authorities, and obligations have been assigned to individuals and states.[155] Keeping in mind the original inferior position of individuals, human rights law has established an impressive list of individual rights and freedoms to protect weaker parties in their relations with sovereign states.

Aiming to cope with a parallel structure of asymmetric relations, international investment law[156] followed a distinctive route and tends to focus on the private law aspects of the relations between host governments and foreign investors. To compensate for the inferior position of foreign investors under domestic law, investment tribunals are generally inclined to level the normative field and are predisposed to attach considerable weight to contractual and semi-contractual

> *Arbitral Tribunal's mission is more mundane, but no less important: to resolve the present dispute between the Parties in a reasoned and persuasive manner, irrespective of the unintended consequences that this Arbitral Tribunal's analysis might have on future disputes in general.* It is for the legal doctrine as reflected in articles and books, and not for arbitrators in their awards, to set forth, promote or criticize general views regarding trends in, and the desired evolution of, investment law.

Romak v Uzbekistan (Award 26 November 2009) PCA Case No. AA280 [emphasis added] <http://italaw.com/sites/default/files/case-documents/ita0716.pdf> accessed 7 March 2015 [171].

151 *Glamis Gold v United States of America* (Award of 8 June 2009) UNCITRAL [emphasis added] <http://italaw.com/sites/default/files/case-documents/ita0378.pdf> accessed 7 March 2015, [3]; and see also [7].

152 Karton (n 96) 100–8.

153 Thomas Schultz and Robert Kovacs, 'The Rise of a Third Generation of Arbitrators' (2012) 28 *Arbitration International* 161, 161–3, 166, 169–70.

154 For an insightful analysis of the history of the public-private divide, see Morton J Horwitz, 'The History of the Public/Private Distinction' (1982) 130 *University of Pennsylvania Law Review* 1423.

155 The public/private divide between international human rights law and investment law also arises from the different scope of application of the relevant rules (*inter-se* vs. *erga omnes* obligations), as well as the cogent and non-reciprocal nature of numerous human rights. See, Hirsch, 'Investment Tribunals and Human Rights: Divergent Paths' (n 54) 108–10.

156 On the tensions between private and public features in international investment law, see Alex Mills, 'Antinomies of Public and Private at the Foundations of International Investment Law and Arbitration' (2011) 14 *Journal of International Economic Law* 469; Stephan W Schill, 'Public or Private Dispute Settlement? The Culture Clash in Investment Treaty Arbitration and its Impact on

arrangements[157] (including various agreements, licenses, and promissory statements that are often made in a contractual environment).[158] This inclination[159] to level the legal field is linked to the dominance of the commercial arbitration paradigm in international investment law, particularly regarding the concept of 'equality of arms'.[160]

The focus on private law aspects of investment relations also constitutes a de-politicizing strategy for investment arbitrators anxious to maintain a neutral position. International investment law presents some ideological disagreements but legal-ideological controversies are much more conspicuous in the sphere of human rights.[161] Thus, the tendency to downplay the role of public interests[162] (including human rights) assists investment arbitrators to evade rulings on divisive issues that may impair the apparent neutrality.

The public/private divide between human rights and investment laws is also revealed in the institutional context in which the respective tribunals operate. Unlike permanent human rights tribunals (like the ECtHR or the Inter-American Court of Human Rights), most investment arbitral tribunals are regularly established on an ad hoc basis, premised on the parties' autonomy and consent.[163] The consensual nature of investment arbitration and the parties' control over the investment proceedings[164] were emphasized in the *Aguas del Tunari v Bolivia* case. A request by an NGO to submit *amicus curiae* briefs (based also on the 1966 ICCPR)[165] was turned down by the tribunal, explaining that:

the Role of the Arbitrator' in Todd Weiler and Freya Baetens (eds), *New Directions in International Economic Law* (Martinus Nijhoff Publishers, 2011) 23.

157 On the legal protection of contractual and semi-contractual arrangements under the 'fair and equitable' clause in investment treaties, see McLachlan, Shore, and Weiniger (n 127) 235–8; Dolzer and Schreuer (n 52) 152–4.

158 During the negotiations towards a contract and the 'entry stage', the gap between the parties' legal capacities is relatively smaller. Following this stage, and during most stages of the implementation of the investment, the superior position of the host state regarding its influence upon the content of both domestic and international law is glaring.

159 For a criticism of the current private law approach adopted by ICSID arbitrators (and particularly regarding the standard of review), see, e.g., William W Burke-White and Andreas Von Staden, 'Private Litigation in a Public Law Sphere: The Standard of Review in Investor-State Arbitrations' (2010) 35 *YJIL* 283, 288, 297, 344–5.

160 See Section IV(a) above.

161 See Moshe Hirsch, 'Conflicting Obligations in International Investment Law: Investment Tribunals' Perspective' in Tomer Broude and Yuval Shany (eds), *The Shifting Allocation of Authority in International Law* (Hart, 2008) 323, 335–7, and the references therein.

162 Park explains the role of the ICSID (in his article that received the OGEMID award the 'IDR-related Article of the Year 2011'): 'The ICSID Convention, Serving to Remove Non-commercial Impediments to the Free Cross-border Flow of Private Investment' [footnote omitted], Park, 'Arbitration in Autumn' (n 96) 289. On the 2011 OGEMID Awards, see TDM, OGEMID Awards 2011, <http://www.transnational-dispute-management.com/ogemidawards/> accessed 7 March 2015.

163 On the major role of the parties' consent in arbitral investment proceedings and the ensuing limited competence to address human rights issues, see also Reiner and Schreuer (n 54) 82.

164 And as Park states: 'Few would disagree that arbitrators must remain faithful to the parties' contract, not create new public policy'. Park, 'Arbitration in Autumn' (n 96) 297. See also Karton (n 96) 79–85.

165 *Aguas del Tunari SA v Bolivia* (n 78).

[I]t is the Tribunal's unanimous opinion that your core requests are beyond the power or the authority of the Tribunal to grant. The interplay of the two treaties involved [the ICSID Convention and the BIT] and *the consensual nature of arbitration places the control of the issues you raise with the parties, not the Tribunal.*[166]

This inclination to follow the private mode of adjudicating disputes is also illustrated in the prevalent confidential features[167] of most investment arbitral proceedings. Generally,[168] investment arbitration proceedings are not open to the public, tribunals do not disclose copies of written pleading and other documents, and oral hearings are closed to the public.[169]

International mechanisms developed to protect human rights are fundamentally different from those established in international investment law. Unlike investors' rights, which are primarily protected by ad hoc arbitral tribunals, states are often pressured to comply with their human rights obligations by NGOs, inter-governmental organizations, and special supervisory bodies established by international conventions.[170] International adjudicatory bodies play a significant role only in certain regional human rights regimes (mainly in Europe and in America).[171] In contrast to investment arbitration, human rights tribunals (like the European and Inter-American courts of human rights) present clear public features: they are permanent courts and their proceedings are regularly open to the public.[172] Unlike the enforcement of investment obligations, exposure of human rights violations to the public is a major instrument for pressuring states to respect their international obligations ('the politics of shame').[173]

[166] *Aguas del Tunari SA v Bolivia* (Letter from President of Tribunal Responding to Petition by NGOs to Participate as amici curiae of 29 January 2003) ICSID Case No. ARB/02/3 [emphasis added] <http://ita.law.uvic.ca/documents/Aguas-BoliviaResponse.pdf> accessed 7 March 2015.

[167] On confidentiality as a core principle of international commercial arbitration and its fundamental link to the principle of party autonomy, see Karton (n 96) 96–8.

[168] On the recent UNCITRAL rules regarding transparency in treaty investment arbitration (which came into effect on 1 April 2014), see UN Commission on International Trade Law, 'UNCITRAL Rules on Transparency in Treaty-based Investor-State Arbitration' (2014) <http://www.uncitral.org/pdf/english/texts/arbitration/rules-on-transparency/Rules-on-Transparency-E.pdf> accessed 7 March 2015. See also the UN Convention on Transparency in Treaty-based Investor-State Arbitration, adopted via UNGA Res 69/116 (18 December 2014) UN Doc A/RES/69/116 <http://www.un.org/ga/search/view_doc.asp?symbol=A/RES/69/116&Lang=E> accessed 7 March 2015. On the significance of these new rules, see Rogers, Ethics in International Arbitration (n 96) 315–17; Esme Shirlow, 'A Step toward Greater Transparency: The UN Transparency Convention' (*Kluwer Arbitration Blog*, 30 March 2015) <http://kluwerarbitrationblog.com/blog/2015/03/30/a-step-toward-greater-transparency-the-un-transparency-convention/> accessed 30 March 2015.

[169] For a comparison between the relevant rules of international arbitration institutions, see Christina Knahr and August Reinisch, 'Transparency versus Confidentiality in International Investment Arbitration' (2007) 6 *International Courts and Tribunals* 97, 98–103. See also Spears (n 136) 1073.

[170] See, e.g., Steiner and Alston (n 51) at 347–50, 456–99, 500–6.

[171] On these regional regimes, see Steiner and Alston (n 51) 563 et seq.

[172] On the difference between international commercial arbitration and international courts, see Mark L Movsesian, 'International Commercial Arbitration and International Courts' (2008) 18 *Duke Journal of Comparative and International Law* 423, 425–7, 437 et seq.

[173] See, e.g., James H Lebovic and Erik Voeten, 'The Politics of Shame: The Condemnation of Country Human Rights Practices in the UNHCR' (2006) 50 *International Studies Quarterly* 861.

One of the most significant factors affecting the limited diffusion of human rights norms to the investment arbitration community relates to the interactions between the two communities. The relationships between the arbitration investment and human rights communities are often characterized by mistrust and antagonism. These hostile relationships were prominent during the attempts to establish the comprehensive Multilateral Agreement on Investment (MAI) that failed in 1998,[174] as well as during the failed negotiations to formulate an additional WTO agreement on investment (1996–2004).[175] Indeed, one of the significant factors leading to these negotiation failures relates to the opposition of human rights and environmental NGOs.[176]

The animosity between these two communities is well illustrated by the reactions to an interim decision rendered by the *Pacific Rim* tribunal in August 2010. Following a decision to reject the preliminary objections of El Salvador,[177] the NGO Network for Justice in Global Investment[178] published a statement regarding investment tribunals:

> [T]his mechanism ... is rarely, if ever, upheld in favor of a national government, suggesting a fundamental imbalance in favor of transnational corporations....
>
> It is outrageous that the government of El Salvador is under attack for protecting the health and safety of its people," said Alexis Stoumbelis, ... *This is the ugly and fundamentally anti-democratic reality of free trade.*[179]

[174] On the MAI and its failure, see Michael J Trebilcock, Robert Howse, and Antonia Eliason, *The Regulation of International Trade* (4th edn, Routledge, 2013) 459–60; Americo Beviglia Zampetti and Pierre Sauvé, 'International Investment' in Andrew T Guzman and Alan O Sykes (eds), *Research Handbook in International Economic Law* (Elgar, 2007) 211, 249–51.

[175] See WTO, Doha Work Programme: Decision Adopted by the General Council on 1 August 2004 (2 August 2004) WT/L/579 <http://www.wto.org/english/tratop_e/dda_e/ddadraft_31jul04_e.pdf> accessed 7 March 2015, Art (g). See also Trebilcock, Howse, and Eliason (n 174) 589–90.

[176] See, e.g., Katia Tieleman *The Failure of the Multilateral Agreement on Investment (MAI) and the Absence of Global Public Policy Network (Case Study for the UN Vision Project on Global Public Policy Networks)* (European University Institute Firenze and Harvard University, 2000) 10–16; Stephen J Kobrin, 'The MAI and the Clash of Globalizations' (Fall 1998) *Foreign Policy* 97, 97–8, 114. On the NGO campaign against the WTO investment agreement, see, e.g., Hannah Murphy, 'NGOs, Agenda-Setting and the WTO' (Australasian Political Studies Association Conference, Monash University 24–6 September 2007) 10–13 <http://www.researchgate.net/publication/241103056_NGOs_Agenda-Setting_and_the_WTO> accessed 7 March 2015; 'WTO: Members Decide On Way Forward in Doha Round' (2003) 7(43) *Bridges Weekly Trade News Digest* 1, 1.

[177] See Pacific Rim Mining Corporation News Release, 'ICSID Tribunal Rejects Government of El Salvador's Preliminary Objection' (3 August 2010) <http://www.marketwired.com/press-release/pacific-rim-mining-corp-icsid-tribunal-rejects-government-el-salvadors-preliminary-objection-tsx-pmu-1298955.htm> accessed 7 March 2015.

[178] On this organization and its opposition to 'unaccountable international arbitration' in the sphere of foreign investments, see Network for Justice in Global Investment, 'About the Project' <http://justinvestment.org/about/> accessed 7 March 2015.

[179] Network for Justice in Global Investment, 'World Bank approves mining company suit against El Salvador' (11 August 2010) [emphasis added] <http://justinvestment.org/2010/08/world-bank-approves-mining-company-suit-against-el-salvador/> accessed 7 March 2015. See also Bilaterals, 'World War 4 Report, World Bank Approves Mining Company Suit Against El Salvador' (9 August 2010) <http://www.bilaterals.org/spip.php?article17848> accessed 7 March 2015.

A prominent figure in the OGEMID discussion list reacted angrily to the above statement, emphasized the biased approach of such NGOs, and raised doubts regarding the *amicus curia* procedures that are available to such groups.[180]

The above analysis of the socio-cultural distance between the investment and human rights communities sheds light on the limited diffusion of norms between these social groups and investment tribunals' general approach to human rights law.[181] In light of the considerable socio-cultural distance between investment and human rights laws, and the deep-rooted tensions between the relevant communities, it is not surprising that investment tribunals are generally reluctant to accord significant weight to human rights treaties in international investment law. Thus, it is plausible that the substantial socio-cultural distance between these socio-cultural settings and significant tensions between the two communities negatively affect the diffusion of norms between these two branches of international law.

V. Dynamic Socio-Cultural Aspects and Future Diffusion of Human Rights Norms

The above conclusion regarding the socio-cultural distance and the reduced prospects for diffusion of norms between investment and human rights laws does not mean that these relationships are not likely to change in the future. Past experience shows that the relationship between various branches of international law is often dynamic (e.g., the interaction between the laws of war and human rights[182] or between the GATT/WTO law and environmental protection).[183] The prospects for diffusion of norms between human rights law and investment law are likely to be affected by various socio-cultural factors and processes. Thus, the existing limited diffusion of norms between the two communities may be improved following changes *within* each of the relevant communities (e.g., demographic composition, change of social structure, or changing values), their mutual interactions, as well as external factors that may affect the approach of investment tribunals to human rights treaties.

[180] OGEMID's rules do not allow me to cite this reaction or attribute it to a particular person. See Transnational Dispute Management, 'OGEMID Rules (Substantive and Technical)', Arts 1–2 <http://www.transnational-dispute-management.com/ogemid/#rules> accessed 7 March 2015.

[181] The above-discussed approach undertaken by investment tribunals is not shared by non-investment tribunals addressing investment disputes which involve human rights treaties. The Southern African Development Community Tribunal discussed international legal rules applicable to expropriations undertaken by the government of Zimbabwe, and the tribunal did not hesitate to grant significant weight to human rights treaties. *Mike Campbell (Pvt) Ltd and Others v Zimbabwe (2/2007)* [2008] SADCT 2 (28 November 2008) <http://www.saflii.org/sa/cases/SADCT/2008/2.pdf> accessed 7 March 2015, 19–21, 47–51.

[182] See, e.g., Christian Tomuschat, 'Human Rights and International Humanitarian Law' (2010) 21 *EJIL* 15.

[183] See, e.g., Trebilcock, Howse, and Eliason (n 174) 665–84.

As to the current tensions between the two communities, the position of investment tribunals vis-à-vis human rights law may change, for instance, following increasing direct interpersonal interactions between the members of the two communities. Social identity empirical studies[184] suggest that interactions between the members of different groups on an interpersonal (rather than inter-group) basis are likely to reduce prejudice. Such interactions cause information about members of other groups to be organized on personal rather than group dimensions, and lead to a generalization of positive attitudes towards the out-group members.[185]

Similarly, the employment of a more common terminology in the two communities may enhance the prospects for diffusion of norms. Thus, for instance, investment literature may assess the injurious consequences of human rights violations in economic terms. Similarly, investment scholars may discuss the negative implications of widespread breaches of human rights for economic development, and may underline the significance of human rights protection for long-term economic development (measured by gross national income (GNI) per capita) and international investment relations. Existing empirical studies reveal that generally, rule of law promotes economic development.[186]

In addition, it seems that legal isolation is somewhat linked to isolation from the public. Thus, recent changes regarding the extent of investment tribunals' exposure to the public may entail a change in investment tribunals' approach to public interest issues, including human rights protection. The prevailing atmosphere of confidentiality in most investment arbitral proceedings tends to intensify the adjudicators' perception that their principal role is settling the particular dispute between the specific parties, and diminish the weight given by the tribunals to broader human rights which are occasionally involved in investment disputes. The current trend to enhance the transparency of investment tribunal proceedings to the public,[187] and greater participation of public interest groups

[184] For a discussion on social identity theory, see Chapter 4, Section II.

[185] To attain the desirable results, these interactions should be undertaken on an equal and cooperative basis. On this technique (and certain additional conditions), see Samuel L Gaertner, John F Dovidio, and Melissa A Houlette, 'Social Categorization' in John F Dovidio and others (eds), *The Sage Handbook of Prejudice, Stereotyping, and Discrimination* (Sage, 2010) 526, 530; Walter G Stephan and Cookie White Stephan, *Intergroup Relations* (Westview Press, 1996) 109–11; Phyllis Anastasio and others, 'Categorization, Recategorization and Common Ingroup Identity' in Russell Spears and others (eds), *The Social Psychology of Stereotyping and Group Life* (Blackwell, 1997) 236, 240; Thomas F Pettigrew, 'Intergroup Contact Theory' (1998) 49 *Annual Review of Psychology* 65, 65–8.

[186] Ronald J Daniels and Michael Trebilcock, 'The Political Economy of Rule of Law Reform in Developing Countries' (2004) 26 *Michigan Journal of International Law* 99, 101–4: Dani Rodrik, Arvind Subramanian, and Francesco Trebbi, 'Institutions Rule, The Primacy of Institutions over Geography and Integration in Economic Development' (2004) 9 *Journal of Economic Growth* 131.

[187] On this trend, see, e.g., *Biwater Gauff v United Republic of Tanzania* (Procedural Order No. 3 of September 29 2006) ICSID Case No. ARB/05/22 <http://italaw.com/sites/default/files/case-documents/ita0089.pdf> accessed 7 March 2015 [114]; Knahr and Reinisch (n 169) 97. On the recent UNCITRAL rules regarding transparency in treaty investment arbitration, see Section IV(b) above.

in investment proceedings, may gradually modify the current role perception of investment arbitrators and enhance the receptivity of human rights norms in the investment community.

The above trend and other relevant social processes, even if intensified, are gradual and a meaningful change in the relationships between the two communities (and between these branches of international law) is likely to take place incrementally and over a long-term period.

VI. Concluding Remarks

This chapter addresses a significant case of limited diffusion of norms between two branches of international law; the unreceptive approach of investment tribunals vis-à-vis human rights norms. An analysis of the investment awards reveals that while these tribunals often incorporate rules of general international law, they adopt a quite consistent approach with regard to the *non*-significant role of international human rights law in investment disputes.

A sociological analysis of the reluctant approach adopted by investment tribunals is informed by the sociological diffusion literature (and particularly regarding 'cultural fit') as well as the conceptual premise of sociology of law that laws are deeply rooted in communities. Thus, the particular legal rules evolved in each branch of international law are affected by the specific socio-cultural features which characterize the relevant social group in which these rules are applied and interpreted; and the prospects of diffusion of norms from one legal community to another is influenced also by the socio-cultural distance between these communities.

More specifically, it was argued that the non-receptive approach of investment tribunals towards human rights norms is influenced by the particular characteristic of the investment arbitration community, the considerable socio-cultural distance between the two social groups, and the negative features that characterize the interactions between the two communities. As to the specific features of the investment arbitration community, the socialization of most investment arbitrators in commercial law firms and the dominance of the commercial arbitration tradition in investment law may explain investment tribunals' ingrained inclination to focus on the private-commercial law aspects of investment disputes—and downplay the role of public interests (including human rights protection). In light of this considerable socio-cultural distance, and the significant tensions between the two communities, it is not surprising that human rights norms have not been meaningfully diffused to the investment arbitration community.

The current limited diffusion of norms between these two communities may change in the future. Past experience shows that the relationship between various branches of international law is often dynamic. Future socio-cultural changes within each community—or changes in the social interactions between the relevant communities—may narrow the socio-cultural distance between the human rights and investment laws communities, and enhance the prospects of diffusion across these branches of international law. Obviously, the relationships between these communities (and the interactions between the legal fields) are not likely to be transformed within a short period but rather gradually and over time.

6

Deviance and Conformity with International Law

[S]ocial groups create deviance by making the rules whose infraction constitute deviance, and by applying those rules to particular people and labelling them as outsiders.

Howard S Becker, *Outsiders: Studies in the Sociology of Deviance*[1]

[1] Howard S Becker, *Outsiders: Studies in the Sociology of Deviance* (Free Press, 1963) 9.

I. Introduction

The subject of compliance with international law has attracted the attention of international law scholars in recent decades. The former, rather sceptical, attitude of many scholars regarding state compliance with international law has largely shifted to a more favourable appraisal. The widespread view in the current literature[2] embraces the famous statement of Louis Henkin that 'almost all nations observe almost all principles of international law and almost all of their obligations almost all of the time'.[3]

Less preoccupied with the question of how much compliance, scholars now pose more intriguing questions as to why compliance is prevalent in the international community, and why some states breach their international obligations. These questions challenge scholars to identify the major factors that motivate states to observe or violate their international obligations. As elaborated below,[4] explanations of compliance or breaches affect strategies developed to enhance compliance with international law. The debate in international legal literature is often associated with two core paradigms in the social sciences: the rational choice, and the sociological approaches. After a brief comparison of these two core perspectives on compliance, the remaining sections of this chapter focus on the sociological context and roots of compliance with[5] or deviance from international law.

'Deviance' has long been considered one of the central topics in sociological literature. Sociological studies emphasize the social context of deviance and seek to understand the social roots of deviant behaviour, why certain activities are

[2] See, e.g., Andrew T Guzman, 'A Compliance-Based Theory of International Law' (2002) 90 *California Law Review* 1823, 1826; Kal Raustiala and Anne-Marie Slaughter, 'International Law, International Relations and Compliance' in Walter Carlsnaes, Thomas Risse, and Beth A Simmons (eds), *Handbook of International Relations* (Sage, 2002) 538, 540; Jana Von Stein, 'The Engines of Compliance' in Jeffrey L Dunoff and Mark A Pollack (eds), *Interdisciplinary Perspectives on International Law and International Relations: The State of the Art* (CUP, 2013) 477; Abram Chayes and Antonia Chayes, *The New Sovereignty: Compliance with International Regulatory Agreements* (Harvard University Press, 1995) 3; Dirk Pulkowski, 'Testing Compliance Theories: Towards US Obedience of International Law in the Avena Case' (2006) 19 *Leiden Journal of International Law* 511, 514; George W Downs, David M Rocke, and Peter N Barsoom, 'Is the Good News About Compliance Good News About Cooperation?' (1996) 50 *International Organization* 379.

[3] Louis Henkin, *How Nations Behave* (2nd edn, Columbia University Press, 1979) 47.

[4] See Section V below.

[5] Compliance is defined by Raustiala and Slaughter as 'a state of conformity or identity between an actor's behaviour and a specified rule'. Raustiala and Slaughter (n 2) 539. On the definition of 'compliance', see also Benedict Kingsbury, 'The Concept of Compliance as a Function of Competing Conceptions of International Law' (1998) 19 *Michigan Journal of International Law* 345, 346–9.

On the relationship between compliance and effectiveness, see Kal Raustiala, 'Compliance and Effectiveness in International Regulatory Cooperation' (2000) 32 *Case Western Reserve Journal of International Law* 387, 411–21; Lisa L Martin, 'Against Compliance' in Jeffrey L Dunoff and Mark A Pollack (eds), *Interdisciplinary Perspectives on International Law and International Relations: The State of the Art* (CUP, 2013) 591, 605.

regarded as deviant, and how those notions of deviance are applied to groups of peoples within society. Deviance is viewed as a universal phenomenon, and some sociological approaches (primarily structural-functional ones) view breach of societal norms as performing certain essential functions.[6] The concept of deviance is applied both to the behaviour of individuals as well as to activities by groups (e.g., corporations), and this chapter addresses breaches of international law committed by both individuals (e.g., international crimes) and other international actors (prominently states).

Section II briefly presents the key assumptions of the rational choice and the sociological approaches to compliance, as well as the premises of the corresponding streams in international relations literature (the realist and the social constructivist perspectives). Following a short introduction to the sociological literature on deviance, Section III offers a broad view of the relevant *rules* (both legally binding and 'soft') and the variety of societal control mechanisms involved in compliance with these rules. Section IV explores sociological factors involved in deviant behaviour and their application to compliance with international law. Three clusters of factors are addressed in this section: constructionist approaches which emphasize the role of labelling; social learning approaches focusing on societal transmission mechanisms (such as socialization and identity); and structural-functional approaches which highlight structural patterns that tend to motivate violations of law. The discussion of these sociological approaches is accompanied by their application to compliance with or breach of international law. Equipped with the above sociological tools, Section V briefly illustrates the practical value of sociological analysis in this sphere by suggesting some strategies that may enhance compliance with international law; mainly those associated with international social control mechanisms, reducing the risk of excessive social labelling and isolation, and reintegrative justice.

II. Compliance and the Inter-Paradigm Debate

Why do international actors obey or violate international legal rules? Two distinct social-science paradigms (which are often contrasted in the literature) provide two different answers to this important question. The rational choice model and the sociological perspective posit different assumptions regarding the motivation for social behaviour in general, and regarding the central factors that affect decision-making processes. Each of those paradigms has spawned theoretical strands in the various disciplines of the social sciences, including in law and international relations.

[6] See Section III(a) below.

a. The rational choice paradigm and the realist approach in international relations literature

The rational choice doctrine views a person as an instrumentally rational and calculating seeker of preference satisfaction. The standard rational choice model assumes that decision-makers are utility maximizers: they have certain goals ('preferences') which they strive to attain through their actions. They have consistent preferences over the goals and they know the outcomes ('utilities') of their alternative actions. Rational decision-makers select the course of action ('strategy') which maximizes their utility, as determined by their goals and the alternative options available to them. The rational choice model takes individual preferences as predetermined goals. The model does not seek to explain which factors motivate a person to adopt a certain aim and how preferences are modified over time. The process of the emergence and change of preferences is exogenous to rational choice theory.[7] Rational choice theory is widely applied in various social science disciplines, most commonly in economics, but also in sociology,[8] political science, international relations, and international law.

The rational choice model is rooted in the realist approach in international relations theory. Realism is the dominant theory in international relations literature. The principal assumptions of the realist school are that nation states are the principal actors in the international system; states are egoistic and rational (they are interested in maximizing their own interests and seek to attain them through rational decision-making processes); the primary interests of states are power and security; and that international politics is essentially anarchic (lacking an overarching authority) and conflictual. Proponents of the realist stream perceive international law as an instrument whereby states seek to attain their interests. Facing common tasks which are not easily amenable to unilateral attainment, national decision-makers treat international legal rules as instruments for fulfilling these common objectives.

According to the realist perspective, compliance with or violation of international norms is dependent upon a comparison of the expected outcomes resulting from these alternative courses of action. Consequently, numerous realist scholars contend that international law has little independent impact on state conduct. International rules are just expressions of power relationships, and they are likely to be ignored or changed when these relationships change. Thus, for instance, international treaties generally bind states to what they would have done anyway.[9]

[7] On the rational choice model, see, e.g., Martin Hollis, *The Philosophy of Social Science* (CUP, 2011) 116–18; Shaun Hargreaves Heap and others, *The Theory of Choice: A Critical Guide* (Blackwell, 1992) 4–5, 62–3; Jon Elster, *Nuts and Bolts for the Social Sciences* (CUP, 1989) 22 et seq.

[8] On the rational choice stream in sociology, see, e.g., Jonathan H Turner, *Contemporary Sociological Theory* (Sage, 2013) 511 et seq.; George Ritzer and Jeffrey Stepnisky, *Sociological Theory* (9th edn, McGraw Hill, 2013) 430–8; James S Coleman, 'Human Action as Rational Choice' in Richard Munch (ed), *Sociological Theory: Developments Since The 1960s* (Nelson Hall Publishers, 1990) 37.

[9] On the realist tradition in international relations and its perspective on international law, see Tim Dunne and Brian C Schmidt, 'Realism' in John Baylis, Steve Smith, and Patricia

Several researchers have employed models of game theory (a formalized strand of rational choice theory) to analyse the prospects of international legal cooperation in various settings[10] or compliance with international law.[11]

b. The sociological paradigm and the social constructivist approach in international relations literature

Unlike the rational choice model, the sociological paradigm[12] generally does not focus on individual decision-makers but rather emphasizes the social environment in which individuals live and act, as well as the relationships between social groups and individuals. Sociology does not assume that individuals' preferences and alternative courses of behaviour ('strategies') are exogenously given—but rather explores their development in a society or in interaction between individuals and society. One of the central assumptions of the classic sociological approach is that individual choices are significantly influenced by social factors and processes (such as norms or socialization). Accordingly, individual preferences alone cannot account for human behaviour in society.[13] Though sociologists generally assume that social factors affect individual attitudes and behaviour, different theoretical streams in sociological literature view differently the constraining influence of such societal patterns (including norms).[14]

Owens (eds), *The Globalization of World Politics* (6th edn, OUP, 2014) 99; Richard H Steinberg, 'Wanted—Dead or Alive: Realism in International Law' in Jeffrey L Dunoff and Mark A Pollack (eds), *Interdisciplinary Perspectives on International Law and International Relations: The State of the Art* (CUP, 2013) 146; Jack Donnelly, 'Realism', in Scott Burchill and others (eds), *Theories of International Relations* (4th edn, Palgrave, 2009) 31;Benjamin Frankel, 'Restating the Realist Case' in Benjamin Frankel (ed), *Realism: Restatement and Renewal* (Frank Cass, 1996) ix, xiv; Guzman, 'A Compliance Based Theory of International Law' (n 2) 1836–7; Kenneth.W Abbott, 'International Relations Theory, International Law, and the Regime Governing Atrocities in Internal Conflicts' (1999) 93 *AJIL* 361, 364–6; Anne-Marie Slaughter, 'International Law and International Relations Theory: A Prospectus' in Eyal Benvenisti and Moshe Hirsch (eds), *The Impact of International Law on International Cooperation* (2004) 16, 21–8. See also Beth A Simmons, 'Compliance with International Agreements' (1998) 1 *Annual Review of Political Science* 75, 79–80; Craig J Barker, *International Law and International Relations* (2000) 70–9.

10 See, e.g., Eyal Benvenisti, 'Collective Action in the Utilization of Shared Freshwater: The Challenges of International Water Resource Law' (1996) 90 *AJIL* 384; Moshe Hirsch, 'Game Theory, International Law, and Environmental Cooperation in the Middle East' (1999) 27 *Denver Journal of International Law and Policy* 75.

11 See, e.g., George Norman and Joel P Trachtman, 'The Customary International Law Game' (2005) 99 *AJIL* 541; Guzman, 'A Compliance-Based Theory of International Law' (n 2); Andrew T Guzman, *How International Law Works: A Rational Choice Theory* (OUP, 2008) 33–69; Moshe Hirsch, 'Compliance with International Norms In the Age of Globalization: Two Theoretical Perspectives' in Eyal Benvenisti and Moshe Hirsch (eds), *The Impact of International Law on International Cooperation* (CUP, 2004) 166, 174–8.

12 On the central tenets of sociology, see Chapter 1, Section II.

13 See, e.g., John J Macionis, *Sociology* (14th edn, Pearson, 2012) 2–3; Richard T Schaefer, *Sociology Matters* (5th edn, McGraw Hill, 2011) 2–3; Martin Hollis, *The Philosophy of Social Science* (n 7) 99–102; Shaun H Heap and others (n 7) 63–4; James Fulcher and John Scott, *Sociology* (4th edn, OUP, 2011) 4–8.

14 On the structure–agency debate in sociological literature, see Chapter 1, Section II.

The social constructivist approach in international relations literature[15] has been significantly influenced by sociological scholarship. From this perspective, states are social actors embedded in social relations which constitute their interests and motivate them. The critical components of the international social structure include shared inter-subjective understandings, expectations, and knowledge. The physical element is part of the international system but is secondary to social and ideational elements which infuse it with meaning, organize, plan, and guide it. International politics and related concepts are human creations and exist as inter-subjective beliefs which are widely shared among people.[16]

Under the constructivist approach, decision-makers are motivated by impersonal social factors such as values, norms, and cultural practices, rather than a calculation of material interests.[17] Legal obligations are perceived in this context as social standards of appropriate behaviour. Thus, norms, socialization, and identities are of major importance for the constructivist understanding of compliance with international law.[18]

Some international law scholars draw on the constructivist literature.[19] Koh's discussion on compliance with international law well illustrates the constructivist link between internalization of norms, definition of state interests, and the habit of obedience:

> Nations thus obey international rules not just because of sophisticated calculations about how compliance or noncompliance will affect their interests, but because a repeated habit of obedience remakes their interests so that they come to value rule compliance.[20]

The above discussion highlights the distinctions between the rational choice and the sociological perspectives on compliance. In practice, however, factors associated with both paradigms are often intertwined in compliance or non-compliance with international law, and occasionally it is impossible to disentangle them.

[15] On the intellectual roots of the social constructivist approach, see Phillip A Karber, 'Constructivism as a Method in International Law' (2000) 94 *American Society of International Law Proceedings* 189.

[16] On the social constructivist approach in international-relations literature, see Chapter 1, Section IV and the references therein.

[17] See, e.g., Raustiala and Slaughter (n 2) 538, 540: Robert O Keohane, 'International Institutions: Two Approaches' (1988) 32 *International Studies Quarterly* 379, 381.

[18] See, e.g., Raustiala and Slaughter (n 2) 540.

[19] For a comprehensive discussion on international law scholars drawing on the constructivist approach, see Jutta Brunnée and Stephen J Toope, 'Constructivism and International Law' in Jeffrey L Dunoff and Mark A Pollack (eds), *Interdisciplinary Perspectives on International Law and International Relations: The State of the Art* (CUP, 2013) 119. See also Pulkowski (n 2) 526–31; Raustiala and Slaughter (n 2) 544-6.

[20] Harold Hongju Koh, 'Why Do Nations Obey International Law?' (1997) 106 *Yale Law Journal* 2599, 2634. See also, Abram Chayes and Antonia Handler Chayes, 'On Compliance' (1993) 47 *International Organization* 175, 179; Vaughn P Shannon, 'Norms are What States Make of Them' (2000) 44 *International Studies Quarterly* 293, 293–4.

III. The Sociology of Deviance and International Social Control Mechanisms

a. The sociology of deviance

Deviance has long been considered one of the central topics in sociological literature.[21] The term 'deviance' refers in sociology to recognized violation of social norms[22] or, similarly, behaviour which violates normative standards governing acceptable conduct in a society.[23] This broad concept includes both violations of society's formally enacted laws ('crimes') as well as breaches of informal rules of behaviour.[24] Sociological studies emphasize the social context of deviance and seek to understand the social roots of deviant behaviour, why certain activities are regarded as deviant, and how notions of deviance are applied to people within society. The concept of deviance is applied in sociological studies both to the behaviour of individuals and to activities by groups.[25]

Sociologists generally view deviance as a universal phenomenon existing in all societies, and some sociological approaches, prominently the structural-functional stream,[26] consider breach of norms as performing certain essential social functions. The structural-functional perspective emphasizes the interdependence of the various components of society and it attaches particular significance to social stability and equilibrium.[27] Every social pattern has some function[28] which it performs in order to preserve the existing society.[29] One of Durkheim's key insights was that there is nothing abnormal about deviance, and deviant acts are inevitable

[21] As Goode explains, '[d]eviance is a fundamental sociological process, as essential to human existence as identity, social structure, status and culture. All human collectivities establish and enforce norms; in all collectivities, these norms are violated; as a consequence, the enforcement of norms ("social control") constitutes the life-blood of all social life'. Erich Goode, 'Deviance', *The Concise Encyclopedia of Sociology* (Wiley-Blackwell, 2011) 135 [hereinafter: 'Goode, "Deviance"'].

[22] The term 'norm' refers in sociology to shared expectation about appropriate behaviour which serve as a common guideline for social action. 'Norm', *Oxford Dictionary of Sociology* (4th edn, OUP, 2014) 519; 'Norm', *The Penguin Dictionary of Sociology* (4th edn, Penguin Books, 2000) 243. See also Steven P Dandaneau, 'Norms', *The Concise Encyclopedia of Sociology* (2011) 426.

[23] Gary Jensen, 'Deviance and Social Control' in Clifton D Bryant (ed), *The Routledge Handbook of Deviant Behaviour* (Routledge, 2011) 11. For a detailed discussion on the definition of deviance in sociological literature, see Erich Goode, *Deviant Behaviour* (9th edn, Prentice Hall, 2011) 6–18 [hereinafter: 'Goode, *Deviant Behaviour*']; Alex Thio, *Deviant Behaviour* (10th edn, Pearson, 2010) 6–13.

[24] Macionis (n 13) 194; Goode, 'Deviance' (n 21) 135; Thio (n 23) 13. On interactions between legal rules and social norms, see Section III(b) below.

[25] Fulcher and Scott (n 13) 232. See, e.g., on corporate deviance, Goode, *Deviant Behaviour* (n 23) 226–34; Thio (n 23) 336–40.

[26] On the structural functional approach in sociological theory, see Chapter 2, Section IV(b).

[27] Émile Durkheim, *The Rules of Sociological Method* (Steven Lukes, ed, Free Press, 1982) 87–93.

[28] On manifest and latent functions of social patterns, see Robert K Merton, *Social Theory and Social Structure* (enlarged edn, Free Press, 1968) 105, 114–23.

[29] Durkheim (n 27) 23 et seq. See also, Turner (n 8) 35 et seq.; Macionis (n 13) 12–13; Anthony Giddens and Philip W Sutton, *Sociology* (7th edn, Polity, 2013) 18–19.

and a necessary element of modern societies.[30] Thus, structural-functionalists[31] contend that what appears on the surface to undermine social order accomplishes the reverse, and deviance often contributes to the social system.[32] Deviant acts can provoke collective responses that reinforce social norms, clarify moral boundaries, enhance group solidarity, and encourage social change.[33] Erikson emphasized the social functions of censuring and punishing deviators and the ritual aspects of this process:

> The community's decision to bring deviant sanctions against an individual is not a simple act of censure. It is a sharp rite of transition … The ceremonies which accomplish this change of status … arrange a formal confrontation between the deviant suspect and representative of his community … ; they announce some *judgment* about the nature of his deviancy … Such ceremonies tend to be events of wide public interest and ordinarily take place in a dramatic, ritualized setting.[34]

The functional approach is echoed in Adler-Nissen's discussion of the role stigma[35] in the construction of international society. According to that approach, international society does not require unanimous acceptance of fundamental values but it does require stigmatization of norm breakers to specify those that threaten order. Thus, stigmatizing states also secures 'the performative enactment of the normal'.[36]

b. Compliance with hard and soft law

As noted, the sociological term 'deviance' includes behaviour that violates both legal rules and informal norms.[37] The sociological perspective on international law explores the whole range of rules reflecting normative standards of behaviour in the international community, including international legally binding rules (such as treaty provisions or international tribunals' judgments), and various softer international norms accepted by the international community (or a particular group of states).

[30] Durkheim (n 27) 101–5. See also Nachman Ben-Yehuda, 'Social Change and Deviance' in Clifton D Bryant (ed), *The Routledge Handbook of Deviant Behaviour* (Routledge, 2011) 38–9; Giddens and Sutton (n 29) 924; Macionis (n 13) 197; Goode, 'Deviance' (n 21) 135.

[31] See, e.g., Kai T Erikson, 'Notes on the Sociology of Deviance' (1962) 9 *Social Problems* 307, 310–12.

[32] Ibid., 309–10; Paul Rock, 'Sociological Theories of Crime' in Mike Maguire, Rod Morgan, and Robert Reiner (eds), *The Oxford Handbook of Criminology* (OUP, 2002) 69.

[33] Ibid., 69; Ben-Yehuda (n 30) 40–1; Macionis (n 13) 197; Giddens and Sutton (n 29) 924; Erikson (n 31) 309–12.

[34] Ibid., 311.

[35] On labelling and stigma in international law, see Sections IV(a) and V(b) below.

[36] Rebecca Adler-Nissen, 'Stigma Management in International Relations: Transgressive Identities, Norms and Order in International Society' (2014) 68(1) *International Organization* 143, 150.

[37] See Section III(a) above.

Soft instruments often attract wide participation of states and introduce new international norms through broad approval.[38] Such wide endorsement frequently exerts social pressure on policy-makers to comply with norms included in these instruments.[39] The latter soft rules include 'best practices', 'codes of conduct', 'guidelines', and 'recommendations' which are prevalent in various branches of international law (e.g., international finance,[40] environmental protection,[41] human rights,[42] and international investment law).[43]

The examination of compliance with international legal rules, international soft law, and international norms necessitates a brief discussion of the interactions between these categories. Numerous international *legally binding* rules overlap with international norms and such legal rules also constitute standards of acceptable behaviour in the international community. This is the case, for example, concerning the prohibition of crimes against humanity[44] or the obligation to treat prisoners of war humanely.[45] International treaties often also include more 'technical' rules, such as obligations to lower tariffs on imported products.[46] Though the latter 'technical' treaty rules do not reflect prominent social norms, they often generate social expectations that the contracting parties will adhere to their voluntarily undertaken obligations. Similarly, an international actor's consent to abide by decisions rendered by an international tribunal regularly engenders social expectations concerning compliance with such tribunals' judgments. In such cases, some social mechanisms which promote compliance with *norms* (such as 'social control')[47] may also support compliance with internationally binding legal rules.

[38] See, e.g., Chris Brummer, *Soft Law and the Global Financial System: Rule-Making in the 21st Century* (CUP, 2012)118; Allan Boyle, 'Soft Law in International Law-Making' in Malcolm D Evans (ed), *International Law* (3rd edn, OUP, 2010) 124–5.

[39] Brown Weiss concludes that '[g]enerally the research confirmed that consensus about the norm positively affected compliance'. Edith Brown Weiss, 'Conclusions: Understanding Compliance with Soft Law' in Dinah Shelton (ed), *Commitment and Compliance: The Role of Non-Binding Norms in the International Legal System* (OUP, 2000) 537.

[40] See, e.g., Brummer (n 38) 115–19.

[41] On the role of soft law in international environmental protection, see, e.g., Alexandre Kiss, 'Commentary and Conclusions' in Dinah Shelton (ed), *Commitment and Compliance: The Role of Non-Binding Norms in the International Legal System* (OUP, 2000) 223.

[42] On the role of soft law in international human rights law, see, e.g., Dinah Shelton, 'Commentary and Conclusions' in Dinah Shelton (ed), *Commitment and Compliance: The Role of Non-Binding Norms in the International Legal System* (OUP, 2000) 449.

[43] Andrea K Bjorklund, 'Assessing the Effectiveness of Soft Law Instruments in International Investment Law' in Andrea K Bjorklund and August Reinisch (eds), *International Investment Law and Soft Law* (Elgar, 2012) 51.

[44] The Rome Statute of the International Criminal Court (adopted 17 July 1998, entered into force 1 July 2002) 2187 UNTS, 90 Art 7.

[45] Geneva Convention (III) relative to the Treatment of Prisoners of War (adopted 12 August 1949, entered into force 21 October 1950) 75 UNTS 135 (Third Geneva Convention) Art 13.

[46] See, e.g., The General Agreement on Tariffs and Trade, (adopted 30 October 1947, entered into force 1 January 1948) 55 UNTS 194 (hereinafter GATT 1947) Art 2.

[47] On international social control mechanisms, see further below.

Non-legally binding rules[48] that reflect international norms are not regularly enforced by legal mechanisms (like the ICJ),[49] but conformity to such soft rules is likely to be promoted by a variety of social mechanisms (discussed below). Some international soft instruments do *not* reflect international norms and are not accompanied by social expectations that they will be followed.[50] Compliance with such non-legally binding instruments is not expected to be supported by international social control mechanisms that promote compliance with international norms. In certain limited cases, some societal processes (such as social identity or socialization) may motivate international actors to comply with such soft law that does not represent social norms. Thus, for example, self-perception and the aspiration to present itself as an outstanding actor in some sphere may lead an international actor to comply with soft law that does not necessarily embody an international norm.

In some less frequent cases, *binding* international legal rules do not reflect international norms and they are not accompanied by the social expectation that they will be followed by international actors. In those infrequent cases, social control mechanisms which regularly support compliance with international norms are not likely to support compliance with such binding international legal rules. And finally, in rare cases, an international norm may contradict an international legal obligation. In such cases, international social control mechanisms are likely to undermine compliance with legally binding obligations. Thus, for example, international tribunals that face such a contradiction may employ their discretionary powers (e.g., concerning the admissibility of the case) in order *not* to enforce a binding legal rule that contradicts a significant societal norm, or rather re-interpret the legal rule in accordance with the prevailing norm in the international society.[51]

The above distinction between 'soft' and 'hard' laws is often not sustained and rules belonging to these categories are frequently interwoven in the real-life fabric of international law; the borderline between rules is frequently blurred.[52] This

[48] Brown Weiss notes that in the absence of domestic legislation or a customary international law rule, domestic institutions for enforcing law (such as the judiciary) cannot be employed to enforce 'soft law'. Brown Weiss (n 39) 536. See also Dinah Shelton, 'Editor's Concluding Note: The Role of Non-Binding Norms in the International Legal System' in Dinah Shelton (ed), *Commitment and Compliance: The Role of Non-Binding Norms in the International Legal System* (OUP, 2000) 554, 556. See also Gregory Shaffer and Mark A Pollack, 'Hard and Soft Law' in Jeffrey L Dunoff and Mark A Pollack (eds), *Interdisciplinary Perspectives on International Law and International Relations: The State of the Art* (CUP, 2013) 197, 215.

[49] Non-legally binding rules that reflect international norms may influence decisions of international tribunals (and other international institutions like the Security Council) that interpret vague legal rules, such as 'due diligence'. Such vague legal concepts are discussed in Section IV(a) below.

[50] Some international non-legally binding instruments do not intend or create normative obligations. See, e.g., Dinah Shelton, 'International Law and Relative Normativity' in Malcolm D Evans (ed) *International Law* (3rd edn, OUP, 2010) 168.

[51] On inconsistency between *national* norms and international legal obligations, see Section IV(c) below.

[52] Shelton, 'International Law and Relative Normativity' (n 50) 165–6; Dinah Shelton, 'Law, Non-Law, and the Problem of "Soft Law"' in Dinah Shelton (ed), *Commitment and Compliance: The Role of Non-Binding Norms in the International Legal System* (OUP, 2000) 10–12.

is particularly prominent where treaties refer to 'soft' instruments,[53] or where 'soft' instruments provide detailed rules required for the implementation of binding international legal rules or for their interpretation.[54] Furthermore, some non-legally binding instruments are accompanied by supervisory mechanisms which traditionally monitor binding instruments.[55] Such monitoring mechanisms are of major importance for compliance.[56]

c. Social control mechanisms

Every society deploys diverse social control mechanisms, that is, the means to encourage and enforce conformity to societal norms (including addressing norm violation).[57] Social control involves a myriad of disciplinary mechanisms, both formal means authorized by the criminal justice system (e.g., police, courts, and prison officials) and less organized informal mechanisms (including expressions of praise or social disapproval, contempt, ridicule, or isolation).[58] Society's 'weapons' of social control are often divided between coercive forms of control (including direct physical constraints) and softer forms of control (including direct persuasion)[59] or certain features of the social media that affect ideas and attitudes.[60] From this perspective, law constitutes one aspect of social control.[61]

Sociological analysis of compliance or breach of international law explores not only the role of coercive means of social control (such as sanctions imposed by the Security Council), but also a broad range of positive and negative rewards employed by the international community to exert its influence in promoting conformity.

[53] On the interaction between the WTO Agreement on the Application of Sanitary and Phytosanitary Measures and non-binding international standards, see, e.g., Peter Van Den Bossche and Werner Zdouc, *The Law and Policy of the World Trade Organization* (3rd edn, CUP, 2013) 910–12; Melaku Desta and Moshe Hirsch, 'The African Countries in the World Trading System: International Trade, Domestic Institutions and the Role of International Law' (2012) 61 *International and Comparative Law Quarterly* 127, 145–7.

[54] See, e.g., Boyle (n 38) 127–8. See also Shaffer and Pollack (n 48) 207–8.

[55] Shelton, 'International Law and Relative Normativity' (n 50) 165–6. See also Dinah Shelton, 'Normative Hierarchy in International Law' (206) 100 *AJIL* 291, 319. On surveillance and peer review of OECD economic recommendations, see Martin S Edwards, 'Can Economic Surveillance Make a Difference? Insights from the OECD' (15 April 2013) *Global Policy Journal* <http://ssrn.com/abstract=2273283> accessed 17 March 2015.

[56] See, e.g., Brown Weiss (n 39) 538, 548.

[57] Goode, *Deviant Behaviour* (n 23) 49–50; Goode, 'Deviance' (n 21) 135; Mathieu Deflem, *Sociology of Law: Visions of a Scholarly Tradition* (CUP, 2008) 227 et seq.; Jensen (n 23) 14.

[58] Goode, 'Deviance' (n 21) 136; Goode, *Deviant Behaviour* (n 23) 50–2; Robert Agnew, 'Control and Social Disorganizational Theory' in Clifton D Bryant (ed), *The Routledge Handbook of Deviant Behaviour* (Routledge, 2011) 114, 115–16.

[59] On the role of persuasion in compliance with international law, see Ryan Goodman and Derek Jinks, 'How to Influence States: Socialization and International Human Rights Law' (2004) 54 *Duke Law Journal* 621, 635–8, 642–4.

[60] 'Social Control' in *Oxford Dictionary of Sociology* (n 22) 693–4; Robert J Brym and John Lie, *Sociology* (Wadsworth, 2003) 494.

[61] See, e.g., Talcott Parsons, 'The Law and Social Control' in William M Evan (ed), *The Sociology of Law: A Social-Structural Perspective* (Free Press, 1980) 60. Reprinted from William Evan (ed), *Law and Sociology* (Free Press, 1962) 56–72.

International social control mechanisms include various statements expressing condemnation or approval by international bodies (such as widely approved resolutions of the UN General Assembly,[62] Security Council Presidential Statements,[63] or decisions of the Financial Action Task Force regarding money laundering);[64] 'peer review' procedures employed by a variety of international institutions;[65] admission (or refusal to admit) new members to certain international institutions or groups; or expulsion from international institutions or groups.[66]

International social control mechanisms are more likely to be rigorously operated against violators of international rules (either 'soft' or 'hard' rules) that reflect fundamental norms of the international society (such as genocide, apartheid, and other international crimes). Generally, where the correlation between international rules and international norms is stronger, international social control mechanisms are more likely to promote compliance with such rules. As previously noted, international treaties also prescribe certain 'technical' rules, and often generate social expectations that the parties will abide by their voluntarily accepted obligations. Thus, some international social control mechanisms may also be involved in response to violations of such less value-laden treaty obligations

IV. The Social Causes of International Deviance

The ubiquitous nature of deviance in society[67] led sociologists to explore the societal context and roots of deviance. Different approaches in the sociology of deviance emphasize various factors involved in deviance and societal reactions to deviant behaviour. *Constructionist* approaches highlight the role of subjective processes affecting the definition of certain behaviours as 'deviant', how these definitions are applied to individuals and social groups, and the ramifications of such labelling.[68] A cluster of sociological explanations focuses on *social learning* mechanisms conducive to deviant behaviour, prominently socialization and identity.[69]

[62] See, e.g., UNGA Res 67/262 regarding the 'situation in the Syrian Arab Republic', (15 May 2013) UN Doc A/RES/67/262 Arts 1–2 <http://www.un.org/en/ga/search/view_doc.asp?symbol=A/RES/67/262> accessed 15 March 2015.

[63] See, e.g., UNSC 'Statement by the President of the Security Council (regarding Syria)' (2 October 2013) UN Doc S/PRST/2013/15 paras 6–9 <http://daccess-dds-ny.un.org/doc/UNDOC/GEN/N13/496/85/PDF/N1349685.pdf?OpenElement> accessed 15 March 2015. On the Security Council's presidential statements, see Henry G Schermers and Niels M Blokker, *International Institutional Law* (5th edn, Nijhoff, 2011) 827.

[64] On the practice of the Financial Action Task Force in this sphere, see Brummer (n 38) 150.

[65] On peer review mechanisms and peer pressure, see, e.g., Fabricio Pagani, 'Peer Review as a Tool for Cooperation and Change' (2002) 11 *African Security Review* 15, 16–17.

[66] On expulsion from international institutions as an instrument of international social control, see Section V(b) below.

[67] See Section III(a) above.

[68] See, e.g., Joel Best, 'Constructing Deviance' in Clifton D Bryant (ed), *The Routledge Handbook of Deviant Behaviour* (Routledge, 2011) 17–20; Giddens and Sutton (n 29) 927–8; Goode, *Deviant Behaviour* (n 23) at 48–9.

[69] See, e.g., Thio (n 23) 23–6; Ronald Weitzer, *Deviance and Social Control* (McGraw Hill, 2002) 26–7.

Structural-functional approaches emphasize structural factors which affect the likelihood of deviant behaviour, and seek to explain why such behaviour is more prevalent in certain social groups.[70] No single approach accounts for all deviant activities, and no single perspective dominates the sociology of deviance.[71]

a. Labelling theory

Labelling theory is the prominent constructionist approach and is widely used in the sociology of deviance.[72] The approach does not aim to explain the origin of the deviant act itself but rather focuses on how judgments of deviance are made, how they are applied to individuals and social groups, and the consequences of such labelling.[73] Deviance is a product of social interaction[74] between individuals and labelling theory emphasizes that a person cannot be deviant in the abstract, without a reference to how an audience does or would label it.[75] Thus, the determination of whether a particular act constitutes a breach of a norm is not objectively given, and the labelling process is affected not only by the properties of the particular act but also by subjective cultural factors.[76] In a widely cited passage, Becker states:

> [D]eviance is not a quality of the act the person commits, but rather a consequence of the application by others of rules and sanctions to an 'offender'. The deviant is one to whom that label has successfully been applied; deviant behaviour is behaviour that people so label.[77]

The labelling process is undertaken not only by public agencies which are legally authorized to label a particular person as deviant (like the judiciary) but also by informal actors like peer groups, the media,[78] and religious or other institutions.[79] Assuming that deviance is culturally and temporarily relative, sociologists seek to understand the interactionist process through which deviance is defined.[80] Though

[70] Goode, *Deviant Behaviour* (n 23) 24–6; Thio (n 23) 16–23.

[71] Giddens and Sutton (n 29) 923; Goode, *Deviant Behaviour* (n 23) 57.

[72] Ryken Grattet, 'Labelling Theory' in Clifton D Bryant (ed), *The Routledge Handbook of Deviant Behaviour* (Routledge, 2011) 121, 126. See also Malcolm Waters, *Modern Sociological Theory* (1994) 29.

[73] Goode, *Deviant Behaviour* (n 23) 54.

[74] Labelling theory is closely related to the symbolic-interactionist approach in sociological theory. On the symbolic-interactionist approach see Chapter 2, Section IV(c).

[75] Categories of audiences include society at large, 'significant others' of particular individuals, or official agents of social control. Goode, *Deviant Behaviour* (n 23) 54. See also Grattet (n 72) 121.

[76] Rock (n 32) 7; Goode, 'Deviance' (n 21) 135.

[77] Becker (n 1) 9.

[78] On the role of the mass media in labelling, see, e.g., David L Altheide, 'The Media and Deviance', *Blackwell Encyclopedia of Sociology* (Wiley-Blackwell, 2007) vol 3, 1107; Stuart Henry, 'Social Construction of Crime' in J Mitchell Miller (ed), *21st Century Criminology* (Sage, 2009) 296, 297–8.

[79] On labelling by institutions, see Richard Jenkins, *Social Identity* (4th edn, Routledge, 2014) 187–90.

[80] Goode, 'Deviance' (n 21) 135. See also Giddens and Sutton (n 29) 927; Macionis (n 13) 196–200.

it is possible to resist or modify deviant designations when attempts are made to apply them, once publicly identified as a deviant it becomes difficult for a person to return to the conventional world.[81] As discussed below, being labelled a deviant may amplify deviant behaviour.[82]

The labelling approach turns our attention to the fact that international mechanisms entrusted with the enforcement of international law also function as international labelling agencies: determining whether a particular actor is tagged as an international law-breaker. An authoritative finding that a particular state has breached certain international obligations (particularly grave norms) may stigmatize that country in the international community[83] and may entail far-reaching consequences in various spheres. The international labelling process is not only carried out by international judicial institutions (like the ICJ or ICC) which authoritatively attach a label of rule-breaker to a particular actor. Additional international labelling agencies include inter-governmental bodies such as the UN Security Council regarding the tag of 'aggression',[84] ad hoc commissions of inquiry,[85] and certain non-governmental organizations concerning international crimes.[86]

From the labelling perspective, it is clear that determinations regarding a breach of international law and the identity of the violator are not objectively given, and that the international labelling process relates not only to the particular features of the specific act but also to certain socio-cultural factors. It is thus plausible that individuals taking part in international labelling processes are also affected by various subjective factors, such as the socio-cultural background of the adjudicators or the conceptions of justice prevailing in their social group.

The definition of numerous international obligations is ambiguous and the application of such legal rules is particularly susceptible to being influenced by socio-cultural factors. Thus, for example, international bodies frequently apply vague legal concepts like 'due diligence' in the law of state responsibility,[87] 'legitimate expectations' in international investment law,[88] or 'legitimate interests' under the WTO Agreement on Trade-Related Aspects of Intellectual Property Rights.[89] International tribunals (or other international control mechanisms),

[81] Rock (n 32) 72. [82] See Section V(b) below.

[83] See, e.g., on 'the terrible stigma' associated with the crime of genocide, William A Schabas, *Genocide in International Law* (CUP, 2000) 12.

[84] UN Charter Art 39.

[85] See, e.g., UNGA, 'Report of the International Commission of Inquiry on Darfur to The United Nations Secretary-General Pursuant to Security Council Resolution 1564' (18 September 2004) <http://www.un.org/news/dh/sudan/com_inq_darfur.pdf> accessed 17 March 2015.

[86] See, e.g., the Amnesty International Report stating that 'The Syrian Government is Responsible for Mass Violations Amounting to Crimes Against Humanity.' Amnesty International, 'Syria: From All-out Repression to Armed Conflict in Aleppo', 1 August 2012 <https://listserv.buffalo.edu/cgi-bin/wa?A2=JUSTWATCH-L;ba6b5312.1208> accessed 18 March 2015.

[87] See, e.g., *Case Concerning Pulp Mills (Argentina v Uruguay)* (Judgment) [2010] ICJ Rep 14 [101].

[88] See, e.g., Moshe Hirsch, 'Between Fair and Equitable Treatment and Stabilization Clause' (2011) 12 *Journal of World Investment and Trade* 783; Rudolf Dolzer and Christoph Schreuer, *Principles of International Investment Law* (2nd edn, OUP, 2012) 130 et seq.

[89] Trade-Related Aspects of Intellectual Property Rights, (adopted 15 April 1994, entered into force 1 January 1995) 1869 UNTS 299.

which apply such vague concepts in order to determine whether a particular person or state has breached international law, are particularly likely to be influenced by socio-cultural factors.[90]

Finally, it is noteworthy that international labelling is not necessarily a unilateral process. When the identification of a particular rule-breaker is not undertaken by international judicial institution but rather by less-legalized labelling agencies (such as the UN General Assembly) or the mass media, international actors may contest the undesirable label.[91]

b. Social learning and identity

A cluster of sociological explanations of deviance focuses on cultural transmission of behavioural patterns. Sociologists assume that humans need social experience to learn their culture. Socialization is the lifelong process by which individuals learn to become members of society, both by internalizing society's norms and values, and also by learning how to perform their social roles.[92]

Sutherland's 'differential association theory' is one of the important social learning approaches in the sociology of deviance. Sutherland's point of departure is that criminal behaviour is learned, like the way members of society learn to speak their language. Criminal behaviour is learned in interaction with other people in a process of communication, and the principal part of the learning of criminal behaviour occurs within interpersonal groups. When criminal behaviour is learned, motives, rationalization, and techniques of committing the crime (sometimes complicated) are all transmitted. Favourable or unfavourable attitudes regarding lawful behaviour ('definitions') are also learned in such groups. In some groups, an individual is surrounded by people who define the legal code as rules to be observed, while in others she/he is surrounded by people whose definitions are favourable to violating the legal code. Thus, an individual's tendency towards conformity or criminal behaviour depends on the amount of association with others who favour either abiding by the law or violating the law.[93]

[90] The WTO panel noted with regard to the term 'legitimate interests' in Art 30 of TRIPS Agreement: 'To make sense of the term 'legitimate interests' in this context, that term must be defined in the way that it is often used in legal discourse—as a normative claim calling for protection of interests that are 'justifiable' in the sense that they *are supported by relevant public policies or other social norms*' [emphasis added] WTO, *Canada—Pharmaceutical Patents* (17 March 2000) WT/DS114/R [679].

[91] For a discussion of the strategy of 'stigma rejection' in international relations, see Adler-Nissen (n 36) 160–5. For a sociological analysis of contesting stigmas by groups in the larger society, see Abdi M Kusow, 'Contesting Stigma: On Goffman's Assumptions of Normative Order' (2004) 27 *Symbolic Interaction* 179.

[92] See, e.g., 'Socialization', *Oxford Dictionary of Sociology* (4th edn, OUP, 2014) 710; Macionis (n 13) 102–3. On socialization, see also Chapter 1, Section II.

[93] Edwin H Sutherland, *Principles of Criminology* (4th edn, Lippincott Company, 1947) 6–7. See also Goode, *Deviant Behaviour* (n 23) 35–6; Thio (n 23) 23–4; Robert J Franzese, *The Sociology of Deviance: Differences, Tradition, and Stigma* (Thomas Pub, 2010) 79–80. On Sutherland's differential approach and Aker's social learning theory, see Wesley G Jennings and Ronald L Akers, 'Social Learning Theory' in Clifton D Bryant (ed), *The Routledge Handbook of Deviant Behaviour* (Routledge, 2011) 106.

The concept of *acculturation* is closely related to socialization. Goodman and Jinks define acculturation as 'the general process by which actors adopt the beliefs and behavioural patterns of the surrounding culture'.[94] Acculturation parallels several features of the process of socialization: it involves a dual process of cultural and psychological changes occurring as a result of contact between two or more cultural groups; but it takes place *after* an individual's initial socialization into her/his original culture (thus, it may also be viewed as a process of re-socialization or secondary socialization).[95] Goodman and Jinks explain that, when successful,[96] the acculturation process is propelled by internal and social pressures that impel actors to adopt socially legitimated attitudes, beliefs, and behaviours.[97] Internal pressures are associated with the social-psychological outcomes of nonconformity (including anxiety, regret, and guilt) as well as the benefits of conforming to group norms (including cognitive comfort). Social pressures include the positive and negative responses which the group applies.[98]

Identity literature indicates that one of the consequences of the formation of a group's identity relates to compliance with the group's norms.[99] As discussed in Chapter 4,[100] identification with a group demands some loyalty and behavioural conformity, and group members orient their behaviour towards other members.[101] Scholars belonging to the social constructivist approach in international relations literature[102] emphasize that states' decision-makers learn the prevailing norms in their group and the expectations of appropriate behaviour.[103] Identity is one of the central concepts employed by social constructivist scholars and, from this perspective, norms either affect the formation of identities in the first place or

[94] Goodman and Jinks, 'How to Influence States' (n 59) 626. See also Ryan Goodman and Derek Jinks, 'Incomplete Internalization and Compliance with Human Rights Law' (2008) 19 *EJIL* 725, 725–6; Ryan Goodman and Derek Jinks, *Socializing States* (OUP, 2013) 25 et seq.

[95] John W Berry, 'Acculturation' in Joan E Grusec and Paul D Hasting (eds), *Handbook of Socialization: Theory and Research* (Guilford Press, 2007) 543.

[96] Goodman and Jinks acknowledge that international actors do not always bow to social pressure. On some factors influencing the likelihood of success of social pressure (according to the 'social impact theory'), see Goodman and Jinks, 'How to Influence States' (n 59) 642.

[97] Goodman and Jinks, 'How to Influence States' (n 59) 640–2.

[98] Goodman and Jinks, 'How to Influence States' (n 59) 641. See also Goodman and Jinks, *Socializing States* (n 94) 26–8.

[99] Goodman and Jinks highlight the link between identity and acculturation: 'The touchstone of this mechanism is that identification with a reference group generates varying degrees of cognitive and social pressures—real or imagined—to conform.' Goodman and Jinks 'How to Influence States' (n 59) 626. See also Goodman and Jinks, 'Incomplete Internalization and Compliance' (n 94) 726.

[100] See Chapter 4, Sections II(c) and IV(b).

[101] Jenkins (n 79) 152, 157–8.

[102] On the social constructivist approach in international relations literature, see Section II(b) above.

[103] See, e.g., Martha Finnemore 'Constructing Norms of Humanitarian Intervention' in Peter J Katzenstein (ed), *The Culture of National Security: Norms and Identity in World Politics* (Columbia University Press 1996) 153, 158–9; Raustiala and Slaughter (n 2) 546. For a constructivist account of the process of international socialization regarding international human rights norms, see Thomas Risse and Kathryn Sikkink, 'The Socialization of international Human Rights Norms into Domestic Practices: Introduction' in Thomas Risse, Stephen C Ropp, and Kathryn Sikkink (eds), *The Power of Human Rights: International Norms and Domestic Change* (CUP, 1999) 1, 5, 11–17.

they prescribe behaviours for already constituted identities.[104] The link between identity and compliance with international norms is particularly significant with regard to 'constitutive norms' that define group membership.[105]

Socialization is one of the most influential sociological processes in the international system[106] and it significantly affects the general rate of compliance with international law. The major agents of international socialization[107] include regional or ideological groups of states, a particular nation with which the particular actor is identified[108] (e.g., a former colonial power or contemporary ideological ally), and certain non-state actors. International institutions (global, regional, and others) often play a significant role in international socialization, and it is particularly notable, regarding the long accession process to certain international organizations (such as the EU, WTO, or OECD)[109] as well as the interaction between the members following the accession.[110]

Notwithstanding the importance of social learning for compliance with international law, it is clear that such processes do not guarantee compliance in all cases. International socialization is a gradual process,[111] and compliance with international law may improve over time.[112] Thus, 'incomplete internalization'[113] may particularly characterize new governments or fresh policy-makers. Such decision-makers, particularly in new states or states in transition, may not have sufficient time to fully internalize the norms prevailing in the international community and be more prone to violate international legal rules. Thus, for instance, several long-established rules regarding the protection of diplomats were violated by the new government of Iran in November 1979, a short period after the revolution.[114]

[104] Peter J Katzenstein, Ronald L Lepperson, and Alexander Wendt, 'Norms, Identity, and Culture in National Security' in Peter J Katzenstein (ed), *The Culture of National Security: Norms and Identities in World Politics* (Columbia University Press, 1996) 11, 54.

[105] Rawi Abdelal, Yoshiko M Herrera, and Alastair Iain Johnston, 'Identity as a Variable' (2006) 4 *Perspectives on Politics* 695, 697–8.

[106] Raustiala and Slaughter state that '[s]ocialization is the causal mechanism or pathway through which norms operate'; Raustiala and Slaughter (n 2) 546.

[107] On agents of socializations in society, see Chapter 1, Section II.

[108] On the impact of 'reference groups' on compliance with international law, see, e.g., Moshe Hirsch, 'The Impact of the Advisory Opinion on Israel's Future Policy: International Relations Perspective' (2004/5) 1 *Journal of International Law and International Relations* 319, 340–1.

[109] On accession to international organizations and international socialization, see Frank Schimmelfenning, 'International Socialization in the New Europe: Rational Action in an Institutional Environment' (2000) 6 *EJIR* 109; Ann Kent, 'China's International Socialization: The Role of International Organizations' (2002) 8 *Global Governance* 343; Petr Drulák and Lucie Königová, 'The Czech Republic: From Socialist Past to Socialized Future' in Trine Flockhart (ed), *Socializing Democratic Norms: The Role of International Organizations for the Construction of Europe* (Palgrave, 2005) 149.

[110] On socialization in international institutions, see Section V(b) below.

[111] On the stages of socialization, see, e.g., Macionis (n 13) 105–9.

[112] See, e.g., regarding international human rights law, Goodman and Jinks, 'Incomplete Internalization and Compliance' (n 94) 727, 731–3.

[113] On the notion of 'incomplete internalization, see Goodman and Jinks, 'Incomplete Internalization and Compliance' (n 94) 727.

[114] The ICJ stated in that regard: 'In its Order of 15 December 1979, the Court made a point: *'There is no more fundamental prerequisite for the conduct of relations between States', the Court there said, 'than the inviolability of diplomatic envoys and embassies, so that throughout history nations*

In addition, the *prior* social environment of a decision-maker, particularly during her/his formative political period, may affect the prospects of compliance with international rules. Policy-makers who have been involved in long violent conflicts during their early political socialization process are thus less likely to rapidly internalize the international norm prohibiting the use of force. Further studies may explore the links between the establishment of new states (or emergence from a violent revolution) or fresh policy-makers and the extent of violations of international law. Furthermore, international socialization may lead international actors to breach international norms. In parallel to Sutherland's differential association theory, previously discussed, non-compliance with international law may arise from the association of a particular state with a group of states which tend to violate global rules in a certain sphere. In such cases, the new member-state may gradually socialize (or re-socialize) into the deviant group of states and internalize the norm of *non*-conformity with those international legal rules.[115]

As noted above, conformity with norms is often linked to the group identity. Thus, for instance, international human rights norms define the identity of some international groups,[116] and human rights protection constitutes a 'constitutive norm' for the European Union (EU).[117] Consequently, members of such international groups, and particularly actors which are more concerned about maintaining their legitimate role in the group, are more likely to comply with international legal rules that define their group identity. It is noteworthy that identity-driven compliance does not necessarily depend on social control mechanisms, and conformity with international norms may take place where the actor's activity is not visible to other members of the group.

International identity, however, does not ensure that the group's norms will not be breached. A member whose bond with the group is weak (or socially alienated from the group) is less likely to be committed to the group's norms.[118] In addition, group members are less likely to comply with the group's norms in their interaction with non-member states ('out-group').[119] Such a motive, for example, appears to have played a role in Italy's decision to use prohibited chemical weapons against Ethiopia in 1935–6.[120]

of all creeds and cultures have observed reciprocal obligations for that purpose.' Case Concerning US Diplomatic and Consular Staff in Teheran (USA v Iran) (Judgment) [1980] ICJ Rep 3, [91] [emphasis added, reference omitted]; and see also [67], [92].

115 On subcultures that facilitate a breach of norms, see Section V(b) below.

116 See, e.g., Risse and Sikkink (n 103) 12.

117 See, e.g., Marise Cremona, 'Values in the EU Foreign Policy' in Malcolm Evans and Panos Koutrakos (eds), *Beyond the Established Legal Orders: Policy Interconnections between the EU and the Rest of the World* (Hart 2011) 307. For a discussion on the central role of human rights in the EU's identity, see Chapter 4, Section IV(b).

118 On the link between weak bond to society and non-compliance, see, e.g., Rock (n 32) 57; Macionis (n 13) 202.

119 On the interactions between 'in-group' and 'out-group' members, see Chapter 4 Section II(c).

120 Price and Tannewald's research reveals that the origins of the chemical weapons 'taboo' were implicated in exclusionary practices that distinguished between 'civilized' and 'uncivilized' areas of the globe. Richard Price and Nina Tannenwald, 'Norms and Deterrence: The Nuclear and Chemical Weapons Taboos' in Peter Katzenstein (ed), *The Culture of National Security: Norms*

Furthermore, in certain cases, identity with a particular group of states may *encourage* breach of some international norms vis-à-vis *non-member* states. Social-psychological and sociological studies reveal that identification with a group is often accompanied by the tendency to grant in-group members better treatment ('favouritism') and discriminatory treatment towards out-group members.[121] Such discrimination is inconsistent with diverse international legal rules, prominently those relating to the prohibition on racial discrimination,[122] discrimination against non-nationals (e.g., in human rights[123] or trade treaties),[124] or between different states.[125] Thus, for example, policy-makers' identification with a specific nation or regional group may lead them to discriminate against individuals or states which do not belong to their identity group.

c. Structural approaches

Structural theories of deviance highlight societal structures that are likely to motivate individuals to violate laws. According to the *anomie approach*, individuals are assumed to be characterized by insatiable and potentially destructive desires, and if they are not restrained, society is at risk of degeneration into a state of anomie (in which institutionalized norms lose their force).[126] People living in social groups, periods, or areas[127] characterized by disruption of social order or weak social regulation face fewer moral restraints and are correspondingly freer to deviate.[128]

The anomie approach may shed light on widespread breaches of international law in areas undergoing significant disruptions of order. Such disturbances in social order may take place either within a state or in some groups of states. Numerous international treaties bind governments to enforce international legal rules on individuals and groups within their territory.[129] Consequently,

and Identity in World Politics (Columbia University Press, 1996) 130–2. And see the discussion in Chapter 4 Section IV(a).

121 Michael A Hogg, Deborah J Terry, and Katherine M White, 'A Tale of Two Theories: A Critical Comparison of Identity Theory with Social Identity Theory' (1995) 58 *Social Psychology Quarterly* 255, 260, 262; Jan E Stets and Peter J Burke, 'Identity, Theory and Social Identity Theory' (2000) 63 *Social Psychology Quarterly* 224, 232; Jenkins (n 79) 7.

122 See, e.g., International Convention on the Elimination of All Forms of Racial Discrimination (opened for signature 7 March 1966, entered into force 4 January 1969) 660 UNTS 195 Art 2.

123 See, e.g., International Covenant on Civil and Political Rights (adopted 19 December 1966, entered into force 23 March 1976) 999 UNTS 171 (ICCPR) Art 26.

124 See, e.g., GATT 1947 Art III.

125 See, e.g., GATT 1947 Art I.

126 Timothy Brezina, 'Anomie-Strain Theory' in Clifton D Bryant (ed,), *Routledge Handbook of Deviant Behaviour* (Routledge, 2011) 99. See also Agnew (n 58) 118.

127 On the 'Chicago school' that highlighted the impact of zones characterized by social disorganization (particularly 'zones in transition') on deviance rates, see, e.g., Goode, *Deviant Behaviour* (n 23) 29–30; Rock (n 32) 61–2; Agnew (n 58) 118–19. See also Rodney Stark, 'Deviant Places' in Ronald Weitzer (ed), *Deviance and Social Control* (McGraw Hill, 2002) 45.

128 Rock (n 32) 52–3; Franzese (n 93) 35, 79; Waters (n 72) 29–30.

129 See, e.g., Convention on the Elimination of Racial Discrimination (n 122) Art 2(1)(d); Convention on the Elimination of All Forms of Discrimination Against Women (opened for signature 18 December 1979, entered into force 3 September 1981) 1249 UNTS 13 (CEDAW) Arts 2(b) and 2(e); Convention on the Rights of the Child (adopted 20 November 1989, entered into force

a breakdown of order within a state (e.g., during a civil war) leaves individuals and groups freer to breach international legal rules and it often constitutes fertile ground for widespread violations of international law.[130] For instance, the lack of order in Somalia since 1991 led to wide-ranging violations of human rights,[131] and piracy;[132] while the breakdown of order in the Former Yugoslavia during the 1990s led to extensive breaches of international criminal law (including genocide).[133] People living in such states characterized by anomie are thus more prone to breach international laws.

An application of the anomie approach to international law also suggests that governments and individuals in areas less exposed to *international* social control agencies are more likely to breach international legal rules. Actors located in regions that are largely eclipsed from the supervision of various inter-governmental organizations, NGOs, and the media thus face fewer international social restraints and are correspondingly freer to violate international law.

Strain theory was developed by the influential structuralist sociologist Robert Merton who emphasizes that certain social patterns exert pressure on individuals to engage in deviant activities. Such social pressures may originate from strain (or disassociation) between culturally defined *goals* involving varying degrees of prestige and sentiment—and social structures defining the acceptable *means* of achieving these goals.[134] A strain exists where 'a system of cultural values extols, virtually above all else, certain *common* success-goals *for the population at large* while the social structure rigorously restricts or completely close access to approved modes of reaching these goals *for a considerable part of that same population*'.[135] Merton contends that such disjuncture exists in US society whose norms strongly encourage individuals to gain material wealth but does not provide suitable opportunities for everyone to accomplish that goal.[136] Conformity is achieved through pursuing conventional goals by approved means. But people

2 September 1990) 1577 UNTS 3 Art 3. On such obligations in international environmental law, see, e.g., Malcolm Shaw, *International Law* (7th edn, CUP, 2014) 618–20.

[130] On the vulnerability of states characterized by a poor capacity to maintain public order and prevent various activities which constitute breaches of international law, see, e.g., Edward Newman, 'Failed States and International Order' (2009) 30 *Contemporary Security Policy* 421, 429–30.

[131] See, e.g., Human Rights Watch, 'You don't Know who to Blame'—War Crimes in Somalia' (15 August 2011) <http://www.hrw.org/reports/2011/08/15/you-don-t-know-who-blame> accessed 18 March 2015.

[132] See, e.g., UNSC Res 1918 (27 April 2010) UN Doc S/RES/1918.

[133] See, e.g., *Case Concerning the Application of the Genocide Convention (Bosnia v Serbia)* (Judgment of 26 February 2007) [2007] ICJ Rep 43 [297].

[134] Robert K Merton, 'Social Structure and Anomie', reproduced in Ronald Weitzer (ed), *Deviance and Social Control* (McGraw Hill, 2002) 64. See also Goode, *Deviant Behaviour* (n 23) 32–3; Brezina (n 126) 99–101; Thio (n 23) 17–19.

[135] Merton, *Social Theory and Social Structure* (n 28) 146 [emphasis in the original].

[136] Merton states in that regard that 'such antisocial behaviour is in a sense "called forth" by certain conventional values of the culture and by the class structure involving differential access to the approved opportunities for legitimate, prestige-bearing pursuits of the culture goals'. Robert K Merton, 'Social Structure and Anomie' (1938) 3 *American Sociological Review* 672. See also Clifton D Bryant, 'Theories of Deviance—Overview' in Clifton D Bryant (ed), *The Routledge Handbook of Deviant Behaviour* (Routledge, 2011) 89.

who grow up in social groups in which they see little hope of attaining society's goals if they 'play by the rules', are more likely to attempt attaining these aims by illegal activities.[137]

An additional structural explanation for deviance relates to the concept of 'role strain' (or 'role conflict').The concept of 'role' refers to social expectations attached to a person in a particular social position.[138] Role strain[139] arises when an individual having two (or more) roles faces incompatible expectations attached to her/his different roles. Such a role conflict is more frequent in contemporary societies, since individuals hold multiple roles simultaneously, and different social obligations derive from these distinct roles (e.g., mother and employee).[140] Such role strain may lead individuals to breach social expectations attached to one of their conflicting roles.[141]

The concept of 'role strain' is pertinent to non-compliance with international law. Breaches of international legal rules may arise from the fact that policy-makers (and states) are often members of two (or more) social groups. National decision-makers occasionally face inconsistent norms prevailing in their respective internal social system, as well as the norms and legal rules prevailing in the international community. Increasing participation of states in various international socio-cultural frameworks is likely to increase the likelihood of such strains. Such conflicts of norms may lead national policy-makers to conform to the national norm and breach international legal rules. For example, deeply rooted norms[142] in domestic societies regarding inequality between women and men[143] are often inconsistent with obligations prescribed by the Convention on the Elimination of Discrimination against Women.[144] The Convention's text

[137] Merton, *Social Theory and Social Structure* (n 28) 188–9; Goode, *Deviant Behaviour* (n 23) 33; Macionis (n 13) 197–8.

[138] See, e.g., 'Role', *Oxford Dictionary of Sociology* (4th edn, 2014) 652.

[139] On types of role strain, see William J Goode, 'A Theory of Role Strain' (1960) 25 *American Sociological Review* 483, 483–5.

[140] Goode, 'Theory of Role Strain' (n 139) 485; 'Role', *Penguin Dictionary of Sociology* (4th edn, 2014) 301–2. On role strain in work relationships, and particularly in large organizations, see J Diedrick Snoek, 'Role Strain in Diversified Role Sets' (1966) 71 *American Journal of Sociology* 363. See also Stephen R Marks, 'Multiple Roles and Role Strain: Some Notes on Human Energy, Time and Commitment' (1977) 42 *American Sociological Review* 921.

[141] On the link between role strain and conformity with norms, see Goode, 'Theory of Role Strain' (n 139) 484. On techniques for reduction of role strain, see 486–90.

[142] On the relationship between compliance with international treaties and domestic legal culture, see Ljiljana Biukovic, 'Compliance with International Treaties-Selective Adaptation Analysis' (2006) 44 *Canadian Yb Intl L* 451.

[143] The Human Rights Committee noted in General Comment No. 28 that '[i]nequality in the enjoyment of rights by women throughout the world is deeply embedded in tradition, history and culture, including religious attitudes.' UN Human Rights Committee (HRC), 'General Comment No. 28: Article 3 (Equality of rights between men and women)' (29 March 2000) UN Doc. CCPR/C/21/Rev.1/Add.10, para 5 <http://tbinternet.ohchr.org/Treaties/CCPR/Shared%20Documents/1_Global/CCPR_C_21_Rev-1_Add-10_6619_E.pdf> accessed 18 March 2015. And Hutn states in that regard: '[g]ender discrimination has been a remarkably consistent feature of most cultures'. Mala Hutn, 'Culture, Institutions, and Gender Inequality in Latin America' in Lawrence E Harrison and Samuel P Huntington (eds), *Culture Matters* (Basic Books, 2000).

[144] Convention on the Elimination of All Forms of Discrimination Against Women (n 129). For a detailed description of religious approaches to gender inequality and the obligations prescribed

points out that the drafters were well aware of some inconsistencies between social norms existing in some societies and the Convention's obligation regarding gender equality.[145] Similar strains and non-compliance derive from inconsistent norms prevailing in some states' societies regarding racial discrimination (e.g., regarding the caste system),[146] slavery,[147] and the prohibitions against such practices under international law.[148]

This section focuses on the societal context and roots of non-compliance with international law. The way breaches are understood affects strategies developed to enhance compliance with international legal rules.

V. Enhancing Compliance with International Law

Sociological analysis may not only cast new light on social factors and processes involved in compliance/non-compliance; it may also offer some practical suggestions concerning promoting compliance with international law. This section briefly illustrates the practical value of sociological analysis by offering some proposals that may reduce breaches of international law.

a. Surveillance and publicizing rule-breakers

Structural theories (and particularly the anomie approach) posit that where individuals and groups are not adequately restrained, the deviance rate is liable to

by this Convention, see, Gila Stopler, 'Countenancing the Oppression of Women: How Liberals Tolerate Religious and Cultural Practices that Discriminate Against Women' (2003) 12 *Columbia Journal of Gender and Law* 154.

[145] Art 5(a) of the Convention requires state parties to take all appropriate measures '[t]o modify the *social and cultural patterns* of conduct of men and women, with a view to achieving the elimination of prejudices and customary and all other practices which are based on the idea of the inferiority or the superiority of either of the sexes or on stereotyped roles for men and women' [emphasis added]. Art 2(f) of the Convention requires state parties to pursue a policy of eliminating discrimination against women, and to this end they are required '[t]o take all appropriate measures, including legislation, to modify or abolish *existing* laws, regulations, *customs and practices* which constitute discrimination against women' [emphasis added]. See also CEDAW (n 129) 14th recital of the Preamble.

[146] On the social structures of the caste system in several countries and the relevant international legal obligations, see Jeremy Sarkin and Mark Koenig, 'Ending Caste Discrimination in India: Human Rights and the Responsibility to Protect Individuals and Groups from Discrimination at the Domestic and International Levels' (2010) 41 *George Washington International Law Review* 101. See also Narula Smita, 'Equal by Law, Unequal by Caste: The "Untouchable" Condition in Critical Race Perspective' (2008) 26 *Wisconsin International Law Journal* 255; Annapurna Waughray, 'Caste Discrimination: A Twenty-First Century Challenge for UK Discrimination Law?' (2009) 72 *Modern Law Review* 182.

[147] On long-term social practices that violate international treaties regarding slavery, see, e.g., *Hadijatou Mani Koraou v The Republic of Niger (ECOWAS Community Court of Justice)* (27 October 2008) Application No. ECW/CCJ/APP/08/08, Judgment No. ECW/CCJ/JUD/06/08, [63], [78], [85] <http://www.unodc.org/res/cld/case-law/ner/h_m__v__republic_of_niger_html/Hadijatou_Mani_v._Republic_of_Niger_Community_Court_of_Justice.pdf> accessed 18 March 2015.

[148] On the states' obligation to address cultural obstacles for the realization of international human rights, see Henry Steiner, 'International Protection of Human Rights' in Malcolm D Evans (ed), *International Law* (3rd edn, OUP, 2010) 784, 806–11.

increase. The international community has developed diverse international social control mechanisms which identify rule-breakers and express social disapproval.[149] Improving compliance with international law calls for treaty and institutional design which enhance various international social control mechanisms. The establishment of robust enforcement bodies that impose harsh sanctions on rule-breakers is likely to enhance the prospects of compliance (particularly from the rational choice perspective), but they are occasionally not politically or economically feasible.[150] Reliable surveillance mechanisms which *collect and publicize* information about compliance with international legal obligations and identifying rule-breakers are of significant importance for applying social pressure vis-à-vis non-compliant actors. International monitoring bodies include not only authoritative organs established in a binding legal text; informal and external bodies (like NGOs)[151] may also play a significant role in collecting information regarding non-compliance. Such informal or external bodies may cooperate with the officially authorized international institutions.[152]

Furthermore, *disseminating* information on the specific rule-breaker's identity is of considerable importance for exerting social pressure. Once the identity of the rule-breaker is widely publicized, the particular violator is more likely to be stigmatized in the international community. 'Naming and shaming' techniques are well-known in international human rights law[153] and are also employed in other spheres of international law.[154] Brummer explains the logic of naming and shaming in international financial law (employed by the Financial Action Task Force): '[r]egulators in the identified jurisdictions are thus publicly ostracized and isolated from the members of the organization publishing the list'.[155] And regarding the WTO Trade Policy Review Mechanism (TPRM),[156] Van den Bossche

149 See Section III(c) above.

150 On the economic and political costs of sanctions designed to enhance enforcement with international law, see, e.g., Anu Bradford and Omri Ben-Shahar, 'Efficient Enforcement in International Law' (2012) 12 *Chicago Journal of International Law* 375, 409–12.

151 On collection of information by NGOs regarding human rights see, Molly Beutz-Land, 'Networked Activism' (2009) 22 *Harvard Human Rights Journal* 205.

152 On the provision of compliance data by NGOs to international organizations, see Jennifer Shkabatur, 'A Global Panopticon? The Changing Role of International Organizations in the Information Age' (2011) 33 *Michigan Journal of International Law* 159, 168–9.

153 On 'naming and shaming' in international human rights law, see James Meernik and others, 'The Impact of Human Rights Organizations on Naming and Shaming Campaigns' (2012) 56 *Journal of Conflict Resolution* 233. See also, e.g., Lesley Wexler, 'The International Deployment of Shame, Second-Best Responses, and Norm Entrepreneurship: The Campaign to Ban Landmines and the Landmine Treaty' (2003) 20 *Arizona Journal of International and Comparative Law* 561, 566; Sandeep Gopalan and Roslyn Fuller, 'Enforcing International Law: States, IOs, and Courts as Shaming Reference Groups' (2014) 39 *Brooklyn Journal of International Law* 73.

154 On the evolution of this technique in international financial law and particularly by the Financial Action Task Force, see Brummer (n 38) 151. On this technique in the climate change instruments, see Duyck, Sébastien, 'MRV in the 2015 Climate Agreement: Promoting Compliance Through Transparency and the Participation of NGOs' (2014) 3 *Carbon and Climate Law Review* 175.

155 Brummer (n 38) 151.

156 Annex 3 of the Marrakesh Agreement: Trade Policy Review Mechanism <http://www.wto.org/english/docs_e/legal_e/29-tprm.pdf> accessed 18 March 2015. Art A(i) of the WTO

clarifies: 'by *publicly* deploring inconsistencies with WTO law of a Member's trade policy or practices, the TPRM intends to 'shame' Members into compliance'.[157]

In sum, strengthening diverse mechanisms which collect information on non-compliance and widely disseminating the identity of the specific rule-breakers are likely to reduce violations of international legal rules. From this perspective, it would be desirable that various treaty monitoring bodies invest significant efforts in reaching out to the mass media and highlighting the identity of the main rule-breakers in the particular sphere. Expressions of praise also constitute a significant component of international social control, and it is desirable that international reports also underscore the identity of actors that excel in compliance with the specific regime's obligations.

b. The risk of excessive social labelling and isolation

The above discussion indicates that international social control mechanisms are often influential in enhancing compliance with international law. Sociological studies, however, also indicate that under certain circumstances, a community's reaction to deviance may intensify deviant behaviour. Society's reaction to labelling—prominently one which involves attributing negative traits to members of a group ('stereotyping')[158]—may limit the lawful options available to rule-breakers and create impediments to their reintegration into society.[159] Under certain circumstances, labelling may become a 'self-fulfilling prophecy'.[160]

Some people manage to resist or modify deviant designations but others that are brought into disrepute may modify their self-concept and identity.[161] In the latter case, 'primary deviation' (i.e. engaging in deviant behaviour in the first place) may lead to social exclusion of the deviant from her/his social network and engaging in 'secondary deviation'.[162] Once societal reactions lead to 'secondary deviation', it becomes difficult for an individual to return to the conventional world.[163] These outcomes of labelling, particularly isolation from mainstream

instrument on TPRM states that this mechanism 'is not, however, intended to serve as a basis for the enforcement of specific obligations under the Agreements or for dispute settlement procedures, or to impose new policy commitments on Members.'

[157] Van Den Bossche and Zdouc (n 53) 94–5.

[158] On stereotyping, see, e.g., Stephan Worschel and Hank Rothgerber 'Changing the Stereotype of the Stereotype' in Russell Spears and others (eds), *The Social Psychology of Stereotyping and Group Life* (Blackwell, 1997) 72, 74–8. On stereotyping and group identity, see Chapter 4, Sections II(c) and IV(c)(ii).

[159] Goode, *Deviant Behaviour* (n 23) 56–7; Grattet (n 72) 124.

[160] Goode, *Deviant Behaviour* (n 23) 57. It is noteworthy that negative labelling does not always have this self-fulfilling outcome. Goode, *Deviant Behaviour* (n 23) 57.

[161] Rock (n 32) 71; Macionis (n 13) 200.

[162] Macionis (n 13) 200; Mindy S Bradely-Engen, 'Stigma and the Deviant Identity' in Clifton D Bryant (ed), *The Routledge Handbook of Deviant Behaviour* (Routledge, 2011) 190, 191–2; Goode, *Deviant Behaviour* (n 23) 54. As Rock explains: 'When a person begins to employ his deviant behaviour or a role based upon it as a means of defence, attack, or adjustment to the overt and covert problems created by the consequent societal reaction to him, his deviation is secondary'. Rock (n 32) 72.

[163] Ibid., Giddens and Sutton (n 29) 927–8.

society and restricted lawful options, may impel rule-breakers to associate with a social group which is also stigmatized by society.[164] As noted previously, a person's tendency towards conformity or deviance is also affected by the amount of contacts with others who encourage or reject lawful behaviour.[165]

The influence of people's social environment on the prospects of breaching law is related to the concept of *subculture*. This term is used to describe a subsection of the mainstream population whose cultural norms and values differentiate the subgroup from wider society. Subcultures borrow (and often distort) symbols, values, and beliefs prevalent in the larger population. Sociologists of deviance are particularly interested in subcultures that condone, promote, or otherwise facilitate breaches of norms: members of such subcultures are particularly prone to deviant activities.[166]

These sociological studies turn our attention to the limits of international social control mechanisms, and to the perils of excessive social stigmatization and isolation of international law-breakers. Such risks are noticeable with regard to legal rules and practices concerning membership in international institutions. Some international law scholars (such as Lang[167] and Cho)[168] emphasize that international institutions also constitute social environments in which member states' delegates interact and participate in the process of exchanging information, sharing normative beliefs, and diffusing social norms. Several social constructivist studies have provided evidence that international organizations also influence state behaviour through the process of international socialization.[169] One of the principal empirical insights of acculturation studies is that the degree to which a

[164] Goode, *Deviant Behaviour* (n 23) 53–4.

[165] See Section IV(b) above.

[166] Keith Hayward and Jonathan Ilan, 'Deviant Subcultures' in Clifton D Bryant (ed), *The Routledge Handbook of Deviant Behaviour* (Routledge, 2011) 233; Rock (n 32) 73; Giddens and Sutton (n 29) 924. On subcultures formed as a response to social frustration or humiliation, see Hayward and Ilan, 234.

[167] Andrew T F Lang, 'Some Sociological Perspectives on International Institutions and the Trading System' in Colin B Picker, Isabella D Bunn, and Douglas W Arner (eds), *International Economic Law:The State and Future of the Discipline* (Hart Publishing, 2008) 73, 78. Lang and Scott discuss three major functions of WTO bodies (particularly the Services Council and the Committee on Sanitary and Phytosanitary Measures): (i) production of collective knowledge through information exchange; (ii) facilitating technical assistance and regulatory learning; and (iii) norm elaboration. Andrew Lang and Joanne Scott, 'The Hidden World of WTO Governance' (2009) 20 *EJIL* 575, 582–4.

[168] Cho emphasizes that the members of the WTO community convey their thoughts and ideas through an interactive and ritualized discourse, and eventually institutionalize them as norms. Sungjoon Cho, 'Beyond Rationality: A Sociological Construction of the World Trade Organization' (2012) 52 *Virginia Journal of International Law* 321, 327. See also Sungjoon Cho, *The Social Foundations of World Trade: Norms, Community, and Institutions* (CUP, 2015) 101–43.

[169] See, e.g., Brian Greenhill, 'The Company You Keep: International Socialization and the Diffusion of Human Rights Norms' (2010) 54 *International Studies Quarterly* 127; David H Bearce and Stacy Bondanella, 'Intergovernmental Organizations, Socialization, and Member-State Interest Convergence' (2007) 61 *International Organization* 70; Jon C Pevehouse, 'Democracy from the Outside-In? International Organizations and Democratization' (2002) 56 *International Organization* 515.

state is embedded in international organizations is associated with the state's conformity to international models of appropriate behaviour.[170]

Expulsion of deviant states from international groups (including institutionalized ones) may increase the pressure to comply with certain legal rules but can also contribute to their isolation from the international society. Such exclusion may push the banished actors to bond with persistent deviant actors and join an international subculture characterized by condoning, promoting, or otherwise facilitating the breach of international legal rules in a particular sphere.

These perils should not negate the positive impacts of certain social control measures that take the form of certain restrictions on membership in international institutions,[171] but rather highlight the need to balance between the two competing aims of enhancing compliance through social control and reducing the risk of excessive isolation. From this perspective, it is plausible that while some temporary measures against violating members (such as suspension of certain procedural rights) may be desirable, a long-term expulsion from significant international institutions should generally be avoided. The fact that states' participation in international institutions often reflects or strengthens collective identities[172]—and the above-noted link between international identity and compliance[173]—reinforces the case for inclusive strategies and avoids extensive exclusion from significant international groups.

c. Reintegrative justice

Where a particular state has persistently breached certain significant international legal rules, the international community should take into account not only factors relating to social control but also considerations of 'restorative justice',[174] that is, the need to reintegrate rule-breakers back into the community of law-abiding states. From this perspective, it is desirable that the particular community's responses

[170] Goodman and Jinks, 'How to Influence States' (n 59) 667–8. See also Martha Finnemore, 'Norms, Culture, and World Politics: Insights from Sociology's Institutionalism' (1996) 50 *International Organization* 325, 328–30.

[171] On conditioned and inclusive membership in international institutions and their impacts in this sphere, see, e.g., Goodman and Jinks, 'How to Influence States' (n 59) 656. On conditioned membership in the EU and conditions relating to human rights, see Chapter 4, Section IV(b). On admission and exclusions in international organizations (relating to observance of human rights and democratic governance), see Alison Duxbury, *The Participation of States and International Organizations: The Role of Human Rights and Democracy* (CUP, 2011) 106 et seq.

[172] See Chapter 4, Section IV(b). [173] See Section IV(b) above.

[174] On restorative justice, see, e.g., Rock (n 32) 72–3; Carrie Menkel-Meadow, 'Restorative Justice: What Is It and Does It Work?' (July 2007) 3 *Annual Review of Law and Social Science* 161.

Miller explains the aim of rituals of restoration: 'The purpose of these rituals is to restore the normal condition of a person when it has been compromised by some error or offense. These rituals purport to realign the individual and social identities, and thereby reduce the threat to society that the continued existence of a disparity between these identities would create'. Geoffrey P Miller, 'The Legal Function of Ritual' (2005) 80 *Chicago-Kent Law Review* [footnote omitted] 1181, 1220.

(including harsh sanctions) are accompanied by a signal that once the persistent violator ceases non-compliance, there is a sincere willingness to accept it as a respected member of the community. It is also desirable that suspension of rights in international institutions should be clearly limited to a certain period (even if renewable by the institutions' members). The need to reintegrate violators into the particular international social group (global or regional) suggests that while 'naming and shaming' techniques are often effective in reducing non-compliance in certain spheres, it is important to avoid humiliating or dehumanizing rhetoric that could reduce the likelihood of future reintegration into the international community.

VI. Concluding Remarks

The preceding sections shed some light on certain sociological factors influencing conformity or breach of international norms. The sociological term 'deviance' is broader than violation of legal rules and the sociological perspective on international law explores not only the breach of legally binding instruments but also soft international norms prevailing in the international community (or in a group of states). Where international rules (either legally binding or soft ones) overlap with international norms, compliance with these rules is supported by various international social control mechanisms. Where international rules do not reflect international norms (including the social expectation to follow voluntarily undertaken obligations), they are not likely to trigger such social control mechanisms. International social control mechanisms are more likely to be rigorously applied against violators of international rules embodying the fundamental norms of the international community but they are also often active with regard to other obligations (such as those relating to the protection of diplomats).

Different approaches in the sociology of deviance emphasize different factors involved in deviant behaviour and societal reactions to such conduct. The labelling perspective suggests that diverse international labelling agencies are often influenced by certain socio-cultural factors, prominently where these agencies apply vague legal concepts (such as 'good faith'). Social learning approaches emphasize the importance of international socialization which often takes place within international institutions. Such socialization processes, however, do not guarantee compliance with international law. Situations characterized by incomplete socialization or a particular state's association with international rule-breakers illustrate the potential adverse effects of international socialization on the compliance rate.

Similarly, international identity often leads to conformity with international legal rules but identification with a particular group (either domestic or international) is often accompanied by discrimination vis-à-vis 'out-group' members. Such discriminatory behaviour is occasionally inconsistent with international legal rules regarding non-discrimination. Strain theory, and particularly the notion of 'role strain', underlines that non-compliance may be triggered by the fact that policy-makers often belong to two (or more) social groups. Thus, national decision-makers who encounter inconsistent norms prevailing in their internal social system and international legal rules (e.g., concerning gender equality) may conform to national norms and breach international law.

Sociological analysis of non-compliance may offer strategies to enhance compliance with international legal rules. Consequently, certain methods of institutional and treaty design may aim to reduce breaches of international law, including certain improvements in international social control mechanisms (particularly regarding dissemination of information concerning the identity of rule-breakers, as well as increasing praise for obedient actors). Sociological analysis indicates that certain international social control operations may undermine compliance, prominently in cases of excessive stigmatization and isolation of rule-breakers. Thus, for example, while expulsion from significant international institutions may increase the pressure to comply, it can also contribute to the isolation of the banished state and push it to join international subcultures that facilitate violations of certain international legal rules. These perils do not negate the desirable impacts of international social control mechanisms, but rather highlight the need to strike a balance between the two competing aims of enhancing compliance through social pressure and reducing the risk of excessive isolation and amplifying violations.

Designing and improving international social control mechanisms should also take into account the need to reintegrate persistent violators back into the community of law-abiding states ('restorative justice'). Consequently, economic and social sanctions should be accompanied by a signal that once the particular rule-breaker ceases non-compliance, there is sincere readiness to accept it as a legitimate member of the international community.

Sociological analysis of compliance or non-compliance with international law generates diverse hypotheses that may be tested in further studies. Thus, for example, the social learning approach may lead to empirical studies exploring the link between the formation of new states (or dramatic regime changes in existing states) and the extent of violations of international law. The anomie approach may lead researchers to examine whether actors located in zones that are largely eclipsed from international social control mechanisms are more prone to violate international law. Similarly, Sutherland's differential theory invites an empirical examination of the link between an individual state's association with other states who favour violation of certain international legal rules and further breaches of these legal rules by that particular state.

7
Some Conclusions

The preceding chapters demonstrate that international law emerges and operates in social groups, and that the particular features of these communities infuse international legal rules and institutions. International legal actors often constitute social groups, and sociological processes taking place within these groups (such as socialization or identity) are intertwined with legal rules constructed in these communities. This presumption applies not only to formal international actors (like states or international institutions) but also to less formal actors (such as the international investment community or human rights groups) which substantially affect international law.

Turning to the relationships between individuals and their societies, it is plain that diverse decisions adopted by individual decision-makers (such as adjudicators) regarding international law are influenced by the social structures of their respective groups; and vice versa, international legal rules often 'emerge from below', from social interactions between individual legal decision-makers. Thus, casting light on the social factors and processes operating within the decision-makers' social environment (such as norms or collective memory) as well the social interactions between these decision-makers is vital for understanding the formation, interpretation, and implementation of international law.

International law also emerges from and operates in various interactions *between* social groups (which often also constitute international legal actors), such as regional economic blocks or professional groups. This aspect is prominent, for example, regarding the diffusion of legal rules between different branches (and communities) of international law. The features characterizing social interactions between socio-legal communities affect the content of international legal rules developed in these contexts. Hence, sociological literature regarding inter-groups relations (such as in-group/out-group processes) may be valuable for analysing international legal rules operating in such inter-group contexts.

These and additional fundamental links between international law and social factors and processes point out that the sociological analysis of international law is often essential for understanding complex international legal phenomena; and ignoring or underestimating the social context in which international law evolves may often lead to an incomplete understanding of the real-life international law.

As with any useful instrument, users should be aware of its limitations. The valuable contribution of the sociological analysis of international law should not blur the limits of international law or the sociological discipline. The previous chapters reveal that the mere establishment of a new international legal obligation does not guarantee a significant behavioural change, and certain socio-cultural factors occasionally inspire resistance to the internalization or implementation of particular international rules. The previous chapters also highlight some limitations of the sociological investigation itself. While socio-cultural factors often affect the mindset and behaviour of international legal actors, it is noteworthy that such factors are not determinative. The presence of certain sociological factors and processes (like social control mechanisms or socialization) may constitute a fertile ground for some behaviour and make certain activities more likely to happen—but sociological analysis does not pretend to yield precise predictions regarding social behaviour. This substantial limit of sociological inquiry relates, inter alia, to the fact that such behaviour is often influenced by more than one sociological factor, individuals are frequently members of two or more social groups, and sociological factors are often entangled with non-sociological factors (e.g., psychological considerations). Thus, intricate social phenomena like the evolution or implementation of international law are not likely to be precisely anticipated by sociological studies of international law.

Sociological analysis can shed light on significant factors motivating and constraining international legal behaviour (like conformity or nonconformity with some international legal norms) but the results of such investigations may change over time. Though international legal rules often institutionalize certain socio-cultural characteristics and are relatively stable, they are not immune to social changes. Significant changes undertaken in the pertinent social groups are likely to engender some international legal changes; and the latter may take the form of new international instruments, reinterpretation of existing instruments, or non-implementation of previously enacted rules. While it is important not to lose sight of the dynamic aspects of sociological analysis, social changes are mostly incremental, and do not usually unfold within a short period.

The first part of the book sketched out the broad contours of the sociological landscape and the following parts presented some insights gained from research 'expeditions' into four regions of sociology and international law. These expeditions do not aim to cover all significant areas of the sociological realm but rather to invite readers to undertake further journeys to this relatively under-explored (but fascinating) dimension of international law. As Berger states in the last part of his well-known *Invitation to Sociology*:

> This book has been an invitation to attend a certain party. In issuing such an invitation, it is not customary to include a full dossier on all the people that the putative guest will find at the party. All the same, the latter will want to know a little more about those people, or at least about where he [or she] can go to find out.... Obviously it is up to the reader how far he [or she] wants to go in response to this invitation. He [or she] has already been warned that such an undertaking is not without risk.[1]

[1] Peter Berger, *Invitation to Sociology: A Humanistic Perspective* (Anchor Books, 1963) 177.

Selected Bibliography

Abbott, AF, 'Latin America and International Arbitration Conventions: The Quandary of Non-Ratification' (1976) 17 *Harvard International Law Journal* 131

Abbott, KW, 'International Relations Theory, International Law, and the Regime Governing Atrocities in Internal Conflicts' (1999) 93 *AJIL* 361

Abdelal, R, YM Herrera, and AI Johnston, 'Identity as a Variable' (2006) 4 *Perspectives on Politics* 699

Abrams, D, and MA Hogg, 'Social Identity and Self-Categorization' in JF Dovidio and others (eds), *Prejudice, Stereotyping and Discrimination* (Sage, 2010) 177

Acheson, K, and C Maule, 'Culture in International Trade' in VA Ginsburgh and D Throsby (eds), *Handbook of the Economics of Art and Culture* vol 1 (Elsevier, 2006) 1141

Adair, WL, and JM Brett, 'Culture and Negotiation Processes' in MJ Gelfand and JM Brett (eds), *The Handbook of Negotiation and Culture* (Stanford University Press, 2004) 158

Adler, E, 'Cognitive Evolution: A Dynamic Approach for the Study of International Relations and Their Progress' in E Adler and B Crawford (eds), *Progress in Postwar International Relations* (Columbia University Press, 1991) 43

Adler, E, and M Barnett, 'A Framework for the Study of Security Communities' in E Adler and M Barnett (eds), *Security Communities* (CUP, 1998) 29

Adler-Nissen, R, 'Stigma Management in International Relations: Transgressive Identities, Norms, and Order in International Society' (2014) 68 *International Organization* 143

Agnew, R, 'Control and Social Disorganizational Theory' in CD Bryant (ed), *The Routledge Handbook of Deviant Behaviour* (Routledge, 2011) 114

Anastasio, P, and others, 'Categorization, Recategorization and Common Ingroup Identity' in R Spears and others (eds), *The Social Psychology of Stereotyping and Group Life* (Blackwell, 1997) 236

Anderson, K, and H Norheim, 'Hilstory, Geography, and Regional Integration' in K Anderson and R Blackhurst (eds), *Regional Integration and the Global Trading System* (St. Martin's Press, 1993) 19

Ang, JS, Y Cheng, and C Wu, 'The Role of Social Capital and Cultural Biases in the Investment Behaviour of Foreign High-Tech Firms' (2011) <http://ssrn.com/abstract=1786535>

Appelrouth, S, and LD Edles, *Classical and Contemporary Sociological Theory* (Pine Forge Press, 2008)

Appiah, KA, 'The State and the Shaping of Identity' (Tanner Lectures on Human Values, Cambridge, 30 April 2001)

Assmann, A, 'Canon and Archive' in A Erll and A Nünning (eds), *Cultural Memory Studies: An International and Interdisciplinary Handbook* (Walter de Gruyter, 2008) 97

Assmann, A, and J Czaplicka, 'Collective Memory and Cultural Identity' (1995) 65 *New German Critique* 125

Baldwin, R, 'Preferential Trading Arrangements' in A Narlikar, M Daunton and R Stern (eds), *The Oxford Handbook on the World Trade Organization* (OUP, 2012) 632

Banakar, R, and M Travers (eds), *An Introduction to Law and Social Theory* (Hart, 2002)

Barager, JR, 'The Historiography of the Rio de la Plata Area Since 1830' (1959) 39 *The Hispanic American Historical Review* 588

Barker, CJ, *International Law and International Relations* (Continuum, 2000)
Barnett, M, 'Social Constructivism' in J Baylis, S Smith, and P Owens, *The Globalization of World Politics* (6th edn, OUP, 2014) 155
Bartels, L, *Human Rights Conditionality in the EU's International Agreements* (OUP, 2005)
Bartels, L, 'Human Rights and Sustainable Development Obligations in EU Free Trade Agreements' (September 2012) Legal Studies Research Paper Series University of Cambridge Faculty of Law 1
Bartels, L, 'A Model Human Rights Clause for the EU's International Trade Agreements' (17–18 February 2014) German Institute for Human Rights and MISEREOR 10, <http://ssrn.com/abstract=2405852>
Barth, F, 'Introduction' in F Barth (ed), *Ethnic Groups and Boundaries: The Social Organization of Culture Difference* (Little, Brown and Company, 1969) 9
Baud, M, 'State and Society in Argentina: Change and Continuity under the Kirchners' (2013) 95 *European Review of Latin American and Caribbean Studies* 114
Baylis, J, S Smith, and P Owens, *The Globalization of World Politics* (6th edn, OUP, 2014)
Bearce, DH, and S Bondanella, 'Intergovernmental Organizations, Socialization, and Member-State Interest Convergence' (2007) 61 *International Organization* 70
Becerra, M, S Marino, and G Mastrini, *Mapping Digital Media: Argentina* (Open Society Foundation, 2012)
Becker, HS, *Outsiders: Studies in the Sociology of Deviance* (Free Press, 1963)
Benedek, W, 'Drago-Porter Convention' (1907), in R Wolfrum (ed), *Max Planck Encyclopedia of Public International Law* (OUP, 2007)
Benson, J, *Working More Creatively with Groups* (Routledge, 2000)
Benvenisti, E, 'Collective Action in the Utilization of Shared Freshwater: The Challenges of International Water Resource Law' (1996) 90 *AJIL* 384
Ben-Yehuda, N, 'Social Change and Deviance' in CD Bryant (ed), *The Routledge Handbook of Deviant Behaviour* (Routledge, 2011) 38
Berger, P, *Invitation to Sociology: A Humanistic Perspective* (Anchor Books, 1963)
Berman, PS, 'From International Law to Law and Globalization' (2005) 43 *Columbia Journal of Transnational Law* 485
Berman, PS, 'The Enduring Connections between Law and Culture' (2009) 57 *American Journal of Comparative Law* 101
Berry, JW, 'Acculturation' in JE Grusec and PD Hasting (eds), *Handbook of Socialization: Theory and Research* (Guilford Press, 2007) 543
Best, J, 'Constructing Deviance' in CD Bryant (ed), *The Routledge Handbook of Deviant Behaviour* (Routledge, 2011) 17
Beutz-Land, M, 'Networked Activism' (2009) 22 *Harvard Human Rights Journal* 205
Bhagwati, J, *Termites in the Trading System: How Preferential Agreements Undermine Free Trade* (OUP, 2008)
Bhala, R, *Modern GATT Law* (Sweet & Maxwell, 2005)
Bishop, RD, J Crawford, and WM Reisman, *Foreign Investment Disputes: Cases, Materials and Commentary* (Kluwer, 2005)
Biukovic, L, 'Compliance with International Treaties-Selective Adaptation Analysis' (2006) 44 *Canadian Yb Intl L* 451
Bjorklund, AK, 'Assessing the Effectiveness of Soft Law Instruments in International Investment Law' in AK Bjorklund and A Reinisch (eds), *International Investment Law and Soft Law* (Elgar, 2012) 51
Blumer, H, *Symbolic Interactionism: Perspective and Method* (Prentice Hall, 1969)

Böckstiegel, KH, 'Commercial and Investment Arbitration: How Different are they Today?: The Lalive Lecture 2012 (2012) 28 *Arbitration International* 577

Bourhis, RY, JC Turner, and A Gagnon, 'Interdependence, Social Identity and Discrimination' in R Spears and others (eds), *The Social Psychology of Stereotyping and Group Life* (Blackwell, 1997) 273

Boyle, A, 'Soft Law in International Law-Making' in MD Evans (ed), *International Law* (3rd edn, OUP, 2010) 122

Bradford, A, and O Ben-Shahar, 'Efficient Enforcement in International Law' (2012) 12 *Chicago Journal of International Law* 375

Bradely-Engen, MS, 'Stigma and the Deviant Identity' in CD Bryant (ed), *The Routledge Handbook of Deviant Behaviour* (Routledge, 2011) 190

Branstetter, L, 'Is Foreign Direct Investment a Channel of Knowledge Spillovers? Evidence from Japan's FDI in the United States', (2006) 68 *Journal of International Economics* 325

Brewer, MB, 'The Social Self: On Being the Same and Different at the Same Time' (1991) 17 *Personality and Social Psychology Bulletin* 475

Brewer, MB, 'The Many Faces of Social Identity: Implications for Political Psychology' (2001) 22 *Political Psychology* 155

Brezina, T, 'Anomie-Strain Theory' in CD Bryant (ed), *Routledge Handbook of Deviant Behaviour* (Routledge, 2011) 99

Brown Weiss, E, 'Conclusions: Understanding Compliance with Soft Law' in D Shelton (ed), *Commitment and Compliance: The Role of Non-Binding Norms in the International Legal System* (OUP, 2000) 537

Brummer, C, *Soft Law and the Global Financial System: Rule-Making in the 21st Century* (CUP, 2012)

Brunnée, J, 'Europe, The United States, and the Global Climate Regime: All Together Now?' (2008) 24(1) *Journal of Land Use and Environmental Law* 1

Brunnée, J, and SJ Toope, 'International Law and Constructivism: Elements of an International Law Theory of International Law' (2000) 20 *Columbia Journal of Transnational Law* 27

Brunnée, J, and SJ Toope, 'Constructivism and International Law' in JL Dunoff and MA Pollack (eds), *Interdisciplinary Perspectives on International Law and International Relations: The State of the Art* (CUP, 2013) 119

Bruter, M, 'Winning Hearts and Minds for Europe: The Impact of News and Symbols on Civic and Cultural European Identity' (2003) 36 *Comparative Political Studies* 1148

Bryant, CD, 'Theories of Deviance—Overview' in CD Bryant (ed), *The Routledge Handbook of Deviant Behaviour* (Routledge, 2011) 89

Brym, RJ, and J Lie, *Sociology* (Wadsworth, 2003)

Burke-White, WW, and A Von Staden, 'Private Litigation in a Public Law Sphere: The Standard of Review in Investor-State Arbitrations' (2010) 35 *YJIL* 283

Buzan, B, *From International to World Society?* (CUP, 2004)

Cahn, S, and D Schimmel, 'The Cultural Exception: Does It Exist in GATT and GATS Frameworks' (1997) 15 *Cardozo Arts and Entertainment Law Journal* 281

Calhoun, C, and others (eds), *Contemporary Sociological Theory* (Blackwell, 2002)

Carmona, BR, 'The International Centre for Settlement of Investment Disputes (ICSID): An Empirical Research on the Voting Behaviour of Arbitrators' (28 November 2009) <http://ssrn.com/abstract=1514882>

Carty, A, 'Sociological Theories of International Law', *Max Planck Encyclopedia of Public International Law* (last updated March 2008), <http://opil.ouplaw.com/

view/10.1093/law:epil/9780199231690/law-9780199231690-e735?rskey=uV9ZYR&result=1&prd=EPIL>

Casey, ES, *Remembering: A Phenomenological Study* (2nd edn, Indiana University Press, 2000)

Cassese, A, *International Criminal Law* (3rd edn, OUP, 2013)

Chase, O, *Law, Culture and Ritual* (New York University Press, 2005)

Chayes, A, and AH Chayes, 'On Compliance' (1993) 47 *International Organization* 175

Chayes, A, and AH Chayes, *The New Sovereignty: Compliance with International Regulatory Agreements* (Harvard University Press, 1995)

Checkel, JT, 'Norms, Institutions and National Identity in Contemporary Europe' (1999) 43 *International Studies Quarterly* 83

Checkel, JT, and PJ Katzenstein, *European Identity* (CUP, 2009)

Cho, S, 'Breaking the Barrier between Regionalism and Multilateralism' (2001) 42 *Harvard International Law Journal* 419

Cho, S, 'Beyond Rationality: A Sociological Construction of the World Trade Organization' (2012) 52 *Virginia Journal of International Law* 321

Cho, S, 'An International Organization's Identity Crisis' (2014) 34 *Northwestern Journal of International Law and Business* 359

Cho, S, *The Social Foundations of World Trade: Norms, Community, and Institutions* (CUP, 2015)

Chorev, N, 'Changing Global Norms through Reactive Diffusion: The Case of Intellectual Property Protection of AIDS Drugs' (2012) 77 *American Sociological Review* 831

Choudhury, B, 'Democratic Implications arising from the Intersection of Investment Arbitration and Human Rights' (2009) 46 *Alberta Law Review* 983

Chow, PYS, 'Culture as Collective Memories: An Emerging Concept in International Law and Discourse on Cultural Rights' (2014) 14 *Human Rights Law Review* 611

Cohen, I, 'Sociological Theory' in BS Turner (ed), *The Cambridge Dictionary of Sociology* (CUP, 2006) 595

Coleman, JS, 'Human Action as Rational Choice' in R Munch (ed), *Sociological Theory: Developments Since The 1960s* (Nelson Hall Publishers, 1990) 37

Collins, R, *Interaction Ritual Chains* (Princeton University Press, 2004)

Costa, JAF, 'Comparing WTO Panelists and ICSID Arbitrators: The Creation of International Legal Fields' (2011) 1(4) *Oñati Socio-Legal Series* 1 <http://www.opo.iisj.net/index.php/osls/article/viewFile/63/207>

Côté, L, 'Reflections on the Exercise of Prosecutorial Discretion in International Criminal Law' (2005) 3 *Journal of International Criminal Justice* 162

Cotterrell, R, *Law, Culture and Society: Legal Ideas in the Mirror of Social Theory* (Ashgate, 2006)

Cottier, T, 'The Challenge of Regionalism and Preferential Relations in World Trade Law and Policy' (1996) 1 *European Foreign Affairs Review* 149

Cover, RM, 'Forward: Nomos and Narrative' (1983) 97 *Harvard Law Review* 4

Craven, MCR, 'The Problem of State Succession and the Identity of States under International Law' (1998) 9 *EJIL* 142

Crawford, JA, 'A New Transparency Mechanism for Regional Trade Agreements' (2007) 11 *Singapore Ybk of Intl L* 133

Crawford, JA, and CL Lim, 'Cast Light and Evil Will Go Away: The Transparency Mechanism for Regional Trade Agreements Three Years After' (2011) 43 *Journal of World Trade* 375

Cremades, B, 'The Resurgence of the Calvo Doctrine in Latin America' (November 2005) 2(5) *Transnational Dispute Management* 2

Cremona, M, 'Values in the EU Constitution: The External Dimension, Centre on Democracy, Development, and the Rule of Law' (2004) 26 *Stanford Institute for International Studies* 1

Cremona, M, 'Values in the EU Foreign Policy' in M Evans and P Koutrakos (eds), *Beyond the Established Legal Orders: Policy Interconnections between the EU and the Rest of the World* (Hart, 2011) 307

Crisp, RJ, 'Prejudice and Perceiving Multiple Identities' in JF Dovidio and others (eds), *Prejudice, Stereotyping and Discrimination* (Sage, 2010) 508

Crystal, D, *How Language Works* (Penguin Books, 2006)

Cullet, P, 'Differential treatment in International Law' (1999) 10 *EJIL* 549

Damrosch, LF, and others, *International Law* (5th edn, West, 2009)

Dandaneau, SP, 'Norms', *The Concise Encyclopedia of Sociology* (Wiley-Blackwell, 2010) 426

Daniels, RJ, and M Trebilcock, 'The Political Economy of Rule of Law Reform in Developing Countries' (2004) 26 *Michigan Journal of International Law* 99

Daws, S, 'The Origins and Development of UN Electoral Groups' in R Thakur (ed), *What is Equitable Geographic Representation in the 21st Century?* (United Nations University, 1999) 11

De Brabandere, E, 'Human Rights Considerations in International Investment Arbitration' in M Fitzmaurice and P Merkouris (eds), *The Interpretation and Application of the European Convention of Human Rights: Legal and Practical Implications* (Martinus Nijhoff Publishers, 2013) 183

De Búrca, G, 'The European Courts and the Security Council: Between Dédoublement Fonctionnel and Balancing of Values: Three Replies to Pasquale De Sena and Maria Chiara Vitucci' (2009) 20 *EJIL* 853

De Búrca, G, 'The Evolution of EU Human Rights Law' in P Craig and G De Burca (eds), *The Evolution of EU Law* (2nd edn, OUP, 2011) 465

Deflem, M, *Sociology of Law: Visions of a Scholarly Tradition* (CUP, 2008)

Delbrück, J, 'Max Huber's Sociological Approach to International Law Revisited' (2007) 18 *EJIL* 97

De Lombaerde, P, A Estevadeordal, and K Souminen, 'Governing Regional Integration for Development: Introduction' in P De Lombaerde, A Estevadeordal, and K Souminen (eds) *Governing Regional Integration for Development* (Ashgate, 2008) 1

Desta, MG, 'EC-ACP Economic Partnership Agreements and WTO Compatibility: An Experiment in North-South Inter-Regional Agreements?' (2006) 43 *Common Market Law Review* 1343

Desta, M, and M Hirsch, 'The African Countries in the World Trading System: International Trade, Domestic Institutions and the Role of International Law' (2012) 61 *International and Comparative Law Quarterly* 127

Devine, PG, and LB Sharp, 'Automaticity and Control in Stereotyping and Prejudice' in TD Nelson (ed), *Handbook of Prejudice, Stereotyping, and Discrimination* (Taylor & Francis, 2009) 61

Dezalay, Y, and BG Garth, *Dealing in Virtue: International Commercial Arbitration and the Construction of a Transnational Legal Order* (University of Chicago Press, 1996)

Dezalay, Y, and BG Garth, *The Internationalization of Palace Wars: Lawyers, Economists, and the Contest to Transform Latin American States* (University of Chicago Press, 2002)

Dinstein, Y, *War, Aggression, and Self-Defence* (5th edn, CUP, 2011)

Do, VD, and W Watson, 'Economic Analysis of Regional Trade Agreements' in L Bartel and F Ortino (eds), *Regional Trade Agreements and the WTO Legal System* (OUP, 2006) 7

Dobbin, F, 'The Sociological View of the Economy' in F Dobbin (ed), *The New Economic Sociology: A Reader* (Princeton University Press, 2004) 1

Docea, V, 'History, Ideology and Collective Memory' (2010) 1 *Acta Universitatis Sapientiae—European and Regional Studies* 83

Dolzer, R, and C Schreuer, *Principles of International Investment Law* (2nd edn, OUP, 2012)

Donno, D, 'Legalization and Leverage: Human Rights Conditionality in the European Union's Economic Agreements' (American Political Science Association Annual Meeting, New Orleans, September 2012)

Donnelly, J, 'Human Rights: A New Standard of Civilization?' (1998) 74 *International Affairs* 1

Donnelly, J, 'Realism', in S Burchill and others (eds), *Theories of International Relations* (4th edn, Palgrave, 2009) 31

Dovidio, JF, and others, 'Prejudice, Stereotyping and Discrimination: Theoretical and Empirical Overview' in JF Dovidio and others (eds), *Prejudice, Stereotyping and Discrimination* (Sage, 2010) 1

Downs, GW, DM Rocke, and PN Barsoom, 'Is the Good News About Compliance Good News About Cooperation?' (1996) 50 *International Organization* 379

Drulák, P, and L Königová, 'The Czech Republic: From Socialist Past to Socialized Future', in T Flockhart (ed), *Socializing Democratic Norms: The Role of International Organizations for the Construction of Europe* (Palgrave, 2005) 149

Duina, F, *The Social Construction of Free Trade: The European Union, NAFTA, and Mercosur* (Princeton University Press, 2006)

Dullien, S, and U Guérot, 'The Long Shadow of Ordoliberalism: Germany's Approach to the Euro Crisis' (2012) European Council on Foreign Relations Policy Brief <http://ecfr.eu/page/-/ECFR49_GERMANY_BRIEF.pdf>

Dunne, T, and BC Schmidt, 'Realism' in J Baylis, S Smith, and P Owens (eds), *The Globalization of World Politics* (6th edn, OUP, 2014) 99

Dupuy, PM, F Francioni, and EU Petersmann (eds), *Human Rights, International Investment Law and Investor-State Arbitration* (OUP, 2009)

Durkheim, E, *Sociology and Psychology* (Free Press, 1953)

Durkheim, E, *The Rules of Sociological Method* (3rd edn, Free Press, 1982) 6

Dusenberry, W, 'Juan Manuel de Rosas as Viewed by Contemporary American Diplomats' (1961) 41 *The Hispanic American Historical Review* 495

Duxbury, A, *The Participation of States and International Organizations: The Role of Human Rights and Democracy* (CUP, 2011)

Duyck, S, 'MRV in the 2015 Climate Agreement: Promoting Compliance Through Transparency and the Participation of NGOs' (2014) 3 *Carbon and Climate Law Review* 175

Dyson, K, *The Politics of the Euro-Zone* (OUP, 2000)

Eder, K, 'A Theory of Collective Identity' (2009) 12 *European Journal of Social Theory* 427

Edwards, GE, 'Assessing the Effectiveness of Human Rights Non-Governmental Organizations (NGOs) From the Birth of the United Nations to the 21st Century' (2009) 18 *Michigan State Journal of International Law* 165

Edwards, MS, 'Can Economic Surveillance Make a Difference? Insights from the OECD' (15 April 2013) *Global Policy Journal* <http://ssrn.com/abstract=2273283>

Eldridge, JET, *Max Weber: The Interpretation of Social Reality* (Nelson, 1972)

Elster, J, *Nuts and Bolts for the Social Sciences* (CUP, 1989)

Eltringham, N, '"We are not a Truth Commission": Fragmented Narratives and the Historical Record at the International Criminal Tribunal for Rwanda' (2009) 11 *Journal of Genocide Research* 55

Eppinger, ME, K Knop, and A Riles, 'Diplomacy and Its Others: The Case of Korean Comfort Women' (18 April 2014) <http://ssrn.com/abstract=2411610>

Erikson, KT, 'Notes on the Sociology of Deviance' (1962) 9 *Social Problems* 307

Ethier, WJ, 'The New Regionalism' (1998) 108 *The Economic Journal* 1149

Fabbricotti, A, 'The ASEAN Free Trade Area (AFTA) and its Compatibility with GATT/WTO' (2003) 8 *Asian Ybk Intl L* 37

Falvey, R, N Foster, and D Greenaway, 'North-South Trade, Knowledge Spillovers and Growth' (2002) 17 *Journal of Economic Integration* 650

Featherstone, K, 'The Greek Sovereign Debt Crisis and EMU' (2011) 49 *Journal of Common Market Studies* 193

Felbermayr, G, and F Toubal, 'Cultural Proximity and Trade' (2010) 54 *European Economic Review* 279

Ferguson, N, *The Ascent of Money: A Financial History of the World* (Penguin Books, 2009)

Finnemore, M, 'Constructing Norms of Humanitarian Intervention' in PJ Katzenstein (ed), *The Culture of National Security: Norms and Identity in World Politics* (Columbia University Press, 1996) 153

Finnemore, M, 'Norms, Culture, and World Politics: Insights from Sociology's Institutionalism' (1996) 50 *International Organization* 325

Fiorentino,RV, L Verdeja, and C Toqueboeuf, 'The Changing Landscape of Regional Trade Agreements: 2006 Update' (2007) WTO Discussion Paper 12 <http://www10.iadb.org/intal/intalcdi/PE/2010/05129.pdf>

Fischer-Lescano, A, and G Teubner, 'Diversity or Cacophony?: New Sources of Norms in International Law Symposium', (2004) 25 *Michigan Journal of International Law* 999

Fitzmaurice, M, 'Treaties' in R Wolfrum (ed), *Max Planck Encyclopedia of Public International Law* (OUP, 2010)

Foucault, M, *Language, Counter Memory & Practice: Selected Essays and Interviews* (Cornell University Press, 1997)

Franck, TM, *The Power Of Legitimacy Among Nations* (OUP, 1990)

Frankel, B, 'Restating the Realist Case' in B Frankel (ed.), *Realism: Restatement and Renewal* (Frank Cass, 1996) ix

Frankel, JA, Regional Trading Blocs in the World Economic System (Institute for International Economics, 1997)

Fransman, L, 'Commonwealth Subjects and Nationality Rules', in R Wolfrum (ed), Max Planck Encyclopedia of Public International Law (OUP, 2009)

Franzese, RJ, *The Sociology of Deviance: Differences, Tradition, and Stigma* (Thomas Pub, 2010)

Freund, C, and E Ornelas, 'Regional Trade Agreements' (2010) World Bank Policy Research Working Paper 5314 <http://papers.ssrn.com/sol3/papers.cfm?abstract_id=1612091>

Friedman, L, 'Some Comments on Cottorrell and Legal Transplants' in D Nelken and J Feest (eds), *Adapting Legal Cultures* (Hart, 2001) 93

Friedman, LM, *Law and Society: An Introduction* (Prentice Hall, 1977)

Froehlich, A, 'Cultural Matters in Investment Agreements and Decisions' in A Reinisch and C Knahr (eds), *International Investment Law in Context* (Eleven, 2007) 141

Fulcher, J, and J Scott, *Sociology* (4th edn, OUP, 2011)

Fulponi, L, M Shearer, and J Almeida, 'Regional Trade Agreements—Treatment of Agriculture' (2011) OECD Food, Agriculture and Fisheries Working Paper 44 <http://www.oecd-ilibrary.org/docserver/download/5kgg53fmnjxv.pdf?expires=1426232987&id=id&accname=guest&checksum=1F8EDE25AAF5BC4BAEDDA44E6E7C1D26>

Gaertner, SL, JF Dovidio, and MA Houlette, 'Social Categorization' in JF Dovidio and others (eds), *The Sage Handbook of Prejudice, Stereotyping, and Discrimination* (Sage, 2010) 526

Gammage, C, '(Re)conceptualizing International Economic Law' in A Perry-Kessaris (ed), *Socio-Legal Approaches to International Economic Law* (Routledge, 2013) 64

Garcia-Bolivar, OE, 'The Latin American Struggle With the International Law of Foreign Investment: Is It a Demand for a More Balanced System?' (December 2009) 6(4) *Transnational Dispute Management* 1

Garibaldi, OM, 'Carlos Calvo Redivivus: The Rediscovery of the Calvo Doctrine in the Era of Investment Treaties' (December 2006) 3(5) 3 *Transnational Dispute Management* 14

Gathii, JT, 'African Regional Trade Agreements as Flexible Legal Regimes' (2010) 35 *North Carolina Journal of International Law and Commercial Regulation* 571

Gaukrodger, D, and K Gordon, 'Investor-State Dispute Settlement: A Scoping Paper for the Investment Policy Community' (2012) OECD Working Papers on International Investment 2012/03 <http://www.oecd-ilibrary.org/docserver/download/5k46b1r85j6f.pdf?expires=1425725077&id=id&accname=guest&checksum=06EAC135D4DEA10B912459D398F8F6DA>

Geelhoed, A, F Amtenbrink, and S Kingston, 'Economic, Monetary and Social Policy' in PJG Kapteyn and others (eds), *The Law of the European Union and the European Communities* (4th edn, Kluwer, 2008)

Ghemawat, P, 'Distance Still Matters' (2001) 79 *Harvard Business Review* 137

Gibbs, M, S Wagle, and P Ortega, *The Great Maze: Regional and Bilateral Free Trade Agreements in Asia* (UNDP Asia-Pacific Trade and Investment Initiative, 2005)

Giddens, A, *New Rules of Sociological Method: A Positive Critique of Interpretative Sociologies* (Basic Books, 1976)

Giddens, A, *The Constitution of Society: Outline of the Theory of Structuration* (University of California Press, 1984)

Giddens, A, and P Sutton, *Sociology* (7th edn, Polity, 2013)

Gilpin, R, *Global Political Economy* (Princeton University Press, 2001)

Ginsburg, T, 'The Culture of Arbitration' (2003) 36 *Vanderbilt Journal of Transnational Law* 1335

Ginsburg, T, 'Eastphalia and Asian Regionalism' (2010) 44 *University of California Davis Law Review* 859

Giorgetti, C, 'Towards a Revised Threshold for Arbitrators' Challenges Under ICSID?' (*Kluwer Arbitration Blog*, 2 July 2014) <http://kluwerarbitrationblog.com/blog/2014/07/03/towards-a-revised-threshold-for-arbitrators-challenges-under-icsid/>

Goh, G, 'The ASEAN Way: Non-Intervention and ASEAN's Role in Conflict Management' (2003) 3 *Stanford Journal of East Asian Affairs* 113

Gonzalez, G, and S Haggard, 'The United States and Mexico: A Pluralistic Security Community?' in E Adler and M Barnett (eds), *Security Communities* (CUP, 1998) 295

Goode, E, *Deviant Behaviour* (9th edn, Prentice Hall, 2011)

Goode, WJ, 'A Theory of Role Strain' (1960) 25 *American Sociological Review* 483

Goodman, CL, 'Uncharted Waters: Financial Crisis and Enforcement of ICSID Awards in Argentina' (2007) 28 *University of Pennsylvania Journal of International Economic Law* 452

Goodman, R, and D Jinks, 'Toward an Institutional Theory of Sovereignty' (2003) 55 *Stanford Law Review* 1749

Goodman, R, and D Jinks, 'How to Influence States: Socialization and International Human Rights Law' (2004) 54 *Duke Law Journal* 621

Goodman, R, and D Jinks, 'Incomplete Internalization and Compliance with Human Rights Law' (2008) 19 *EJIL* 725

Goodman, R, and D Jinks, *Socializing States* (OUP, 2013)

Gopalan, S, and R Fuller, 'Enforcing International Law: States, IOs, and Courts as Shaming Reference Groups' (2014) 39 *Brooklyn Journal of International Law* 73

Gotz, N, 'Western Europeans and Others: The making of Europe at the United Nations' (2008) 33 *Alternatives: Global, Local, Political* 366

Gowan, R, and F Brantner, 'A Global Force for Human Rights? An Audit of European Power at the UN' (2008) European Council on Foreign Relations Policy Paper <http://kms2.isn.ethz.ch/serviceengine/Files/RESSpecNet/91657/ipublicationdocument_singledocument/12CA5C36-C4CC-46BD-B38F-B1CB7717F217/en/Global_Force_Human_Rights_EU_0908.pdf>

Graham, FD, *Exchange, Prices, and Production in Hyper-inflation: Germany, 1920–1923* (Russell and Russell, 1967)

Granovetter, M, 'Economic Action and Social Structure: The Problem of Embeddedness' in R Swedberg (ed), *Economic Sociology* (Edward Elgar, 1996) 239

Grant, JH, and C Parmeter, 'Has the World Trade Organization Promoted Successful Regional Trade Agreements?' (BePress Selected Works, 2010) <http://works.bepress.com/parms/27>

Grattet, R, 'Labelling Theory' in CD Bryant (ed), *The Routledge Handbook of Deviant Behaviour* (Routledge, 2011) 121

Gray, J, 'Politics and Patronage: The Function of Dysfunctional Regional Trade Agreements' (Conference on 'The Politics of Preferential Trade Agreements', Princeton University, April 30-May 1, 2010) <http://www.princeton.edu/~pcglobal/conferences/ptas/Gray_pta_paper.pdf>

Greenhill, B, 'The Company You Keep: International Socialization and the Diffusion of Human Rights Norms' (2010) 54 *International Studies Quarterly* 127

Greenwald, BC, and JE Stiglitz, 'Keynesian, New Keynesian and New Classical Economics' (1987) 39 *Oxford Economic Papers* 119

Grieco, JM, 'Systemic Sources of Variations in Regional Institutionalization in Western Europe, East Asia, and the Americas' in ED Mansfield and HV Milner (eds), *The Political Economy of Regionalism* (Columbia University Press, 1997) 164

Grip, L, and J Hart, 'The Use of Chemical Weapons in the 1935–36 Italo-Ethiopian War' (October 2009) SIPRI Arms Control and Non-proliferation Programme 6, <http://www.sipri.org/research/disarmament/chemical/publications/ethiopiapaper>

Grusec, JE, and PD Hasting, 'Introduction' in JE Grusec and PD Hasting (eds), *Handbook of Socialization* (Guilford Press, 2007)

Guiso, L, P Sapienza, and L Zingales, 'Cultural Biases in Economic Exchange' (2009) 124 *Quarterly Journal of Economics* 1095

Gurowitz, A, 'The Diffusion of International Norms: Why Identity Matters' (2006) 43 *International Politics* 305

Guzman, AT, 'A Compliance-Based Theory of International Law' (2002) 90 *California Law Review* 1823

Guzman, AT, *How International Law Works: A Rational Choice Theory* (OUP, 2008)

Guzman, AT, and JHB Pauwelyn, *International Trade Law* (Kluwer, 2012)

Halbwachs, M, *On Collective Memory* (Lewis A Coser tr, University of Chicago Press, 1992)

Hansen-Magnusson, H, and J Wustenberg, 'Forging a European Memory: The Treaties of Rome as a Common Tradition in the Making?' (Biennial Conference of the European Union Studies Association, Boston, 3–5 March 2011) <http://www.euce.org/eusa/2011/papers/1g_wustenberg.pdf>

Harpaz, G, and E Rubinson, 'The Interface between Trade, Law and Politics and the Erosion of Normative Power Europe' (2010) 35 *European Law Review* 551

Hays, S, 'Structure and Agency and the Sticky Problem of Culture' (1994) 12 *Sociological Theory* 57

Hayward, K, and J Ilan, 'Deviant Subcultures' in CD Bryant (ed), *The Routledge Handbook of Deviant Behaviour* (Routledge, 2011) 233

Hazelzet, H, 'Suspension of Development Cooperation: An Instrument to Promote Human Rights and Democracy?' (August 2005), European Centre for Development Policy Management

Heap SH, and others, *The Theory of Choice: A Critical Guide* (Blackwell, 1992)

Hecht, G, *The Radiance of France: Nuclear Power and National Identity After World War II* (MIT Press, 2009)

Heilmann, S, and N Schulte-Kulkmann, 'The Limits of Policy Diffusion: Introducing International Norms of Anti-Money Laundering into China's Legal System' (2011) 24 *Governance* 639

Hellinger, DC, *Comparative Politics of Latin America* (Routledge, 2011)

Hemmer, C, and PJ Katzenstein, 'Why is There No NATO in Asia? Collective Identity, Regionalism, and the Origins of Multilateralism' (2002) 56 *International Organization* 575

Henkin, L, *How Nations Behave* (2nd edn, Columbia University Press, 1979)

Henrard, K, 'Minorities, International Protection' in *R Wolfrum (ed), Max Planck Encyclopedia of Public International Law* (OUP, 2008)

Henry, S, 'Social Construction of Crime' in JM Miller (ed), *21st Century Criminology* (Sage, 2009) 296

Heritage, J, *Garfinkel and Ethnomethodology* (Polity Press, 1984)

Herndon, T, M Ash, and R Pollin, 'Does High Public Debt Consistently Stifle Economic Growth? A Critique of Reinhart and Rogoff' (2013) Political Economy Research Institute, Working Paper 322 <http://www.peri.umass.edu/fileadmin/pdf/working_papers/working_papers_301-350/WP322.pdf>

Hirsch, M, 'Game Theory, International Law, and Environmental Cooperation in the Middle East' (1999) 27 *Denver Journal of International Law and Policy* 75

Hirsch, M, 'Compliance with International Norms In the Age of Globalization: Two Theoretical Perspectives' in E Benvenisti and M Hirsch (eds), *The Impact of International Law on International Cooperation* (CUP, 2004) 166

Hirsch, M, 'The Impact of the Advisory Opinion on Israel's Future Policy: International Relations Perspective' (2004/5) 1 *Journal of International Law and International Relations* 319

Hirsch, M, 'The Logic of North-South Economic Integration' (2005) 32 *Legal Issues of Economic Integration* 3

Hirsch, M, 'Conflicting Obligations in International Investment Law: Investment Tribunals' Perspective' in Tomer Broude and Yuval Shany (eds), *The Shifting Allocation of Authority in International Law* (Hart, 2008) 323

Hirsch, M, 'Investment Tribunals and Human Rights: Divergent Paths' in PM Dupuy, FF Francioni, and EU Petersmann (eds), *Human Rights in International Investment Law and Arbitration* (OUP, 2008) 97

Hirsch, M, 'The Sociology of International Economic Law: Sociological Analysis of the Regulation of Regional Agreements in the World Trading System' (2008) 19 *EJIL* 277

Hirsch, M, 'Interactions between Investment and Non-Investment Obligations' in P Muchlinski, F Ortino, and C Schreuer (eds), *The Oxford Handbook of International Law on Foreign Investment* (OUP, 2008) 154

Hirsch, M, 'The Interaction between International Investment Law and Human Rights Treaties: A Sociological Perspective' in Y Shany and T Broude (eds), *Multi-Sourced Equivalent Norms* (Hart, 2011) 211

Hirsch, M, 'North-South Regional Trade Agreements: Prospects, Risks and Legal Regulation' in YS Lee and T Broude (eds), *Law and Development Perspective on International Trade Law* (CUP, 2011) 225

Hirsch, M, 'Between Fair and Equitable Treatment and Stabilization Clause' (2011) 12 *Journal of World Investment and Trade* 783

Hirsch, M, 'The Sociology of International Investment Law' in Z Douglas, J Pauwelyn, and JE Viñuales (eds), *The Foundations of International Investment Law: Bringing Theory into Practice* (OUP, 2014) 143

Hirst, P, 'Pluralism' in W Outhwaite (ed), *Modern Social Thought* (Wiley, 2006)

Hodaka, M, and S Maroš, *Symbols, Group Identity and the Hold-Up Problem* (30 November 2011) <http://ssrn.com/abstract=1966354>

Hoekman, B, 'Supply Chains, Mega-Regionals and Multilateralism: A Road Map for the WTO' (2014) Robert Schuman Centre for Advanced Studies Research Paper No. RSCAS 2014/27 <http://papers.ssrn.com/sol3/papers.cfm?abstract_id=2406871>

Hoekman, BM, and MM Kostecki, *The Political Economy of the World Trading System* (3rd edn, OUP, 2009)

Hofmann, T, and SY Kim, 'Designing Reciprocity: The Politics of Dispute Settlement Mechanisms in Asia's PTAs' (Workshop on The Politics of Trade Agreements, the Niehaus Center for Globalization and Governance, Princeton University, April 30, 2010) <http://www.princeton.edu/~pcglobal/conferences/ptas/KH_pta_paper.pdf>

Hogg, MA, and DJ Terry, 'Social Identity Theory and Organizational Process' in MA Hogg and DJ Terry (eds), *Social Identity Process in Organizational Context* (Psychology Press, 2001) 1

Hogg, MA, DJ Terry, and KM White, 'A Tale of Two Theories: A Critical Comparison of Identity Theory with Social Identity Theory' (1995) 58 *Social Psychology Quarterly* 255

Hollis, M, *The Philosophy of Social Science* (CUP, 2011)

Hoover, KD, 'New Classical Macroeconomics', *The Concise Encyclopaedia of Economics* (2nd edn, Liberty Fund Inc, 2008)

Hopf, T, 'The Promise of Constructivism in International Relations Theory' (1998) 23 *International Security* 171

Horwitz, MJ, 'The History of the Public/Private Distinction' (1982) 130 *University of Pennsylvania Law Review* 1423

Howarth, D, and P Loedel, *The European Central Bank: The New European Leviathan?* (Palgrave Macmillan, 2003)

Howarth, D, and C Rommerskirchen, 'A Panacea for all Times? The German Stability Culture as Strategic Political Resource' (2013) 36 *West European Politics* 750

Hume, J, 'Memory Matters: The Evolution of Scholarship in Collective Memory and Mass Communication' (2010) 10 *Review of Communication* 181

Hurd, I, 'Constructivism' in C Reus-Smit (ed), *The Oxford Handbook of International Relations* (OUP, 2008) 298

Hurwitz, DR, 'Lawyering for Justice and the Inevitability of International Human Rights Clinics' (2003) 28 *YJIL* 505

Hutn, M, 'Culture, Institutions, and Gender Inequality in Latin America' in LE Harrison and SP Huntington (eds), *Culture Matters* (Basic Books, 2000) 189

Hymans, JEC, *The Psychology of Nuclear Proliferation: Identity, Emotions, and Foreign Policy* (CUP, 2006)

Ioannidis, M, 'Naming a State: Disputing over Symbols of Statehood at the Example of Macedonia' 14 *Max Planck Yearbook of United Nations Law* (OUP, 2010) 507

Irwin, MD, and JD Kasarda, 'Trade, Transportation, and Spatial Distribution' in NJ Smelser and R Swedberg (eds), *The Handbook of Economic Sociology* (Princeton University Press, 1994) 342

Jackson, R, and G Sørensen, *Introduction to International Relations: Theories and Approaches* (4th edn, OUP, 2010)

Jamieson, B, 'Trade Liberalization: Culture, Identity and Social Cohesion' (2001) Department of Canadian Heritage: Paper prepared on behalf of the PRI-GCON Working Group on World Trade Issues <http://citeseerx.ist.psu.edu/viewdoc/download?doi=10.1.1.199.7336&rep=rep1&type=pdf>

Jenkins, R, *Social Identity* (4th edn, Routledge, 2014)

Jenks, C, 'Culture: Conceptual Clarifications', *The Concise Encyclopedia of Sociology* (Wiley-Blackwell, 2010)

Jennings, WG, and RL Akers, 'Social Learning Theory' in CD Bryant (ed), *The Routledge Handbook of Deviant Behaviour* (Routledge, 2011) 106

Jensen, G, 'Deviance and Social Control' in CD Bryant (ed), *The Routledge Handbook of Deviant Behaviour* (Routledge, 2011) 11

Jetten, J, and others, 'Rebels with a Cause: Group Identification as a Response to Perceived Discrimination from the Mainstream' (2001) 27 *Personality and Social Psychology Bulletin* 1204

Jones, E, 'Identity and Solidarity' in E Jones, A Menon, and S Weatherill (eds), *The Oxford Handbook of the European Union* (OUP, 2012) 690

Jones, ME, 'Forging an ASEAN Identity: The Challenge to Construct a Shared Destiny' (2004) 26 *Contemporary Southeast Asia* 140

Jönson, K, 'Unity-in-Diversity: Regional Identity Building in Southeast Asia' (2010) 29 *Journal of Current Southeast Asian Affairs* 42

Juillard, P, 'Calvo Doctrine/Calvo Clause' in R Wolfrum (ed), *Max Planck Encyclopedia of Public International Law* (OUP, 2012)

Kabaalioglu, H, 'The Turkish Model of Association: Customs Union before Accession' in P Demaret, JF Bellis, and GG Jimenez (eds), *Regionalism and Multilateralism after The Uruguay Round* (European Interuniversity Press, 1997) 115

Kahler, M, 'Legalization as Strategy: The Asia-Pacific Case' (2000) 54 *International Organization* 549

Kahn-Freund, O, 'On Uses and Misuses of Comparative Law' (1974) 37 *Modern Law Review* 1

Kapeliuk, D, 'The Repeat Appointment Factor—Exploring Decision Patterns of Elite Investment Arbitrators' (2010) 96 *Cornell Law Review* 47

Karber, PA, 'Constructivism as a Method in International Law' (2000) 94 *American Society of International Law Proceedings* 189

Karton, J, *The Culture of International Arbitration and the Evolution of Contract Law* (OUP, 2013)

Kasarda, JD, and M Janowitz, 'Community Attachment in Mass Society' (1974) 39 *American Sociological Review* 328

Katz, E, 'Cultural Diffusion' in JR Hall, L Grindstaff, and MC Lo (eds), *Handbook of Cultural Sociology* (Routledge, 2010) 668

Katzenstein, PJ, 'Introduction: Alternative Perspectives on National Security' in PJ Katzenstein (ed), *The Culture of National Security: Norms and Identity in World Politics* (Columbia University Press, 1996) 1

Katzenstein, PJ, RL Lepperson, and A Wendt, 'Norms, Identity, and Culture in National Security' in PJ Katzenstein (ed), *The Culture of National Security: Norms and Identities in World Politics* (Columbia University Press, 1996) 11

Kent, A, 'China's International Socialization: The Role of International Organizations' (2002) 8 *Global Governance* 343

Keohane, RO, 'International Institutions: Two Approaches' (1988) 32 *International Studies Quarterly* 379

Khan, FH, *Eating Grass: The Making of the Pakistani Bomb* (Stanford University Press, 2012)

Kim, M, 'Inspecting the Termites: Market Structure and WTO's Consideration Process of PTAs' (APSA Annual Meeting, Chicago, August–September 2013) <http://ssrn.com/abstract=2299655>

King, R, 'Institutionalizing Collective Memories of Hate: Law and Law Enforcement in Germany and the United States' (2005) 111 *American Journal of Sociology* 579

Kingsbury, B, 'The Concept of Compliance as a Function of Competing Conceptions of International Law' (1998) 19 *Michigan Journal of International Law* 345

Kirton, JJ, *G20 Governance for a Globalized World* (Ashgate, 2013)

Kiss, A, 'Commentary and Conclusions' in D Shelton (ed), *Commitment and Compliance: The Role of Non-Binding Norms in the International Legal System* (OUP, 2000) 223

Klotz, A, *Norms in International Relations: The Struggle Against Apartheid* (Cornell University Press, 1995)

Klotz, A, 'Norms Reconstituting Interests: Global Racial Equality and U.S. Sanctions Against South Africa' (1995) 49 *International Organization* 451

Knahr, C, and A Reinisch, 'Transparency versus Confidentiality in International Investment Arbitration' (2007) 6 *International Courts and Tribunals* 97

Kobrin, SJ, 'The MAI and the Clash of Globalizations' (Fall 1998) *Foreign Policy* 97

Koh, HH, 'Why Do Nations Obey International Law?' (1997) 106 *Yale Law Journal* 2599

Koji, T, 'Emerging Hierarchy in International Human Rights and Beyond' (2001) 12 *EJIL* 917

Kolben, K, 'Foreign Investment and Human Rights Link' in *Human Rights, Trade and Investment Matters* (Amnesty International, May 2006) <http://www.amnestyusa.org/sites/default/files/pdfs/hrtradeinvestmentmatters.pdf>

Kowert, P, and J Legro, 'Norms, Identity and Their Limits: A Theoretical Reprise' in PJ Katzenstein (ed), *The Culture of National Security: Norms and Identity in World Politics* (Columbia University Press, 1996) 451

Kriebaum, U, 'Privatizing Human Rights: The Interface between International Investment Protection and Human Rights' (2006) 5 *Transnational Dispute Management* 1

Krueger, AO, 'Free Trade Agreements versus Customs Unions' (April 1995) NBER Working Paper No. 5084 <http://www.nber.org/papers/w5084.pdf>

Kugelmann, D, 'Refugees' in R Wolfrum (ed), *Max Planck Encyclopedia of Public International Law* (OUP, 2010)

Kumar, R, 'Culture and Emotions in Intercultural Negotiations', in MJ Gelfand and JM Brett (eds), *The Handbook of Negotiation and Culture* (Stanford University Press, 2004) 13

Kusow, AM, 'Contesting Stigma: On Goffman's Assumptions of Normative Order' (2004) 27 *Symbolic Interaction* 179

Kymlicka, W, *Contemporary Political Philosophy* (2nd edn, OUP, 2002)

Landheer, B, *On the Sociology of International Law and International Society* (Nijhoff, 1966)

Landsman, S, *Crimes of the Holocaust* (University of Pennsylvania Press, 2005)

Lang, ATF, 'Some Sociological Perspectives on International Institutions and the Trading System' in CB Picker, ID Bunn, and DW Arner (eds), *International Economic Law: The State and Future of the Discipline* (Hart Publishing, 2008) 73

Lang, A, and J Scott, 'The Hidden World of WTO Governance' (2009) 20 *EJIL* 575

Langer, MJ, and JE Viñuales, 'Foreign Investment in Latin-America: Between Love and Hatred' (2010) <http://ssrn.com/abstract=1652736>

La Porta, R, and others 'Trust in Large Organizations' (1997) 87 *American Economic Review* 333

Lastra, RM, and JV Louis, 'European Economic and Monetary Union: History, Trends, and Prospects' (2013) *YB Eur L* 1

Lawrence, RZ, *Regionalism, Multilateralism, and Deeper Integration* (Brookings Institute, 1996)

Lebovic, JH, and E Voeten, 'The Politics of Shame: The Condemnation of Country Human Rights Practices in the UNHCR' (2006) 50 *International Studies Quarterly* 861

Lee, SH, O Shenkar, and J Li, 'Cultural Distance, Investment Flow, and Control in Cross-border Cooperation' (2008) 29 *Strategic Management Journal* 1117

Lee, YS, *Reclaiming Development in the World Trading System* (CUP, 2006)

Leung, K, and KK Tong, 'Justice Across Cultures: A Three-Stage Model for Intercultural Negotiation', in MJ Gelfand and JM Brett (eds), *The Handbook of Negotiation and Culture* (Stanford University Press, 2004) 313

Lewis, DK, *The History of Argentina* (Palgrave Macmillan, 2001)

Lewis, MK, 'The Politics of Indirect Effects of Asymmetrical Bargaining Power in Free Trade Agreement' in T Broude and others (eds), *The Politics of International Economic Law* (CUP, 2011) 19

Linzert, T, D Nautz, and U Bindseil, 'The Longer Term Refinancing Operations of the ECB' (2004) ECB Working Papers Series No. 359 <http://www.ecb.europa.eu/pub/pdf/scpwps/ecbwp359.pdf>

Lipson, C, *Standing Guard: Protecting Foreign Capital in the Nineteenth and Twentieth Centuries* (University of California Press, 1985)

Lockhart, NJS, and AD Mitchell, 'Regional Trade Agreements Under GATT 1994: An Exception and its Limits' in AD Mitchell (ed), *Challenges and Prospects for the WTO* (Cameron May, 2005) 217

Loedel, PH, *Deutsche Mark Politics* (Boulder, 1999)

Louis, JV, 'Monetary Policy and Central Banking in the Constitution' in *Legal Aspects of the European System of Central Banks* (European Central Bank, 2005) 27

Lowenfeld, AF, 'The International Monetary System: A Look Back Over Seven Decades' in T Cottier and JH Jackson (eds), *International Law in Financial Regulation and Monetary Affairs* (OUP, 2012) 52

Lu, IC, 'Curtain Call at Closing: The Multi-Dimensional Legacy of the International Criminal Tribunal for Rwanda' (2014) 34 *University of Pennsylvania Journal of International Law* 859

Luban, D, 'A Theory of Crimes Against Humanity' (2004) 29 *Yale Journal of International Law* 85

Lucarelli, S, 'Introduction: Values, Principles, Identity and European Union Foreign Policy' in S Lucarelli and I Manners (eds), *Values and Principles in European Union Foreign Policy* (Routledge, 2006) 1

Lucarelli, S, 'Values, Identity and Ideational Shocks in the Transatlantic Rift' (2006) 9 *Journal of International Relations and Development* 304

Maccoby, EE, 'Historical Overview of Socialization Research and Theory' in JE Grusec and PD Hasting (eds), *Handbook of Socialization* (Guilford Press, 2007)

Macionis, JJ, *Sociology* (14th edn, Pearson, 2012)

Mackenzie, R, and P Sands, 'International Courts and Tribunals and the Independence of the International Judge' (2003) 44 *HJIL* 271

Macklem, P, 'Rybná 9, Praha 1: Restitution and Memory in International Human Rights Law' (2005) 16 *EJIL* 1

McLachlan, C, L Shore, and M Weiniger, *International Investment Arbitration: Substantive Principles* (OUP, 2007)

Madeira, JL, 'Blood Relations: Collective Memory, Cultural Trauma, and the Prosecution and Execution of Timothy McVeigh' (2008) Indiana Legal Studies Research Paper No. 102, 9 <http://ssrn.com/abstract=1007041>

Madsen, MR, 'Sociological Approaches to International Courts' in C Romano, K Alter, and Y Shany (eds), *Oxford Handbook of International Adjudication* (OUP, 2014) 338

Magliveras, KD, *Exclusion from Participation in International Organisations* (Kluwer, 1999)

Mahmoudi, S, 'Organization of the Islamic Conference', in R Wolfrum (ed), *Max Planck Encyclopedia of Public International Law* (OUP, 2009)

Maier, P, *Political Pressure, Rhetoric and Monetary Policy* (Elgar, 2002)

Maier, P, and T Knaap, 'Who Supported the Deutsche Bundesbank?: An Empirical Investigation' (2002) 24 *Journal of Policy Modeling* 831

Maio, GR, and others 'Attitude and Intergroup Relations' in JF Dovidio and others (eds), *Prejudice, Stereotyping and Discrimination* (Sage, 2010) 261

Malintoppi, L, 'Independence, Impartiality, and Duty of Disclosure of Arbitrators' in P Muchlinski, F Ortino, and C Schreuer (eds), *Oxford Handbook of International Investment Law* (OUP, 2008) 789

Mamdani, M, 'Race and Ethnicity as Political Identities in the African Context' in M Mamdani and others (eds), *Keywords: Identity* (Other Press, 2004)

Manners, I, 'The Constitutive Nature of Values, Images, and Principles in the European Union' in S Lucarelli and I Manners (eds), *Values and Principles in European Union Foreign Policy* (Routledge, 2006) 19

Mansfield, ED, 'Preferential Peace: Why Preferential Trading Arrangements Inhibit Interstate Conflict' in E Mansfield and BM Pollins (eds), *Economic Interdependence and International Conflict* (University of Michigan Press, 2003) 222

Mansfield, ED, and JC Pevehouse, 'Trade Blocks, Trade Flows, and International Conflict' (2000) 54 *International Organizations* 775

Markovits, I, 'Selective Memory: How the Law Affects What We Remember and Forget about the Past: The Case of East Germany' (2001) 35 *Law and Society Review* 513

Marks, SR, 'Multiple Roles and Role Strain: Some Notes on Human Energy, Time and Commitment' (1977) 42 *American Sociological Review* 921

Martín, FE, and ML Astrada, 'Argentine Strategic Culture' (Florida International University, Applied Research Center, Miami, 2010)

Martin, LL, 'Against Compliance' in JL Dunoff and MA Pollack (eds), *Interdisciplinary Perspectives on International Law and International Relations: The State of the Art* (CUP, 2013) 591

Martin, P, T Mayer, and M Thoenig, 'The Economics and Politics of Free Trade Agreements' (Research-based policy analysis, 2010) <http://www.voxeu.org/article/free-trade-agreements-do-they-help-keep-peace>

Mason, E, 'Value Pluralism' in Edward N Zalta (ed), *The Stanford Encyclopedia of Philosophy* (Fall 2011 edn) <http://plato.stanford.edu/entries/value-pluralism/>

Mathis, JH, *Regional Trade Agreements in the GATT/WTO* (Asser Press, 2002)

Matsushita, M, and YS Lee, 'Proliferation of Free Trade Agreements and Some Systemic Issues—In Relation to the WTO Disciplines and Development Perspectives' (2008) 1 *The Law and Development Review* 23

Matsushita, M, TJ Schoenbaum, and PC Mavroidis, *The World Trade Organization: Law, Practice, and Policy* (2nd edn, Oxford International Law Library, 2006)

Mattli, W, *The Logic of Regional Integration: Europe and Beyond* (CUP, 1999)

Maupin, JA, 'Public and Private in International Investment Law: An Integrated Systems Approach' (2014) 54 *Virginia Journal of International Law* 367

Mautner, M, 'Three Approaches to Law and Culture' (2011) 96 *Cornell Law Review* 839

Mavroidis, PC, 'If I Don't Do It, Somebody Else Will (or Won't)' (2006) 40 *Journal of World Trade* 187

Mavroidis, PC, 'Always Look at the Bright Side of Non-Delivery: WTO and Preferential Trade Agreements, Yesterday and Today' (2011) 10 *World Trade Review* 375

Mavroidis, PC, *Trade in Goods: The GATT and the Other Agreements Regulating Trade in Goods* (2nd edn, OUP, 2012)

May, T, *Situating Social Theory* (OUP, 1996)

McWhinney, E, 'Julius Stone and the Sociological Approach to International Law' (1986) 9 *University of New South Wales Law Journal* 14

Meckenstock, CA, *Investment Protection and Human Rights Regulation* (Nomos, 2010)

Meernik, J, and others, 'The Impact of Human Rights Organizations on Naming and Shaming Campaigns' (2012) 56 *Journal of Conflict Resolution* 233

Meierhenrich, J, 'A Question of Guilt' (2006) 19 *Ratio Juris* 314

Melucci, A, 'The Process of Collective Identity' in H Johnston and B Klandermans (eds), *Social Movements and Culture*, vol 4 (University of Minnesota Press 1995) 41

Menkel-Meadow, C, 'Restorative Justice: What Is It and Does It Work?' (July 2007) 3 *Annual Review of Law and Social Science* 161

Mercurio, B, 'TRIPS-Plus Provisions in FTAs: Recent Trends' in L Bartel and F Ortino (eds), *Regional Trade Agreements and the WTO Legal System* (OUP, 2006) 215

Meron, T, 'Judicial Independence and Impartiality in International Criminal Tribunals' (2005) 99 *AJIL* 359

Mertes, M, 'Germany's Social and Political Culture: Change through Consensus?' (1994) 123 *Daedalus* 1

Merton, RK, *Social Theory and Social Structure* (enlarged edn, Free Press, 1968)

Merton, RK, 'Social Structure and Anomie' (1938) 3 *American Sociological Review* 672

Meshel, T, 'Human Rights in Investor-State Arbitration: The Human Right to Water and Beyond' (2015) 6 *Journal of International Dispute Settlement* (forthcoming)
Meyer, JW, FO Ramirez, and YN Soysal, 'World Society and the Nation-State' (1997) 103 *American Journal of Sociology* 144
Meyer, JW, FO Ramirez, and YN Soysal, 'World Expansion of Mass Education, 1870–1980' (1992) 65 *Sociology of Education* 128
Miles, K, *The Origins of International Investment Law* (CUP, 2013)
Miller, GP, 'The Legal Function of Ritual' (2005) 80 *Chicago-Kent Law Review* 1181
Mills, A, 'Antinomies of Public and Private at the Foundations of International Investment Law and Arbitration' (2011) 14 *Journal of International Economic Law* 469
Minaverry, CM, 'International Arbitration as a Dispute Resolution Mechanism: The Argentine Case in ICSID' (*Observatory on Latin America*, 2013) <http://www.observatorylatinamerica.org/en/programs/pnk/334-international-arbitration-as-a-dispute-resolution-mechanism-the-argentine-case-in-icsid>
Misztal, BA, *Theories of Social Remembering* (Open University Press, 2003)
Mochizuki, MM, 'Japan Tests the Nuclear Taboo' (2007) 14 *Non-proliferation Review* 306
Molnar, T, 'A Sociology of Names' (1999) *The Intercollegiate Review* 39
Mortenson, JD, 'Is the Vienna Convention Hostile to Drafting History?' (2013) 107 *AJIL* 780
Mourra, MH, 'The Conflicts and Controversies in Latin American Treaty-Based Disputes', in MH Mourra (ed), *Latin American Investment Treaty Arbitration* (Kluwer, 2008) 5
Movsesian, ML, 'International Commercial Arbitration and International Courts' (2008) 18 *Duke Journal of Comparative and International Law* 423
Mullin, BA, and MA Hogg, 'Motivations for Group Membership: The Role of Subjective Importance and Uncertainty Reduction' (1999) 21 *Basic and Applied Social Psychology* 91
Nelken, D, 'Towards a Sociology of Legal Adaptation' in D Nelken and J Feest (eds), *Adapting Legal Cultures* (Hart, 2001) 3
Nelken, D, 'Using the Concept of Legal Culture' (2004) 29 *Australian Journal of Legal Philosophy* 1
Newcombe, AP, and LP Paradell, *Law and Practice of Investment Treaties* (Kluwer Law International, 2009)
Newman, E, 'Failed States and International Order' (2009) 30 *Contemporary Security Policy* 421
Nicolaidis, K, and R Howse, 'This is my EUtopia ...: Narrative as Power' (2002) 40 *Journal of Common Market Studies* 767
Niemann, A, and PC Schmitter, 'Neo-functionalism' in A Wiener and T Diez (eds), *European Integration Theory* (2nd edn, OUP, 2009) 45
Noam, G, 'Allocation of Judicial Power between Domestic and International Courts and Tribunals—Some Guidelines for the International Criminal Law System' (PhD Dissertation, Hebrew University, 2013)
Noland, M, 'Affinity and International Trade' (2005) Institute for International Economics Working Paper No. WP 05-3 <http://iie.com/publications/wp/wp05-31.pdf>
Nora, P, 'Between Memory and History: Les Lieux de Mémoire' (1989) 26 *Representations* 15
Norman, G, and JP Trachtman, 'The Customary International Law Game' (2005) 99 *AJIL* 541
Norton, B, 'Language, Identity, and the Ownership of English' (1997) 31 *TESOL Quarterly* 419

Nowak, M, 'Human Rights 'Conditionality' in Relation to Entry to, and Full Participation in the EU' in P Alston (ed), *The EU and Human Rights* (OUP, 1999) 687
Nye, JS, *Soft Power* (Public Affairs, 2004)
Oberschall, A, 'Theories of Social Conflict' (1987) 4 *Annual Review of Sociology* 291
O'Callaghan, P, 'Collective Memory in Law and Policy: The Problem of the Sovereign Debt C-risis' (2012) 32 *Legal Studies* 642
Oelsner, A, 'The Institutional Identity of Regional Organizations, Or Mercosur's Identity Crisis' (2013) 57 *International Studies Quarterly* 115
Olick, JK, 'Collective Memory: The Two Cultures' (1999) 17 *Sociological Theory* 333
Olick, JK, *The Politics of Regret: On Collective Memory and Historical Responsibility* (Routledge, 2007)
Olick, JK, 'Collective Memory', *International Encyclopedia of the Social Sciences* (2nd edn, Macmillan, 2008)
Olick, JK, and J Robbins, 'Social Memory Studies: From "Collective Memory" to the Historical Sociology of Mnemonic Practices' (1998) 24 *Annual Review of Sociology* 105
Olick, JK, V Vinitzky-Seroussi, and D Levy, 'Introduction' in JK Olick, V Vinitzky-Seroussi, and D Levy (eds), *The Collective Memory Reader* (OUP, 2011) 3
O'Neill, B, 'Nuclear Weapons and National Prestige' (February 2006) Cowles Foundation Discussion Paper No. 1560 <http://ssrn.com/abstract=887333>
Onuf, N, *World of Our Making* (University of South Carolina Press, 1989)
Osiel, MJ, *Mass Atrocity, Collective Memory and the Law* (Transaction, 1997)
Osler, A, and J Zhu, 'Narratives in Teaching and Research for Justice and Human Rights' (2011) 6 *Education, Citizenship and Social Justice* 223
Paasch, A, 'Human Rights in EU Trade Policy—Between Ambition and Reality' (December, 2011) *Ecofair Trade Dialogue Discussion Paper*
Pagani, F, 'Peer Review as a Tool for Cooperation and Change' (2002) 11 *African Security Review* 15
Palmer, CL, 'Which Cues Matter? The Implications of Stereotype Appeals and Explicit Predispositions for Group-Centric Issue Opinion' (August 2010) <http://ssrn.com/abstract=1664772>
Park, I, and S Park, 'Cultural Affinity, Political Ties, and Endogenous Regional Trade Agreements' (GEP China Conference on Structural Change and Trade Efficiency, the Nottingham Centre for Research on Globalisation and Economic Policy, 7–8 November 2013) <http://www.nottingham.ac.uk/gep/documents/china/conferences/2013-14/ningbo/park.pdf>
Park, WW, 'Arbitrator Integrity: The Transient and the Permanent' (2009) 46 *San Diego Law Review* 629
Park, WW, 'Arbitration in Autumn' (2011) 2 *Journal of International Dispute Settlement* 287
Parsons, T, 'The Law and Social Control' in WM Evan (ed), *The Sociology of Law: A Social-Structural Perspective* (Free Press, 1980) 60
Paul, JR, 'Cultural Resistance to Global Governance' (2001) 22 *Michigan Journal of International Law* 1
Pauwelyn, J, 'WTO Panelists Are From Mars, ICSID Arbitrators Are From Venus: Why? And Does it Matter?' (1 January 2015) <http://ssrn.com/abstract=2549050> accessed 7 March 2015
Pedemonte, DF, 'Media Cases and Social Memory in Argentina post 2001' (2012) 5 *Journal for Communication Studies* 61
Pelliccia, S, 'Repsol, YPF, and Argentina: A Hypothetical Look at the Pending ICSID Arbitration over YPF' (2013) ExpressO: <http://works.bepress.com/stephen_pelliccia/1>

Pervou, I, 'The Convention for the Protection of All Persons from Enforced Disappearance: Moving Human Rights Protection Ahead' (2012) 5 *European Journal of Legal Studies* 120

Peterson, LE, 'Human Rights and Bilateral Investment Treaties: Mapping the Role of Human Rights Law within Investor-State Arbitration' (2009) *Rights and Democracy* <http://publications.gc.ca/collections/collection_2012/dd-rd/E84-36-2009-eng.pdf>

Peterson, LE, 'Argentina by the Numbers: Where Things Stand with Investment Treaty Claims Arising Out of the Argentine Financial Crisis' (1 February 2011) *Investment Arbitration Reporter* <http://www.iareporter.com/articles/argentina-by-the-numbers-where-things-stand-with-investment-treaty-claims-arising-out-of-the-argentine-financial-crisis/>

Peterson, LE, 'After Settling some Awards, Argentina takes more Fractious Path in Bond-Holder Case, with New Bid to Disqualify Arbitrators' (30 December 2013) 6(24) *Investment Arbitration Reporter* <http://www.iareporter.com/articles/20131230/print>

Pettigrew, TF, 'Intergroup Contact Theory' (1998) 49 *Annual Review of Psychology* 65

Pevehouse, JC, 'Democracy from the Outside-In? International Organizations and Democratization' (2002) 56 *International Organization* 515

Picker, CB, 'Regional Trade Agreements v. the WTO: A Proposal for Reform of Article XXIV to Counter this Institutional Threat' (2005) 26 *University of Pennsylvania Journal of International Economic Law* 267

Picker, CB, 'Comparative Legal Cultural Analyses of International Economic Law: A New Methodological Approach' (2013) 1 *Chinese Journal of Comparative Law* 21

Pirker, B, 'Interpreting Multi-Sourced Equivalent Norms: Judicial Borrowing in International Courts', in Y Shany and T Broude (eds), *Multi-Sourced Equivalent Norms in International Law* (Hart, 2011) 93

Pisani-Ferry, J, and AS Posen, *The Euro at Ten: The Next Global Currency?* (Institute for International Economics, 2009)

Polaski, S, 'Linking Trade and Investment Agreements to Improvements in Labor Rights' in *Human Rights, Trade and Investment Matters* (Amnesty International, May 2006) <http://www.amnestyusa.org/sites/default/files/pdfs/hrtradeinvestmentmatters.pdf>

Polletta, F, '"It Was like a Fever …" Narrative and Identity in Social Protest' (1998) 45 *Social Problems* 137

Poole, R, 'Memory, History and the Claims of the Past' (2008) 1 *Memory Studies* 149

Potter, PB, 'Legal Reform in China: Institutions, Culture, and Selective Adaptation' (2004) 29 *Law & Social Inquiry* 465

Pratt, MG, 'Social Identity Dynamics in Modern Organizations' in MA Hogg and DJ Terry (eds) *Social Identity Process in Organizational Context* (Psychology Press, 2001) 13

Price, RM, *The Chemical Weapons Taboo* (Cornell University Press, 1997)

Price, R, and N Tannenwald, 'Norms and Deterrence: The Nuclear and Chemical Weapons Taboos' in P Katzenstein (ed), *The Culture of National Security: Norms and Identity in World Politics* (Columbia University Press, 1996) 114

Prieto, GC, 'Constructing regionalism in South America: The Role of Ideas in the Andean Community and MERCOSUR Projects' (2003) 1 *Colombian Economic Journal* 267

Puig, S, 'Social Capital in the Arbitration Market' (2014) 25 *EJIL* 387

Pulkowski, D, 'Narratives of Fragmentation: International Law between Unity and Multiplicity' (Founding Conference of the European Society of International Law, Florence, 2004) <http://www.esil-sedi.eu/fichiers/en/Pulkowski_670.pdf>

Pulkowski, D, 'Testing Compliance Theories: Towards US Obedience of International Law in the Avena Case' (2006) 19 *Leiden Journal of International Law* 511

Qingjiang, K, 'Is the European Experience Duplicable in East Asia?' in R Wolfrum and V Röben (eds), *Developments of International Law in Treaty Making* (Springer, 2005) 297

Quaglia, L, *Central Banking Governance in the European Union: A Comparative Analysis* (Routledge, 2007)

Raustiala, K, 'Compliance and Effectiveness in International Regulatory Cooperation' (2000) 32 *Case Western Reserve Journal of International Law* 387

Raustiala, K, and AM Slaughter, 'International Law, International Relations and Compliance' in W Carlnaes and others (eds), *Handbook of International Relations* (2002) 538

Reiner, C, and C Schreuer, 'Human Rights and International Investment Arbitration' in PM Dupuy, F Francioni, and EU Petersmann (eds), *Human Rights in International Investment Law and Arbitration* (OUP, 2008) 82

Reinisch, A, 'The Proliferation of International Dispute Settlement Mechanisms: The Threat of Fragmentation vs. the Promise of a More Effective System?' in I Buffard and others (eds), *International Law between Universalism and Fragmentation: Festschrift in Honour of Gerhard Hafner* (Martinus Nijhoff Publishers, 2008) 107

Reus-Smit, C, *The Moral Purpose of the State* (Princeton University Press, 1999)

Richards, DL, RD Gelleny, and DH Sacko 'Money with a Mean Streak? Foreign Economic Penetration and Government Respect for Human Rights in Developing Countries' (2011) 45 *International Studies Quarterly* 219

Riles, A, 'Comparative Law and Socio-Legal Studies' in M Reimann and R Zimmermann (eds), *Oxford Handbook of Comparative Law* (OUP, 2006) 775

Risse, T, 'The Euro between National and European Identity' (2003) 10 *Journal of European Public Policy* 487

Risse, T, *A Community of Europeans? Transnational Identities and Public Spheres* (Cornell University Press, 2010)

Risse, T, and K Sikkink, 'The Socialization of International Human Rights Norms into Domestic Practices: Introduction' in T Risse, SC Ropp, and K Sikkink (eds), *The Power of Human Rights* (CUP, 1999) 1

Ritzer, G, *Introduction to Sociology* (2nd edn, Sage, 2015)

Ritzer, G, and DJ Goodman, *Modern Sociological Theory* (6th edn, 2004)

Ritzer, G, and J Stepnisky, *Sociological Theory* (9th edn, McGraw Hill, 2013)

Roberts, A, 'Clash of Paradigms: Actors and Analogies Shaping the Investment Treaty System' (2013) 107 *AJIL* 45

Rock, P, 'Sociological Theories of Crime', in M Maguire, R Morgan, and R Reiner (eds), *The Oxford Handbook of Criminology* (OUP, 2012) 57

Rodrik, D, A Subramanian, and F Trebbi, 'Institutions Rule, The Primacy of Institutions over Geography and Integration in Economic Development' (2004) 9 *Journal of Economic Growth* 131

Rogers, CA, 'Emerging Dilemmas in International Economic Arbitration: The Vocation of the International Arbitrator' (2005) 20 *American University International Law Review* 957

Rogers, CA, *Ethics in International Arbitration* (OUP, 2014)

Rogers, EM, *Diffusion of Innovations* (5th edn, Free Press, 2003)

Romero, LA, *A History of Argentina in the Twentieth Century* (Pennsylvania State University Press, 2002)

Rosamond, B, *Theories of European Integration* (St. Martin's Press, 2000)

Rosen, L, *Law as Culture: An Invitation* (Princeton University Press, 2006)

Rosenberg, CB, 'The Intersection of International Trade and International Arbitration: The Use of Trade Benefits to Secure Compliance with Arbitral Awards' (2013) 44 *Georgetown Journal of International Law* 503
Rowley, EE, *Hyperinflation in Germany: Perceptions of a Process* (Scholar Press, 1994)
Ruggie, J, *Constructing the World Polity* (Routledge, 1998)
Rublee, MR, *Non-Proliferation Norms: Why States Choose Nuclear Restraint?* (University of Georgia Press, 2009)
Rumelili, B, 'Constructing Identity and Relating to Difference: Understanding the EU's' (2004) 30 *Review of International Studies* 27
Ryvkin, B, 'Saving the Euro: Tensions with European Treaty Law in the European Union's Efforts to Protect the Common Currency' (2012) 45 *Cornell International Law Journal* 227
Sagan, SD, 'Why Do States Build Nuclear Weapons? Three Models in Search of a Bomb' (1996) 21 *International Security* 54
Salacuse, JW, 'Negotiating: The Top Ten Ways That Culture Can Affect Your Negotiation' (September/October 2004) *Ivey Business Journal* <http://iveybusinessjournal.com/publication/negotiating-the-top-ten-ways-that-culture-can-affect-your-negotiation/>
Salacuse, JW, 'The Emerging Global Regime for Investment' (2010) 51 *Harvard International Law Journal* 427
Sandoz, Y, and others (eds), *Commentary on the Additional Protocols of 8 June 1977 to the Geneva Conventions of 12 August 1949* (Martinus Nijhoff Publishers, 1987)
Sarfaty, GA, 'International Norm Diffusion in the Pimicikamak Cree Nation: A Model of Legal Mediation' (2007) 48 *Harvard International Law Journal* 441
Sarfaty, GA, 'Why Culture Matters in International Institutions: The Marginality of Human Rights at the World Bank' (2009) 103 *AJIL* 647
Sarfaty, GA, *Values in Translation: Human Rights and the Culture of the World Bank* (Stanford University Press, 2012)
Sarkin, J, and M Koenig, 'Ending Caste Discrimination in India: Human Rights and the Responsibility to Protect Individuals and Groups from Discrimination at the Domestic and International Levels' (2010) 41 *George Washington International Law Review* 101
Sasse, G, 'EU Conditionality and Minority Rights', EUI Working Papers 2005/16 <http://cadmus.eui.eu/bitstream/handle/1814/3365/05_16.pdf?sequence=1>
Saurugger, S, and F Mérand, 'Does European Integration Theory Need Sociology?' (2010) 8 *Comparative European Politics* 1
Sauvé, P, and K Steinfatt, 'Towards Multilateral Rules on Trade and Culture: Protective Regulation or Efficient Protection?' (Achieving Better Regulation of Services Conference, Canberra, November 2000) <http://www.pc.gov.au/research/completed/better-regulation/abros.pdf>
Savelsberg, JJ, and RD King, 'Law and Collective Memory' (2007) 3 *Annual Review Law Social Science*
Savelsberg, JJ, and RD King, 'Institutionalizing Collective Memories of Hate: Law and Law Enforcement in Germany and the United States' (2005) 111 *American Journal of Sociology* 189
Savelsberg, JJ, and RD King, *American Memories: Atrocities and the Law* (Sage Foundation, 2011)
Schabas, WA, *Genocide in International Law* (CUP, 2000)
Schaefer, RT, *Sociology Matters* (5th edn, McGraw Hill, 2011)
Scheller, HK, *The European Central Bank: History, Role and Functions* (2nd edn, European Central Bank, 2006)

Schermers, HG, and NM Blokker, *International Institutional Law* (5th edn, Martinus Nijhoff Publishers, 2011)

Schiff, MW, and LA Winters, *Regional Integration and Development* (World Bank and OUP, 2003)

Schill, SW, 'W(h)ither Fragmentation? On the Literature and Sociology of International Investment Law' (2011) 22 *EJIL* 875

Schill, SW, 'Public or Private Dispute Settlement? The Culture Clash in Investment Treaty Arbitration and its Impact on the Role of the Arbitrator' in T Weiler and F Baetens (eds), *New Directions in International Economic Law* (Martinus Nijhoff Publishers, 2011) 23

Schimmelfennig, F, 'International Socialization in the New Europe' (2000) 6 *EJIR* 109

Schreuer, C, L Malintoppi, A Reinisch, and A Sinclair, *The ICSID Convention: A Commentary* (2nd edn, CUP, 2009)

Schultz, T, and R Kovacs, 'The Rise of a Third Generation of Arbitrators' (2012) 28 *Arbitration International* 161

Schwartz, B, *Abraham Lincoln and the Forge of National Memory* (University of Chicago Press, 2000)

Seidendorf, S, 'Defining Europe Against its Past?—Memory Politics and the Sanctions Against Austria in France and Germany' (2005) 6 *German Law Journal* 439

Sen, N, and BG Nair, 'Human Rights Provisions in the forthcoming Indian-EU Free Trade Agreement' (2011) 4 *National University for Juridical Science Law Review* 417

Servais, D, and R Ruggeri, 'The EU Constitution: Its Impact on Economic and Monetary Union and Economic Governance' in *Legal Aspects of the European System of Central Banks* (European Central Bank, 2005) 43

Shadikhodjaev, S, 'Keeping Regionalism Under "Control" of the Multilateral Trading System: State of Play and Prospects' (2013) 19 *Law and Business Review of the Americas* 327

Shaffer, G, and MA Pollack, 'Hard and Soft Law' in JL Dunoff and MA Pollack (eds), *Interdisciplinary Perspectives on International Law and International Relations: The State of the Art* (CUP, 2013) 197

•Shan, W, 'From North-South Divide to Private-Public Debate: Revival of the Calvo Doctrine and the Changing Landscape in International Investment Law' (2007) 27 *Northwestern Journal of International Law and Business* 631

Shannon, VP, 'Norms are What States Make of Them' (2000) 44 *International Studies Quarterly* 293

Shaw, M, *International Law* (7th edn, CUP, 2014)

Shdaima, CS, 'What's in a Name?: Cause Lawyers as Conceptual Category' (2006) Bepress Legal Series Paper 903 <http://law.bepress.com/cgi/viewcontent.cgi?article=4436&context=expresso>

Shea, DR, *The Calvo Clause: A Problem of Inter-American and International Law Diplomacy* (University of Minnesota Press, 1955)

Shelton, D, 'Law, Non-Law, and the Problem of "Soft Law"' in D Shelton (ed), *Commitment and Compliance: The Role of Non-Binding Norms in the International Legal System* (OUP, 2000) 1

Shelton, D, 'Commentary and Conclusions' in D Shelton (ed), *Commitment and Compliance: The Role of Non-Binding Norms in the International Legal System* (OUP, 2000) 449

Shelton, D, 'Editor's Concluding Note: The Role of Non-Binding Norms in the International Legal System' in D Shelton (ed), *Commitment and Compliance: The Role of Non-Binding Norms in the International Legal System* (OUP, 2000) 554

Shelton, D, 'Normative Hierarchy in International Law' (2006) 100 *AJIL* 291

Shelton, D, 'International Law and Relative Normativity' in MD Evans (ed), *International Law* (3rd edn, OUP, 2010) 141

Shenkar, O, Y Luo, and O Yeheskel, 'From "Distance" to "Friction": Substituting Metaphors and Redirecting Intercultural Research' (2008) 33 *Academy of Management Review* 905

Shi, J, *Free Trade and Cultural Diversity in International Law* (Hart, 2013)

Shkabatur, J, 'A Global Panopticon? The Changing Role of International Organizations in the Information Age' (2011) 33 *Michigan Journal of International Law* 159

Shumway, JM, 'Sometimes Knowing How to Forget is Also Having Memory: The Repatriation of Juan Manuel de Rosas and the Healing of Argentina', in LL Johnson (ed), *Death, Dismemberment, and Memory: Body Politics in Latin America* (University of New Mexico Press, 2004) 105

Sicurelli, D, *The European Union's Africa Policies* (Ashgate, 2010)

Siegel, JI, AN Licht, and SH Schwartz, 'Egalitarianism, Cultural Distance, and FDI: A New Approach' (2013) 24 *Organization Science* 1174

Simma, B, 'Foreign Investment Arbitration: A Place for Human Rights?' (2011) 60 *International & Comparative Law Quarterly* 573

Simmons, BA, 'Compliance with International Agreements' (1998) 1 *The Annual Review of Political Science* 75

Simmons, BA, F Dobbin, and G Garret, 'Introduction: The International Diffusion of Liberalism' (2006) 60 *International Organization* 781

Simmons, BA, and Z Elkins, 'The Globalization of Liberalization: Policy Diffusion in the International Political Economy' (2004) 98 *American Political Science Review* 171

Sjursen, H, 'Why Expand? The Question of Legitimacy and Justification in the EU's Enlargement Policy' (2002) 40 *Journal of Common Market Studies* 491

Skonieczny, A, 'Constructing NAFTA' (2001) 45 *International Studies* 433

Slaughter, AM, 'International Law and International Relations Theory: A Prospectus' in E Benvenisti and M Hirsch (eds), *The Impact of International Law on International Cooperation* (CUP, 2004) 16

Slaughter, J, *Human Rights, Inc: The World Novel, Narrative Form, and International Law* (Fordham University Press, 2007)

Small, ML, DJ Harding, and M Lamont, 'Reconsidering Culture and Poverty' (2010) 629 *Annals of the American Academy of Political and Social Science* 6

Smita, N, 'Equal by Law, Unequal by Caste: The 'Untouchable' Condition in Critical Race Perspective' (2008) 26 *Wisconsin International Law Journal* 255

Smith, PH, *Talons of the Eagle* (4th edn, OUP, 2013)

Smits, R, *The European Central Bank: Institutional Aspects* (Kluwer, 1997)

Snoek, JD, 'Role Strain in Diversified Role Sets' (1966) 71 *American Journal of Sociology* 363

Somers, MR, 'Narrative, Narrative Identity, and Social Action: Rethinking English Working-Class Formation' (1992) 16 *Social Science History* 591

Sornarajah, M, *The International Law on Foreign Investment* (2nd edn, CUP, 2004)

Spar, D, 'Foreign Investment and Human Rights' (1999) 42 *Challenge* 55

Spears, SA, 'The Quest for Policy Space in a New Generation of International Investment Agreements' (2010) 13 *Journal of International Economic Law* 1037

Stangor, C, and JT Jost, 'Commentary: Individual, Group and System Levels of Analysis and their Relevance to Stereotyping and Intergroup Relations' in R Spears and others (eds), *Social Psychology of Stereotyping and Group Life* (Blackwell, 1997) 346

Stark, R, 'Deviant Places' in R Weitzer (ed), *Deviance and Social Control* (McGraw Hill, 2002) 45

Steinberg, RH, 'Wanted—Dead or Alive: Realism in International Law' in JL Dunoff and MA Pollack (eds), *Interdisciplinary Perspectives on International Law and International Relations: The State of the Art* (CUP, 2013) 146

Steinberg, R, and J Zasloff, 'Power and International Law' (2006) 100 *AJIL* 64

Steiner, H, 'International Protection of Human Rights' in MD Evans (ed), *International Law* (3rd edn, OUP, 2010) 784

Steiner, HJ, and P Alston, *International Human Rights in Context: Law, Politics and Morals* (3rd edn, OUP, 2008)

Stephan, WG, and CW Stephan, *Intergroup Relations* (Westview Press, 1996)

Sterling-Folker, J, 'Competing Paradigms or Birds of a Feather? Constructivism and Neoliberal Institutionalism Compared' (2000) 44 *International Studies Quarterly* 97

Stets, JE, and PJ Burke, 'Identity, Theory and Social Identity Theory' (2000) 63 *Social Psychology Quarterly* 224

Stets, JE, and PJ Burke, 'A Sociological Approach to Self and Identity' in M Leary and J Tangney (eds), *Handbook of Self and Identity* (Guilford Press, 2002) 228

Stone, C, 'Common but Differentiated Responsibility in International Law' (2004) 98 *AJIL* 276

Stopler, G, 'Countenancing the Oppression of Women: How Liberals Tolerate Religious and Cultural Practices that Discriminate Against Women' (2003) 12 *Columbia Journal of Gender and Law* 154

Strang, D, and JW Meyer, 'Institutional Conditions for Diffusion' (1993) 22 *Theory and Society* 487

Stryker, S, and PJ Burke, 'The Past, Present, and Future of an Identity Theory' (2000) 63 *Social Psychology Quarterly* 284

Suh, DC, 'Trade and Financial Liberalization in South Asia' in D Singh and RY Siregar (eds), *ASEAN and Korea* (Institute for Southeast Asian Studies, Singapore 1997) 19

Sutherland, EH, *Principles of Criminology* (4th edn, Lippincott Company, 1947)

Sutherland, P, and others, *The Future of the WTO: Addressing Institutional Challenges in the New Millennium—Report by the Consultative Board to the Director-General Supachai Panitchpakdi* (WTO, 2004)

Swidler, A, *Talk of Love: How Culture Matters* (University of Chicago Press, 2001)

Szasz, PC, 'The Investment Disputes Convention and Latin America' (1970–1) 11 *Virginia Journal of International Law* 256

Tajfel, H, *Human Groups and Social Categories: Studies in Social Psychology* (CUP, 1981)

Tajfel, H, and JC Turner, 'The Social Identity of Intergroup Behaviour' in S Worchel (ed), *Psychology of Intergroup Relations* (Nelson-Hall, 1986) 7

Teitel, RG, *Transitional Justice* (OUP, 2000)

Thio, A, *Deviant Behaviour* (10th edn, Pearson, 2010)

Thomas, CA, 'The Concept of Legitimacy and International Law' (December 2013) LSE Law, Society and Economy Working Papers <http://eprints.lse.ac.uk/51746/1/__libfile_repository_Content_Law,%20society%20and%20economics%20working%20papers_2013_WPS2013-12_Thomas.pdf>

Tieleman, K, The Failure of the Multilateral Agreement on Investment (MAI) and the Absence of Global Public Policy Network (Case Study for the UN Vision Project on Global Public Policy Networks) (European University Institute Firenze and Harvard University, 2000)

Titi, C, 'Investment Arbitration in Latin America: The Uncertain Veracity of Preconceived Ideas' (2014) 30 *Arbitration International* 357

Tivey, T, 'Robert Dahl and American Pluralism' in LJ Tivey and A Wright (eds), *Political Thought Since 1945* (Elgar, 1992) 91
Tomohiko, S, 'Japan's Nuclear Policy: Between Non-Nuclear Identity and US Extended Deterrence' (May 2009) Austral Policy Forum <http://nautilus.org/wp-content/uploads/2009/12/Tomohiko-PDF.pdf>
Tomuschat, C, 'Human Rights and International Humanitarian Law' (2010) 21 *EJIL* 15
Tönnies, F, *Community and Society* (Transaction Publishers, 2004)
Torney, D, 'Assessing EU Leadership on Climate Change: The Limits of Diffusion in EU Relations with China and India' (2012) KFG Working Paper Series <http://userpage.fu-berlin.de/kfgeu/kfgwp/wpseries/WorkingPaperKFG_46.pdf>
Torriani, R, 'The Dynamics of National Identity' (2002) 37 *Journal of Contemporary History* 559
Trachtman, JP, 'Decision of the Appellate Body of the World Trade Organization: Turkey-Restrictions on Import of Textile and Clothing Products' (2000) 11 *EJIL* 217
Trachtman, JP, 'Toward Open Recognition? Standards and Regional Integration under Article XXIV of GATT' (2003) 6 *Journal of International Economic Law* 459
Trachtman, J, 'Regional Trade: Regionalism' in AT Guzman and AO Sykes (eds), *Research Handbook in International Economic Law* (Elgar, 2007) 151
Trakman, L, 'Legal Traditions and International Commercial Arbitration' (2006) 17 *American Review of International Arbitration* 1
Trebilcock, MJ, *Understanding Trade Law* (Elgar, 2011)
Trebilcock, MJ, R Howse, and A Eliason, *The Regulation of International Trade* (4th edn, Routledge, 2013)
Tuori, KH, 'The European Financial Crisis: Constitutional Aspects and Implications' (2012) EUI Working Papers Law 2012/28 <http://cadmus.eui.eu/bitstream/handle/1814/24301/LAW_2012_28_Tuori.pdf?sequence=1>
Turner, JC, and others, 'Self and Collective: Cognition and Social Context' (1994) 20 *Personality and Social Psychology Bulletin* 454
Turner, JC, and RS Onorato, 'Social Identity, Personality, and the Self-Concept: A Self-Categorization Perspective' in TR Tyler, RM Kramer, and OP John (eds), *The Psychology of the Social Self* (Erlbaum Publishers, 1990) 38
Turner, JH, *Contemporary Sociological Theory* (Sage, 2013)
Van den Bossche, P, and W Zdouc, *The Law and Policy of the World Trade Organization: Text, Cases and Materials* (3rd edn, CUP, 2013)
Vandevelde, KJ, *United States Investment Treaties: Policy and Practice* (Kluwer, 1992)
Vandevelde, KJ, 'Sustainable Liberalism and the International Investment Regime' (1997) 19 *Michigan Journal of International Law* 373
Van Grasste, C, 'The Political Economy of Services in Regional Trade Agreements' (2011) OECD Trade Policy Papers, No. 112 <http://www.oecd-ilibrary.org/docserver/download/5kgdst6lc344.pdf?expires=1426232123&id=id&accname=guest&checksum=BA2ECF5DA8C111B436F5B6B6AF9E522B>
Van Harten, G, *Investment Treaty Arbitration and Public Law* (OUP, 2007)
Van Harten, G, 'The (Lack of) Women Arbitrators in Investment Treaty Arbitration' (2012) 59 *Columbia FDI Perspectives* <http://ccsi.columbia.edu/files/2014/01/FDI_59.pdf>
Van Langenhove, L, *Building Regions: The Regionalization of the World Order* (Ashgate, 2011)
Vicard, V, 'Trade, Conflicts, and Political Integration: Explaining the Heterogeneity of Regional Trade Agreements' (2012) 56 *European Economic Review* 54

Viner, J, *The Customs Union Issue* (Carnegie Endowment for International Peace, 1950)

Vinitzky-Seroussi, V, 'Commemorating a Difficult Past: Yitzhak Rabin's Memorial' (2002) 67 *American Sociological Review* 30

Viñuales, JE, *Foreign Investment and the Environment in International Law* (CUP, 2012)

Voeten, E, 'International Judicial Behaviour' in CP Romano, KJ Alter, and Y Shany (eds), *Oxford Handbook of International Adjudication* (OUP, 2014) 550

Von Der Haar, CM, *Social Psychology: A Sociological Perspective* (Pearson 2005)

Von Stein, J, 'The Engines of Compliance' in JL Dunoff and MA Pollack (eds), *Interdisciplinary Perspectives on International Law and International Relations: The State of the Art* (CUP, 2013) 477

Voon, TS, *Cultural Products and the World Trade Organization* (CUP, 2007)

Wagner-Pacifici, R, and B Schwartz, 'The Vietnam Veterans Memorial: Commemorating a Difficult Past' (1991) 97 *American Journal of Sociology* 376

Waibel, M, 'Interpretive Communities in International Law' (2014) University of Cambridge Faculty of Law Research Paper No. 62/2014 <http://ssrn.com/abstract=2513411>

Waibel, M, and Y Wu, 'Are Arbitrators Political?' (2001) ASIL Research Forum Working Paper

Waisman, CH, 'The Dynamics of National Identity Frames: The Case of Argentina in the Twentieth Century' in Louis Roniger and Mario Sznajder (eds), *Constructing Collective Identities and Shaping Public Spheres: Latin American Paths* (Sussex Academic Press, 1998) 149

Wälde, TW, 'The Present State of Research Carried Out by the English-Speaking Section of the Centre for Studies and Research' (2007) *Hague Academy Report on International Investment Law*

Wälde, TW, 'Procedural Challenges in Investment Arbitration under the Shadow of the Dual Role of the State: Asymmetries and Tribunals Duty to Ensure, Pro-actively, the Equality of Arms' (2010) 26 *Arbitration International* 3

Wallerstein, I, *The Modern World System I: Capitalist Agriculture and the Origins of the European World-Economy in the Sixteenth Century* (Academic Press, 1974)

Walsh, DF, 'Structure/Agency' in C Jenks (ed), *Core Sociological Dichotomies* (Sage, 1998) 8

Waters, M, *Modern Sociological Theory* (Sage, 1994)

Waughray, A, 'Caste Discrimination: A Twenty-First Century Challenge for UK Discrimination Law?' (2009) 72 *Modern Law Review* 182

Weber, M, *The Theory of Social and Economic Organization* (OUP, 1947)

Weiler, JHH, 'Cain and Abel—Convergence and Divergence in International Trade Law' in JHH Weiler (ed), *The EU, The WTO And The NAFTA: Towards a Common Law of International Trade?* (OUP, 2000)

Weiler, T, 'Balancing Human Rights and Investor Protection: A New Approach for a Different Legal Order' (2004) 27 *Boston College International and Comparative Law Review* 429

Weitzer, R, *Deviance and Social Control* (McGraw Hill, 2002)

Wendt, A, 'Anarchy is What States Make of It' (1992) 46 *International Organization* 391

Wendt, A, 'Collective Identity Formation and the International State' (1994) 88 *American Political Science Review* 385

Wendt, A, *Social Theory of International Politics* (CUP, 1999)

Wexler, L, 'The International Deployment of Shame, Second-Best Responses, and Norm Entrepreneurship: The Campaign to Ban Landmines and the Landmine Treaty' (2003) 20 *Arizona Journal of International and Comparative Law* 561

Whalley, J, 'Recent Regional Agreements: Why so Many, so Fast, so Different and Where are they headed?' (2006) Centre for International Governance Innovation Working Paper 9 <http://www.cigionline.org/sites/default/files/recent_regional_agreements.pdf>

Whitaker, AP, *The United States and Argentina* (Harvard University Press, 1954)

Wilson, RA, *Writing History in International Criminal Trials* (CUP, 2011)

Woodward, K, *Understanding Identity* (Hodder Education 2002)

Worchel, S, 'A Developmental View of the Search for Group Identity' in S Worschel and others (eds), *Social Identity: International Perspectives* (Sage, 1998) 53

Worchel, S, and H Rothgerber, 'Changing the Stereotype of the Stereotype' in R Spears and others (eds), *The Social Psychology of Stereotyping and Group Life* (Blackwell, 1997) 72

Zampetti, AB, and P Sauvé, 'International Investment' in AT Guzman and AO Sykes (eds), *Research Handbook in International Economic Law* (Elgar, 2007) 211

Zelizer, B, 'Why Memory's Work on Journalism Does not Reflect Journalism's Work on Memory' (2008) 1 *Memory Studies* 79

Zerubavel, E, 'Social Memories: Steps to a Sociology of the Past' (1996) 19 *Qualitative Sociology* 283

Zerubavel, Y, *Recovered Roots* (University of Chicago Press, 1995)

Zwagemakers, F, 'The EU's Conditionality Policy: A New Strategy to Achieve Compliance' (January 2012) IAI Working Papers 12/03 <http://www10.iadb.org/intal/intalcdi/PE/2012/09808.pdf>

Index